D1611674

THE WORK OF CHRIST

BOOKS BY G. C. BERKOUWER

MODERN UNCERTAINITY AND CHRISTIAN FAITH

RECENT DEVELOPMENTS IN ROMAN CATHOLIC THOUGHT

THE TRIUMPH OF GRACE IN THE THEOLOGY OF KARL BARTH

THE SECOND VATICAN COUNCIL AND THE NEW CATHOLICISM

STUDIES IN DOGMATICS SERIES —

THE PROVIDENCE OF GOD

FAITH AND SANCTIFICATION

FAITH AND JUSTIFICATION

FAITH AND PERSEVERANCE

THE PERSON OF CHRIST

GENERAL REVELATION

DIVINE ELECTION

MAN: THE IMAGE OF GOD

THE WORK OF CHRIST

Studies in Dogmatics

The Work of Christ

BY

G. C. BERKOUWER

PROFESSOR OF SYSTEMATIC THEOLOGY
FREE UNIVERSITY OF AMSTERDAM

WILLIAM B. EERDMANS PUBLISHING COMPANY
GRAND RAPIDS, MICHIGAN

Library of Congress Catalog Card No. 64-22032

ISBN 0-8028-3036-6

Translated by Cornelius Lambregtse
from
the Dutch edition, *Het Werk van Christus*,
published by J. H. Kok N.V., Kampen, The Netherlands

First printing, December 1965
Fifth printing, January 1980

PHOTOLITHOPRINTED BY EERDMANS PRINTING COMPANY
GRAND RAPIDS, MICHIGAN, UNITED STATES OF AMERICA

CONTENTS

ABBREVIATIONS

Ench.	– Augustine, *Enchiridion*
Geref. Dog.	– Bavinck, *Gereformeerde Dogmatiek*
Inst.	– Calvin, *Institutes of the Christian Religion*
K.D.	– Barth, *Kirchliche Dogmatik*
Q.	– Question
Stud. Cath.	– *Studia Catholica*
TWNT	– Kittel (ed.), *Theologisches Wörterbuch zum Neuen Testament*

CHAPTER ONE

INTRODUCTION

WHEN WE study the biblical message concerning the work of Christ, and examine the countless questions and answers, theories and viewpoints which this work has called forth in the history of the Church and theology, we are surprised that the many answers to the question, "Whom do men say that I the Son of man am?" (Matt. 16:13) reveal such a striking parallel with the various theories concerning the nature and meaning of Christ's *work.* The words of Scripture, which depict this work in its ultimate import, seem to present a simple, unmistakable message: "For ye know the grace of our Lord Jesus Christ, that, though he was rich, yet for your sakes he became poor, that ye through his poverty might become rich" (II Cor. 8:9). Here the work in question is seen to be accomplished through the depths of utmost poverty, but the *goal* in the midst of this poverty is the distribution of a far greater wealth which overcomes all things.

But in the history of dogmatics, speculation on the work of Christ is far removed from this simplicity. We encounter all kinds of theories, particularly when "atonement" is mentioned (consider, e.g., the objective and subjective theories of atonement); indeed, there is hardly one aspect of the multilateral work of Christ which commands general agreement. It is true that some have tried to avoid this alarming situation by resorting to the unapproachable "mystery" of this work. All theories, they have maintained, are attempts to formulate that which in essence cannot be formulated, and hence they have at best only a relative validity. The result is a pluriformity of approaches to Christ's work; one kind of approach does not exclude but rather completes the others, and thus Paul's prayer is answered that we "may be strong to apprehend with all the saints what is the breadth and length and height and depth and to know the love of Christ which passeth *knowledge*" (Eph. 3:18, 19).

It is apparent however, that these advocates of relativity meet with one great stumblingblock, namely, the confession of the

Church, whose great desire it was to confess the work of her Lord clearly, positively, and definitively. Thus was manifested the urge of faith to know, and to confess, and to preach what Christ has *done.* We think of the blind men who requested a concrete act: "Have mercy on us thou son of David," and of whom Christ asked, "*Believe ye that I am able to do this?*" (Matt. 9:27, 28; cf. Matt. 20:32, "What will ye that I shall do unto you?"). For, indeed, the object is not a purely theoretical knowledge but a profitable, wholesome knowledge of the salvation of God in Jesus Christ.

No matter how deeply the Church was convinced that she would never be able to fathom the mystery of the love of God in Christ, still she could not be satisfied with a vague assimilation of all theories concerning the work of Christ into one irrational whole. Rather, she returned again and again to the testimony of Scripture, which in penetrating words taught the excellence of the work of Christ. The multitude of theories should never induce us to say that we are still groping in the dark for the real meaning of the work of Christ.

The description of dogmatic reflection as being *repetitio Sacrae Scripturae* may contain more problems than appear at first glance; yet the message of Scripture will be the sole, final, and real viewpoint in the midst of all confusion. We recall how, among the many ideas concerning the person of Christ, Peter's confession alone evoked a beatitude. And when we realize that Peter's answer was, "Thou art the Christ," that is to say, the Anointed One, the bearer and fulfiller of the Messianic office, then we understand that Scripture inseparably connects the true knowledge of Christ's office with salvation. Our own flesh and blood does not yield this knowledge either. It is possible to have this knowledge only by the Father's revelation, who omnipotently penetrates our subjective confusion and leads us to the knowledge of Christ, to the knowledge of the breadth and length, height and depth, of his love in his work.

Since only the illumination of the Holy Spirit imparts the right insight into the profound significance of Christ's work, we realize the great danger connected with human interpretation and construction. Nowhere are the words of I Cor. 2:14, "Now the natural man receiveth not the things of the Spirit of God: for they are foolishness unto him, and he cannot know them, because they are *spiritually* judged," more fitting than with respect to the work of Christ. Human thinking is not excluded, but it certainly is not sufficient. Without the aid of the Holy Spirit it is possible to interpret Christ's work falsely and to reverse its meaning, just as the Pharisees explained Christ's casting out of evil spirits as a demonic act (Luke 11:15). It is possible to consider the word of the cross foolishness and the crucified Christ can become an offense and stumblingblock.[1]

Most interpretations of Christ's work are, indeed, appreciative, rather than indications of offense. Within the Church and theology there is even wide agreement as to the unique value of Christ's work. Nevertheless we also find far-reaching divergencies, which can be traced to differing opinions concerning his person. One who confesses the deity of Christ will, for example, interpret his redemptive work differently from another who, like Arius, emphatically rejects this confession. Again, the monophysite, who believes that Christ's human nature is wholly absorbed by the divine nature, will judge differently about Christ's work from one who, agreeing with Chalcedon, confesses not only the *vere Deus* but also the *vere homo.* It would not be difficult to prove from history that the consequences of Arianism, adoptianism, docetism, and modernism abound in ideas concerning the work of Christ. This does not mean that one can arrive at a correct conception of Christ's work merely by drawing logical conclusions from a theory concerning his person. Our previous study, *The Person of Christ,* itself depended upon a consideration of Christ's works. So here again we must follow the only correct way, which is to hear the testimony of Scripture and thus be safeguarded from the deceitfulness of the human heart. Under the guidance of the Spirit we may again understand that these Scriptures testify of him (John 5:39), and thus we are freed from the temptation to place Christ only at the end of our thinking, remembering that he has said, "*I* am the first and the last" (Rev. 22:13).

A self-made conception of Christ is very dangerous because it is religiously tinted, as Israel showed when it wished to crown Christ king according to its confused Messiah-conception. Such projections and ideals of the mind may easily turn into their opposites (Crucify him!) because the first "valuation" of Christ

1. Christ's calling Peter blessed in Matt. 16 corresponds with the beatitude pronounced upon everyone who shall not be offended in Christ (Matt. 11:6).

was not based upon a true knowledge of Christ in his person and work, but rather upon an image derived from the desires of the human heart.

Not only the history of theology but Scripture itself characterizes the work of Christ in diverse ways. At times the different theories concerning Christ's work have been directly connected with this variation in Scripture. Bavinck states that Scripture shows Christ's suffering and death again and again from different angles, each time bringing a new aspect to light. He emphasizes that there are "several valuations of the person and work of Christ to be found" in the New Testament.[2] This is not to say, however, that for Bavinck these valuations are merely subjective or relative. On the contrary, these different aspects of the scriptural message do not contradict but complement each other. They emphasize the broad scope of the work of Christ. "The work of Christ is so many-sided that it cannot be described by one single word or summarized in one single formula." It is thus – according to Bavinck – that each book of the New Testament portrays another significance of Christ's death and that all of them together contribute to "a deep impression and clear understanding of the richness and many-sidedness of Christ's mediatorial work." The point at issue is variation, but in this variation there is the harmony of one, multilateral work. Thus it becomes possible to test "variations" in the history of theology by the variation in the harmony as presented by Holy Scripture. Holy Scripture emphasizes the inexhaustible richness and real aspects of one mediatorial work, whereas the more recent variations of theological thought frequently accentuate the one-sidedness and isolation of one or more aspects of the biblical message.

It is not difficult to point out this one-sidedness in various expositions, which always results in impoverishment of the Christ-conception. For example: frequently the attempt has been made to bring the work of Christ under one theme, e.g., that he is our *example*. It cannot be denied that Scripture does mention this, even in connection with a very concrete and central act of Christ, namely, the washing of the disciples' feet: "For I have given you an example" (John 13:15; cf. I Pet. 2:21). But others, opposing this isolation of certain aspects of Christ's work, have mistakenly neglected his exemplary function, as if his cause could be

2. *Gereformeerde Dogmatiek,* II, 371.

served by combating one-sidedness with neglect! Again, some have placed their whole emphasis on Christ's *obedience*. Christ's obedience certainly is essential in the actuality of his work, for the Church confesses his active and passive obedience. But frequently this obedience has been emphasized while Christ's deity was attacked, and thus his obedience became a kind of conscientiousness belonging to the man Jesus of Nazareth, making him more and more an object of God's favor. The portrait thus created was nothing but the distorted Christ-idea of liberal Christology.

And, finally, we mention the one-sided ideas concerning the love of Christ. Indeed, Scripture is overflowing with this love, and Paul prays that the Church may fully comprehend it, but frequently this love was so over-emphasized that it violated God's righteousness and so could no longer be a correct description of the work of Christ. The entire representation became so distorted that finally God's wrath was pushed entirely into the background; it was said that God's wrath is only a misconception on our part, from which Jesus Christ came to deliver us by his message that *this* love was God.

This theological situation concerning the work of Christ could only result in confusion and impoverishment. Each one-sided presentation was allegedly based upon Scripture, thus creating the impression that Christ was being represented according to the unequivocal testimony of Scripture. This explains the influence which some of the very one-sided Christ-ideas have had in the course of history. But at the same time the attack upon the confession of the Church intensified. When reflecting upon this criticism from so many sides the Church must continually and seriously ask herself whether she has truly freed herself from this one-sidedness, and whether she herself is not also projecting ideas instead of listening to the Word of God. Her preaching can be a truly comforting and encouraging light only if she is willing – in this respect also – to bring into captivity every thought to the obedience of Christ (II Cor. 10:5). By doing so, it is true, she will never be able to exhaust this richness and she will be continually reminded of John's statement that not all of Jesus' works can be described (John 21:25), but at the same time she will be on her guard against the danger that her preaching will deteriorate in one way or another, so that the Christ-idea of the congregation will not become unrecognizably obscured.

It is not for nothing that Paul speaks of the height and depth, the breadth and length, of the love of Christ (Eph. 3:18). This passage touches upon the inexhaustibleness of Christ's work and the many ways in which it profits us. When God opens the windows of his revelation, then its richness proclaims and testifies that this is the Christ, the Light of the world.

It is obvious that the confession of the authority of Scripture is of decisive importance in order to have a correct conception of the unity of Christ's work. If one should suppose, e.g., that the biblical record is itself fragmented, that the various authors merely give subjective and theologically biased views of Christ, then of course he will have little reason to look for a fundamental unity in the diversity. In this connection the variations between John and the other Gospels and between Paul and Hebrews, etc., have been pointed out. The new biblical research, however, has become aware of the unity of the various New Testament testimonies, a viewpoint which we find, for example, in Sevenster's *Christologie.*[3] A tendency is noticeable not to let one aspect eliminate another too quickly. If one does not respect the authority of Scripture, he is inclined to interpret the emphasis in one particular book of the Bible in such a way that the impression is created that all other biblical emphases have been neglected or

3. G. Sevenster, *De Christologie van het Nieuwe Testament,* 1946, p. 313, where he speaks of "a striking unity in the N.T. testimony concerning Christ." "No matter which book we open, as far as the essential is concerned, it is always the same theme – of Jesus Christ – which presents itself to us." Cf. also p. 339 where Sevenster points out the relationship between the message concerning Christ in the epistle to the Hebrews and the rest of the N.T. books. This message, however, does stress the diversity. Hebrews especially is "a typical document of the diversity of the N.T. Christ-revelation" (cf. p. 340). But this diversity does not imply a contrast. Cf. also his ideas on John and the Synoptists. It is "one powerful testimony concerning the coming of Jesus Christ and his atoning death, which we meet in the N.T." (p. 355). Cf. H. N. Ridderbos on Sevenster's book in *Gereformeerd Theologisch Tijdschrift,* 1947, pp. 54ff., and the criticism by G. J. Heering, who was disappointed because "it maintains, almost throughout, the tradition of the church, which sees throughout the entire N.T. the influence of the same Christology" (Heering, *Theologie en Practijk,* June and July, 1948). He speaks of the influence of the tradition of the church which is quite strong in our days and which must be resisted, according to him.

even denied by its author.[4] But Holy Scripture should not be atomized; attention should be given to all emphases, because they are all concerned with one message concerning the work of the one Lord.

In considering the work of Christ we do not intend to be biblicistic, to neglect or belittle the light which the Church has accumulated in her history of many ages. We may freely say that no one any longer approaches Scripture as if it were a blank sheet of paper. The confessions and hymns of the Church, and especially her preaching, are indeed relevant. The ties of faith will not create an obstacle if only we maintain obedience to the normative Word of God. Thus it will be possible in any era to re-inquire about the meaning of the work of Christ for all times, and thereby remain conscious of the fact that it is impossible to understand the mystery of this work "for us" without believing in abstract-theoretical reflection.

It certainly would be an exaggeration to say that today the voice of liberal theology is no longer heard in Christology, in spite of Albert Schweitzer's influential criticism of the liberal Jesus-idea. Nevertheless, we must fully realize that, if not instead of, then certainly alongside of, the modern Christ-conception a new idea has appeared. Every era raises new questions and offers new answers which clearly reflect the nature of a certain phase of history. In the general realm of theological thinking this has been most clearly evidenced by the radical eschatology of Christendom. Pressed by the catastrophic events in our age, attention has been focused once more on the transcendence of God's kingdom, on the origin and destiny of the cosmos, and on the advent of God, instead of on the "inner evolution of the world."

The question arises whether this influence upon dogmatic reflection, resulting from the nature of contemporary events, has

4. A striking example, and a difference in attitude towards Scripture, may be found in connection with Heb. 13:20. We frequently read that the epistle to the Hebrews does not know or accept the resurrection of Christ. Sevenster, however, reasons quite differently. The fact that the resurrection is mentioned only once "does not in the least imply a negation of this part of the doctrine of Christ. On the contrary, the entire epistle presupposes, of course, the resurrection and this is, moreover, explicitly mentioned in one place .(*Christologie*, p. 314).

also extended to the meaning of Christ and his work. It cannot be denied that this is indeed the case. The question has become actual again: What can be the meaning of Jesus Christ, not for the gray past, but for *today*? Perhaps more than ever before, attention has been focused on the words which should shine as a light over every valley of temporality, "Jesus Christ is the same *yesterday* and *today,* yea and *for ever*" (Heb. 13:8). The breach with the past, in so many respects absolute, has increasingly urged the question, what Christ *now* means to, and does in, a world which apparently has been irretrievably given over to the unconquerable powers of destruction and doom.

And in times when new sufferings like an avalanche descended upon human life, causing unprecedented terror and utmost desertion and loneliness, the question arose with renewed urgency: What can the *passio magna* of Jesus Christ mean for a torn world whose "humanity," so passionately sought for, had hardly been able to alleviate, let alone eliminate its suffering? Is the cross then indeed more than just a symbol of the Church, a symbol of tragedy and at the same time of oppression, a symbol of the evil in the world? Is it more than romanticism, which had not been able to make headway against the outrages of a realistic era? And is the cross (and resurrection) of this Person a real comfort in the futility and senselessness of our "existence," for the first time discovered in its hopelessness and absurdity?

We realize that these questions are not exclusively scientific, even though they also play a part in the realm of theology. We are first of all concerned with questions which touch the core of the preaching of the Church and which cry out there for an answer. The reality of present-day life cannot be helped and comforted by shiftings in a New Testament science which has replaced the liberal Jesus-idea with that of the eschatological Jesus and his imagination of the approaching Kingdom of God, the Jesus Christ who had been grossly mistaken in his great expectation. It was exactly this shifting which caused the problem of history to be a big question mark; it failed utterly to transform history into a divine answer, a big exclamation mark! Not simply a new theory, nor even a new theological theory was needed, but a real answer to the perplexing complications of present history. What about Jesus Christ's presence and authority in a harassed world? What about his holy office, the *munus triplex* in the past, but especially at present in a situation wherein the threats simply could be called "multiplex"? Could the Church, here and now, in connection with the work of Christ, continue to remind men of his assurance, "All authority hath been given unto me in heaven and on earth" (Matt. 28:18) and "Lo, I am with you always, even unto the end of the world" (Matt. 28:20)? Was it justified to deal with this presence and these promises: and how and where were they manifest and experienced? Thus the danger arose that again Jesus Christ would be viewed from the perspective – or rather the perspectivelessness of this world. Was the confession of the Church still justified – the confession of the *euaggelion*, the glad tidings – and could Christmas still mean more than just an ornament in a secularized world, which no longer simply accepted the "Glory to God" from the "mythical" realm of angels?

On the other hand, it is noteworthy to observe that a crisis took place in the mind of many people with respect to the optimistic belief in evolution and that at the same time theology became concerned again with the *eschaton*, the last things, the future, the judgment, and the wrath of God. Whereas the optimism of the nineteenth century had all but erased the consciousness of the wrath of God, our era seemed to call up the idea of God's wrath again, and countless are the studies dealing once more with God's justice, his holiness, and his wrath. Rudolf Otto's book on "that which is holy," which appeared in 1917, had, by 1926, its 13th printing. A fierce opposition became evident against all immanent world-explanation, and God's transcendence was again silhouetted against the lightnings of his judgment. When gradually the false comfort of the nineteenth century had been discerned as a deception, attention was again focused on Jesus Christ and his work. In connection with God's holiness the mystery of God was discussed again, in contrast with the historically shallow and psychologically approachable "presence and evidence" of the God of nineteenth-century theology. The controversy between God and the world was brought up again, as well as the grace which could come to us only thus and because it penetrated the reality of God's judgment.

Somehow Christ was again seen as standing at the crossing of the two lines: judgment and grace; and what no one would have expected, happened: his vicarious suffering was mentioned again, a confession which had more and more faded into the background because of the increasing criticism since the days of Socinianism up until the nineteenth century.

Frequently this revival of the idea of a "vicarous" suffering developed in a so-called *theopaschitic* sense. It was asserted that it was God himself who, in Christ, had taken the suffering upon himself and thus entered the world and its guilt. The idea of the suffering God, formerly entertained occasionally by border-groups of the Church, reappeared with renewed force from different sides, and this, in my opinion, is becoming one of the striking aspects of present-day theological thinking. "The suffering God" – the influence of this idea (which spread in England after the first World War) reflects the temper of our present era. It seems that no longer the aspects of power and might, but more and more those of impotence, are placed in the foreground; not the *majesty*, but the *kenosis*. The idea of this "God himself" betrays the longing desire for divine compassion as the answer to all life's problems of suffering and death. Needless to say, this effect upon present-day theological thinking confronts the Church with the great responsibility, especially with respect to her preaching, to publish the fulness of Christ and to do so by preaching the Scriptures. All dogmatic reflection, if it truly wants to be based upon the Word of God, can and will be subservient only to this message. It will have to realize that the light of Christ shines in the darkness and that he came to seek *that which is lost*. And the more human life seems to be "lost" in the process of the modern secularization, the more urgent must the preaching of the object of his coming become. It will not be permissible to picture him according to the schemes of human distress and strain, but the message of Christ does retain, especially in times darker than ever before, all its actuality. Then everything receives new meaning: his power, his presence, his sacrifice, his victory. "Remember Jesus Christ, risen from the dead" (II Tim. 2:8). The remembrance of his suffering and death (in the Lord's supper) and of his resurrection is essentially one and is the antithesis of secularization, which essentially is *forgetting* Christ, because secularization is the isolation of the world within its own immanence. To remember Christ here in his death and resurrection is an assignment in which first of all the preaching, but also all dogmatic reflection, should participate. And in this way the cross will still be a *skandalon,* unless the illumination of the Spirit enlightens the eyes, and it is understood again that "the foolishness of God is wiser than men; and the weakness of God is stronger than men" (I Cor. 1:25).

CHAPTER TWO

THE MOTIVE OF THE INCARNATION

IN OUR discussion of the person of Christ we repeatedly pointed out that, in the study of Christ and his salvation, it is impossible to separate his *person* from his *work*. There is such an inseparable connection between his person and work that any separation causes us to go astray with respect to both his person and his work. For he manifests himself in his work as the Mediator between God and men (II Tim. 2:5), so that even the slightest abstract notions of his work and of the valuable influences and impulses proceeding from Jesus of Nazareth immediately derogate from the real essence of his work. Moreover, an isolated consideration of his person "as such" is impossible and illegitimate, because he can be fully known only in connection with his holy work.

When we do differentiate between Christ's person and his work, then we are likely to misunderstand either or both of them. Scripture often does speak of his person and answers the question who he is, and it does deal with the nature of his work, but it is always one and the same message it brings us. To mention Christ's name is to point to his work, and to mention the blessing of his work is, if it be well, to deal with the work of him of whom the Church in adoration confesses: *vere Deus, vere homo.* Towards the end of our study of the person of Christ we could remind ourselves of the unity and harmony expressed in Christ's own words, "These things have I spoken unto you, that in me ye may have peace" (John 16:33). These words apparently do not refer to a *general* idea of peace, happiness or bliss, but to the peace *in him,* viz., such a peace as is contained and founded only *in him.* It is a peace which would depart from us and become unrecognizable just as soon as it is isolated from his person. This peace can be known only in communion with his person, the communion which Calvin called the *mystica communicatio,* or, of which the Form for the Lord's Supper says, that we seek our life apart from ourselves in Jesus Christ, who fills us with his blessing. And in the prayer before the celebration of the Lord's supper it is mentioned that we, with true confidence, give ourselves up unto Jesus Christ, "in order that our burdened and contrite hearts, through the power of the Holy Spirit, may be nourished and refreshed with his true body and blood, *yea with him,* true God and man, the only heavenly bread" (John 6:58).

In human relationships it is possible – out of ingratitude – to isolate the gift from the giver and still enjoy it, and there are also "unknown" givers who remain in the background. But Christ is not such an unknown giver. He gives himself, and therefore his gift is never an isolated richness. Every gift would lose its richness and vivifying power when isolated and considered apart from his person. The objective of preaching Christ may never be a neutral happiness, or general immortality, or anything else which might appear desirable outside of Christ. No more than the object may be an abstract ontological interest in Christ's person, may his work, his Word, his influence, as such, be the source of any truly Christian faith. Preaching Christ must always be centered around *his* work, and his *work.*

Many may consider the preceding remarks self-evident, yet the history of the Church and of theology has unmistakably proven that we are confronted here with very important questions, which at various times have played an important role in the consideration of the Christ-message. Moreover, we see that these questions, when wrongly answered, cause shadows to descend upon the Church. The general problem here, as we shall call it, is "the motive of the incarnation." That is, we want to know the connection between the incarnation of the Son of God and the sum total of God's acts of salvation. Does the incarnation originate in and is it motivated by the lost condition of mankind, or would it also have occurred if there had not been a fall of mankind, or, at least, would it have been conceivable and possible?

In the latter case the deliverance from guilt and destruction would have been a *secondary* motive, which historically – because of the fact of the fall – must indeed be considered very important, but which nevertheless would not be the deepest or *primary* motive. Thus the inquiry concerning the motive of the incarnation takes on this special form: Would there have been an incarnation *without the fall?* Upon hearing this question we might be inclined *a priori* to call it merely speculative and thus dismiss it; yet the fact remains that this question, "incarnation, even without sin?" has often been answered in the affirmative. This simple and probably surprising fact already compels us to a closer examination, since it naturally brings up immediately the question concerning the significance of the work of Christ. We may even say that by answering this question we approach a far-reaching conclusion regarding the work of Christ.

When the above question is answered in the affirmative there is every reason to examine the motives for such an answer, for the issue at stake is not the fact of the incarnation of the Word, but its primary motivation. According to this view the great mystery, "God manifest in the flesh," may absolutely not be made dependent on the fact of the *fall*. The miracle of the incarnation simply cannot be a mere *response* to an act of human apostasy! Would rebellion have the "power" to "cause" this unique act of Christ's emptying himself? Such a dependence – even though it be associated with the unity of God's decree – is considered incommensurate with the stupendous reality of Christmas. True, the incarnation is *historically* connected with deliverance, but from this it may not be concluded, it is asserted, that there would have been no incarnation without the fall.

Once this idea of "incarnation even without a fall" is accepted, it soon follows that a special meaning is ascribed to the incarnation as such. This incarnation becomes the subject, without immediately connecting it with Christ's suffering and his obedience unto death. The connection between incarnation and cross is recognized as a historical fact, but it is a "connection" in a condition which developed later, viz., of man's lost condition and guilt. Apart from this it is possible to concentrate one's attention specifically on the incarnation of the Word, which, for that purpose, is often referred to as Christ's "becoming *man*." It is obvious that this preference of some people for the expression "becoming man" instead of "becoming *flesh*" has something to do with the fact that "becoming flesh" reminds us of *fallen* mankind while "becoming man" allows for a coming of Christ, a *unio personalis,* without necessarily having the shadows of sin and guilt descend on it.

As a result the connection between incarnation and cross becomes much looser, and reflection on the incarnation reveals a specific trend. Kuyper has pointed out that this idea of "incarnation even without a fall" has always been considered heretical in the history of the Church. Even though it showed up here and there – sometimes hesitantly, then again positively – in dogmatic thinking, it remained a border-opinion in the Christian Church and Kuyper was of the opinion that the Church intuiitively felt that this meant a deviation from the confession concerning Christ, even though the essence of the incarnation was not denied.

Guided by this intuition, the Church refused to accept the idea that this view would result in a deeper insight into the mystery of the incarnation. In addition, those theologians who entertained this idea were not of the sort to inspire confidence that the confession would be kept pure. We are thinking of such people as Osiander, Socinus, and several *Vermittlungstheologen* (mediation-theologians) of the nineteenth century,[1] the majority of whom were of the opinion that Christ would have become man even if there had not been sin and guilt. This opinion, to be sure, could not be proven by specific scriptural statements, but it was pointed out that the fact of the incarnation, the *idea* that God had become man, contained a thought which as such must be considered and worked out. It is the idea of the connection between God and man (or the divine and the human) which as such was of great import.[2] Moreover, it was sometimes pointed out that the incarnation had already been incorporated in the eternal decree, so that the historic correlation between incarnation and cross might not be projected back into eternity in order to conclude that the incarnation was "motivated" exclusively by the fall. Some were of the opinion that the Church had overemphasized the connection between the incarnation and the need for deliverance, a connection which some-

1. Cf. A. Kuyper, *De Vleeswording des Woords*, 1887, p. 28. Kuyper speaks of "the strange, objectionable thesis" which he had found in Origen, Tertullian, Duns Scotus, and others (p. 28) and adds that more than once the attempt has been made to ascribe the same idea to others, as, for instance, Augustine, Thomas, and the Reformed theologian Zanchius, which, according to Kuyper, was possible only by "untrue quotations" (p. 30). Kuyper speaks also of a contra-scriptural and pantheistic error and considers the question, "incarnation, even without sin" a *senseless, useless, foolish* speculation (p. 10) because Scripture "does not know of any other incarnation but the one *for sinners*" (p. 10).
2. Althaus writes that "the entire history of Christian thinking is concerned with the question whether the incarnation of Christ would not be necessary, apart from sin." In our opinion this generalizing statement is too strong. Althaus, *Theol. Aufs.*, II (1935), 51.

times has been called a hamartiologic or hamartiocentric conception, to which they vigorously objected.[3]

It was asserted that thus Christ was considered solely as the restorer of what sin had ruined. God's acting through Christ, it was alleged, was no more than a divine reaction; and the divine initiative, God's personal acting, on the basis of his own motives, was put in the background. God acted only because man, in rebellion, had acted first. Thus God's action in the incarnation does not sovereignly precede all human action, but follows it. It was no longer an *aprioristic* acting of God. That is why it is called a hamartiocentric conception of history and Christology, over against which the idea and the possibility of an "incarnation" even without a fall is placed. It is believed that the idea of the incarnation as such can be treated and considered as something meaningful without immediately endangering the reconciliation through the cross. The incarnation as such has its own motive without immediately connecting it with the motive of redemption and restoration.

All this presses the urgent question whether such an anti-hamartiocentric conception within the Church may be considered legitimate, or whether we are dealing here with a *speculation* which obscures rather than clarifies the dogmatic perspectives in Christology.

Before we attempt to answer this question in the light of Holy Scripture we wish first of all to point out that this idea of "incarnation even without sin" is frequently found in certain theological and philosophical connections far removed from the ancient confession of the Church. This was especially the case in the nineteenth century, during which the speculative philosophy of Hegel strongly dominated theology and specifically Christology. This philosophy strongly accentuated the idea of God's becoming *man,* far more than the Word becoming *flesh,* and the incarnation was explained as the gradual unification of God and man by a gradual process of evolution. Orthodox Christology was sharply attacked because of its mythical elements (the real incarnation of the Word in the historic Jesus of Nazareth) since it arbitrarily limited the unity of God and man

3. The expression "hamartiocentric" is especially used by H. W. Schmidt (Althaus, p. 52).

to Jesus Christ.[4] It is obvious that in this line of thinking the idea of incarnation-even-without-sin (or rather, becoming-one, even without sin) found ready acceptance and was vigorously defended.

Several nineteenth-century theologians show clear traces of this idea. The idea of becoming-man (or: becoming-one) as such becomes an object of reflection. Martensen, for instance, is of the opinion that the object of history, regardless of sin, is the "idea of the world-completion," viz. "that humankind will be united with God," so that he concludes, "In this sense we say that, even if sin had not entered in, Christ still would have come."[5] Martensen argues that Christ has metaphysical significance and "so his coming cannot be determined by sin only."[6]

Van Oosterzee, too, defends the idea of "incarnation even without sin." Those who disagree, he says, consider Christ solely as the Lamb of reconciliation, so that the sacrifice would not have

4. That which the Church considered "once-and-for-all" had to be taken as general. According to Strauss this is the key of Christology. See, among others, J. A. Dorner, *Entwicklungsgeschichte der Lehre von der Person Christi,* 1853, II, 1118ff. This matches the well-known expression of Strauss, "To pour its entire fullness into (just) *one* object would not be the way at all in which the Idea would be realized." Here humanity is made God-become-man (Dorner, p. 1119).
5. H. Martensen, *Die Chr. Dogmatik,* 1897, pp. 208-211.
6. *Ibid.,* p. 209; cf., "Must we accept, then, that the most glorious thing in the world could only have been occasioned by sin, so that, if there had not been sin, there would not have been a place in humanity for the glory of the only-begotten?" (p. 209). We must, "even when we disregard sin," ask the question, "who is the complete God-man in this realm?" Martensen bases his ideas on Eph. 1:10ff. and Col. 1:15ff., which mention Christ's cosmic significance (p. 210). Cf. on Martensen, e.g., E. Günther, *Die Entwicklung der Lehre von der Person Christi im XIX. Jahrhundert,* 1911, pp. 232ff. We find similar ideas especially in Dorner. Cf. Günther, *op. cit.,* p. 237. "That he agrees with the central idea of the speculative Mediation-Theory is evidenced by his conviction of the necessity of the God-man, regardless of the fact of the fall and the work of redemption." As to Dorner himself, see Dorner, II, 1259 (who refers to Col. 1:15-17). The same motive is to be found in Liebner, who wants to transcend the exclusive hamartiologic-soteriologic to the "theanthropologic" motive (Dorner, II, 1245). It is remarkable to find the idea in Liebner that already creation is to be considered "Christologically." In the 19th Century the idea was even voiced that if Adam had not fallen the incarnation would still have proceeded (Dorner, II, 1247). The idea that the incarnation of God is given with the *idea* of mankind was quite widespread in the 19th century.

been necessary if there had not been sin. Van Oosterzee, however, is of the opinion that Christ was not only the Mediator of reconciliation, but "it is no less true that He at the same time is the highest revelation of the invisible Godhead and that originally man was destined to be like unto God."[7] Even without sin man would have had to be lifted up to higher perfection. "And why would we not be allowed to believe that the means which the highest Love would have employed to this end would have included the sending of his Son in human flesh?" He, too, argues that the incarnation cannot be an "incidental" reaction. "An incident so amazing as the incarnation of God in Jesus Christ, the Lord, can hardly be only the result of a phenomenon not absolutely necessary, viz., sin."[8] God's plan to gather all together in his Son does not originate at the time of the fall but from eternity (*ibid.*, p. 86). According to Van Oosterzee this idea would have been more generally accepted "if it had not been protected and recommended by Pelagian and Socinianistic theologians even though it has not the least connection with their reprehensible heresies."[9]

These examples make it sufficiently clear that the idea of "incarnation even without sin" is opposed to the *exclusive-soteriologic* motive of the incarnation.[10] Attention is called to

7. J. J. van Oosterzee, *Christologie,* III (1861), 85.
8. *Ibid.,* p. 86. The stubborn attempt to point out the basis for this idea in Scripture is evident when he quotes Paul's statement as proof, "that was not first which is spiritual, but that which is natural; and afterward that which is spiritual. The first man is of the earth, earthy: the second man is the Lord from heaven" (I Cor. 15:46, 47; cf. the distorted reasoning in connection with this word: *ibid.,* p. 86).
9. *Ibid.,* p. 89. Van Oosterzee mentions Irenaeus, Tertullian, Origen, Thomas Aquinas, Duns Scotus, and Osiander as champions of this idea. The latter wrote in 1550, "an filius Dei fuerit incarnandus, si peccatum non introivisset in mundum." Further; Liebner, and in the Netherlands: J. J. de Roy. It is remarkable that Van Oosterzee concludes his discussion of this problem with these words, "But why should we any longer lose ourselves in the inquiry concerning a deduced possibility or impossibility. Sin has entered the world. . ." (*ibid.,* p. 90).
10. We further mention J. H. Gunning, *Blikken in de Openbaring,* III (1868), 133, who writes, "Jesus is the fulfillment of man; He is the Man, the chosen One *par excellence.* The relationship between the Son and mankind is eternal. He would have become man also if sin had not come in between, and that would only have materialized in the course of time, in human history, what He, in essence, has been from eternity. The great marvel of Bethlehem is only this, that he became *flesh,* and partook of our *weakness* resulting from sin. His becoming

Christ's mediatorship or his universal and cosmic significance, and this significance is regarded as limited and threatened if considered on the basis of the soteriological motive. Even the doctrine of God's image and the way of man to perfection are brought up in the argument from which, too, is concluded that the Son of God would have become man even if the world had not fallen.

Long before the nineteenth century, however, similar ideas had appeared in Christian theology. We find them, for instance, already in Duns Scotus and the Scotists, in contrast to the Thomists, who, like their teacher, reject the idea of an "incarnation even without sin." Thomas, indeed, had considered the problem, but answered the question "incarnation even without sin?" in the negative, basing this on the *patres,* but also, as Kreling states, "simply on Holy Scripture."[11]

The Scotists accused the Thomists of not sufficiently honoring

---

man, therefore, had been decreed from eternity." Cf. also Vol. I, 316ff. for the general background which shows that Gunning has been influenced by such motives as are to be found in Duns Scotus; although it is my opinion that specific 19th-century influences cannot be denied. It would be very interesting to examine the backgrounds of the "Christologic" motives in the doctrine of creation with Duns Scotus, Gunning, and Barth.

11. P. Kreling, "Het Motief der Menswording," *Studia Catholica,* 1939, p. 90. Thomas deals with the problem in his *Summa Theologica III,* 1, 3. (Utrum si homo non peccasset, Deus incarnatus fuisset). He considers several arguments (that human nature after sin is receptive to the grace of the communion with God and therefore it would have been so also outside of the fall; that the predestination is from eternity and therefore it was necessary, even before sin, that God's Son became man "ad hoc quod Dei praedestinatio impleretur"). However, over against this he places the words of Luke 19:10 and I Tim. 1:15, because we cannot know anything of the things which proceed "ex sola Dei voluntate nisi quatenus in Sacra Scriptura traduntur." And because Scripture everywhere (*ubique*) points out the "ratio incarnationes ex peccato primi hominis" it is more proper (*convenientius*) to say, that God appointed the work of the incarnation "in remedium contra peccatum," so that "peccato non existente, incarnatio non fuisset." Neither is Thomas convinced by the argument on the basis of the *praedestinatio,* because "praedestinavit opus incarnationis in remedium humani peccati." Concerning these questions see also P. Kreling, *Incarnatie en Verlossing,* Het Schild, XXIX ed., p. 76; further Zacharias, *Het Geheim van de Menswording in Oosten en Westen,* Het Schild, XXIX ed., p. 125, and my *Conflict With Rome,* "Incarnatie en Katholicisme"; and *Dict. Theol. Cath. VII,* 2, s.v. *Incarnation,* pp. 1480ff.

Paul's word, which depicts Christ as the firstborn of the entire creation, by whom all things are created (Col. 1:16). The Scotists called attention to the fact that Christ is the head of angels and that the entire creation points to Christ,[12] and they accused the Thomists of degrading Christ, "making him the means of man's deliverance, a means to an end" (Kreling, *Studia Cath.*, 1939, pp. 90ff.). Kreling points out that Thomas certainly realized the import of such Scripture passages but that he did not conclude an "incarnation even without sin" from them. Neither, apparently, did the argument that Christ thus was degraded to a "means to an end" impress him. From the cosmic significance of Christ it cannot in the least be concluded that he would have become flesh even without the fall.

The words of Scripture concerning this cosmic significance do not appear isolated but in immediate connection with the certainty and the fulness of God's salvation in Jesus Christ. According to Thomas one may not isolate one element of the way of salvation from the sum total in order to turn the incarnation, on the basis of the predestination, into an absolute, necessary idea that would be independent of the fall. There is a remarkable similarity in Thomas', Calvin's, and Kuyper's defenses; they all surrender to the superior power of Scripture.

Calvin came across this idea of the "incarnation even without sin" in Osiander.[13] Calvin's sharp attack is very remarkable, the

12. In my opinion it cannot be denied that to a certain extent Duns Scotus' ideas occupy a separate place in the frequently rather strange connections in which the idea of the "incarnation, even without sin" comes up in the course of history (especially with Osiander and the Mediation Theology). The issue with Scotus is the dogmatic problem in connection with the predestination of Christ. If God, in the predestination of Christ, first of all decreed Christ's utmost glory, then this election must have *preceded* that of other men and certainly the foreknowledge of the fall, so that it can no longer be said that sin is presupposed by the incarnation. There would not have been *redemptio*, "nisi homo peccasset, sed non propter solam istam causam videtur Deus praedestinasse illam animam ad tantam gloriam." We see, therefore, that the issue with Duns Scotus is the order in the *praescientia Dei*, which is the same kind of problem as was at stake later on in the controversy between supra- and infralapsarianism. Duns considers it absurd to suppose that God had sooner foreseen the fall of Adam than predestined Christ to glory. Concerning the entire problem see Duns Scotus, *Sententiae*, Lib. III, VII, Qu. 3, and on him, P. Kreling, "Het Motief der Menswording," *Stud. Cath.*, 1939.

13. Calvin, *Institutes*, II, XII, 5ff.; cf. W. J. Aalders, *De Incarnatie*, 1933, pp. 178, 179.

more so since he unconditionally confessed the predestination and apparently refused to draw a line from this divine initiative to the ideas of Osiander, and he could not at all accept the separation of the incarnation as an "idea" from the historical connection among God's acts of salvation. It is Calvin, who had such a keen insight into God's aprioristic activity (which truly is not just an activity "out of reaction") who rejected Osiander's idea as an unjustified speculation. He emphatically pointed out that the essential "motive" of the incarnation was the deliverance from sin and death, and he was convinced that Scripture clearly indicated that. He points out that Christ himself has declared the reason for his coming and asks the question why, then, Christ is not called the *first* Adam, but the *second.* Because he is the theologian of election, Calvin's thinking is unconditionally historical, and he avoids all speculation when he points out that Paul places the fall between the first and second Adam. The entire Scripture exclaims that Christ has been clothed with our flesh in order to become a Savior. To think up another reason or motive shows exceeding rashness, according to Calvin. Never has the Mediator been promised without the shedding of blood, and all the apostles unanimously agreed about the purpose of his coming.

It is not necessary to examine all the connections in which this idea of "incarnation even without sin" has functioned in the course of history. But the preceding examples prove sufficiently that the object of all this variation is always the same splitting of the motive of Christ's coming into the world, by separating this coming from the exclusively-soteriological framework. Thus it is impossible to avoid a dualistic motivation: one for the historic reality which entered in (the fall), and for a hypothetical situation, which nevertheless would also have called for the fact of the incarnation. It must not in the least surprise us, therefore, that later on the idea of the incarnation "as such" was disconnected from the connections in which it appeared in Scotistic theology and thus became the first stage of the deification of man in Osiander, and stronger yet, in nineteenth-century speculative reflection.

The development of nineteenth-century theology and its "mankind-Christology" makes us realize even more how much it was the duty of the Church at that time to be on her guard against all kinds of speculation, because this idea of "incarnation even without sin" took on such proportions that the actuality of the incarnation of the Word was hardly mentioned any more.

When studying this question we are inevitably reminded of all those passages of Scripture which so clearly deal with the immediate connection between Christ's coming in the incarnation of the Word and the salvation from our sin and lost condition. It is true, the angels laud the miracle of Christmas itself, and it is indeed the fulfillment of the prophecy concerning *Immanuel* (Isa. 7:14), but *this* "God with us" has nothing to do with the speculative theology of God and man becoming one *in general.* Never is a marvelous event *as such* the subject of a doxology by either men or angels, as though they consider it a cosmic theanthropic mystery. The salvation of God in his Son does not allow for any speculation. Neither can the incarnation be isolated from the further career of Christ. When considering the incarnation, that is to say, the Word becoming *flesh,* it is impossible — in the light of the scriptural connections — to speak first of Christ's *cosmic* significance, ontology, and the anthropologic "elevation" of human nature to this unification; rather, the reality of Immanuel must be seen as the fulfillment of the prophecy of salvation, and full attention must fall on God's Son descending and the heavens' rending.

The message of the incarnation is never a thing by itself; it preaches not the *elevatio* of human nature but its *deliverance* and *restoration* by him whom the Father had sent. Already in the Gospels we see the shadows descend upon the pathway of the Babe of Bethlehem, concerning which Simeon prophesies even while the joy about the Messiah, who had just come, still fills his heart (Luke 2:34). From the very beginning it is evident that Immanuel's coming is historically decreed and that it does not merely have a "general" meaning which can be described as a "unity between God and man." The Divine object is peace and good will when the fulness of time has come. Just as soon as Messiah is born opposition arises. This child is set for the fall and rising again of many in Israel; and for a sign which shall be spoken against (Luke 2:34). We nowhere find this Christmas event presented as a thing by itself, as an Immanuel-idea, but we read of the signs of poverty, by which the shepherds will know him (Luke 2:12). The entire gospel message clearly preaches the object of his coming. No matter how variegated this object may be designated, it is always presented in connection with the salvation of God.

His coming is *soteriological,* or, if the word were not so overcharged already, we could say *anthropocentric.* Man is the center in this coming, not of course in an anthropocentric sense as opposed to a theocentric sense, (the song of the angels!), but nevertheless man is a real, actual center (cf. Tit. 3:8). Thus we learn from the message of Scripture that Christ came to give his soul, his life, a ransom for many (Matt. 20:28; cf. John 12:27); not to be ministered unto, but to minister (Mark 10:45); to destroy the works of the devil (I John 3:8; cf. Gal. 4:4, Rom. 8:3); and to do the will of God (Heb. 10:7, cf. Ps. 40). He came to save sinners (I Tim. 1:15), to seek that which was lost (Luke 19:10), to call sinners to repentance (Mark 2:17), and to bear witness unto the truth (John 18:37). His being sent and his coming are unto *salvation* and *deliverance.* Nowhere is mentioned a "meaning" of his coming as such, nor an "idea" of the incarnation apart from this salvation; there is no mention of an Immanuel apart from Isaiah's prophecy of salvation, nor of an event by itself which would justify the speculative argument: "incarnation even without sin." There simply is no cosmological, anthropological, or theanthropological problem whatsoever. It is true that with respect to the fulness of time, and eschatologically, the point at issue is God's dwelling with men (cf. John 1:14 and Rev. 21:3), but that is the dwelling of the true God, the Covenant God, and the God of salvation. The Bible is obviously not at all afraid to depict God's act as a holy acting *in reaction,* viz., *against* man's guilt and lost condition. The biblical message is so historical in character that the historical viewpoint of the destroying work of Satan and mankind *precedes* the redemptive work of Christ, which is also historical, and God's response to the fall is a deed of supreme reaction, "*I* will put enmity" (Gen. 3:15)! True, Christ's redemptive work is not merely an incidental reaction in the midst of the course of history, and Scripture does bring up unfathomable depths and unlimited perspectives in connection with God's decree[14], but that does not

14. Eph. 1:4 (Has he not chosen us in him before the foundation of the world?); I Pet. 1:20. God's "reaction" does not preclude that this divine act of salvation primarily originates in God's good pleasure and that this good pleasure would not in a human, casual sense be dependent on human decisions and thus lose its aprioristic character. That is why Paul can say that God has chosen us in Christ before the foundation

change the fact that Christ's coming and his work may never be separated from the motive of his coming, which had been fixed within the scope of history and time, and which is *reaction* against rebellion and guilt.

His coming is truly curing and saving. It is a coming in and with the peace which surpasses all understanding, and even the naming of the Messiah expresses this motive, "Thou shalt call his name *Jesus*: for he shall save his people from their sins" (Matt. 1:21). This Jesus had been expected, his coming had been prophesied, and he had come as the Messiah, the Anointed; who could, for a moment, take this anointing in an abstract sense and disconnect it from his historical filling of his office? It is, therefore, impossible to separate his birth from his cross or even to imagine these being separated, or to speak of an incarnation as such, which should have significance apart from guilt.

The mystery, which was kept secret since the world began, but now made manifest (Rom. 16:25) is designated as "God manifest in the flesh," but is described *in* history: justified in the Spirit, seen of angels, preached unto the Gentiles, believed on in the world, received up into glory (I Tim. 3:16).

We need not be surprised that this speculation concerning the "incarnation even without sin" places the cross more or less in the shadows. The twofold motive of Christ's coming makes these shadows inevitable. Once the connection between incarnation and redemption has been severed, be it only *in abstracto* and hypothetically, then it cannot be reconstructed afterwards. The *idea* of the incarnation must simply continue to fascinate the mind and cause one ultimately to accept the elevation of man by means of this *unio*. The dominating aspect of the incarnation thus becomes the ascension of man rather than the *kenosis,* the descent of the Son of God into the depths of the flesh, which is presented to us as the act of mercy which finds its completion in death, even the death of the cross (Phil. 2:8).

On the basis of the confession of the Church, her confession of guilt and her doxology, the criticism which alleges that she has been too much influenced by "hamartiocentric" thought

---

of the world (Eph. 1:4), but to conclude from this that history and man's decisions are irrelevant would be changing the relationship between divine and human acts according to a merely human scheme of rational synthesis.

simply fails to impress us any longer. For the divine enmity expressed the promise to the woman by which the Bible opens the windows to the history of reconciliation, shows how serious the living and holy God considers the historic rebellion,[15] which he places in the "center" of his reconciliatory action. Christ's coming is indeed a divine response, not to a suppliant asking – He is found of them that sought him not (Isa. 65:1) – but to the guilt of a rebellious heart, and history may never be considered relative on the basis of God's decree. It is exactly the historical relationship between fall and redemption which God's revelation reveals unto us. What has the "thinking away" of sin to do with this (Martensen, p. 209)? That which has been critically called the hamartiocentric conception of history is nothing but the recognition of the reality of the historic reconciliation. This criticism is a misjudgment of the connection between guilt and redemption and severs the historical relationship between Christ's coming and man's guilt.[16]

15. We are referring to the expression, "o felix culpa," frequently ascribed to Augustine, and which refers to Adam's sin, by which Jesus Christ was revealed as the Reconciler in the way of deliverance: "O felix culpa quae tantum et talem meruit habere redemptorem." Quick is of the opinion that "those who think it wrong to utter it, have not understood the fulness of the gospel" (O. C. Quick, *Doctrines of the Creed,* 1949, p. 211), which, in my opinion, is an incorrect verdict, because it is fully well possible to confess the greatness of the *Redemptor* and the *redemptio,* without considering the "felix culpa" an acceptable expression in that connection. Thomas quotes this expression together with Rom. 5:20 (But where sin abounded, grace did much more abound), but Paul does not express the "felix culpa." On the matter of ascribing this expression to Augustine, cf. A. Sizoo, "*Felix culpa,*" *Gereformeerd Theologisch Tijdschrift,* 1944. Thomas quotes from the "benedictio cerei paschalis." Cf. the footnote in the Thomas edition Marietti, 1939, Rome: "habetur in ordine romano sine nomine, sed Ambrosio tribuitur eius compositio" (with Thomas, *Summa Theol.* III, Qu. 1, art. IV).

16. Paul Althaus writes in connection with his own theology that he is attempting to liberate theology "from the scheme of hamartiocentric theology" (*Theol. Aufsätze,* II, [1935], 53) without falling into the idealistic conception of history, which does not attach any *essential* significance to the historic facts with respect to the salvation of man, because these have only symbolic or illustrative significance. It is quite evident, however, that Althaus' attempt to *transcend* the hamartiocentric viewpoint is closely connected with his critical viewpoint with respect to the historical character of the fall. There does not appear to be a "tertium" between the "hamartiocentric" and the "idealistic" conception. One may object to the expression "hamartiocentric" since sin can hardly

It goes without saying that to accept the inseparable connection between Christ's coming and our salvation is entirely in harmony with the age-old confession of the Church, as we find this expressed in the Nicean Confession, which states that *he descended for our sakes.* This silences all speculation, and the Church has respected this viewpoint, both in her dogma and no less in her hymns.[17] No one can very well raise the objection that the point at issue is the motive, which, after the actual entrance of sin, was indeed connected with his coming. For the Church never knew of any other motive, neither hypothetical nor as secondary motive, besides this motive of Christ's coming unto salvation. She saw the incarnation in historical unity with the cross. Kreling mentions that Catholic theology has frequently been accused of having become mired in the incarnation doctrine. This accusation is incorrect, according to him. We may leave this statement for what it is, but we welcome his assertion that incarnation and redemption may never be separated, as so often happened in Eastern theology.[18] The incarnation is not an isolated phase of the way of salvation, followed by a second and new phase, viz., the cross. The hymn of the silent and holy night reaches its full depth at the prospect of the salvation of the millions, and after this joyful prospect it returns again to the stable in Bethlehem (Dutch version of *Silent Night*). The way of the Church, therefore, is that of faith, which directs itself to the message of the entire way of the incarnated Word, the Messiah, in his coming and in the complete fulfillment of his one, holy office. Let the Church be on her guard at the border of the mystery now manifested. For speculation – any speculation – falsifies the *tone* of the gospel, the tone which resounds *guilt* and *grace* from beginning to end. Immanuel's coming is integral

---

be called the "center," but the *fact* it indicates may not embarrass us. That which the history of criticism of the "hamartiocentric" has produced is in many respects so startling that we may discard this criticism with an easy conscience.

17. Cf. J. K. Mozley, *Christologie und Soteriologie,* in *Mysterium Christi;* Christol. Studien britischer und deutscher Theologen, 1931, pp. 209-236, esp. p. 218; and D. M. Baillie, *God Was in Christ,* An Essay on Incarnation and Atonement, 1948, pp. 157ff.

18. Cf., e.g., S. Zankow, *Das orthodoxe Christentum des Ostens,* 1928, who says that the Eastern church, since its earliest days, has been more concerned with the being and person of the God-Man than with soteriology" (p. 47). Cf. also Zankow, *Die orthodoxe Kirche des Ostens in oekumenischer Sicht,* 1946, p. 33.

to the prospect of salvation; this is entirely different from saying that Christ first became *man,* then secondly became *flesh* and brought salvation. The Church confesses in the same breath that he was born of the virgin Mary and suffered.

There is no other "elevation" of man possible than through reconciliation and restoration. It is the restoration of the imitation, which, according to Paul, is only feasible against the background of reconciliation in its self-denial and humiliation (Phil. 2:5ff.), "Let this mind be in you, which was also in Christ Jesus." Immediately our attention is called to the transition from the the form of God into the form of a servant to the poverty of the cross. His service is manifest in the world in this kind of coming and with this goal in mind. Through this transition from glory to poverty and forsakenness the debt is paid, demonry broken, and the way opened to the throne of grace. His coming is not our elevation but the *communion* with him, "Behold, the tabernacle of God is with men, and he shall dwell with them, and they shall be his people, and God himself shall be with them, and be their God" (Rev. 21:3). Here the purpose of Christ's coming shines in eschatological glory and the "motive" of the incarnation in its reality becomes once more fully evident. Even in the book of visions, the book of time and eternity, the sharp contours of history are still not erased: "Worthy is the *Lamb* that hath been *slain* to receive the power, and riches, and wisdom, and might, and honor, and glory, and blessing" (Rev. 5:12).

CHAPTER THREE

HUMILIATION AND EXALTATION

IT WILL NOT be surprising that we proceed at once to consider that particular distinction which, both in the Church's preaching and hymnology and in dogmatic discussion, came to the fore again and again, viz., the distinction between the two *states* of Christ's life: humiliation and exaltation. Bavinck remarks that the formal discussion of the doctrine of the two states took place among the Lutherans in order to bring the *communicatio idiomatum* into agreement with the humiliation of Christ, but that this distinction soon was accepted by the Reformed theologians in spite of other important confessional differences.[1] This already indicates that ultimately this distinction was not the result of a dogmatic construction.[2] The agreement of opinion

1. H. Bavinck, *Geref. Dog., III,* 398.
2. That does not mean that in the manner of developing dogmatic ideas certain motives may not play an important role, as is apparent especially in the Lutheran discussion of the doctrine of the two states. The communication of the divine attributes to human nature indeed plays an important role here, since this made it difficult to take the humiliation seriously and distinguished it sharply from the exaltation. Especially important to the Lutherans was the distinction between the *incarnation* and the – at least logically – following *exinanitio.* In the *exinanitio* the God-Man Jesus Christ had, in a certain sense, put off the divine attributes (cf. H. Bavinck, *op. cit.,* III, 237, and H. Schmid, *Die Dogmatik der evang-luth. Kirche.* 1893, pp. 271ff.). This distinction between incarnation and exinanition was linked up with Phil. 2, but essentially its purpose was to save the doctrine of the two states which had been jeopardized by the Lutheran idea of the *communicatio idiomatum,* and to prove a distinction between humiliation and exaltation. "The dogmatists find the state of exinanition described in Philipp. 2:5-8" (Schmid, p. 277). Thus there is no such thing as a kenosis of the Logos and the subject of the kenosis is not the Logos, but the *God-Man* Jesus Christ. In between "incarnation" and "exinanition" is the element of voluntariness which created the possibility of distinguishing between humiliation and exaltation. Cf. Jac J. Müller, *Die Kenosisleer in die Kristologie sedert die Reformasie,* 1931, pp. 16ff. Directly connected with this problem is, later on, the controversy between *Giesseners* and *Tubingers.*

with respect to the meaning of this distinction is undoubtedly based upon irrefutable scriptural evidence.[3] The distinction between humiliation and exaltation is meant to do justice to the testimony of Scripture concerning the historical progress of Christ's life from humiliation to exaltation, through suffering to glory. The doctrine of the two states is, therefore, not at all a dogmatic construction which only originated later on from a need to schematize. We find the idea of the two states in essence and principle already in the Apostolicum and throughout the practice of faith and the preaching of the ancient Church. When, therefore, under the influence of Schleiermacher's sharp criticism the doctrine of the two states was abandoned or drastically changed, this caused a radical breach in the confessional continuity of the Church. A new Christological thought announced itself which violated the evidence of the testimony of Scripture.

Schleiermacher's criticism was especially aimed at the idea of *humiliation.* In the first place, "the expression *humiliation* presupposes, strictly speaking, a former higher state, which cannot be allowed if we maintain the unity of his Person."[4] Schleiermacher's objection is not exegetical but entirely dogmatic in character, which is evident when he states, "only, no humiliation can be ascribed to the most High, and eternal, and consequently the unchangeable One."

On the basis of this "impossibility" the *kenosis* (emptying) and humiliation are rejected. When Schleiermacher asks what the origin may be of the doctrine of the two states, he finds that its "only basis" is derived from Philippians 2:6-9, which, according to him, cannot be decisive in this respect because this particular part of Scripture is *ascetic* and *rhetoric* in character. Thus reasoning, he concludes, "Therefore, when passing on doctrine this part may just as well be omitted and left to history to keep it." This clearly evidences a disregard for scriptural evidence on the basis of a dogmatic *a priori* and also how inseparably the ensuing criticism of the doctrine of the two states is connected with a complete modification in Christological thinking. This criticism directly touches that which, according to Scripture, is exactly the great mystery: *God* manifest in the flesh.

Against this widely accepted criticism[5] it must be maintained

3. "The Christian faith has always maintained the humiliation and exaltation" (K. Müller, *Doppelter Stand Christi, Realencyklopädie für protestantische Theologie und Kirche,* XVIII, p. 755).
4. Schleiermacher, *Glaubenslehre, II* (1884), 149.

that the doctrine of the two states did not in the least proceed from a schematic attempt to divide Christ's life into two distinct phases and periods, as is done in biographies, but from the plainness with which Scripture calls our attention to this distinction. The Bible portrays a historically decisive turn and progress in Christ's life which is inseparably connected with the significance of his work. True, Paul's statement in Philippians 2 is by no means the only basis, as Schleiermacher very superficially asserts, but we may say that few doctrines in dogmatics have corresponded so verbally with the direct and explicit testimony of Scripture as does the doctrine of the two states.

How difficult it is to evade the evidence of this testimony becomes apparent when we hear Schleiermacher make the statement that Paul actually speaks only of the *appearance* of humility in Christ (*op. cit.*, p. 152). But introducing this idea of "appearance" removes all basis for Paul's admonition to imitate Christ. On the contrary, Paul makes Christ's unique "emptying himself" and humiliation the basis for the believers' mode of life. Paul clearly depicts humiliation and exaltation as the progress of Christ's life through the death of the cross. He calls our attention to a caesura, but it is not a caesura as in a biography, which, as a scheme of description, distinguishes childhood and adulthood, or adulthood and old age. On the contrary, he wants to bring out a progress which portrays the content of Christ's work as manifesting the divine action. Humiliation and exaltation do indeed point to that which was present in the historical reality of Christ's life, but it is history which can be understood in its deep and universal meaning only on the basis of the divine program. There is a *unique* connection between humiliation and exaltation. After Paul depicts the way of humiliation as ending in death, even the death of the cross, then he immediately adds, "Wherefore also God highly exalted him, and gave him a name which is above every name."[6]

This statement from Paul has always been regarded as one

5. For further criticism of the doctrine of the two states I mention the sharp criticism from the adherents of Ritschl, for instance, from Horst Stephan, *Glaubenslehre,* 1928, p. 170, who considers it an impossible attempt to make the ancient doctrine of the two natures agree with the Jesus the Gospels portray. Cf. also J. Kaftan, *Dogmatik,* 1920, pp. 420ff.

6. Phil. 2:9-10. It is not in the least my contention to infer the connection between humiliation and exaltation exclusively from this "wherefore" (διὸ), nor to use the word "causal" here in a simplistic man-

of the foundations of the doctrine of the two states. The Church has never been concerned with a historical "life of Jesus" in a biographical sense, describing the various important phases which deserve special attention, but with a correct understanding of this historical progress in connection with God's action and the nature of Christ's work in this world. Anyone able to compose a better and purer definition to describe the nature of this progress than the two "states" of Christ's life, will certainly not be opposed by the Church or theology, provided that he does not replace the doctrine of the two states by a "life of Jesus" which removes the Divine perspective from it, so that the connection, the unique relationship between humiliation and exaltation, begins to disappear and the real meaning of Christ's life completely fades away.[7]

The progress of Christ's life through humiliation to exaltation is certainly not to be found only in the well-known pericope of Paul, but it is the continuous and ever-returning theme of the entire apostolic message, when this points out and preaches the way through suffering to glory as the way of salvation. This becomes evident immediately after the day of Pentecost in the interpretation and explication of this historical course of life, when Peter says that God has exalted Jesus Christ at his right hand and he is that *same* Jesus – whom ye have crucified – who by this exaltation has been made both Lord and Christ (Acts 2:33-36).

It is the act of God in Christ's exaltation, through suffering to glory in spite of what men may do, which the apostles constantly keep in mind (cf. Acts 2:22-24; 2:32, 36; 4:10, 28; 17:3; 26:23).

---

ner. But I do not understand how Streeder can write: "Paul cannot have meant with his admonishments to point out that shown meekness guarantees divine reward. This would cultivate disguised pride" (G. J. Streeder, *De Gemeente in Christus Jezus. De Brief aan de Philippenzen,* 1948, p. 39). Neither Ewald's idea (*Zahn Commentary*) nor the reference to Calvin make the difference between "result" and "cause" clear. Cf. S. Greijdanus (*Commentary on Philippians,* p. 197), who speaks of "in connection with and on account of and with an eye to" his preceding self-emptying and self-humiliation. G. Sevenster speaks of "the Divine sanctioning of Christ's sacrifice" (*De Christologie van het N. T.*, 1946, p. 278).

7. Cf. on the "biography of Jesus" the noteworthy comments by A. Kuyper, *Encyclopaedie der H. Godgeleerdheid,* III (1909), 159ff. Kuyper considers the very idea "repugnant" and denies this kind of biography a place in theology. He speaks of its impossibility (p. 159), but also of its unlawfulness (p. 161).

This progress is, indeed, absolutely historical reality and passes through places and periods such as Gethsemane, Golgotha, the Mount of Olives, and Pentecost; and it may be freely said that one phase *follows* the other.[8] Nevertheless this succession reveals God's doings, and sheds light on the meaning and depth of these phases.

The content of the apostolic message is this humiliation and exaltation. Not selected parts of Christ's life but the totality of his humiliation and exaltation is incorporated and passed on in the *kerygma,* just as they follow each other in holy and gracious order. It has indeed been hours, and days, and years, which passed, but the mystery of this progress can be discerned only in the light of revelation and, therefore, in the light of faith. Without this light there remains nothing but offense, or perhaps some interest in this still curious history from the gray past. But this light reveals that the tensions and emotions of this progress are the result of the divine "must" and the unavoidability of the Father's command and the goal he had set. These determine the caesura in Christ's life: humiliation-exaltation. In this caesura salvation becomes historical reality for all times. For in the way of humiliation he has blotted out the handwriting which threatened us, and he has done so by nailing it to his cross. Thus he disarmed principalities and made a show of them openly and triumphed over them (Col. 2:14, 15).

It is not necessary to mention all the scriptural passages which more or less refer to the way that led through humiliation to exaltation. Sometimes they occur in connection with a practical admonition, derived from Christ's reconciling death (Phil. 2:5ff.), then again in a doxology on the glory which becomes his after accomplishing his sufferings.[9] The emphasis is on the glory which is given him in the raising up from the dead (I Pet. 1:21)

8. Cf. Acts 1:3 concerning Christ's appearances "*after* his passion" and I Pet. 1:11, where Peter says that the Spirit of Christ signified in the prophets concerning the sufferings of Christ "and the glory that should follow."
9. Cf. e.g., Heb. 1 on the Son of God, who, "when he had made purification of sins, sat down on the right hand of the Majesty on high" (1:3ff.), and the inheritance which Christ obtained (1:4). Cf. Heb. 2:9, where we see "Jesus, who was made a little lower than the angels for the suffering of death, *crowned with glory and honor,* that he by the grace of God should taste death for every man." See also Heb. 2:10 (through sufferings to perfection) and 4:15; 9:26; 12:25; 13:12.

and in the receiving up into glory (I Tim. 3:16). All this must be seen in connection with the real historical progress in which salvation is directly connected with the power of this historic event in God's dealings, exactly as the old creed, without any intellectualization, confesses the "*natus ex virgine*," the "*sub Pontio Pilato*," cross, resurrection, and ascension, just before the *forgiveness of sins*.

It is quite logical that the consideration of the states of Christ focused again and again on the *connection*, which, according to the apostolic message, existed between humiliation and exaltation. The "wherefore" of Philippians 2 has already been discussed in this connection, and the question was raised whether a *causal* connection must be understood here, and if so, what the nature of this "causality" might be.

On this point the Church has been accused of trying to rationalize the mystery of Christ's earthly course, but this has never caused her to shrink back. On the contrary, she understood that Scripture clearly emphasized this unique connection. In it she discerned essentially the same message as in the Old Testament prophecy concerning the suffering Servant of the Lord, the Man of Sorrows of Isaiah 53. There too, we observe in the historic progressive development of the life of God's Servant the depth and indissolubility of the connection: the pleasure of the Lord proceeds in and through his suffering and therefore "he shall see of the travail of his soul" and receive a portion with the great, "because he poured out his soul unto death, and was numbered with the transgressors" (Isa. 53:11-12; cf. also 52: 13, 14).

With the "wherefore" of Paul and the "because" of Isaiah we touch upon the same meaning of the progress from humiliation to exaltation. The mere "succession" of two phases does not in the least contribute to a right understanding of this progressive development if the historic-temporal is not incorporated in a divine connection. Christ himself points out this connection when he expounds to the disciples on the way to Emmaus, beginning at Moses, that the prophets had spoken of the suffering of the Messiah, "Behooved it not the Christ to suffer these things, and to enter into his glory?" (Luke 24:26ff.). There is marvelous unity in both Christ's life and death, and this unity becomes fully apparent exactly *in* the caesura between humiliation and exaltation, in the progress from humiliation to exaltation. Of this the apostles soon become witnesses (Luke 24:45ff., and 48). Christ himself always saw his life in the sharp light of this caesura and thus he knew that he was not delivered up unto arbitrariness, but that he was subject to the command of his Father. He mentions this transition in his prayer to the Father (John 17:5), he knows this when entering the week of suffering by a conscious knowledge of the reality of this historical course (John 13:1), and already when announcing his suffering he mentions the darkness of the approaching suffering, but also the "thereafter" of his glorification (Mark 10:34, and elsewhere). And the clarity of this knowledge did not diminish as his suffering more and more grieved his soul, even unto death.

Important in this connection is the chapter which brings Christ's glorification into immediate relationship with his death, viz., John 12. When certain Greeks had come who desired to see Jesus, he spoke of the hour which had come, that the Son of man should be glorified (John 12:23; Bultmann points out the connection with verse 19, "lo, the world is gone after him," *Ev. des Joh.*, p. 324). He is not referring to human but to divine glorification. Christ realizes that this glorification would not materialize as Satan's temptation suggested (Matt. 4:1-11; 16:21-23), by way of eliminating the suffering, but only *by* and *through* the suffering.

Immediately after mentioning his glorification he speaks of the dying grain of wheat, "Verily, verily, I say unto you, Except a grain of wheat fall into the earth and die, it abideth by itself alone; but if it die, it beareth much fruit" (John 12:24). In the midst of his words full of glory he points to the shadows of his approaching death. Therefore, when his soul is stirred with emotion and he contemplates, "What shall I say? Father, save me from this hour!" the realization that the connection is unavoidable flashes through his mind, "but for this cause came I unto this hour. Father, glorify thy name" (12:27-28).[10] This, too, shows clearly that the historical progress is the realization of the divine plan, of the "must," and that his going to the Father has a purpose. Christ does not speak exclusively of the progress of his own life, but he knows that this progress is connected with the fruit of his death and the salvation of the world. The glory

10. Cf. F. W. Grosheide, *Commentary on John* 12, p. 221. Cf. the divine answer in v. 28, "I have both glorified it, and will glorify it again."

which is mentioned cannot be measured according to human standards, but it is the glory which results from his atoning, fruitful death.[11] This contains the meaning and mystery of his life. "And I, if I be lifted up from the earth, will draw all men unto myself."[12] Therefore the Greeks remain in the background. Pentecost has not yet come. The emphasis is on the light of the revelation that already here is cast on the pathway of the Son of men.[13] Grosheide states (p. 217), "The end is grievous, and yet it does not bring grief but life."

Christ also mentioned his exaltation on other occasions, as is evident especially from the Gospel of John. Already in John 3 we read of a comparison between the lifting up of the serpent by Moses in the desert and Christ's exaltation, "even so must the Son of man be lifted up" (3:14). Though there is difference of opinion about whether the evangelist is referring to the lifting up in the sense of glorification or of hanging on the cross,[14] yet there is hardly any disagreement that Christ, either directly or indirectly, is referring to the blessing of his work which will become manifest in his exaltation.

11. Cf. also Christ's expression, "This voice hath not come for my sake, but for your sakes" (John 12:30).
12. John 12:32. Cf. Bultmann, *Commentary on John,* p. 325, "Jesus' δοξασθηναι is not a mythical occurrence which concerned him only, but an event connected with the history of salvation: part of his δοξα is the gathering of the church." For the entire pericope cf. especially Grosheide *ad hoc.*
13. Grosheide, II, p. 215: the coming of the Greeks gives Christ "occasion to preach that he can obtain glory only in the way of suffering and death."
14. The dilemma is this: the local lifting up on the cross or the exaltation after the resurrection. This refers especially to John 12:33, where the evangelist writes, in connection with Christ's statement, "And I, if I be lifted up from the earth, will draw all men unto me": "This he said, signifying what death he should die." Grosheide rejects a lifting up on the cross (cf. his commentary on the words in question) also with respect to John 12:33, but he accepts a lifting up *in a dogmatic sense.* It is very difficult, it seems to me, to explain especially John 12:33 entirely this way and to combine both aspects in the one word "exaltation." This difference in exegesis, however, is irrelevant to the problem with which we are concerned. Cf. also Grosheide, p. 466 on John 18:32 (no lapidation but crucifixion), who refers to John 12:32 and continues, "This prophecy is, at any rate, less clear. That this being lifted up may not exclusively be taken to mean being crucified has been explained when dealing with verse 32." The expression "exclusively" indicates that Grosheide does not read a contrast in it.

Now it has been frequently asserted that especially the Gospel of John is not intended to be historically accurate, and therefore cannot give us a correct insight into the meaning of the *historical* connection between humiliation and exaltation. It is John who continually points to the glory irradiating from Christ's historical life. It is also believed that a projection of later date is frequently attached to it, creating a picture of Christ's glory which obscures the historical contours of Christ's earthly life.

It is very remarkable, however, that in this Gospel as well the historical aspect of the relationship between humiliation and exaltation is brought out. So, for instance, we read that the Holy Spirit was not yet present *"because Jesus was not yet glorified."*[15] This "not yet" fully recognizes the historical progress, and the temporary absence of the Holy Spirit is specifically connected with this, just as elsewhere in this Gospel the coming of the Comforter is connected with Christ's having to depart first (cf. John 14:19). The coming of the Comforter is not an event which merely *follows* Christ's death in historical succession, but he is sent by Christ himself (John 14:16, 25, 26; 16:13) in the historical progress of his work as the *fruit* of his death, so that it is expedient for the Church that he departs (John 15: 26; 16:7).[16]

The indications concerning the import of humiliation and exaltation in Christ's life are so numerous and so dominant in apostolic teaching that it must surprise us that there has been, and still is, such a disagreement concerning this dominance and this theme. It is no exaggeration to say that the dispute concerning the work of Christ always includes this caesura in Christ's life: cross – resurrection, suffering – glory, humiliation – exaltation.

In the nineteenth century it was extremely difficult to recognize the significance of the doctrine of the two states, because this doctrine is so decidedly historical and therefore a stumblingblock to anyone who is ruled by an idealistic interpretation of history. The influence of idealistic thought as expressed in the statement,

15. John 7:39. Cf. in this connection the indications in John 2:18ff., "*When therefore he was risen* from the dead, his disciples remembered that he had said this unto them concerning the destruction of the temple" (2:22); and John 12:16, where is said, in connection with Jesus' entry into Jerusalem, that the disciples did not understand it. However, when Jesus was "glorified" then they remembered the prophecy of Zech. 9:9, and that this had been written with respect to Christ, and that they had done these things to him.

16. John 16:7; RSV: "It is to your advantage that I go away."

"Incidental facts of history can never be the proof for necessary truths of reason," must not be underestimated.[17] The alleged fortuity and contingency of historic facts were an insurmountable obstacle to combining Christian faith with history. Today this idealistic interpretation of Christian faith no longer has full sway, but it has not vanished completely. Attempts have been made to find a synthesis between the elements of truth in idealism and the Christian faith. But it becomes more and more evident that there is no such synthesis, because idealism, on the basis of its starting-point, can ascribe no greater significance to historical events than their power to illustrate the eternal idea.

In opposition to this the Christian faith confesses an unbreakable tie between faith and history, and is thus in accord with Paul, whose conviction was that everything would fade and disappear if Jesus Christ had not risen from the dead.

It is quite obvious that the progress from humiliation to exaltation had to be the main target of idealism's attack, because it was this *historical* progress that had become the theme of the apostolic preaching. Neither need we in the least be surprised that present-day "demythologizing" centers especially upon the relationship between humiliation and exaltation, between cross and resurrection. This is quite evident in Bultmann, who, via *Entmythologisierung* (demythologizing), replaces the progress of Christ's life from suffering to glory with the soteriological significance of the cross. Just as the dispute concerning the person of Christ centered upon the two natures of Christ,[18] so the dispute concerning the work of Christ centers upon the two states, and it must be agreed that in essence it is the very same problem. There is every reason to go further into this point now, since this still-continuing argument raises not only theoretical problems but also directly concerns the life of the Church in her faith and preaching.

The problems are so serious for this reason: Bultmann does not deny the significance of history, and he does speak of God's *activity*, even of the decisive *soteriological* work of God *in* the cross of Jesus Christ. It may be said that the confession of this activity of God takes the place of the confession of the two states. What lies behind this feeling, which lately, especially in

17. Cf. L. van der Zanden on Lessing, in *Christelijke Religie en Historische Openbaring*, 1928, pp. 7ff.
18. Cf. my *The Person of Christ*, Introduction, also concerning the *Entmythologisierung* in general.

the German churches, has evoked so much unrest, so much approval, and so much criticism?

We have pointed out before[19] that according to Bultmann the mythical and historical are mixed through each other in the New Testament. To the mythical belong Christ's pre-existence, incarnation, resurrection, ascension, and return; but the *cross* of Christ belongs to the historical, and has nothing to do with the mythical. The cross, it is true, is depicted and described in the New Testament in a special way and is represented in a mythical form, but that only indicates the *significance* of the cross. Actually, however, the cross belongs to history, and the point is to understand correctly the meaning of this cross.

It is necessary, however, to introduce at once Bultmann's conception of the resurrection. There the situation is quite different from that of the cross. The resurrection certainly belongs to the mythical elements of the New Testament and may not be considered a historic reality. That is why Bultmann concentrates all his attention on this relationship between *cross* and *resurrection* in the New Testament. He simply must agree that this theme in the New Testament is extremely central. "Ultimately everything is concentrated on the main question concerning cross and resurrection."[20] He states, moreover, that they indeed belong together and must be connected with each other: "Indeed, cross and resurrection are, as cosmic events, a unity" (p. 63). It soon becomes evident, however that Bultmann does not intend in the least to defend the doctrine of the two states with this declaration. He emphatically denies "that the cross as such may be considered the death and destruction of Jesus, which was then followed by the resurrection, after death had been abandoned" (p. 63). The New Testament frequently does picture it as a "confirmed miracle" (p. 64), for instance in the legends of the empty tomb and the appearances of Christ, but that may not determine our conception of the resurrection. For the point at issue is not Christ's resurrection as historical event,[21] but the Easter-*faith*. The historical event is the *faith* of the first witnesses. How that faith originated — psychologically from the

19. *The Person of Christ,* p. 15.
20. Bultmann, *N.T. und Mythology,* 1941, p. 60, now incorporated in *Kerugma und Mythos I,* 1948, pp. 14-54.
21. "The Easter event as the resurrection of Christ is not a historical event" (p. 66).

disciples' affection for Christ (p. 67) – is entirely unimportant. "The Christian Easter-faith is not interested in the historical problem." The point at issue, says Bultmann, is *only* and *exclusively* that the faith in the resurrection is actually a faith *in the cross*. "The resurrection faith is nothing else but the faith in the cross as a soteriological event." Christ's death is not the tragic death of a noble man, but it is God who acts in the cross, and that is the eschatological event. Bultmann also calls both death and resurrection eschatological events (p. 66), but does not mean that they are both historical in the same sense. The point at issue is much rather cross and *faith*. The cross, as historical fact, reveals to faith God's doings, which are non-mythical. For we are not dealing here with a "miraculous, supernatural event" (p. 68) but with a *historical* occurrence in space and time. When we thus "remove the mythological cloak" (p. 68) we rediscover, according to Bultmann, the deepest intention of the New Testament, viz., that God's eschatological ambassador is "a concrete, historical man."

God acts, and is present with his grace, in him – Jesus of Nazareth – and in him he reconciles the world with himself (p. 68). Everything that takes place in the New Testament around this eschatological proceeding only accentuates the decisive seriousness of this occurrence. The disciples' faith after the crucifixion was an "act of decision."[22] The decision of this "Easter-faith" showed that the cross was not arbitrary but that it made sense "in connection with the history of salvation" (*ibid.*, p. 46). To Paul the issue was death *and* resurrection (p. 289), but essentially that means the *cross*, and the word of the cross, even though Paul interprets Christ's death "analogically after the death of a mystery deity" (p. 293), and even though he describes this death as "in the gnostic myths," namely that the coming and departure of the Redeemer are "his humiliation and exaltation" (p. 293). Exactly that which was the decisive theme of the apostolic preaching, and that which the confession of the Church expressed in inseparable relationship with the salvation of God, and that which had been incorporated in the hymns of the Church of all ages, is here excluded. That which is left is the cross.[23] Only *that* is not mythical, but historical reality. One can continue to live by the soteriologic significance of the

22. Bultmann, *Theol. des N.T.*, 1948, p. 46.
23. Cf., on Philipp. 2, *ibid.*, pp. 293 and 174ff.

cross in the modern condition of the world, because this historic cross is stripped of all mythic elements.

The "demythologizing" of the New Testament removes all the stumblingblocks of the gospel for modern man, and aims to confront him with the real *skandalon*: God's reconciling dealings in this concrete crucified man Jesus of Nazareth. For modern man, too, it is possible to believe without violating his scientific mind. He can approach the *real kerygma*, which penetrates the mythical forms. It is no longer necessary for man to accept a number of historical facts and truths at the cost of a *sacrificium intellectus* in order to come to faith, but the word of the cross demands of man "whether he wants to consider himself co-crucified and consequently co-resurrected."[24] In the cross of Jesus Christ, God passes absolute judgment on man's "inessential" being, and when man accepts the *kerygma* of the cross, then Christ's death becomes significant to him through his acceptance of it *as his own cross;* thus he takes the way of God's grace and mercy. That is being co-crucified and co-resurrected.

Bultmann does not *isolate* the person of Jesus, as though that which happened to him was something by itself.[25] The cross as such, as a fact in the past, is not an occurrence in our our life, but preaching places it once more in the present. Bultmann stresses so strongly that our present life is concerned with salvation that he even states, "It is a soteriological event not because it is the cross of Christ, but it is the cross of Christ because it is a soteriological event" (p. 50). The object of the word of the cross is not the preaching of the reality of reconciliation in the cross, but in preaching the soteriological event is re-enacted again and again. It is exactly in this respect eschatalogical, "that is does not become a fact of the past, but continually repeats itself in the present."[26]

How does it become clear that the object of the preaching of the soteriological event is the salvation of God? That is not obtained by reasoning or by means of instruction in the divineness of this event.[27] It is the offense, the stumblingblock which is being overcome in the existential decision as *acceptation* (*Anerkennung*). This takes place when one accepts the requirement "to surrender the self-conception one has always had, and

24. *N.T. und Mythologie*, p. 67.
25. *Kerugma und Mythos, I,* 143.
26. Bultmann, *Th. des N.T.*, p. 267.
27. *Ibid.*, p. 298.

to accept the cross, allowing it to be the directing force of his life, and to let himself be crucified with Christ" (p. 298). So the point is not at all to accept the great value of an isolated fact (Golgotha), but to be incorporated in the eschatological occurrence. "God has made the crucifixion on Golgotha an eschatological event, so that it, elevated above every limitation of time, is re-enacted in everyone's presence, both in preaching and sacraments."[28] Thus the cross of Christ is no longer prior, since it has been disconnected from the historic resurrection of Christ. At first it seemed that after the removal of the "mythical" element of the New Testament (the resurrection), the historicity of the cross would be fully honored. But the eschatological has crowded out this concrete historicity as well from the preaching of the gospel. The decisive actuality which now constitutes salvation is the modern man's contact with the eschatological-soteriological occurrence; and that, then, is what finally is left of Paul's message of being crucified and resurrected with Christ.

It is clearly evident that the object of the demythologizing of the New Testament is the self-explication (*Selbstverständnis*) of human existence, and Heidegger is to be the philosopher whose categories must remove the obstacles for modern man, not only the obstacle of the mythical world-conception of the past but also that of the *sacrificium intellectus* with its acceptation of isolated historical facts.[29]

The doctrine of the two states, the confession of Christ's humiliation and exaltation is nowhere more seriously attacked and endangered by contemporary theology than in Bultmann's presentation of the eschatological fact of salvation in the cross.

It stands to reason that in the numerous discussions of Bult-

28. *Ibid.*, p. 298. Because of its formal analogy one is constantly reminded here of all kinds of Roman Catholic dissertations on the mass, which carry the sacrifice of the cross into history and make it "effective" there. It is not in the least my intention to insinuate that there is a relationship between Bultmann and Roman Catholic doctrine, but it certainly cannot be denied that at any rate there is – against a very different background – a *tertium comparationis* in connection with the historicity and the "once-and-for-all" of the sacrifice of the cross. It struck me that Karl Barth exactly with respect to *cross* and *preaching* (the re-enactment!) writes, "I am concerned about the similarity to all kinds of Catholic death mysticism which Bultmann's presentation suggests" (K. Barth, *Rudolph Bultmann. Ein Versuch ihn zu verstehen. Theol. Studien*, Vol. 34, 1952, p. 20).

29. Cf. on Bultmann and Heidegger: K. Barth, *ibid.*, pp. 34ff.

mann's theology[30] the question has been raised frequently whether it leaves anything at all of a real *kerygma.*

It is remarkable that this question has been raised not only by the more conservative elements but also by the ultra-liberal. Fritz Buri, for one, asks whether demythologizing would not logically result in "de-kerygmatizing."[31] He considers this an unavoidable consequence of Bultmann's program and specifically denies that the *kerygma* could mean the soteriological act of God in the cross of Golgotha. "Salvation has no connection whatsoever with *any* historical fact." Whatever the New Testament says concerning this also belongs to the realm of mythology, according to Buri. "This offensive assertion that the soteriological fact is once-and-for-all is again nothing but the result of the usual mythical thinking of the New Testament" (p. 97).

Now Bultmann realized that many protests against his program were motivated by the fear that its consistent application would make it impossible to speak of *any* activity of God in history.[32] He is convinced, however, that there is no reason for such fear if only God's activity is not taken in a mythical, miraculous, or supernatural sense, but as a hidden activity in our reality, wherever and whenever a merely *natural* happening is visible (p. 197). The point at issue in faith is the paradox that it sees a natural happening "at the same time as an act of God," although, *as* an act of God "it is not universally visible and cannot be determined as such." *Faith* sees Jesus Christ in the world, in history

30. Of the overwhelming abundance of literature I mention the following: *Kerugma und Mythos, I* (1948); *Kerugma und Mythos, II* (1952); H. N. Ridderbos, *De Nieuwste Mythologische Interpretatie van het N. T.;* J. H. Bavinck, *"Het Probleem der "Entmythologisierung"* (*Vox Theol.,* 1951); W. Klaas, *Der moderne Mensch in der Theologie R. Bultmanns.* (*Theol. Stud.,* Vol. 24, 1947); G. J. Heering, *De Verwachting van het Koninkrijk Gods,* 1952, pp. 109-132; Ernst Steinbach, *Mythos und Geschichte,* 1951; H. Frey, *Das Wort ward Fleisch,* 1952; *Zur Entmythologisierung. Ein Wort lutherischer Theologie* (E. Kinder) 1952; G. Bornkamm – W. Klass, *Mythos und Evangelium,* 1951.

31. F. Buri, *Entmythologisierung oder Entkerugmatisierung der Theol.* In *Kerugma und Mythos, II* (1952), 96.

32. Bultmann, *Die Rede vom Handeln Gottes. Kerugma und Mythos, II,* 196. It is remarkable that Bultmann, when answering all kinds of objections, does not mention Buri at all. From this it may certainly not be concluded, when surveying Bultmann's complete book, that he does not have an answer. Throughout he makes a clear distinction between demythologizing and "de-kerygmatizing"; indeed, this distinction is the basis of his entire theology.

as the eschatological act of God by which grace concretely and now comes to us. The once-and-for-all lies not in the past but in the present nature of God's activity, in the eschatological *now!*

Thus, according to Bultmann, Christology is completely freed from the bondage of the ontology of objectivizing thinking (p. 206). True faith knows that it has nothing in its hand and possesses no proof except for the Word of God. In this way grace can be proclaimed to modern man. To be crucified with Christ reveals *the true understanding of one's self.* So Bultmann does not leave anything of what the Church considered essential.[33]

The freeing of human existence does not need these objectivizings. Bultmann's Christology may frequently be sharply opposed to the liberal Jesus-theology of the nineteenth century with its reduction method, but as far as the confession of Christ's work is concerned, the result is the same. Bultmann's theology is even more dangerous because it does not contra-idealistically attack and deny the significance of history, but he makes history – God's activity – to fit in by stripping it of all "mythical" elements.

The transition from the world's condition to the grace of God has no basis. The correlation between the cross of Christ and our being crucified with him is so understood that there is no room in this correlation for a historical "before," as is the case with Paul, who always fully honors the temporal aspect and who speaks of Christ, who died for us, *while we were yet sinners* (Rom. 5:8). It will be difficult to deny the correctness of Buri's conclusion that this demythologizing *must* lead to de-kerygmatizing.[34]

33. H. N. Ridderbos, *op. cit.*, p. 7 and Stauffer in *Kerugma und Mythos, II.*
34. See Barth's sharp criticism of Bultmann, and his question, "why we should exactly on the basis of an existentialistic conception (of Heidegger, and then only a specific phase of his thinking!) have to consider the New Testament as though that would be *the* obligatory, prerequisite knowledge for understanding the New Testament?" (K. Barth, *R. Bultmann,* 1952, p. 39). I consider Barth's attempt to explain Bultmann on the basis of Lutheranism unsuccessful (*op. cit.*, pp. 46f.). According to Barth, Luther's Christology (Galatians!) all but dissolves into soteriology. These ideas are far too aphoristic to be considered justified, the more so since Barth, after having made some fairly definite statements, again speaks of "a very thin line." This connection certainly cannot be construed from the relationship between Christology and

According to the gospel Christ went through suffering to glory, and the darkness of judgment and forsakenness is swallowed up by the light of the resurrection. Whoever tries to find salvation outside of this history is only groping in the darkness of the cross. God's activity is one in the midst of history, and is just as historic as man's guilt and lost condition. Idealism denies man's guilt and searches for a therapy which can never heal the damage because it bypasses this historical reality. But Bultmann's representation of God's activity in the cross also simply minimizes the significance of this history. An enormous amount of idealism continues to dominate the entire field, just as, moreover, natural scientific determinism dominates to a large extent the teachings of "demythologizing." The question in all this is not simply a matter of some scientific problems, but we see the battle focusing around the crucial matter of finding God where he *let* himself be found.

Over and over again there has been a flight from history to the heights of ideas (*eternal* ideas) or to the depths of the human soul as the places to find and meet the living God. It seemed easier to find him there than in the raw reality of history. To the apostles, history made all the difference: to Paul, when he sees how all the shadows of our lost condition draw together if Christ be not raised (I Cor. 15:18), or to John, when he speaks of the antichrist, if *this* history be denied (I John 4:3). These apostolic emphases and admonitions have not lost their deep earnestness. The confession of the two states of Christ's life means to express the value of history, of *this* history. It is true that the gospel can be historized and the history of Jesus can be so presented that the gospel message has disappeared from it. The holy land with its many memories and reminders truly is no "fifth gospel" as it has been called at times.[35] Whoever places this "gospel" beside the others, neglects the true meaning of the gospel.

But this message is inseparably connected with history. The accounts of God's action in Jesus Christ incorporate a multitude of local references, to specific places and events. Of course, no

---

soteriology and from the fact that the quest for the *applicatio salutis* was the real quest of Luther and Lutheranism. When reasoning thus even Bultmann can be traced back to Paul (being co-crucified).

35. Cf. on this expression Th. C. Vriezen, *Palestina en Israël*, 1951 (Bijbelse Herinneringen).

Christian means quite what the Jew means, when he sings out his longing for his country: If I forget thee, O Jerusalem![36] The objective of Christian faith is not a world of sentiments or memories, but the message to the travelers towards the holy land and to those who will never reach it, certainly is related to the history of that land. The well-known song "On mountains and in valleys, and everywhere is God" may never be used to contradict this historic and local limitation. Whoever would do so would deny the special act of God in this history, the act of the Father of Jesus Christ. Neither the idea, nor the illustration, nor mysticism, nor the experience of the "Infinity" can replace that which "took place" here. The Word of God makes us understand why there needed to be missionary journeys of Paul, and why Christ's life and death are temporally connected with names such as Mary and Peter, Herod and Caiaphas, Pilate and Simon of Cyrene. This history is fully emphasized in this message. One may be amazed that God's way runs through a *country* and does not rather touch the world in a far different, "ubiquitous" manner. But then one forgets that for blind eyes light dawns upon the world — somewhere in the Orient — in a manner which to men is incalculable, just as is the election of Israel in the world of nations. *This* is the way salvation comes, and this way is incorporated as a real constituent in the message and is proclaimed by heralds in the world. "*Tertium non datur*" between idealism and historic Christianity.

If the confession of humiliation and exaltation be not a dry schematizing but a summarizing of the gospel according to Scripture, then one can understand why the Church of all ages has shown a profound interest in the nature of the connection between humiliation and exaltation. Frequently this connection has been called "causality." Kittel, for instance, speaks of "the causal connection between the dying and the fruit-bearing of the corn.[37] But the word "causal" draws opposition here, since it has a certain mechanical flavor unsuitable to this historic mystery of the connection between humiliation and exaltation.

36. Cf. the question of Zionism, whether another country than Palestine would be able to satisfy the longing. The idea of Uganda (in British East Africa) was considered treason by many Zionists, and when Herzl wanted to settle for Uganda the later president of Israel, Weizmann, made a glowing speech in favor of Palestine.

37. Kittel II, p. 252, s.v. δόξα.

Nevertheless, this is not a conclusive objection, since the word can be used in non-mechanistic senses as well.[38] It may be used to point out that the exaltation did not just follow after the humiliation, but followed it *on the basis of God's activity.* The analogy of the dying and fruit-bearing corn indicates this connection. There is a holy and divine "necessity" in this transition, not in a deterministic sense, but proceeding from the Father's heart. It is not a necessity which supersedes God as a fate to which he is subject, and it is least of all contrary to God's love. It is a necessity of an entirely *unique* character which corresponds with the uniqueness of this event, of which Scripture says that it was not *possible* that Jesus Christ should be held by death (Acts 2:24). The mystery of this compulsion, this necessity in the progress from humiliation to exaltation, is free from all arbitrariness because of the personal mercifulness and justice of God. Over against the arbitrariness of man and sin is the "unarbitrariness" of God's love which condemns all arbitrariness of sin *in the flesh of the Son of Man.* The style of God's action here crosses the stylelessness of sin, and over against the curse of the evil deed, which continually causes new evil, we have here the holy, productive progress of God's deeds, which manifests itself as God's order over against the world's disorder. This is the "causal" relationship between suffering and glory, and in pointing out *this* cause the cause of every lost condition is manifested at the same time.[39]

It does not surprise us, therefore, that throughout the centuries there has been such controversy concerning the character of this relationship, because here man is confronted with the full reality of salvation. We remember the heated arguments concerning the "merits" of Christ. It has often been thought that this expression revealed a juridical and legalistic schematization which left no room for God's love and mercy. All of salvation seemed to shrivel down to a meritorious "achievement." Again and

38. Then, too, Scripture calls Christ in the same connection "cause" (Engl. *author, αἴτιος*): "and when He had reached the end, he became a *cause* of eternal salvation unto all them that obey Him" (Heb. 5:9, Dutch version).

39. Cf. the expression in the form for the Lord's Supper: "the *cause* of our eternal hunger and distress, namely sin"; cf. in the same connection Christ's sacrifice as the "only ground and foundation of our salvation."

again reference was made to the typical Reformed doctrine which, after a hard battle, had once and for all removed the merit-concept from religion, so that mentioning Christ's "merit" – in the way of humiliation – meant nothing but an intolerable "alien body" within Reformed thinking. Is it possible to resist the meritoriousness of good works and at the same time base all of the work of salvation on the fact of a meritorious achievement?

There have been times that, under the influence of these questions, there was a tendency not to speak of Christ's merits but to say instead that he came to glory *in the way* of obedience.[40] But it is evident that this solution offers no clear difference from the idea of merit. Therefore most theologians speak freely of Christ's merit, as do also the confessions,[41] without detracting in the least from the objections to the legalistic meritoriousness of good works. Calvin specifically deals with this question in a separate chapter, "That it has been justly said that Christ has merited God's grace and salvation for us," and he further warns against the misplaced sagacity of those who do acknowledge that we receive salvation through Christ, but who do not want to accept the word "merit."[42] They are of the opinion that this obscures God's grace. Calvin, however, considers it incorrect to contrast Christ's merit with God's mercy. He knows that Christ's merit is connected only with God's grace and is therefore just as much opposed to human righteousness as is grace. God's *good pleasure* is also present in Christ's pathway from suffering to glory. That is why there is no arbitrariness in this way; the normative structures of God's love and justice are fully maintained.

When we speak thus of "merit" it must strike us that the Church spoke of this merit in a very special sense, viz., as merit

40. So, e.g., Wollebius, "Exaltatiomem hanc Christus consecutus est, obedientia sua, *non tamquam merito,* sed tamquam via et medio" (cf. Heppe, *Dogmatik*). However, Wollebius certainly does not wish to consider the exaltation a historic result of the humiliation without essential connection.

41. See, e.g., the Heidelberg Catechism, Question 21 (freely and merely of grace; only for the sake of Christ's merits) and Q. 84 (same phrase). Obviously the same is meant as what we read in Q. 126, "for the sake of Christ's blood." Cf. the Belgic Confession, Art. 22, 24 (the merits of the suffering and death of our Savior); Art. 35 (same). Finally, the Canons of Dort I, rejection of errors, III (the remonstrant doctrine renders God's good pleasure and Christ's merit ineffective).

42. Calvin, *Institutes* II, XVII, pp. 1ff. Cf. my *Faith and Justification.*

to *our* benefit. Especially Calvin emphasizes this and says that the point at issue is not a course which Christ ran (the suffering) in order to merit something for *himself*. "The Father is not said to have consulted the advantage of his Son in his services, but to have given him up to death and not spared him, because he loved the world" (*Inst.* II, XVII, 6).

Calvin devotes special attention to the fact that *we* are the objective of Christ's work. Christ – so says Calvin when clearly defining what he means – did not think of himself but sanctified himself for *our* sakes (John 17:19). He merits nothing for himself but applies the fruit of his holiness unto others. Indeed, to dedicate himself wholly to our salvation, to a certain extent he *forgot himself*. In this connection Calvin does not consider the "wherefore" of Philippians 2 as the "cause" of Christ's exaltation but simply as an indication of the sequence so that it would serve as an example for us.

Paul's meaning is the same as what Christ told the disciples on the way to Emmaus, that he ought to enter into his Father's glory through suffering. Calvin creates the impression that here "sequence" is more justified than "cause." But it is difficult to see what has been gained this way, because also in these words to the disciples the way through suffering to glory is subjected to the divine "ought." Calvin correctly wishes to reject the idea that Christ's suffering was motivated by his coming glory and that this motivation was the purpose of his suffering.[43] He forgot himself – with these words we may, with Calvin, praise Christ's *love*. It is impossible to measure the holiness of Christ's soul on the basis of our selfishness. But this love which is directed to us is not in conflict with Christ's prayer to the Father to be glorified with the glory which he had with the Father before the world was (John 17:5). His self-denying love and the prospect of the glory after the bitter period of suffering were inseparably connected in the Son of the Father, as we see this unfathomable harmony manifested in the institution of the Lord's supper when he, in the midst of the approaching shadows (the blood of the New Covenant), looks into the future, "Verily . . . I shall no more drink of the fruit of the vine, *until that day* when

43. Cf. John 8:50, "I seek not mine own glory"; cf. verse 54, "If I glorify myself, my glory is nothing: it is my Father that glorifieth me."

I drink it new in the kingdom of God."[44] Human psychology will never fully explain the harmony of Christ's motivation, but we may not allow this failure to lead us into a dualistic contrast between Christ's motives.

It is not possible at this time to discuss the questions which arise in connection with Christ's merit. However, it was necessary to bring up the subject here since Christ's exaltation cannot be considered apart from his work "for us."[45] The exaltation is also soteriological, "For if we have become united with him in the likeness of his death, we shall be also in the likeness of his resurrection" (Rom. 6:5). This again shows that the Church's interest in the way "through suffering to glory" was motivated not by historical curiosity but by faith. This faith is not selfish, but it does concentrate itself, through the power of the Holy Spirit, upon salvation.

Thus at the beginning of our consideration of Holy Scripture it is evident that the history of Christ's "through suffering to glory" is part of God's activity and that for this reason the confession of the two states of Christ's life partakes of the "offense"

44. Mark 14:25; Matt. 26:29. Cf. also his answer to Caiaphas in the midst of the shame of his humiliation, concerning the Son of man sitting on the right hand of power and coming in the clouds of heaven (Matt. 26:64). Heb. 12:2 says that Jesus "for the joy *that was set before him* endured the cross, despising the shame." Grosheide refers this to Christ's heavenly glory (cf. Phil. 2 and II Cor. 8:9) and considers the opinion that this joy would refer to Christ's glory after his finished work unacceptable since it would then synchronize with the following "set down at the right hand of the throne of God." Van Oyen (*Christus de Hogepriester,* p. 249) in agreement with Calvin thinks of the renunciation of all earthly joy. Not so Bengel, *Gnomon N.T.*, 1891, on Heb. 12:2, "pro gaudio proposito, illo scilicet quod mox erat aditurus, crucem tantisper aeque libenter sustinuit" and referring to Acts 2:28. See further B. F. Westcott, *The Epistle to the Hebrews,* 1951, pp. 395f., who associates προκειμένης in verse 2 with τὸν προκείμενον ἀγῶνα and in this connection with the coming glory. Riggenbach, *Der Brief an die Hebräer,* p. 389, contests the idea of the preexistence, because "here the man Jesus is meant." Considering everything, it is difficult for me to surrender to the argument that this joy would synchronize with the *sessio ad dextram* (cf. further H. Windisch, *Der Hebräerbrief,* 1931, p. 109, "and is now sitting at the right hand of God, where he is enjoying this happiness"). If the word does indeed refer to Christ's coming joy, which I am inclined to believe, then it is in line with the discussion above.

45. Cf. in the same connection Heb. 2:10, "in bringing many sons unto glory, to made the author of their salvation perfect through sufferings."

of the word of the cross. That does not mean at all that we consider the Church's confession equal to the gospel. But this is clear, that the Church's confession of Christ's humiliation and exaltation had no other intention than to speak of him who had come not to be ministered unto, but to minister (Mark 10:45), and whose greatness in this ministration was so great and inexpressible that he may proclaim as a marvelous secret, "If any man serve me, him will the Father honor" (John 12:26).

CHAPTER FOUR

CHRIST'S OFFICE

AFTER having focused our attention on the great caesura which is so evident in Scripture, we must now, in this connection, discuss Christ's *office.* For this reaffirms what we observed in the relationship between humiliation and exaltation, viz., that the work of Christ is absolutely free from all arbitrariness. His life and work cannot be understood apart from the light of the divine commission of which he himself so emphatically spoke. However, just as it has been said of the doctrine of the two states of Christ, so it has been said that the doctrine of the three offices of Christ reveals schematization and scholasticism. Some have feared that it would cause a spiritual coldness which separates us from the living scriptural witness concerning the one Lord. It may be granted, indeed, that often the three offices of Christ *have* been discussed in a dry, formal manner, and this has evoked a reaction which so far forth is justifiable.

However, when we consider more closely the questions which arise in connection with Christ's office, we soon see that speaking of his offices is no more arbitrary than is the distinction between his states. Those who object to all kinds of distinctions (natures, states, and offices) because they are "scholastic" are in danger of rejecting the facts which these distinctions are meant to explain. At any rate, it must be understood that these distinctions are meant to establish the facts: in the doctrine of the natures that of the *vere Deus, vere homo,* in the doctrine of the states that of the humiliation and exaltation, and in the doctrine of the offices that of his mediatorial work.

It cannot be denied, however, that particularly in connection with Christ's offices there is a danger that such distinctions may remove us from the Christ as pictured in the Gospels. The word "office" has uses outside the realms of theology, and thus to call

Christ's work "official" may readily obscure the dynamic and unique course of his life.[1]

Especially in these times, when there is a marked interest in the irrational depths of "individuality" and "personality," we observe a great aversion to "the official" because it supposedly threatens to turn human life into dead objectivity. Even in the early Church there were fierce reactions against the overestimation of "office" on the ground that under the influence of the Holy Spirit individual religious life is spontaneous. These tensions concerning the offices in the Church broadened to include the preaching of Christ's "offices," preaching which called him the great Office-Bearer and his obedience an official obedience. Such preaching, it was believed, evidenced a certain rigidity that would minimize everything "personal" and "psychological."[2] This controversy contained the danger that the scriptural depth of Christ's office would be lost sight of; both the continuous mentioning of his office as well as the avoidance of this word actually caused a considerable impoverishment. It is advisable to refrain from such impure reactions. Overestimation of Christ's office should never cause us to lose sight of the greatness of this Messianic office, and the only way to avoid this danger is to plumb the richness of the Word of God. The object of the consideration of these offices is never — may never be — an abstraction of his living person. His office does not conflict with the *personal* qualities of his life's work. He himself is the living reality *in* the fulfillment of his office.

This does not in the least remove us from the full reality of his person but it places us in the midst of it, that is, if we do not consider it *in abstracto* but in living faith and under the con-

1. Cf. J. D. Dozy, "Onze Hoogste Profeet" (in: *Het Ambt van Christus*, 1942, p. 4), "The expression (triple office) undoubtedly sounds abstract and theoretical," although Dozy adds at once that it is not the Church's intention to put up an abstract theoretic scheme into which Christ's work must neatly fit.
2. Something similar may be found when there is a strong emphasis on the covenant, when the word "obedience" is hardly used anymore but "covenantal obedience" instead, and Christ is called the "Covenant Head." Out of reaction the usage of this word is then more and more avoided, not so much because theological differences are directly involved but because of the *atmosphere* which a certain frequently used word may suggest. Here, too, a new one-sided reaction is worthless and the right way can be retained only by a believing consideration of the Covenant.

tinuous influence of the Word and the guidance of the Spirit. For, truly, the office of Christ is certainly not a Platonic idea, but in the fulfillment of his office we see him run his course from suffering to glory.[3] When considering Christ's office we are confronted with himself, his grace, his sacrifice. Then we see him go his lonely way; we see him bend his knees and wash the disciples' feet; we see him being betrayed, beaten, crowned, and forsaken – completely forsaken on the cross of Golgotha.

Exactly because we are touching upon his complete work when we deal with Christ's office, it stands to reason that this, too, caused a great deal of controversy in the history of the Church and theology. It is remarkable, however, that all three offices (prophetic, priestly, and kingly) were not always subjected to the same intensity of attack.

The fact is that Christ's prophetic office seemed to be attacked least of all. Most of the participants in the controversy were willing to accept Christ as prophet, even though they strongly opposed the term "office." Even ultra-modern Christological circles wanted to honor him, especially in his teaching and his significance to revelation. They accented the truth which he prophetically proclaimed and which they considered of extraordinary significance to the world. Yet behind this recognition of Christ's prophetic role there loomed a profound problem that still involved his "office" directly. For his prophetic proclamation of the truth had, in principle, been detached from his person and thereby took on an independent character. Consequently no justice could be done to his claim, "I am the truth" (John 14:6), which statement now had become incomprehensible and which presented more of a problem than his answer to Pilate, "To this end have I been born, and to this end am I come into the world, that I should bear witness unto the truth" (John 18:37).

So the problem regarding his prophetic office was, contrary to appearance, also evident in the modern evaluation of Christ's teaching. This manifested itself particularly in a critical attitude

3. Cf. A. A. v. Ruler, *Bijzonder en algemeen ambt,* 1952, Chap. VI, who emphasizes the significance of Christ's office. In my opinion it is not clear, however, why he writes, "Christ's offices are more important to us than his natures and states," especially in connection with the inseparable relationship between Christ's person and work, which he points out immediately afterwards (p. 71).

towards the priestly aspects of Christ's work, brought on by the isolation of his prophetism, and was revealed more specifically in the rejection of the Church's doctrine of reconciliation. This one-sidedness had to result in devaluating and devoiding Christ's work, as was done by the Ritschlian and liberal theology of the nineteenth century. True, Scripture was frequently quoted for support concerning Christ's revelation of his Father, but these quotations were lifted out of the total picture presented by Scripture. Thus the special emphasis on Christ's prophetism was an attack upon the one *munus triplex.*

One might expect that his priestly office has not been isolated to the same extent. Yet its isolation, too, may be found in circles which accent his suffering and which more or less neglect Christ's prophecies and teaching. We are also thinking of theopaschitic tendencies in theology, which depict God's suffering in Christ as an irrational fact in the divine substitution. Thus the tensions in the *munus triplex* became no less evident.

And finally it is obvious that it is also possible to isolate and render absolute the kingly aspect of Christ's office. Aulén, for instance, elevates the strife-and-victory motif to *the* dominant and exclusive factor of reconciliation (see the comments on Aulén in our last chapter), while this also may be found wherever Christ's kingship is isolated from the whole of his work and the kingly aspects of his office either crowd out his priestly work or obscure it.

Thus it has become evident from these short introductory remarks that the issue at stake in the controversy about the triple office is not the schematization of Christ's life or the protest against it, but the fundamental insights into the nature of his work which were of far-reaching consequences for the practical life of the Church.

It is generally admitted that the elements of the so-called *munus triplex* date back to long before the Reformation, but that does not mean that the triple office was already used then as an established dogmatic expression. Specifically, it is Calvin who developed the idea of the *munus triplex*, and this for the sole purpose of bringing out the greatness of Christ's works. He explains that we, in order to know why Christ was sent by the Father and what he has obtained for us, must specifically consider three things in him: his prophetic, priestly, and kingly office (*Inst.* II, XV, heading). Calvin wishes to bring out the principle that the office with which the Father commissioned Christ has three parts. Calvin fully realizes that the connection of this conception with the actual fact of salvation can soon be lost, and as an illustration he points to these three offices as they had already appeared in papal doctrine, although "they are treated there indifferently and with little result" (*Inst.* II, XV, 1).

The pivotal point in the doctrine of the offices is Christ himself, as his name, Christ, the Anointed One, in analogy with the office-bearers under the Old Covenant, already indicates. It strikes us at once that Calvin does not construe the *munus triplex* on the basis of aprioristic ideas but bases it solely on the testimony of Scripture. Neither is he interested in an abstract or speculative analysis of Christ's appearance, for Christ has filled the office of Savior "in order to obtain our salvation." The office-bearing is not something rigid but has a wondrous and *saving* effect. The name Christ, his official name, is inseparably connected with his name Jesus or Savior (*Inst.* II, XVI). For this reason we do not speak of three separate offices but of one indivisible office, even though, according to Calvin, this consists of three parts. In fulfilling this office he accomplishes the *one* work of salvation. That is why Christ's office does not conflict with his personal spontaneity; in Christ there never existed such a conflict. It was his will to do what his office required; his will was free from the arbitrariness of human autonomy and self-determination. And therefore his office is also connected with his *humiliation*.

The Heidelberg Catechism also calls our attention to the one threefold office, and it strikes us again that this office is seen in connection with the fruit of Christ's labor. The Catechism, treating the *Apostolicum* and explaining the name "Christ," immediately adds, "Why art thou called a Christian?" (Lord's Day XII). And the answer points out that we are members of Christ by faith and thus partakers of *his* anointing. There is no trace of dissolving Christology into soteriology, but it does stress a close relationship. When considering the office we must exclude every thought of rigidity and autonomy, and the best way to do this is to note Christ's anointing in Scripture and how, on the basis thereof, this confession bears fruit in the lives of believers.

We would now be ready to consider the *munus triplex* itself, were it not for Korff's fundamental objection to the very conception. Dogmatics, he asserts, is concerned with the category of *revelation*. And, "now, in our scheme revelation is undoubtedly first of all represented by the prophetic office."[4] But when we place the kingly and priestly office beside the prophetic, then other categories appear which jeopardize the unity of Christ's work.

But Korff's criticism is based on a mistake. The point at issue is not a matter of *new* categories beside the one of revelation, but the correct understanding of Christ's office and its fulfillment from the testimony of Scripture. This testimony is the only basis for the *munus triplex*. To consider the prophetic office as the sole basis for the category of revelation is to depart in principle from the unity of Christ's office, because Christ "is a revelation of God's love both in all of his person and in all of his work,"[5] and this may not be limited to his prophetic office. Korff's criticism of the *munus triplex* as point of departure is not very clear and makes very little sense, the more so because later on he himself – involuntarily – returns to the three-fold office and says, "This scheme is now, entirely incidentally, the result at which we arrive" (*ibid.*, p. 212).

Now the offices appear, also to Korff, not to be separate but one, so there is apparently no longer any danger of speaking of the priestly and kingly offices. It has always been the objective of the doctrine of the *munus triplex*, however, to confess this unity and not to consider Christ's offices as different, independent functions, but as the one *munus* as *triplex*. Any consideration, such as Korff's, which proceeds from one office in order to treat the other ones exclusively on the basis of that one office is unable to maintain the indivisible harmony of the *munus triplex*.[6]

Let us now consider the meaning of the word "office." It obviously expresses the fact that one does not act on his own initiative but fulfills a given *commission*, as the Old Testament already stresses. Anointing was the symbol of this commissioning. The office is always superpersonal, not in the sense that it floats, like an abstract idea, above the living person, but it does come from above and can never be explained in the person, no matter how talented he may be. "Superpersonal" implies that

4. F. W. Korff, *Christologie*, II, 110.
5. Bavinck, III, 353.
6. Cf. in this connection the unity of the offices in the Church; especially K. Dijk, *De Eenheid der Ambten*, 1949, and *De Dienst der Kerk*, 1952, p. 243.

human life itself lacks this authority and can receive it only indirectly in the calling to the fulfillment of a commission.[7] One does not call himself to an office, but he *is* called to a task. The office is always a creaturely function and always presupposes a higher, i.e., a divine authority, which gives it a solid foundation. This is clearly illustrated in the Old Testament anointing. Another person intervenes in God's name and according to his commission. Everything is dependent, even the institution of the office and the act of anointing.[8] In Israel, according to Van Gelderen, the emphasis is always on *ordination by Jehovah.*[9] The accent is on "chosen instruments of the Lord" and on the "anointed of the Lord" (*ibid.,* p. 221). Whoever is truly an "anointed of the Lord" receives in his anointing the seal of divine ordination and qualification."[10]

This authoritative character of the commissioning with an office is strongly accentuated in the example of Cyrus, who in Isaiah 45:1 is called the anointed of the Lord. The point there is divine appointment and qualification for the work that Cyrus will have to accomplish with respect to Israel.[11] God has held his right hand "to subdue nations before him." We are dealing with a special case here because the superpersonal is strongly accented. It is not a case of consciously serving God and gladly accepting a task, but of a work assigned "from above" according to divine providence. "For Jacob my servant's sake, and Israel my chosen, I have called thee by thy name: I have surnamed thee, though thou hast not known me" (Isa. 45:4). This clearly evidences absolute sovereignty, "*I* am the Jehovah, and there is none else; besides *me* there is no God. "*I* will gird thee,

7. Cf. on the office, among others, A. Kuyper, *Encyclopaedie* II, 587ff. and III, 471ff., concerning office and διακονία. Cf. K. Dijk, *De Dienst der Kerk,* 1952, p. 15, on the shifting of the accent of the *diakonia* to man, viz. as a *function* of the religious individual or the religious community. Concerning the authority which is accorded *in* and *with* the ultimate dependency, note the words addressed to Jeremiah, "if thou take forth the precious from the vile, thou shalt be *as my mouth*" (Jer. 15:19). Cf. also K. Dijk, *De Eenheid der Ambten,* 1949.
8. Cf. Exodus 29:7 (the ordination of Aaron as priest); 40:13, "And thou shalt put upon Aaron the holy garments; and thou shalt anoint him, and sanctify him; that he may minister *unto me* in the priest's office"; I Kings 19:15, 16 (Hazael, Jehu, Elisha).
9. Van Gelderen, *I Kings* 19:16 (p. 221).
10. Van Gelderen, *Korte Verklaring,* I, on I Kings, p. 37. Cf. Grosheide in *Bijbelse Encycl.,* s.v. *Zalving.*
11. Cf. Isa. 44:28, "He is my shepherd, and shall perform all my pleasure."

though thou hast not known me" (Isa. 45:5). Every anointing is based on this sovereignty, also when it is accepted and acknowledged in faith and service. The anointing of prophets, priests, and kings reveals God's dealings.

The point at issue is the fulfillment of a task in response to a divine commission.[12] The anointing, moreover, symbolizes the insufficiency of the anointed, since the commission carries with it a promise that the office-bearer will be given the qualifications for his task. Office-glorification, therefore, is a contradiction in terms. It should not be fought by minimizing the office but by showing its essential nature, the fact that it is based on God's sovereignty. Whoever glorifies an office-bearer merely shows that he does not understand the office.[13]

Christology does not speak of the threefold office because it wishes to force the work of Christ into a special scheme, but because of the testimony of Scripture. The pivotal point is the *name* Christ, which means "Anointed One."[14] It is, therefore, not a new name which Jesus of Nazareth receives. He is *the* Christ (Matt. 16:17), and both the Old and New Testaments picture him as the Anointed One. From the beginning the Church has, with Peter, confessed him as such and after Pentecost the prayer of the young Church is, "thy holy child Jesus, *whom thou didst anoint*" (Acts 4:27). The kings of the earth and the rulers stood up against the Lord and his "Christ" (Acts 4:26). It is his holy *servant* (RSV) in whom God's decree was fulfilled by the holiness of his official fulfillment and the accomplishment of his task in this world.

Other texts also place Jesus of Nazareth in the light of the anointing. The Old Testament, for instance, speaks of the Spirit that is upon the Messiah "because Jehovah hath anointed me" (Isa. 61:1). What is meant here is the anointing with the oil of gladness (Ps. 45:7), not the act of anointing as in the Old Testament, but the fulfillment of this anointing, which is the Messiah,

12. Cf. W. P. Berghuis, "Het Begrip Ambt," (*Philos. Reformata,* 1938, p. 231) on the "religious office commission."
13. Cf. A. Kuyper, *E Voto,* I, p. 279, on "the commissioned office" (p. 280) and the over-estimation of the *person* who came to be regarded in such a way "that people could not see why he should not be worthy to exercise the authority given him by men." Kuyper says that thus finally the concept of anointing disappeared (p. 281).
14. Χριω to anoint, cf. "Χριστος" LXX, Lev. 4:3, 5, 16, and especially Isa. 45:1: "*οὕτως λέγει κύριος ὁ θεὸς τῷ χριστῷ μου Κύρῳ.*"

who is truly anointed with the Holy Spirit. Because of this anointing he is the Christ and will fulfill his office in holiness. This fulfillment, it is true, radiates his glory and grace, but also in him the anointing is fully evident in its true essence. The life of the Messiah, too, reflects the divine sovereignty. He did not manifest autonomy, but submission; not his own will and initiative, but subjection and obedience. To speak of Christ's office is not to schematize his life but instead to depict the dark shadows of his *humiliation*.[15]

Now when Christian theology speaks of Christ's *threefold* office, it does so not to separate but to differentiate; and the basis of this differentiation is solely the testimony of Scripture. So, too, when the Heidelberg Catechism speaks of Christ as our highest Prophet (Lord's Day XII), this implies a relationship with the Old Testament prophets but not an identification with them. Christ does appear in the list of prophets[16] but he cannot be explained simply as one of them because prophecy is fulfilled in him and derives its significance only from him. His own coming was prophesied in Deuternomy: "Jehovah thy God will raise up unto thee a prophet from the midst of thee, of thy brethren . . . unto him ye shall hearken."[17] Israel receives the promise of the light of prophecy over against the self-willed desire to penetrate the future by means of oracles and soothsaying. Old Testament prophecy is like a prophetic beam of light, converging in one central point, namely, Christ.[18] "God, having of old time spoken unto the fathers in the prophets by diverse portions and in diverse manners, hath at the end of these days spoken unto us in his Son" (Heb. 1:1).

The Messiah radiates the full light of prophecy. The only begotten Son, who is in the bosom of the Father, has declared the

15. Cf. Kuyper, *E Voto*, I, 282: "The Lord, therefore, here appears in his humiliation, as having become one of us, as man." The decree concerning Jesus is the dispensation of God's good pleasure which from eternity commissioned him to bear as man the full office by which God's power over his kingdom would be executed. Thus he became the Christ" (p. 283).
16. Cf. the parable of the unrighteous husbandmen, Matt. 21:33-46.
17. Deut. 18:15; cf. 18:18, "I will raise them up a prophet from among their brethren, like unto thee; and I will put my words in his mouth, and he shall speak unto them all that I shall command him."
18. Cf. Acts 3:22f.; 7:37.

Father (John 1:18); as the One sent by God, he speaks the words of God (John 3:34); and he came to men with his *witness* (John 5:32). By his being a prophet he is fulfilling his office. Whatever he speaks is free from arbitrariness and selfwilledness. He is the Dependent One, who shows in everything – also in his prophecy – what the office implies. He does not bear witness of himself, but the Father has borne witness of him (John 5:32-37). Moreover, when speaking he cannot do *anything* of himself, "as I hear, I judge" (John 5:30). His doctrine is not his own but his that sent him (John 7:16). Christ even says that any man who does the will of God will know whether Christ's doctrine comes from God or whether Christ speaks of himself![19] The dilemma which defines Christ's office!

Of course, Christ in his office may never be considered an instrument with no will of his own. When the Pharisees accuse him of witnessing to himself he answers, "Even if I bear witness of myself, my witness is true; for I know whence I came, and whither I go" (John 8:14). But these words do not cancel the other fact, because his knowledge and willingness are directed upon and subjected to the Father. He speaks as the Father has taught him (John 8:28) and he keeps *his* word (John 8:55). He received a commandment, what he should say and what he should speak (John 12:49, 50), so that the word which had been heard was not his but the Father's who had sent him (John 14:24; 17:14, "I have given them *thy* word").

How clearly this reveals the nature of Christ's office, his submissiveness and obedience in the fulfillment of the commanded task! Whoever objects to the "official," considering him rigid and a threat to life, let him follow *this* Messiah!

According to John's Gospel, Christ spoke the words of God because he had received the Holy Spirit "not by measure" (3:34). Being submissive and dependent, he was the proclaimer of the kingdom of heaven. The reality of his prophetic office may never be minimized, not even to refute those who honor Christ exclusively as prophet and priest but not as king. The prophetic office is wholly directed to the coming of the kingdom, which in turn is directly connected with the priestly office. Christ does not simply testify of "the truth," but he *is* the Truth; and in his office as prophet he does not simply proclaim

19. John 7:16; cf. 7:18, "He that speaketh from himself seeketh his own glory"; cf. 8:54.

general truths which eventually might be discovered some other way, but he *calls* sinners to repentance (Matt. 9:13; Mark 2:17) and *preaches* the acceptable year of the Lord, the recovering of sight to the blind, liberty to the bruised, and the gospel to the poor (Luke 4:18, 19 [Isa. 61:1, 2]; cf. Luke 4:21; Matt. 11:5).

Christ was fully conscious of this prophetic office. After Nazareth's rejection he knew that the common expression particularly applied to him. "Verily I say unto you, No prophet is acceptable in his own country" (Luke 4:24; cf. Luke 13:33. "Nevertheless I must go on my way today and tomorrow, and the day following: for it cannot be that a prophet perish out of Jerusalem").

His prophecy, therefore, essentially belongs to the commission of him who had sent him. We have no objection to those who emphasize his prophecy, but we do object to the fact that they lift his prophesying from the totality of his person and work and formalize it into the proclamation of a "religious truth."

That is not the objective of his prophecy; for Christ became the prophet of *his own* suffering, just as he was the subject of the prophecy concerning the Man of Sorrows. He did not come merely to proclaim a generalized Kingdom of God. Whoever, therefore, isolates his prophetic task loses its real meaning, for he has separated it from its integral relationship to the *threefold* office of Christ. Christ was never ashamed of his prophetic task, nor did he even consider his submission a burden. He knew what it was to live among a people that kills the prophets, but he did not hide his prophetism. When the Samaritan woman said, "I perceive that thou art a prophet" (John 4:19) and a little later, "I know that Messiah cometh (he that is called Christ): when he is come, he will declare unto us all things" (4:25), then his answer is, "*I* that speak unto thee am *he*" (4:26). This consciousness of his prophetic office stayed with him till the end, when the high priest asked him, "Art thou the Christ, the Son of the Blessed?" (Mark 14:61). And Jesus said, "I am" (14:62), and added the prophetic proclamation of the Kingdom of God.

In his prophetic office he is also Immanuel: God with us. Thus he taught with authority, yet being submissive and dependent![20] The people were deeply impressed by Christ's

20. This word in Matt. 7:29, *ὡς ἐξουσίαν ἔχων*" (and *not* as the scribes); cf. Mark 1:22.

authoritative appearance (Matt. 7:28; 22:33), but still they did not comprehend the full extent of his prophecy. "What is this? A new teaching! with authority. . . ." (Mark 1:27), they exclaimed. They were amazed as they saw the fulfillment of prophecies in the total revelation of his Messianic appearance.[21] But his doctrine was diametrically opposed to the barrenness of the doctrine of Pharisees and Sadducees,[22] basically because Christ could say, "My teaching is not mine, but his that sent me" (John 7:16). From this originated his authority, which was the authority of *God* who spoke through him.

In the light of this background, we can fathom something of the bitterness of the mockery which Christ had to endure as a prophet when he was maltreated and asked, "Prophesy unto us, thou Christ: who is he that struck thee?" (Matt. 26:68). Here Christ's prophetic task is contrasted with forbidden divination (Deut. 18), and he is derided because his prophetic office is entirely misunderstood.[23] Not the insinuation that he did not know who struck him constitutes the cutting derision, but the caricature of his prophetic office, his speaking the things which he had learned *from the Father.* He was derided at a moment when his entire life's work proceeded in the inseparability of his holy office, the *munus triplex.*

How serious was the mistake of those who honored him as prophet on account of his doctrine but who, at the same time, separated his prophetic from his priestly office! In this way he becomes a teacher of wisdom, possibly the greatest of all, but the relationships set forth in Lord's Day XII of the Heidelberg Catechism are abandoned. His doctrine is isolated from *the* truth which he is himself, and is severed from the Messianic Kingdom. Only if we have an eye for these relationships can we understand the peculiar and unique connections which we find everywhere in the Gospels. His preaching is a calling of sinners to conversion, a preaching by which a people in darkness see great light (Matt. 4:16). But his preaching of the kingdom of heaven, his doctrine and proclamation are surrounded by the signs of his Kingship in the healing of the sick (Matt. 4:23,24), the casting out of demons (Matt. 8:16), and the raising of the dead (John 11). Of this Prophet it is written that the Scripture

21. The word concerning "the new doctrine" is remarkably followed by the act of the casting out of the unclean spirit!
22. Matt. 16:12; cf. Kittel, TWNT, II, s.v. διδαχή p. 166.
23. Cf. K. Schilder, *Christ in His Suffering.*

was fulfilled in him: "He hath borne our griefs, and carried our sorrows" (cf. Matt. 8:17; 10:7).

Christ himself directly connects the preaching of the kingdom of heaven with these signs, and it is *this* preaching which has its own place in the fulfillment of the *munus triplex.* Again and again we observe how impossible it is to make a separation in the threefold office of Christ. This will become more evident as we now, in the second place, consider Christ's *priestly office.*

Just as Christ came to call sinners to repentance, so he came also to give his life a ransom for many (Mark 10:45). The offices in the Old Testament were separated, but we should not carry this separation through to Christ's offices. That would mean that we were separating his three "offices" from his person, who throughout the fulfillment of his office was the *one* Messiah, the *one* sent One, for the *one task.*[24] We hope to deal with Christ's sacrifice more in detail. At present we are interested only in showing that the mystery of the *munus triplex* is rooted in the mystery of the Father and the Son and that the fulness of his office is seen only if he is recognized also as *priest.* And finally we consider him in the discharge of his kingly office, of which both the prophecy in the Old Testament, as well as the fulfillment in the New Testament, gives abundant evidence. It is one task, one commission. It is no wonder that Bavinck speaks of the uncertainty of dogmatics concerning the question of exactly what in Jesus' life and work belongs to each particular office.[25] Indeed, frequent attempts have been made to arrive at a sharp distinction, but it often turned out that what had been attached to the one office could just as well have been attached to the other. "It is, therefore, an atomistic viewpoint which isolates certain activities of Jesus' life and classifies some as belonging with the prophetic and others with the priestly and kingly offices" (ibid., p. 351). Bavinck correctly says that Christ does not just perform prophetic, priestly, and kingly activities, but that his whole person *is* prophet, priest, and king, and that everything he is, does, and speaks reveals this threefold dignity.[26]

24. Lord's Day XII clearly illustrates this unity when describing the three offices: 1) the counsel and will of God *concerning our redemption.* 2) He has *redeemed* us by his sacrifice. 3) He preserves us by the purchased *salvation* (redemption).

25. Bavinck, *Gereformeerde Dogmatiek,* III, 351.

26. Undoubtedly there is a connection between the *one munus triplex* and the fact that Peter can call the believers "an holy priesthood"

Now the question could be raised whether thus the doctrine of the *munus triplex* is justified at all.[27] But Bavinck is of the opinion that "differentiation" is indeed possible, since, as he emphasizes, each office has its own characteristics. The question is now in what way such a differentiation can be made. Bavinck bases this differentiation on the idea of *man,* who has this threefold dignity within himself: "he has a head to know, a heart to give himself, and a hand to govern and lead." And whereas sin had radically disturbed the dignity of these three offices, "Christ as Son and image of God had to bear all three offices for himself as well as for being our Mediator and Savior" (*ibid.,* p. 352). It seems to me that this explanation of the *munus triplex* on the basis of an anthropological analogy contributes very little to a correct understanding of it.

In my opinion it is impossible to base the threefold office of Christ — in connection with its differentiation — on the diversities in man's structure. For the office is of a superpersonal character, and although it is true that the object of man's life is the fulfillment of his office, and that through the power of grace man is called again to the threefold office, yet it is obvious that this cannot be based upon a clear separation between head, heart, and hand. Moreover, it is not at all clear why exactly *this* distinction should be the anthropological basis for the differentiation in Christ's threefold office. Indeed, others have offered different anthropological motifs in connection with Christ's triple office in order to make it understandable.[28]

(I Pet. 2:5) but also "a royal priesthood" (I Pet. 2:9); cf. also Rev. 5:10. Remember also, in connection with Christ, the expression: his royal suffering, which is deeply rooted in Scripture if the true essence of Christ's kingship is correctly understood.

27. Bavinck writes that the doctrine of the *munus triplex* has often been attacked "because the one office could not be distinguished from the other" (*ibid.,* III, 351).

28. The distinction between head, heart, and hand itself evokes various questions, especially in connection with the place and function of the *heart.* It seems to me that it must be extremely difficult to maintain the unity of the threefold office when accepting this anthropologic foundation. This will be possible only if the central place of the heart is accepted in any office fulfillment, but this eliminates, in my opinion, the differentiation between head, heart, and hand. Moreover, it is remarkable that Bavinck himself describes the function of the heart as the giving of self; the *service* of man. This I consider correct, but that leaves a problem with respect to head and hand. Kuyper in *E Voto,* I, 286f., speaks of mind (prophet), will (priest), and deed

It is more correct, in my opinion, to consider the threefold character of the office in connection with the nature of the commission given with the office. The office is not first of all a psychological but a *historical* thing, because the office is directly linked to a *task* that is to be performed in history. This historical commission is fully designated by the object of salvation in the revelation of God's Name and Kingdom, the taking away of the guilt, and ultimately the building of the real kingdom in the world. That is why there are various aspects in the one office. It is far better to consider these offices on a historical-soteriological rather than an anthropological basis, and certainly none of the offices may exclusively be associated with the *heart*.[29] At any rate we must take heed not to place the offices in competition with each other, as is suggested when we associate one of them with the heart. These one-sided emphases are not supported by Scripture at all.[30]

One often hears the question whether it is correct to speak not only of Christ's prophetic and priestly offices but also of his

---

(king) in connection with man's office. See also E. L. Smelik (*Het Ambt van Christus,* 1942, p. 13) who says that the *munus triplex* is not only based on the O.T. but that it also has a psychological foundation. According to him it is rooted in "the threefold disposition of man and corresponds with his threefold destination." Cf. p. 15 where this idea is developed: 1) prophecy: the illuminating word, reason; 2) kingship: will, act, power; 3) priesthood: emotions, service of love; priesthood reveals the heart. In my opinion the differences in anthropological formulations clearly reveal that this basis is unsatisfactory. Cf. on these differentiations in connection with Christ's office: O. Noordmans, *Het Koninkrijk der Hemelen,* 1949, p. 87.

29. When Noordmans states that the Messianic offices are not based on creation but on the re-creation *ibid.,* p. 88) then it all depends what he means by that. For, in my opinion, it is possible to reject the anthropological foundation (head, heart, and hand) and still hold that Christ fulfills the office of man (the commission) and that he thus places *us* again in office (Lord's Day XII). This is, to be sure, not basing the Messianic office on creation, but it implies the *restoration* of man's office.

30. There is no objection to what Smelik says, that Christ's priesthood "is the center of Christ's essence and work" (*Het Ambt van Christus,* p. 16) or that the priesthood is *central,* if only the other offices are not kept far from this center. Koopmans correctly points out that we cannot say that one of Christ's offices is "the most important" (*Het Ambt van Christus,* p. 25). He speaks of a perichoresis (inter-relationship): "this reciprocity by which each one of the offices is of significance to and at the same time decisively designated by the two other ones."

kingly office *before* his exaltation. Is it not more correct to relate the prophetic and priestly offices to the humiliation and the kingly office to the exaltation? If one associates kingship with outward splendor and glory he may be inclined to answer in the affirmative. But Scripture does not break up Christ's offices according to a historical succession. The Old Testament anointing, which pertained especially to kings,[31] becomes fully reality in Christ. He is the Messianic King anointed by God himself. Already in the annunciation of Christ's birth the angel says, "the Lord God shall give unto him the throne of his father David: and he shall reign over the house of Jacob for ever; and of his kingdom there shall be no end" (Luke 1:32, 33; cf. Dan. 7:14 as Messianic prophecy).

This kingship of the Messiah is actual *before* his exaltation. We not only hear Nathanael's confession, "thou art the Son of God; thou art King of Israel" (John 1:49), but the matter of Christ's kingship is also specifically mentioned in the controversy with Pilate when Christ himself speaks of his kingdom (John 18:36, "My kingdom is not of this world"), and Pilate in this connection asks, "Art thou a king then?" (John 18:37; Luke 23:3). Christ's answer, "Thou sayest that I am a king" (Luke 23:3, "Thou sayest *it*") contains an affirmation, and because of *this* pretension he was still ridiculed in the last hours (John 19:3; cf. John 18:39). Therefore, the reality of Christ's kingship is undeniable, according to Scripture.[32]

The only question which may arise concerns the *nature* of this kingship. It is remarkable that Christ not once but frequently rejected all kinds of expectations in connection with his kingship. Each time we see him puncture these expectations by preaching his suffering. We are thinking of the request made by the sons of Zebedee to be allowed to sit at his right and left hand in his kingdom. Christ answers this by referring to the cup (Matt. 20:20f.). We further see how Christ evades the tumult and goes to the solitude of the mountains when the crowd wants to make

31. Bavinck, *Gereformeerde Dogmatiek*, III, 350.

32. Cf. further Luke 23:2, "saying that he himself is Christ a King" and John 19:21, where the Jews are saying to Pilate, "Write not, The King of the Jews; but *that he said*, I am King of the Jews" (cf. also verse 15). However, see on this Jewish presentation, Grosheide, *Comm.*, II, 497 (presumably Jesus' own words are being quoted).

him a king.[33] And especially when testifying before Pilate he points out the *nature* of his kingship. It is not *of* this world, nor does it originate from it. If it had been of this world then his servants would have fought "that I should not be delivered to the Jews: but now is my kingdom not from hence."[34] And when Pilate isolates the word "kingdom" and wishes to know whether he really has the pretension of being a *king*,[35] then Christ gives an explanation concerning the object of his coming, "To this end have I been born, and to this end am I come into the world, that I should bear witness unto the truth" (John 18:37). Here we see again that none of the three offices of Christ can be isolated. References concerning his prophetic witness unto the truth are interspersed with those concerning his kingship. Christ's kingship is not limited by his prophetic and priestly offices but instead is designated by them in the unique and unmarred harmony of the *munus triplex*.

Israel misunderstood this Messianic harmony both when they wanted to make him a king and when they reviled him saying, "Hail, King of the Jews!" (John 19:3). They isolated the kingly office from the unity of the Messianic office and seized upon it in a political Messiah-expectation; when Messiah did not fulfill this expectation, his entire *munus triplex* became an object of scorn and indignation. For they identified kingship with "power" and governing, and were therefore unable to see that Messiah's objective is not *this* power, as he did not come to be ministered unto but to *minister*. Their idea of kingship is not his. In their opinion all the marks of true kingship fade when he walks a different way from the one which they consider *royal*, and this is especially the case when he is crowned king[36] and given a purple robe, when he is fully revealed in the poverty for which

33. John 6:14, 15. It is remarkable that they wanted to make Jesus a king when they saw his miracles and said, "This is of a truth the prophet that cometh into the world." Cf. also Matt. 21:9-11.
34. John 18:36. Cf. my *The Providence of God.*
35. The question as to the nature of Christ's kingship apparently does not interest Pilate at all. He actually thinks the same as the Jews (that he *said*) and he only intends to ridicule the Jews with the contents of the superscription (John 19:19) on the cross (Grosheide, *Comm.*). Therefore, Pilate, after the conversion concerning the kingdom of Christ can say, "I find in him no fault" (John 18:38).
36. "And the soldiers platted a crown of thorns, and put it on his head" (John 19:2). Cf. Grosheide (*Commentary* on John 19:5) on the "caricature king."

he came (II Cor. 8:9). But it is exactly here that they go astray, because they do not discern his kingship nor understand the nature of his anointing.

We may not say, however, that it would be better not to speak of kingship in this state of poverty and service. Christ himself mentions it, and in the light of Scripture we are able to understand something of it if only we do not isolate his kingship from his prophetism and priesthood. The kingly office is fully Messianic. It is the fulfillment of the theocracy and of the *historia revelationis.* For the kingship becomes apparent only *in* and *through the sacrifice,* and thus becomes manifest as the beneficial dominion of Christ. It is not incidental that in the midst of the execution of judgment Christ's kingship is the central question. Not Pilate's question, "Shall I crucify your King?" (John 19:15) contains the crisis of his kingship, even though this seems so, but the manifestation of his *true* kingship as faith embraces it as a reality.

If we wish to do justice to this kingship we must not compare it with the deteriorated kingly office as described by Samuel at the beginning of Israel's kingship (I Sam. 8:11-18): it will mean a heavy burden and hard service for "a people of serfs and slaves; it will mean only obligations and no rights."[37] "And ye shall cry out in that day because of your king whom ye shall have chosen you." Instead we shall have to refer to the correct conception of the kingship as we find it in Deuteronomy 17, which depicts the kingship – in Israel – according to God's intention as an *obedient* kingship (Deut. 17:18) which will be a *blessing* to the people, "that he may learn to fear Jehovah his God, to keep all the words of this law . . . to the end that he may prolong his days in his kingdom, he and his children, in the midst of Israel" (Deut. 17:19, 20).

The light of this kingly law radiates in the midst of the deterioration of the theocracy. But already in this light the kingship is *normed.* In Christ's kingly office we no longer see the self-willed way of Israel that chose a king *itself,* but the God-given Messiah whose kingship will not be a heavy but a light burden and an infinite blessing. It is obvious that the law regarding the king in Deuteronomy 17 refers to the kings of Israel, but indirectly it can be fully understood only in connection with Christ. The blessing of his kingship penetrates the deterior-

37. C. J. Goslinga, *Samuel I* (Korte Verklaring), p. 110.

ation. Christ's kingship in inseparable connection with his prophecy and priesthood is a blessing to the world.

Another question, no less important, concerns the execution of Christ's *munus triplex* in his exaltation.[37a] The reality of this *munus triplex* is based on the Father's commission to the mediatorial task, and this task is by no means terminated with Christ' exaltation, according to Scripture. His work, indeed, is "finished," and Scripture continually echos the joyous shout of the "once" revealing the definiteness of God's salvation in Jesus Christ; yet this "once" has an eschatological aspect which implies a further completion. That is why the question concerning the nature of the *munus triplex* in Christ's exaltation is so important. But we must take heed how we continue the line of the *munus triplex* from the humiliation to the exaltation. The progress of the *munus triplex* from humiliation to exaltation involves a progress in Christ's *work*, in the task which the Father had assigned to him.

We are not dealing with a simple continuation, but with a soteriological historical progress which decisively determines the nature of the *munus triplex* in the exaltation. Christ's office does not concern an "idea" which remains the same, but an effective office-fulfillment, and therefore the question concerning the *munus triplex* in the exaltation is so important. No succession may be attached to the unity of Christ's office as though he became prophet and priest first and afterwards king. There is succession, however, in the discharge of his one, threefold office. Here we are confronted with that particular *modality* of the *munus triplex* in the exaltation to which Bavinck refers when he says, "The foundations of the work which he now performs as the exalted Mediator were laid in his cross" (*ibid.*, p. 471). His work now takes on another *form*. We already notice this in his prophetic work during the forty days between resurrection and ascension. It is true, there is no essential change in the contents of the message, but we discover that now there is a *referring back* to the turning point from cross to resurrection. The message concerns the same grace of the Kingdom of God, the same peace of reconciliation, but it is that peace which has now, in cross and resurrection, become a historical reality. This "referring back" is by no means in contradiction with the eschat-

37a. Bavinck, *Gereformeerde Dogmatiek,* III, 352.

ological nature of the apostolic preaching, but all eschatology which is not directed by this referring back is thereby condemned. Oscar Cullmann has correctly emphasized this again and again.[38] The significance of cross and resurrection is decisive not only for the correct understanding of the New Testament eschatology but also for the right insight into Christ's *munus triplex* in his exaltation. Then this office is defined on the basis of the finished work of Christ. The progress of the *munus triplex* is soteriologically and historically determined. It is important to realize what this concretely means in the light of Scripture.

The discussion must obviously proceed by considering the significance and reality of the Church as the people of the Messiah, which he, since the day of Pentecost, calls out of all nations. The aloneness and total forsakenness of God's Messiah are ended. His work radiates its full light on his *ekklesia* (Dan. 7:18, Matt. 16). In this Church many problems kept coming up concerning the office. When we examine these problems closely, we find that they were with the government of the Church in general but were directly connected with the *munus triplex* of Christ. In the history of the Church we notice two clearly evident excesses. On the one hand we see that *because of the nature of Christ's office* any office in the Church held by men is considered an actual degradation of the office. The office *in* the Church – in whatever form – is considered an obstacle to the truly authoritative office-fulfillment by Jesus Christ himself. In the Church there should only be a faithful acknowledging of *his* office and *his* authority, and no human office in the Church should compete with his. These objections concerned not only the Roman Catholic hierarchy but also the office-conception of the Protestant churches, which was considered to create an untenable balance between Christ's office and the office in the Church. The possibility that Christ himself could officially reign through the office in the Church was overlooked. The office, the *work* of the exalted Lord embraced every office in the Church. His "power" does not leave room for any other authority except for that of God's children, who believe in *his* Name (John 1:12). He himself is present in the Church and that constitutes the joy of the Church.

The *munus triplex* tolerates no "competition." Neither is

38. Cf. Chapter 10, *Christ and the Future.*

there any "mediation," since Christ himself is exclusively the Mediator. It is obvious that Rome never had any difficulty in contesting such a view of the ecclesiastical office. It considered this position to be the application of the authority-less principle of the Reformation, which, in Rome's opinion, left no room for the absolute authority of the Church nor for the *office*.

Over against this devaluation of the office Rome pointed, not incorrectly, to the relationship expressed in Christ's words, "Whosoever heareth you heareth me," and to the given commission of the apostolate in the world, and to the offices in the New Testament. According to Rome there was indeed a place for offices in the Church, without their implying any competition with Christ's authority. It sought the solution – and this is the second excess – in establishing a harmony between Christ's office and that in the Church, a harmony which developed into an *identity* rather than a competition. The office in Christ's Church no longer had its definite and solid foundation in Christ's *munus triplex*; but it *corresponded* to Christ's office because it was Christ himself who lived on in his Church as his body. The office in the Church was directly and unproblematically placed under the sanction and protection of the *munus triplex,* with the far-reaching consequence that these offices in the Church were no longer subject to critical correction but obtained an increasingly autonomous character.[39] Thus the picture takes shape of the official hierarchy in the absolute and obvious discharge of its office. The office of the Church contained no *normative* function apart from the function contained in the *fact* of the office itself. The office as such contained the norm. This comprised and still comprises the profound crisis of the Roman Catholic office-conception, because the essence of the office dissolved into the *factuality* of the office as it was accepted and put into action in the Roman Church. A fundamental violation of the *munus triplex* is evident, and since the consideration of the reality of the *munus triplex* – also confessed by Rome – concerns the reality of the Church, there is every reason to examine more closely the dangers involved.

It strikes us at once that the Roman Catholic position regarding the office abuses particularly the prophetic and priestly offices. This is evident especially with respect to the prophetic

39. Cf. A.A. v. Ruler, *Bijzonder en Algemeen Ambt,* 1952, p. 73, who justly says that in Catholicism no fully-developed office-idea is possible.

office. The idea of the *vicariate* more and more mutilated Christ's *munus triplex* and finally threatened to obscure and overshadow the image of Christ's *munus propheticum* completely. It is not possible to discuss here the doctrine of the papal vicariate, but we touch the core when we say that, according to Rome, Peter not only founded the Church but that on good grounds he may be called Christ's *representative.* This word most clearly indicates how much Christ's *munus* really is at stake. When we truly and in faith confess Christ's *munus triplex,* there simply cannot be such a thing as "representation." This has nothing to do with a rejection of offices in the Church, neither yet with an attempt to approach the office individualistically as though we – according to Przywara's interpretation of the Reformation – on the basis of God's all-activity, were deducing his sole activity in Christ. But if the word "representative" is taken even the least bit seriously it indicates a denial of the reality of Christ's office, since he was and is so present in all of his work that even the thought of a representation may not arise.[40]

If this were understood in a purely Reformation sense, the relationship between the church office and Christ's *munus propheticum* would suddenly be realized again. Then, too, the office – according to its character – would be founded again on the exaltation of Jesus Christ with no thought of representing him thereby.[41] We know that Rome itself shrinks from the simple interpretation of "representation" by way of the idea of *identity.* But the retention of the qualification "vicarious" illustrates the denial of the *munus triplex.* Truly, the term "representation" should be reserved for the doctrine of reconciliation!

When the relationship of his office to Christ himself becomes clear, this will show at once the only correct way in which the office in Christ's Church can function without overshadowing *Christ's office.* For then this office is no longer self-evident – on the basis of representation *or* identity – but it is founded on the full *acknowledgment* of *Christ's office.* Then in the entire Church there will be no office or office-bearer that functions by itself or himself without the necessary warning, "Let him that thinketh he standeth take heed lest he fall" (I Cor.

40. Cf. *ibid.,* p. 74, on the *praesentia realis.*
41. Cf. L. Stählin, *Christus praesens* (Beitr. zur ev. Theol., Bd. 3), pp. 47f.; H. Chr. von Hase, *Die Gegenwart Christi in die Kirche,* 1934, p. 33ff.

10:12). This is a very important word, relevant not only for individual members of the Church but also and especially for the office-bearers, since this office only functions justly in the recognition of the authority of Christ himself, who does not allow his Church to be governed independently but who truly governs it himself. Wherever the idea of "representation" is made constitutive of the office-idea, also when formally recognizing the *munus triplex* of Christ, the deterioration of the life of the Church is inevitable. Then, in principle, the source of light of the Church is extinguished, the "church of self-government" takes the place of the "church of obedience,"[42] and actually there is no longer place for Christ *himself* any more.[43] Christ is given his rightful place only when we still realize something of the *instrumentality* of the office, which derives its instrumental function from the fact that it can be truly a blessing to the Church only when it acknowledges the *superiority* and *sovereignty* of the *munus triplex*, which implies a concrete and real activity on the part of Christ (Kuyper, *ibid.*, p. 17). "She is *church* only because of the continuous prophetic, priestly, and kingly activity of Christ, and on earth only so much of the church is evident as her outward appearance radiates and shows forth that continuous, active working of Christ."[44]

For this reason "vicariate" and "*munus triplex Christi*" are irreconcilable. The extent of the conflict between Rome and the Reformation is also sharply and plainly evidenced by this dispute concerning the *munus triplex*.

While this clearly holds with respect to the prophetic office, it is no less evidently true regarding the priestly office of Christ. Here, too, the question must be asked whether a certain conception of the priesthood may not impair the *munus sacerdotale Christi*. It is obvious that when Scripture calls the believers priests this implies no competition with Christ's office whatsoever. In the priesthood of the believers we are not dealing with an independent entity but with the life of faith based on

42. K. Barth, *K.D.* I, 2, 640.
43. Cf. A. Kuyper, *Tractaat van de Reformatie der Kerken*, 1883, p. 15: "It may not be said, therefore, that Christ actually rules as King only in the heavenly church and that on earth he rules his church only by transferring his authority to men, because speaking thus denies and contradicts his Godhead. Christ most certainly is present in his church on earth, present in the truest sense of the word."
44. *Ibid.*, p. 15; cf. A. J. Bronkhorst, *Schrift en Kerkorde*, 1947, p. 210.

the holy sacrifice of the only High Priest, a life of consecration and service. The point here is the fulfillment of a task *in* Christ. It does not compete with Christ's priesthood but *is founded upon it* and is the answer of thanksgiving to it. Here we may apply what we read already the Old Testament, "The sacrifices of God are a broken spirit: a broken and a contrite heart, O God, thou wilt not despise" (Ps. 51:17). It is a priesthood which originates in election (I Pet. 2:9, "a chosen generation, a royal priesthood"), and which is the result of mercy: "Who in time past were no people, but are now the people of God: who had not obtained mercy, but now have obtained mercy" (I Pet. 2:10). No one, in the light of Scripture, can have a misconception of *this* kind of priesthood. It is nothing but a doxology to Christ's priesthood. Schrenk points out that the believers are called priests in that book (Revelation) which knows of no *temple* any more.[45]

The only way in which the priesthood might compete with the *munus Christi* would be for it to commission itself with a task flagrantly contrary to the *munus triplex Christi.* This is exactly the case in the Roman Catholic priestly sacrifice of the mass, because it denies the blessing of Christ's priestly sacrifice and consequently also the unique significance of the *munus triplex.*

With this we touch upon the second serious conflict — besides the one concerning the vicariate — between Rome and the Reformation regarding the office of Christ. The issue at stake in the sixteenth century controversy concerning the Lord's supper was not just a limited locus of doctrine but the *office* and *work* of Christ. Ever since, the battle has flared up again and again concerning the "once" of Hebrews. For no matter what variety of theories there may be concerning the mass in the Roman Catholic camp, there is no difference of opinion regarding the ecclesiastically decreed doctrine that this sacrifice in the mass is a real, though unbloody, sacrifice.[46] There is a continuation of the *munus sacerdotale* in the Church. And this continuation is really not determined by referring back to what took place — which is *the* category in the progress of the *munus triplex* from the humiliation to the exaltation — but Roman Catholic theology presents it as the real daily sacrifice *now.*

45. Kittel, TWNT, III, 265; cf. Rev. 1:6 and 5:10.
46. Cf. my *De Strijd om het R. K. Dogma,* 1950, pp. 255ff.

It is fully realized that the biblical word "once" has played a tremendous role in polemics, because the Epistle to the Hebrews clearly emphasizes the "once" in contrast with the repetition in the Old Testament sacrificial cult. Rome was confronted with the confessional polemics, as for instance in Lord's Day XX of the Heidelberg Catechism, which says that according to Rome Christ is daily offered by the priests and from this it concludes that the mass "at bottom" – fundamentally – is nothing but a denial of the one sacrifice and sufferings of Jesus Christ. Here, in the midst of the practice of celebrating the Lord's supper, the *munus Christi* was at stake. The Lutheran *Confessio Augustana* had also sharply defined its position.[47] It contains the pronouncement that the mass has been abolished, although the Lutherans have – unjustly – been reproached for having actually retained it. The *Augustana* declares explicitly that the holy sacrament has *not* been instituted to provide a sacrifice for sin – because the sacrifice had taken place already – and that there is no other sacrifice than the death of Christ, for which the *Augustana* explicitly quotes Hebrews.[48]

This epistle considers the universal and decisive significance of Christ's sacrifice on the cross to be so tremendous that there can never be such a thing as a repetition.[49] Now there is sanctification and forgiveness, and no sacrifice for sin is necessary any more. Over against this argumentation Rome asserts that the

47. *Confessio Augustana,* Art. 24 (on the "once").
48. On the real sacrifice in the mass, see *Trente Sess.* 22, cap. 2: "Una enim eademque est hostia, idem nunc offerens sacerdotum ministerio, qui seipsum tunc in Cruce obtulit, sola offerendi ratione diversa." In the encyclical of 1935 "Ad catholici Sacerdotii" (ed. Eccl. docens, p. 21) we read, "This is a real sacrifice of a divine offering and not simply a sign. It has, therefore, real power to reconcile mankind with the eternal majesty of God which sin had offended." (Latin text: "vera divinae hostiae sacrificatio haec est" and "habet efficacem vim"). It is amazing how easily an exegesis is produced in order to prove that the priest has a real function as sacrificer under the New Covenant. The encyclical appeals to I Cor. 4:1 ("Let a man so account of us, as of the ministers of Christ, and stewards of the mysteries of God") and continues, "the priest is the steward of Christ, he is, therefore, as the instrument of the Divine Redeemer the perpetual continuation of his marvelous work." And further on: he is "another Christ" (quod jure meritoque dicere solemne habemus) and "takes the place of Christ's person" (cum eius gerat personam).
49. Heb. 9:8, 12, 14, 25, 26; 10:12, 18. Cf. W. v. Loewenich, *Zum Verständnis der Opfergedankens im Hebräerbrief,* Theol. Blätt., 1933.

sacrifice of the mass is not an ordinary repetition nor another, a *new* sacrifice besides the sacrifice of the cross. Every effort is made to show that the sacrifice of the mass does not compete with the sacrifice of the cross. In fact there is *identity* between the two. It is one and the same sacrifice, only it is offered up differently. Thus the attempt is made to harmonize the sacrifice of the mass with the "once," the historically definite fact, in Hebrews. At times there is even an escape into the mysterious, as for instance when Van der Meer says that the mass is indeed a real sacrifice but that we do not know *how* it is such.[50] But it is obvious that this is an escape, after once having assumed the reality of the sacrifice. It is in this light that we must consider such expressions as "the sacrificial knife of the words of consecration" or the separation of Christ's body and blood by "the mystical sword." But back of it all is Trent, and as long as *that* is the case, the "once" of Hebrews remains in force.

Frequently the polemics of the Reformation, for instance Calvin's,[51] are considered no longer relevant in connection with new theories such as Odo Casel's so-called mystery-doctrine. But the problem concerning the *munus sacerdotale* remains acute. Some vehemently attacked Casel's theory, others welcomed it as *the* solution, when he taught that Christ's death as his sacrificial act is *presented anew* in the sacrifice of the mass and that it, therefore, may not simply be called a repetition. In his opinion it concerns the same act, but then in a pneumatic or sacramental form.[52] All these variations do not remove the fact

50. F. v. d. Meer, *Catechismus,* 1941, pp. 416ff.
51. Calvin, *Institutes,* IV, XVIII, 3, we may not add countless sacrifices daily to the sacrifice which Christ made once, because Christ's sacrifice retains its power forever. Calvin wonders whether such sacrifices do not indicate that Christ's sacrifice is imperfect and weak.
52. See, among others, O. Casel, *Heilige Bronnen* (12 Compositions on Liturgy and Monasticism), 1947, especially pp. 35-76 (The Mass as Holy Act of Mystery). Cf. L. Monden, *Het Misoffer als Mysterie,* 1948; Herricus Schillebeeckx, *De Sacramentele Heilsoeconomie,* "Theological examination of St. Thomas' doctrine of the sacraments in the light of tradition and of temporary sacrament problematics," 1952, pp. 215ff. In it he discusses the question whether Casel's doctrine of mysteries is condemned by the encyclical *Mediator Dei* (pp. 230ff.) This was occasioned by the fact that the pope had *rejected* the vague mystery-doctrine (van recentiores scriptores quidam) in this encyclical. The question now is if Casel is meant, just as there was a question exactly who were condemned in the encyclical *Humani Generis.* According to Schillebeeckx, Casel's doctrine is *not* affected by the encyclical (p.

— and that was exactly the point of issue in the Reformation — that in all these variations Christ is being sacrificed. It actually makes very little difference which form is attributed to the reality of the sacrifice of the mass, because back of all these variations lies the necessity of the *real* sacrifice *now* in order to make the sacrifice of the cross effective.

That is why the conflict must again and again concentrate around the *munus sacerdotale.* Sight is lost of the *historical* progress in Christ's work from humiliation to exaltation. What has actually developed is that the priestly office is construed in analogy with the prophetic office and is considered to continue *on the same level.* But the continuation of the prophetic office (Christ and the office in the Church) may not be applied simply to the priestly office (Christ's sacrifice and the priests of the mass). This denies the sacrifice of Christ and necessitates that Christ wishes to become a sacrifice also *in* his members. "He wants to be a sacrifice *in* us."[53] In and after all these discussions and variations the final result remains fundamentally the same. It is Christ himself who "in the holy mass sacrifices his body and blood to the Father" and it is the same sacrifice which he *once* offered up on Calvary. Why is that necessary? asks Steur. Because a remembrance is not sufficient and his suffering itself must truly remain with us.[54] Therefore "the Holy Sacrament of the Altar is the most venerable sacrament, the object and center of all others" (*ibid.,* p. 98). But for this actual sacrifice of Christ himself a *human* priest is engaged (*ibid.,* p. 163). He receives authority to present the sacrifice to God and thus "participates continuously in Christ's priesthood" (*ibid.,* p. 165; cf. p. 166: "transfer of power, authority"). This presents a totally different view of the *munus triplex,* and the priesthood runs parallel with the vicariate. Here the partaking of Christ's anointing does not refer — as in Lord's Day XII — to the complete sacrifice but is constitutive of the sacrifice which is daily

---

232). Cf. Dr. G. Cloen, *De Verhouding Tussen het Offer van Christus in de Heilige Mis en op het Kruis Volgens de Princeiepen van de Encycliek "Mediator Dei." Stud. Cath.,* 1952, pp. 133ff. and H. Chr. v. Hase, *Die Gegenwart Christi in der Kirche,* 1934, pp. 42-48.

53. P. Romualdus, *De Betekenis van de Heilige Eucharistie.* In *Jaarboek Werkgenootschap van Kath. Theol. in Nederland,* 1951, pp. 147ff.

54. K. Steur, *Levende Tekens van God,* 1946, p. 94.

made by the priests.[55] Thus the *munus triplex* is mutilated in the core of its sacramental soteriological economy.

Finally the question remains whether the *munus triplex Christi* in the Roman Catholic Church is also obscured by its interpretation of Christ's kingly office, as it is by the *vicariate* and the *mass.* The fact is that besides the *vicarius Dei* and the priest it does not have a representative kingly figure. This must be because Rome considers the kingly and prophetic offices closely related. Accordingly, its conception of Christ's kingly office is equally obscured with its conception of the prophetic office, as is evidenced by the vicariate. This does not mean, however, that the Roman Catholic Church and theology pay no attention to Christ's kingship. On the contrary, in 1925 the pope even issued a new encyclical particularly dealing with Christ as King and in which a new feast was announced. It speaks at great length of Christ's power and glory.[56] But again we observe that peculiar *limitation.* There is no real permanent obedience to this kingship as proof for its recognition. Christ's identity with his Church at best allows for his supremacy *over the world.* It is very remarkable that this encyclical emphasizes the call to the heads of the nations to obey this *Christus Rex.* It evidently shows confrontation, danger, concern about the undermining and denial of Christ's authority.[57] And undoubtedly it reveals a stronger New Testament attitude. But this confrontation does *not* touch Christ's authority *in his Church.* That is the deplorable thing in this doxology to Christ *as king.* And so also the position concerning Christ's kingly office shows that the conflict between Rome and the Reformation is in fact a conflict concerning the reality of the *munus triplex.*

Thus we see that the controversy concerning Christ's office is not simply an abstract matter, but that it affects the present life of the Church. The office of Christ in his exaltation is full of the fulfillment of his office in the humiliation. For this reason we cannot do justice to any of his three offices if no justice is done to his finished work of redemption. This, too, explains that the progress from humiliation to exaltation is

55. Cf. K. Steur, *op. cit.,* p. 173, "His name is priest, because he, too, is a sacrificer: he is the servant of Jesus Christ when repeating his sacrifice of the cross."

56. *Quas Primas,* December 11, 1925 (Eccl. docens 1940), p. 18.

57. *Ibid.,* p. 29. Cf. *Ubi arcano.*

reflected in the *progress* and *modality* of the *munus triplex*. This office does not contain an abstract idea which may be applied to both the humiliated and the exalted Messiah, but it concerns the one office of Christ in the *progress* of his redemptive work. We see the progress of the prophetic office in the blessing he gives in the pouring out of the Spirit, in the apostolate, and in every office fulfillment by which Christ's prophetic office causes the Church to enjoy the richness of God's full counsel to our salvation. Apostolic preaching refers back to that which has been accomplished. *Anamnesis* – holy remembrance – is a central matter in the New Testament, and that is more than psychology, in spite of Zwingli. In the priestly office there is, in accordance with the nature of Christ's sacrifice, not a continuous sacrificial act as renewal or repetition of that which the eternal High Priest accomplishes, but, as Scripture teaches, the revelation of the power and reality of his sacrifice – once made – before the countenance of God in the intercession for his people and the keeping of them in his priestly heart.

In the kingly dignity of Jesus Christ, faith discovers the royal structure of his kingdom as it is manifested in his exaltation: that kingdom of which he testified before Pilate when still in poverty and totally misjudged. After the resurrection all power is given unto him in heaven and on earth. But this "power" ensued from his complete office-fulfillment, also from his being king in his humiliation, the king who is crucified and crowned. Now he has received the full power and glory, and the Church confesses that he is her eternal king who "governs us by his *word* and *Spirit* and who defends and preserves us in (the enjoyment of) that salvation he has purchased for us" (Heidelberg Catechism, Q. 31).

Later on – when dealing with the *sessio Christi* – we shall have to go further into some of the related questions, but it is clear already how important the questions concerning the *munus triplex* are. We might possibly say that practically all theological questions – and contemporary discussions as well! – are centered around the doctrine of the *munus triplex*. This need not surprise us when realizing the profound implications and wide perspectivies of Jesus Christ's office. For this *munus triplex* points out the way which Christ went and still goes in undiminished faithfulness to the Father. This office became and still is a blessing for the world, even after man's service became perverted into disobedience and appalling self-service. By his office Christ gave *service* back to life again. And far from being an abstract idea or a logical schematization, the doctrine of the threefold office is intended to preserve the right insight into the fruit of Christ's work by which life can and does become restored. Whosoever follows *him* will not walk in darkness but will have the light of life. That which became full reality in him becomes now – in his footsteps – possible again without having one office-fulfillment eliminating or endangering the other.

The unity of the office becomes evident again in the *service* of God and mankind. That is the light which Christ as the Light of the world has kindled, "and didst purchase unto God with thy blood men out of every tribe, and tongue, and people, and nation, and madest them to be unto our God a kingdom and priests; and they shall reign upon the earth" (Rev. 5:9, 10). He has delivered this one office from all demonry and made it one again, directed towards the true goal. It becomes manifest in the ordinary relationships of life and is acknowledged wherever life is lived "without murmurings and questions . . . blameless and harmless" as children of God without blemish in the midst of a crooked and perverse generation, among whom ye are seen as lights in the world" (Phil. 2:14, 15). Such life is no longer lived in fatal self-consciousness which obscures every office-fulfillment, but in the footsteps of the One pointed out by Paul in the same chapter in whom alone everything becomes possible, "having the same love, being of one accord, of one mind," without "vainglory, but in lowliness of mind each counting other better than himself" (Phil. 2:2, 3; cf. 2:5). Whoever understands the absolute "newness" of such a life has also seen the richness of Christ's office. For there is only one explanation for this new life and it has only one source: the dying grain of wheat which bears much fruit.

CHAPTER FIVE

THE GREAT MYSTERY

WHILE discussing the motive for the incarnation (chapter II), we dealt at length with a certain one-sided view which isolates the incarnation from the fact of sin and from that which historically followed Christ's birth, namely his suffering and death. We noted that this view presupposes, in effect, a distinction between becoming-man and becoming-flesh which easily engenders all kinds of heresies. The danger of heresy must not deter us, however, from a full consideration of the unique fact of the incarnation, which the Church throughout the world commemorates especially at Christmas. If we begin to fear a separate study of the incarnation, then Paul's word must strike us, "And without controversy great is the mystery of godliness: He who was manifested in the flesh" (I Tim. 3:16). Even though this mystery which Paul mentions is far from isolated, but has its place in the sum total of sacred history, yet there is room for the adoration of the mystery of God in the birth of Christ as we find it in the words of John, "And the Word became flesh, and dwelt among us" (John 1:14).

The Church confesses this mystery with the surety of faith, and it is part and parcel of the true fear of God. It is not an obvious truth which may be arrived at by way of human reason, but it is God's revelation of him who was sent and has come. It is possible to deny this, and it *has* been denied, and the character of the mysterious has been removed from Christ's birth. The reason might be that no glorious messenger from heaven surrounded with celestial light witnessed concerning his origin; neither was his appearance overwhelmingly majestic. On the contrary, his birth was in poverty and the weakness of the flesh.[1] It is true, John adds, "and we beheld his glory, glory as of the only begotten from the Father, full of grace and truth" (John 1:14). But this "beholding" of his glory is not a mat-

1. Cf. C. H. Lindijer, *Het Begrip Sarx bij Paulus,* 1952, p. 103.

ter of course to anyone[2] who observes his appearance, but it is a seeing by faith after one's eyes have been opened for the mystery of the One who came.[3] That is why to John this "beholding" does not preclude the Word's becoming *flesh,* nor did Paul believe that Christ's being manifest in the flesh precludes the *revelation.*[4]

For it is exactly this that confronts us with the mystery: the *man* Jesus Christ. Faith considers him not just a mysterious figure but *the* mystery, of which Paul says that it was kept secret since the world began, but now is made manifest.[5] It is *God's* mystery, which, to be sure, is the fulfillment of a promise made before the world began (Tit. 1:3), the promise concerning Immanuel; nevertheless this does not dissolve the mystery that has come now, and here, and in this manner, in the lowliness of the flesh,[6] like one of us, Jesus Christ, in all things like unto his brethren (Heb. 2:17), made of a woman, made under the law (Gal. 4:4).

All sorts of attempts have been made to make this miraculous, mysterious birth somewhat acceptable. It has been presented as a uniting of the Logos with the man Jesus Christ, or, in order to establish the real unity, united the Logos with an incomplete human nature, part of which was replaced by the Logos.[7] In both instances serious injustice was done to what Scripture simply teaches: *born, become.* Grosheide remarks that it is not John's intention to explain the *how,*[8] but the entire Scripture pictures the mystery as an indubitable reality, "in him dwelleth all the fulness of the Godhead bodily" (Col. 2:9). The hiding in the flesh does not contradict the revelation, since the Word's becoming flesh is the way of God's mercy in his Son Jesus Christ.

Whoever proceeds from a formal conception of revelation

2. Grosheide, *Comm.* I, p. 96, mentions the Jews who saw Jesus, but not his glory.
3. Cf. I John 1:1 (seeing and handling the Word of life).
4. I Tim. 3:16. Cf. C. Bouma, *Comm.,* p. 149, "The sentence contains something paradoxical. He was placed in the light, manifest in the flesh, which covered and hid his glory."
5. Rom. 16:25, cf. C. H. Dodd, *The Epistle of Paul to the Romans,* 1949, p. 245, "The divine plan of salvation, though it was attested by the prophetic Scripture was, in its full scope, a secret until the coming of Christ"; cf. Eph. 3:9.
6. God sent his Son "in a flesh like unto that of sin."
7. Cf. my *The Person of Christ,* Ch. III.
8. Grosheide, *Comm. Johannes* I, p. 94.

might consider the *revelation* in the *flesh* a contradiction and conclude to a dialectic of concealment and revelation, but Scripture is not concerned with such a formal mystery but with the *revelation* of God's love in *this* way of poverty and in *this* weakness of the flesh.[9] Herein lies the uniqueness of the incarnation of the Word, which has nothing to do with the idea of the God-man presented by nineteenth-century Christology over against the "once-and-for-all" of the incarnation as confessed by the Church. This generalization endangered the whole mystery, and there never will be any synthesis between the confession of the Church and this philosophy.[10] For thus the incarnation is detached from the biblical teaching of Christ's emptying himself, and the gospel loses its essence, namely that the Word became *flesh,* the glad tidings of God's good pleasure (Luke 2:14, Phil. 2:6f.). This good pleasure becomes manifest in the fact of Christ's birth, and again it becomes clear that it is impossible to make a distinction between becoming-man and becoming-flesh or to consider the incarnation *as such.* For the incarnation is not just connected with God's good pleasure, but it is the revelation of him who *in the fulness of time* was born in Bethlehem.

Paul's indication of the time of Christ's birth is inseparably connected with his expression "kept secret since the world began" to bring out the fact that it is *now* revealed. The fulness of time refers to the time when God sends his Son. Christ himself said, "The time is fulfilled."[11] The expression as such may also refer to ordinary circumstances,[12] but in connection with Christ's birth it denotes the coming of that particular moment when God sends his Son to his assigned work. Therefore we may not assume that the fulness of time had come just then because of

9. Cf. F. Gogarten, *Der Mensch zwischen Gott und Welt,* 1952, p. 247ff.
10. Cf. my *The Person of Christ.*
11. Mark 1:15 (πεπλήρωται ὁ καιρὸς); concerning the conceptions καιρὸς and χρόνος see "Chronos and Kairos," in *Het Tijdsprobleem in het N.T.,* 1952 (Sevenster, p. 11; Polman, p. 26f.). Whoever construes a sharp distinction gets into trouble with Gal. 4:4. If καιροι would exclusively indicate the turning-points of God's activity in history, then in Gal. 4:4 we certainly would expect καιρὸς whereas, to the contrary, it has χρόνος. See Polman, p. 27. Note also the connection of χρόνος and καιρὸς with Polman, p. 26.
12. For instance of Elizabeth, when her full time had come that she should be delivered (ἐπλήσθη ὁ χρόνος). In Eph. 1:10 in eschatological connection; in the dispensation τοῦ πληρώματος τῶν καιρῶν.

a religious dissatisfaction or a religious anticipation or redemption.[13] Scripture does not give any such data in this expression.[14] When the Son comes, born of a woman, then is realized the fulfillment of God's time, and thus it is free of any arbitrariness. The emphasis in the fulness of time is on God's decisive action,[15] which is now manifest in history in the sending of his Son Jesus Christ. It is the coming of the Kingdom of God. It is the great mystery *in time,* now manifest, of which Hebrews says that Christ has appeared "now once at the end of the ages."[16] This fulness is also connected with the "once" of Hebrews: the decisive act of God *now* and *here* is Christ's appearance, now that he has come "to take away sin by his sacrifice."

The Gospels testify of this miracle, this mystery of the incarnation, in the historical records of Christ's birth. We see God's counsel focused upon this local event in which appear such names as Augustus, Cyrenius, Joseph and Mary, Simeon and Anna. This historical demarcation has always irritated many who considered it more consonant with the glory and majesty of God if he would have revealed himself in the universality of his wide world rather than in this locality of Bethlehem, and to whom God's omnipresence presents less of a problem than "God manifest in the flesh." Paul and John, however, knew and understood the significance of the historic designation of this revelation of God and did not consider it incompatible with the universal scope of God's activity any more than Israel's election and God's "dwelling" in the temple contradicted the greatness of his divine revelation. The Old Testament already mentions Bethlehem as the birthplace of the Messiah: "But thou,

13. "Modern historians, for instance, dwell on the *preparatio evangelica* found in the unifying agency of the Roman Empire, in the spread of Greek as practically a universal language, in the renascence of faith implied in the influence of Judaism and of certain heathen cults" (G. S. Duncan, *The Epistle of Paul to the Galatians,* 1948, p. 128).

14. Cf. F. W. Grosheide, *De Volheid des Tijds,* Ref. V.U., 1929, e.g., p. 22: The expression does not permit us to say "exactly why at that particular time the time had become full, since the reason for this is not given." Cf. also p. 9.

15. "The supreme event in the divine plan of the ages" (G. S. Duncan, *ibid.*, p. 127).

16. ἐπὶ συντελείᾳ τῶν αἰώνων. Heb. 9:26. Grosheide in this connection refers to Gal. 4:4, *Comm. Hebr.*, p. 265.

Bethlehem Ephrathah, which art little to be among the thousands of Judah, out of thee shall one come forth unto me that is to be ruler in Israel" (Mic. 5:2). This prophecy implies the *glory* of the Messiah-King; he will come as a Ruler, but this glory is of a *peculiar* character. He will come forth out of the very smallest families of Judah, "so small that it can hardly be numbered among them,"[17] which shows forth God's wonder with respect to the historical aspect. It is his incalculable and unexpected miracle which, also in its character, is *his* mystery.

The birth records, however, prove sufficiently that they are not concerned with the mystery and unfathomableness of the event *as such.* On the contrary, they reflect the full light of *revelation.* If one thing becomes clear in these birth records, it is that all the lines of God's providence converge in Bethlehem. That which Micah's prophecy envisioned and indicated becomes historic reality with the birth of Christ against the background of the great world events in the days of Augustus. These world events are not *excluded* but rather *included* in the great mystery (Luke 2:1). Augustus may be compared with Cyrus in the Old Testament, who must serve God's people as an instrument in God's hand. So must Augustus with all his activity for the Roman Empire, and exactly by this activity he paves the way for God's Messiah, a way which begins in Bethlehem. It has been justly said that "matter-of-factness" dominates the Christmas story.[18] That could not be otherwise with respect to a mystery so rooted in history. It is, indeed, the grace of God which appeared, bringing salvation to all men (Tit. 2:11), and the self-denial of him who was made in the likeness of men

17. J. Ridderbos, *De Kleine Profeten* II, p. 95. In this connection Edelkoort refers to Paul's statement that God has chosen the weak things of the world to confound the things which are mighty (I Cor. 1:27), A. H. Edelkoort, *Micha, Een Profeet vol Recht en Heldenmoed,* p. 126. Cf. also his *De Christusverwachting in het O.T.,* 1941, p. 271, where he considers the choice of Bethlehem over against the metropolis in complete agreement with the fundamental law of the Kingdom of God in I Cor. 1:27f. Cf. in this connection what Matt. 2:23 says concerning Christ's dwelling in Nazareth (in accordance with the fulfillment of the prophecy). Cf. H. N. Ridderbos, *Mattheus, K.V.,* I, p. 50 on Jesus' lowly descent.

18. E. Emmen, *De Prediking op het Kerstfeest,* in *Handboek voor de Prediking,* 1948, p. 71; cf. M. A. Beek and J. M. de Jong, *Bijbelse Knooppunten,* 1952, pp. 7ff.

(Phil. 2:7), but it may also be recorded in the framework of Augustus' actions as well.

Not only the birth records, but also the records of his suffering evidence a great difference from all idealism disconnected from history. The issue at stake is the actual birth of Christ, the fact of the incarnation, history without any apocryphal Christmas illumination. This birth does not only evoke Herod's hatred, who causes the shadows of death to descend on the Christmas event, but again and again the confession of this historical fact of Christ's birth has become an object of criticism throughout the ages and evoked an attack upon the true human nature of the Son of God in the flesh. Again and again both romanticism and idealism attack this confession, which is not one of a glorious theophany but of the *in-carnation.* Already during the infancy of the Christian Church this opposition was so sharp and open that John says that *this* is the spirit of anti-christ, when it is denied that Jesus Christ is come in the flesh.[19]

The point at issue is the reality of *history* and of the *flesh.* These cannot be dissociated from the incarnation, any more than the cross can be disconnected from history and still be a significant symbol. The birth records, therefore, make sense only against the background of history. Thus we see the hand of God in numerous details, at times explicitly mentioned,[20] at other times by undeniable implication.[21] The worst thing that can be done is to explain the reality of God's activity as a mythological formulation, whereas nothing less than the "glory to God" and "on earth peace" are at stake. It is certainly not incidental that in immediate connection with the Christmas story Zacharias' unbelief – when the fulness of time had come – is answered by God's judgment and miraculous punishment, "And, behold, thou shalt be silent and not able to speak, until the day that these things shall come to pass, because thou believedst not my words, which shall be fulfilled in their season"

19. I John 4:3, cf. verse 2, "Hereby know ye the Spirit of God: every spirit that confesseth that Jesus Christ is come in the flesh is of God." Also II John 7.
20. In the annunciation of the angel to Zacharias (Luke 1:11ff.) and to Mary (Luke 1:26ff.); in Elizabeth's being filled with the Holy Spirit (Luke 1:41f.); in the message to Joseph (Matt. 1:20); in the warning of the wise men against Herod (Matt. 2:12), the dream of Joseph (Matt. 2:13), the dream at the return from Egypt (Matt. 2:19), and the dream in connection with their settlement (Matt. 2:22).
21. Think of Augustus and the coming of the wise men from the East.

(Luke 1:20). The doubting and unbelieving voice – in striking symbolism – must remain silent until it is heard again in the song of praise to "the tender mercy of our God, whereby the dayspring from on high shall visit us" (Luke 1:78; cf. 1:64).

Faith alone is able to understand the miracle, not as an incidental and miraculous "appearance" but as incarnation, as the beginning of a way (cf. Luke 1:76) on which the Savior is placed for the fall and rising again of many in Israel and for a sign which shall be spoken against (Luke 2:34). This proves again that we are not merely dealing with a general miracle which surpasses human understanding, but with *this* miracle; not with a general paradox, but with *this* act of grace. Great decisions are made here, and Simeon is seeing in the midst of his joy that a sword shall pierce Mary's soul (Luke 2:25) and that the thoughts of many hearts will be revealed (Luke 2:35). The oppositions to the new-born Christ which will become manifest show that the human heart is closed to this humiliation, the humiliation of the Word become flesh. There were times when the Jews perceived some kingly aspect in Jesus; then they immediately wanted to make him a king (John 6:15, cf. Matt. 21:1-11). But his humiliation was an offense to them: "He came unto his own, and they that were his own received him not" (John 1:11). Faith alone sees the glory in the humiliation, and this faith burst out in songs of praise already at the manger when it understood that it was not facing a mysterious incognito but the revelation of divine grace in the flesh and in utmost humiliation.[22] His poverty prevented neither the shepherds nor the wise men from adoring him, and thus the gospel of Christmas points out the relationship between faith and the depth of this mystery, *this* poverty which is the sign of his true Messiahship (Luke 2:12). God's activity is so evident in the birth of Christ that it surpasses every human standard; every human construction is overtaken by the testimony concerning what took place here (Luke 2:15). The humble Anna and Simeon had a proper expectation of the Messiah; they did

22. Dr. G. C. van Niftrik did not go into my objections to the incognito idea in my *The Person of Christ* (last chapter). See G. C. van Niftrik, *Kerk en Theologie*, 3rd ed., 1952, p. 126. He just asks if the denial of the incognito is not a sort of docetism. It is moreover not clear why the argument stops here, since the rejection of the incognito is based on the acceptance of the incarnation of the Word as the revelation of God's grace in this humiliation. This has nothing to do with docetism. Van Niftrik moreover states that I consider docetism more and more to be *the* heresy (see p. 124).

not separate the appearance of the *Ruler* of Micah 5 from the *lowliness* of Bethlehem. Simeon waited for the consolation of Israel (Luke 2:25) and Anna served God with fastings and prayers night and day in the temple (Luke 2:37; cf. "all them that were looking for redemption of Jerusalem," verse 38).

By faith this mystery is understood, now that the Word has become *flesh,* full of grace and truth (John 1:14), just as in the annunciation the giving of the name of the Messiah excludes all human arbitrariness: "and thou shalt call his name Jesus: for it is he that shall save his people from their sins."[23]

The power of God unto salvation will become manifest in him – in the depth of his humiliation – and this salvation enters history as an ineffaceable reality. Christ's way of salvation is one of humiliation and goes contrary to all human glory. Mary, in her song, sings of the power and richness of God. She envisions, so to speak, the terrible happenings in God's power as if they are already taking place.[24] The holy land is not yet full of the sound of the message and the angels have not yet come with the message of peace. But she sees – the fulness of time – God's deeds coming in an overwhelming vision. *Now* everything is going to change. A divine standard will cross all human relationships and standards. The mighty are put down from their seats and the rich are sent away empty. This is not a revolution in blood and tears as we know it from the history of mankind, but a powerful act of God. The proud in the imagination of their hearts are scattered. Just as in Psalm 146 the way of the wicked is turned upside down in the midst of the multifarious blessings of the righteous (vss. 8, 9), so here the proud cannot last in the face of this mystery. This is

23. Matt. 1:21, Luke 1:31. The uniqueness in the name-giving is not the name itself, which was also the name of many others. See Kittel, s.v., 'Ιησους III, p. 285 (very common) and A. Deissmann, "Der Name Jesus" (in *Mysterium Christi,* 1931, pp. 22f.). This name-giving can be understood only by faith and revelation in its unique significance, and in the light which qualifies *this common name.* Deissmann is of the opinion that the name Jesus did not become a "cult name" until after his exaltation and that Matt. 1:21 is the "oldest proof" thereof (p. 23). The name Jesus is, in his opinion, "canonized by the church as a *nomen sacrum;* it became the banner word of the cult of the Savior." When we, on the basis of the gospel, accept that the name-giving has nothing to do with human canonization, then we clearly see the inseparable unity between this proper name and Christ's official name (Luke 2:11). The act of salvation takes place in the fulfillment of his Messiahship.

24. Cf. Mary's song with Hannah's in I Sam. 2.

no general sermon on the virtue of humility. *This* scattering is historically dated and becomes unavoidable reality, judgment, revelation, in what takes place at the manger: for here God does not come with his majesty and supreme power but in grace. That is the reason why the thoughts of many hearts will be revealed: they cannot remain hidden over against this poverty, which leads either to irritation or adoration. Whoever does not gather here with *him* participates in the scattering of the proud.[25] In the fulness of time it is God's order, the order of his grace and tender mercy which as a historical fact breaks through the disorder of sin. His arm is with strength and the bow of the strong is broken, but this does not take place in a fierce battle but by *this* poverty and by this remembrance of his mercy (Luke 1:54).

And the *Word* was made *flesh,* and dwelt among us (John 1:14). The Christmas gospel reveals the full counsel of God "at the end of the ages"; now that peace has come, God preserves it by his immediate interference when Herod attempts to take Christ's life. This gospel of the incarnated Word is God's answer to all proud questions concerning a "theodicy" and the reality of God's love. The light of this revelation radiates in the midst of all the incomprehensible ways of history, all our questions, and everything that surpasses our understanding. There is a limit to what God "allows" in this dark and demonic world. God sets such a limit when he preserves his Christ.[26]

When the early Church expressed her faith in Jesus Christ in the midst of the world, she remained close to the testimony of Holy Scripture by confessing, "who is born of the Holy Ghost and the virgin Mary."[27] This is the original text of the Apostolic Creed, which later was changed to "conceived by the Holy Ghost, born of the virgin Mary."[28] This confronts us with the fact that the Church was not satisfied with simply confessing

25. Matt. 12:30; Luke 11:23: "gathereth means to bring in and gather people to be his followers" (H. N. Ridderbos, *K.V., Matt. I,* 24:1).
26. Matt. 2:12ff. (the flight to Egypt).
27. "Qui natus est de Spiritu Sancto et Maria virgine." Cf. K. Holl, "Zur Auslegung des 2. Art. des sog. apost. Glaubensbekenntnisses," *Gesammelte Aufs. zur Kirchengesch.,* II, (1928), 115ff., and F. Kattenbusch, *Das apostolische Symbol,* II, (1900), 616f.
28. The question concerning the reason for the supplementing of and distinction between *conceptus* and *natus* is of a symbolic-historical character. According to Kattenbusch it is not of an anti-heretical nature (II, p. 880). Cf., "In fact the accentuation of the *conceptio* corresponds with the story in Luke 1:31" (p. 881).

Christ's birth but that she did so in a specific manner, *natus ex virgine Maria*. That no doubt had something to do with the simple clarity of the scriptural story relating the birth of Christ against the background of the relationship of Joseph and Mary and the special revelation by the angel. No one could then have anticipated that such a heated and longlasting argument would ensue especially around *this* particular article of faith. As long as the Holy Scriptures were accepted as the trustworthy Word of God and the Church did not want to go beyond and "above that which is written" (I Cor. 4:6, ὑπὲρ ἃ γέγραπται), the virgin birth of Christ was accepted and confessed without any crisis of conscience.[29] Ever since the attack on the authority of Holy Scripture, however, the door was opened for far-reaching criticism. To many the plain words of the gospels of Matthew and Luke were no longer a safeguard against the objections of an anti-supernaturalistic era to the "miraculous" birth. The result, especially since the nineteenth century, has been a changed situation which still continues.

Towards the end of the second century the virgin birth was not simply incorporated into a "life of Jesus," but was confessed as an essential part of the Christian faith in the creed. Justin defended it against Jewish and pagan attacks, and Ignatius spoke repeatedly of it.[30] Through century after century it was an indisputable part of the treasures of faith in the Church, and was incorporated not only into the old creed but also into many confessions of later date.[31] But ever since the nineteenth century, both Church and theology have raised objections. The old confession, which was directly linked with the mystery of the incarnated Word, became more and more a stumbling block. Together with other points it gave occasion to all kinds of disputes on the validity and reliability of the *Apostolicum*.[32] A critical disposition became more and more evident. The relative scarcity of New Testament evidence of the virgin birth was emphasized, and from this it was concluded that originally it did not belong to the apostolic witness or, at least, was not

29. Cf. Gresham Machen, *The Virgin Birth,* 1932, p. 3.
30. Cf. Ignatius (*ad Smyrn.* 1, 1; *ad Eph.* 19, 1).
31. In the Symbolum Nicaeno-Constantinopolitanum; furthermore in the Confessio Augustana (Art. 3), Confessio Belgica (Art. 18), Heidelberg Catechism (Lord's Day 14), Confessio Gallicana (Art. 14), Confessio Helvetica (Art. 11), and Confessio Anglicana (Art. 2).
32. Cf. Y. Feenstra, *Het Apostolicum in de Twintigste Eeuw,* pp. 33ff.

on a par with the witness of the resurrection of Christ which was so predominant in the apostolic preaching. Moreover, a strong influence was felt from the religious-historical research which supposedly could point out various parallels between the virgin birth and other stories of birth of gods and their offspring.

The idea of the virgin birth was seen as a frequent *motif* in explaining the divine origin of great figures.[33] Thus the virgin birth was placed on a level with heathen myths concerning the miraculous and fantastic penetration of the borders of the mundane by the mythical.[34] The fact that the New Testament had incorporated it was often explained as an attempt of the young Church to express the mystery of Christ's person. In spite of the fact that many objections were voiced[35] against these religious-historic parallels, the general flood of criticism could no longer be stemmed, so that up to this day an outspoken rejection or at least a strongly critical reservedness is noticeable. In addition, the *natus ex virgine* was considered closely related to Roman Catholic Mariology, which caused many to agree that the virgin birth fitted only into the structure of Mariological thought, with the immaculate conception of Mary as its resultant.[36] It was said that the doctrine of the virgin birth presupposes special conceptions of virginity and of original sin in connection with sexuality, and that these conceptions put the Christian confession in a questionable light.

In view of the fact that so many voices were raised against this article of faith it is necessary, especially in our day, to reflect upon this confession. What is the nature of this "stumbling-block"? Is the Church merely perpetuating a tradition, or does her confession still witness responsibly in the midst of the

33. Cf. *Die Religion in Geschichte und Gegenwart,* s.v., virgin birth.
34. Cf., among others, H. Gunkel, *Zum religionsgeschichtlichen Verständnis des N. T.*, 1930-33, p. 65, "This motif is, as theology has proven long ago, essentially mythologic; fundamentally it is the same as what the nations round about relate concerning their heroes." It cannot be denied that the way the virgin birth was defended at times evoked this misconception. This is true with respect to Justin, who states that the virgin birth of Christ need not seem strange compared with what heathendom teaches concerning the sons of Zeus (*Apol.*, I, 12). Cf. Origen, *Contra Celsum,* I, 37.
35. Among others by Harnack, who himself rejected the virgin birth but who considered the religious-historical explanations insufficient, "This design-book is highly disagreeable" (*History of Dogma,* I, p. 75) Cf. F. Büchsel, *Der Geist Gottes im N.T.*, 1926, pp. 192, 193.
36. In 1854.

world? Originally, this confession was not the result of speculative or mythological motives in Christian thinking, but rather referred simply to the teaching of Scripture. It is this simplicity of the Church which is at stake.

It is not our intention to deal with all the objections raised in the nineteenth and twentieth century against the virgin birth, but we may not ignore some of the main arguments brought up in contemporary theology. It was especially Brunner who vehemently re-attacked the *natus ex virgine.* Even though he was, as early as 1924, the ruthless opponent of Schleiermacherian subjectivism, placing the Word[37] over against this bottomless mysticism, his appeal to the "Word of God" in connection with the virgin birth did not imply that he meant to break away from the critical tendencies of the nineteenth century. Already in his Christology of 1927 he emphatically opposed the virgin birth. He came to the conclusion that the confession of the incarnation had been burdened from the outset with a representation that obscures[38] its fundamental idea, namely the "natus ex *virgine* Maria." For Brunner the scriptural basis of this dogma is inadequate, especially since the New Testament foundation is rather precarious; neither Paul nor John mentions it at all.[39]

Furthermore, there are ever so many indications "that also the opening words of Matthew and Luke once sounded entirely different in this connection."[40] The idea of the virgin birth does not originate in this historic *kerygma* but owes its origin to *dogmatic* motives, and . . . "this tells us exactly where this question belongs and comes from."

The "virgin birth" would have been abandoned long ago if it were not for such dogmatic motives. Without seriously examining the testimony of Scripture, Brunner thus puts the confession of the Church under suspicion of "dogmatic" construction and, further, attempts to show that his criticism does not originate from a rationalistic denial of the miracle, but, on the contrary, from the desire to maintain fully the miracle of the incarnation. The concrete wonder of God took place in the incarnation, and

37. E. Brunner, *Die Mystik und das Wort,* 1924.
38. E. Brunner, *Der Mittler,* 1927, p. 288.
39. *Ibid.,* p. 289, "Except for the two places in Scripture, namely Matt. 1:18-25 and Luke 1:35, the entire N.T. bears not a trace of this representation, neither any sign of interest in it."
40. Cf. Thomas Walker, *Is Not This the Son of Joseph?,* p. 84.

this real miracle may not be denied. But the *natus ex virgine* attempts to explain this miracle by means of inserting a *biological factor*. "'This biological interpretation is the crux of the argument."[41] We may not attempt to penetrate the impenetrable. We must be satisfied with the *fact* of the incarnation. "The *how* is God's secret." The Son of God partook completely and wholly of our human nature, which also includes his being the "product of the two sexes." Therefore, whoever holds to the virgin birth does not respect the miracle but tries to explain it; he does not *magnify* but *minimize* it and seizes it in order to make it transparent.[42] By asserting that the Son of God did not come into the world in a human, natural way, one becomes the tragic victim of the docetistic conception concerning Jesus Christ's origin. The rejection of this confession is not a sign of unbelief but a victory over imperfect faith and shows a profound respect for the great mystery that the Word became *flesh*.[43]

Many years later, Brunner took up this subject once more in his dogmatics. Emphasizing again the *fact* of the incarnation, he acknowledges that there is a New Testament tradition which seems to deal with the *how* of the incarnation, and he makes an attempt to understand this tradition. After close examination he comes to the conclusion that neither Matthew nor Luke was concerned with the *how* of the incarnation at all but with the genesis of the person of Jesus Christ. At this point they knew nothing about the eternal Son, and thus they represent a stage of Christology wherein the theme of the incarnation *had not yet become actual.* They were dealing with the origin of Jesus, and gave the virgin birth as the answer. In fact, if we were to take the text literally, it would exclude "a pre-existence of a Son of God."[44] What we read here is not in harmony with Paul's

41. E. Brunner, *Der Mittler*, p. 290.
42. "The representation of a parthenogenesis is an attempt to explain the miracle of the incarnation" (*ibid.*, p. 290). Cf. concerning the dogmatic motive in connection with original sin, p. 291.
43. "We do not want to explain anything of the *how* of the miracle, but simply marvel at the fact without having to connect any curious biological ideas with it" (*Der Mittler*, p. 291). Brunner makes the remark — strangely enough, because what else is his criticism aiming at? — that he does not want to war against the virgin birth but simply express his "indifference."
44. Brunner, *Dogmatik* II, p. 417.

and John's teachings concerning the incarnation, but is rather an *alternative* to the incarnation. There is a "clear antithesis,"[45] and it is for this reason that the Church, if it wants to confess the incarnation, can never accept the virgin birth. For the idea of the "begetting" in the records of his birth actually comes from Arian thinking, namely that Jesus was "begotten" and by God created in time by means of the "begetting" in Mary's womb.[46]

Later on the Church may have interpreted the birth accounts as being identical or at least immediately related to the *assumtio carnis,* but actually there is no connection because this "Arianism" has nothing to do with the incarnation. Brunner does not think it impossible that the prologue of the Gospel of John actually takes a stand *against* the doctrine of the virgin birth.[47] Therefore this doctrine is not part of the New Testament *kerygma* of the incarnation, which explains why it plays no future role in the New Testament. The apostles either did not know about it or they knew it but considered it unimportant or incorrect. Brunner considers it a remarkable fact that this doctrine, which plays hardly any role in the apostolic testimony, could, by its incorporation in the creed, become the norm of the doctrine of the Church and an established part of the Christian faith (*ibid.,* p. 419). Thus the confession of the Church still contains an "alien body" which fundamentally contradicts the confession of Christ's becoming *man.* It is, according to Brunner, a denial of the true human nature of Christ and a sanctioning of a docetic

45. *Ibid.,* p. 417; cf. the criticism of this by Sevenster in *Christologie,* p. 135, who cannot see any contradiction between the stories of the virgin birth and the N.T. texts on pre-existence and incarnation. According to him there is no conflict. Cf. also p. 138, where he says that he does not intend to hunt for problems on the basis of a dogmatic apriorism. "On the contrary, I explicitly declare that the virgin birth — if I may say so — fits entirely in with the N.T. witness concerning Christ."

46. We find a similar argument with Martin Werner with respect to the confession of Christ's deity. He is of the opinion that the idea of "begetting" is of gnostic origin (*Die Entstehung des kirchlichen Dogmas,* 1941, p. 533). Cf. p. 531, "The gnostic theory is rejected but sooner or later its basic ideas are accepted." Cf. on the *homousie* idea, Werner, pp. 591ff.

47. Brunner, *Dogmatik,* p. 417. In view of the fact that Jesus is called "the son of Joseph" Brunner considers it probable that John was acquainted with this doctrine but *rejected* it (p. 418). Cf. his *Der Erfüller,* in *Zwischen den Zeiten,* 1930, "Is not Jesus the son of Joseph? The Bible gives us a clear answer: Yes, he is."

element in Christology.[48] This doctrine is based on a negative evaluation of sex which is more hellenistic and ascetic than biblical; it furthers ascetic tendencies and thus becomes one of main pillars of Mariology.[49]

Barth, however, stands diametrically opposed to this criticism of Brunner. In the same year (1927) that Brunner criticized this article of the *Apostolicum,* Barth defended it in the Prolegomena of his dogmatics.[50] Since then he has maintained the same view.

Barth writes that his disagreement with Brunner on this point is the result of their different *theologies.* Especially relevant is Brunner's doctrine of the "point of connection," which is determined by his view concerning the relationship between nature and grace. For this reason it is important to examine the basis of Barth's defense, the more so since he has correctly pointed out many weak points in Brunner's criticism. It must be acknowledged that – apart from his own solution – Barth's departure from the general critical tradition has brought a revival of interest in this old article of faith.[51]

48. Here Brunner repeats an accusation made in 1927 (Brunner, II, p. 419).
49. *Finally* Brunner makes a few remarks on the *text* of the gospels. The historical trustworthiness is not of such a nature that we are compelled to silence our theological objections. Brunner bases his argument on the following: the genealogies indicate a male procreator; the other witnesses in the N.T. are silent about it; most likely an incorrect translation of Isa. 7:14 in the Septuagint played a role, and there is a Syrian translation which also points into a different direction. Everything indicates the presence of a legend, which is confirmed by the fact that only two prologues contain the information. We believe in the incarnation of the eternal Son of God *in spite of* and not *because of* the birth accounts (p. 421). Finally, it is remarkable that Brunner declares at the end of his criticism that the idea of the virgin birth "expresses a strong interest of faith" (p. 421), namely that Jesus is God "by nature" and he "appreciates" this doctrine as Christendom's first attempt at proclaiming the mystery of Jesus' person. As such this idea deserves "respectful appreciation."
50. K. Barth, Prolegomena to *Die Lehre vom Worte Gottes,* 1927, pp. 272ff.
51. Cf. S. U. Zuidema, "Stellingen over Ontvangen van de Heilige Geest, Geboren uit de Maagd Maria" (*Polemios,* Dec. 17, 1949). Thesis 2: Also on account of Barth's action the doubt as to the scriptural foundation of this dogma on the basis of exegetical and text-critical arguments— which is one of the motives used by Kohnstamm and Brunner – had to make place for a renewed acknowledgement of the scriptural basis." Cf. for criticism of Barth's solution: theses 19-23.

The core of Barth's defense is this: he sees the virgin birth as a *sign* of God's *new* and *sovereign* activity in Jesus Christ.

The *mystery* of Christmas, both in Scripture and dogma, is "indicated by referring to the miracle of Christmas."[52] The words of the old creed are very significant. The real mystery of the incarnation is that Jesus Christ is both true God and true man. But the testimony concerning this mystery is given to us in a special *form.* The *natus ex virgine* is "only the form and appearance of the witness concerning the true deity and human nature of Christ," and from the beginning the Church has heard this testimony exactly in *this* form.[53] Barth clarifies the meaning of this sign-character of the virgin birth by referring to the incident in Mark 2 where Jesus heals the palsied man and says, "But that ye may know that the Son of man hath authority on earth to forgive sins (he saith to the sick of the palsy), I say unto thee, Arise, and take up thy bed, and go unto thy house."[54] *Sign* and *issue!* The emphasis is on the *issue* (the incarnation), but the *sign* calls attention to it.

The question now arises, however, why it is the *virgin birth* that points as a sign to the mystery of the incarnation. According to Barth it is not the *foundation* of the incarnation which is at stake, because it has its foundation in itself and needs no supplement in the doctrine of the virgin birth. The mystery of this birth does not have an ontological (concerning *being*) but a noetic (concerning *knowing*) significance, that is to say, according to its nature it points to the mystery. A "creation" takes place with respect to Mary. The human element is eliminated because the man is set aside.[55] The fact that not the woman but the man is eliminated constitutes the "striking and characteristic nature of this miracle" (*ibid.*). To this the *significance* of the *sign* is closely related. For it is a fact that in the history of mankind it is the man who well-nigh exclusively takes the lead in the realm of world history, art, science, and business. Most great and outstanding accomplishments have been achieved by men, not by women.

52. Barth, *K.D.*, I, 2, 189.
53. Barth, *De Apostolische Geloofsbelijdenis,* 1935, p. 80.
54. Mark 2:10, 11. Cf., "In like manner must we understand the connection between the mystery of the incarnation and the miracle of the birth-from-the-virgin" (*ibid.,* p. 87).
55. "The elimination of the participation of the man in a natural relationship" (Proleg., p. 277).

Now when God begins a *new* history and starts off a sovereign activity in the old world, then this takes place in the birth of Christ, but it is no longer a man's world. Man's creations and ingenuity do not come into consideration.[56] Barth even goes as far as to say that *justice* falls on the man and that woman becomes the object of God's new and sovereign activity, she is the receiving one: *natus ex virgine*.[57] Thus the virgin birth becomes a *sign*. It shows us what takes place and points out the mystery to us (*ibid.*, p. 90). Mary's virginity is the negation, not of man, "but of his possibility, his fitness, his capability for God" (*K.D.* I, 2, 206). The object is a completely *new beginning*. The incarnation comes into being "only in the person of the virgin Mary, but that means: only in the person who is non-willing, non-accomplishing, non-creative, non-sovereign; only in the person who can but receive, who can but be willing and ready, who can but have something done to her and with her" (*K.D.* I, 2, 207).

The emphasis on this sign-character was very evident when in 1938 Barth raised the question whether history indeed is predominantly masculine or whether the feminine factors have not been just as powerful (*K.D.*, p. 211). But even if this were the case, the fact remains that the *consciousness* of nations, states, and cultures begins with the patriarchy and, as far as we can see, the activity of the man decides the history of the world. With respect to the *sign* this is sufficient, because the elimination of the man thus indicates God's *judgment* on this active, creative humanity, and the sign of God's free and sovereign grace is the "indication thereof."[58] It thus became the *form* in which the matter (of the incarnation) is presented to us in Scripture. Over against those who might think that this sign, this form of the miracle, is not necessary and that sign and matter may be separated, Barth contends that they are inseparable.[59] It is in

56. Prolegomena, p. 279. Cf. *De Apostolische Geloofsbelijdenis*, 1935, p. 89, "the man as bearer of humanity, human dominion, self-development, and self-realization" and as the representative of mankind.
57. *De Apostolische Geloofsbelijdenis*, p. 89, not simply "the sign of Eros" but the function of the man is eliminated (K.D., I, 2, 211).
58. *K.D.*, I, 2, 212; cf. Otto Weber, *Karl Barth's Kirchl. Dogmatik*, 1950, p. 43, and G. C. van Niftrik, *De Belijdenis Aller Eeuwen*, 1949, p. 90: "It is God who makes history and not the man who thinks that with his energy he can make history."
59. Stronger yet is Heinrich Vogel's formulation (*Gott in Christo*, 1951, p. 647) which contests the idea that Christ could have also been born of

this *form* that the Church has heard the message concerning the mystery of the incarnation," and always, as far as we can look back in the history of the Church, whenever the form was abandoned, the contents, the matter itself, too, became lost."[60]

But even though this close connection between form and contents, between sign and fact, is maintained, the virgin birth remains "only a sign" ("Nur die Bezeichnung" – *K.D.* I, 2, 195), a *noetic* and not an *ontological* datum in the message. Barth is not concerned with the foundation of the incarnation or Christ's sinlessness but with the *indication* of the miracle. Barth draws here a parallel with the empty tomb. The mystery of Christ's resurrection is "designated" by the tomb. And he asks in analogy with the virgin birth, "Was it revealed to them [the disciples] in any other way than by means of the sign of the outward facts?" And is the mystery of the resurrection truly accepted "if it is believed that the message of the empty tomb is but a superfluous form of the real fact which may just as well be omitted or left up to Christian liberty, in order to be seriously concerned only with the fact itself?" (*ibid.*, p. 195).

The signs have not been chosen at random, Barth contends over against those who are willing to accept the fact – the incarnation – but *not* the sign. Is it not an abstraction to be

---

Joseph and Mary. *This* idea concerning Christ's origin "which would truly make him in all things like unto his brethren, according to its champions, would rob the miracle of the incarnation of its *sign*" (with reference to Barth). He further adds, "Our thinking in this respect neither has to be mythical nor contrary to reason" (p. 647). Cf. also, on the inseparableness of sign and miracle, G. C. van Niftrik, *De Belijdenis Aller Eeuwen*, 1949, p. 91.

60. K. Barth, *De Apostolische Geloofsbelijdenis*, 1935, p. 80. Barth's connecting *sign* and *issue* clearly reveals his opposition to the critical tradition. It is remarkable that Barth says that form and contents cannot be separated for reasons which cannot be made wholly clear (p. 91). I have great difficulty in finding in Barth's interpretation of the sign any – be it ever so slight – obvious cause why they cannot be separated. It seems to me that Barth is under the influence of the fact that he always finds that a "natural theology" underlies the rejection of the virgin birth by these theologians who on the basis of the "natural ability" to know God restrict God's sovereign grace. To Barth there is a real connection between the rejection of the virgin birth and the doctrine of the "point of connection" (*De Apostolische Geloofsbelijdenis*, p. 90). Undoubtedly Barth is referring to Brunner. However, *on the basis of Barth's view* it remains vague why *this* sign is necessary for the indication of the mystery of the revelation.

concerned only with the contents, the "pivotal matter" of the revelation in distinction from the "outward" things? Is it not the objective of him who rejects the sign to have other *contents* as well?[61]

In spite of Barth's concern not to separate "sign" (virgin birth) from "fact" (incarnation), he actually does make a separation by his distinction between *noetic* and *ontological.* It is remarkable that Barth, illustrating the sign-fact relationship refers to the miracle of Mark 2 (healing-forgiving), but neglects to show why the miracle of Christ's incarnation may be taken as a relevant parallel. Neither has Barth pointed out where in Scripture this noetic "sign"-character of the virgin birth is indicated. The only sign of the birth of Christ in the Christmas story is the swaddling clothes by which the shepherds will recognize the fulfillment of the promise! It is, moreover, difficult to see why the Gospels do not say more about the virgin birth if it were of such far-reaching significance. True, the virgin birth reveals the new and sovereign activity of God in his Son's assuming human nature, but to contrast *noetic* with *ontological* is to make an *a priori* separation in the one mystery, all aspects of which (incarnation and virgin birth) are intertwined according to the testimony of the Gospels. That which Barth calls "sign" may not for a moment be singled out as a relatively independent element in the Christmas story. It is not the case that God wanted by this "form" to signify something special concerning the fact of the incarnation, but rather, the fact of the virgin birth is made known unto us as part of an *indivisible totality.*

Moreover, the parallel with the empty tomb proves to be fallacious at the crucial point.[62] Barth overlooks the fact that the empty tomb was not just a significant accompanying sign — noetic rather than ontological — but a *fact* which was inseparably connected with the corporeal resurrection of Christ.

Therefore, the virgin birth of Christ may not be burdened with

61. Barth. *K.D.* I, 2, 196. We may conclude that Barth is strongly opposed to the reasoning of G. van de Leeuw (*Dogmatische Brieven*), who considers the virgin birth a myth. The mystery is Christ's birth. "It does not make any difference whether he was born of Mary alone or of both Mary and Joseph."

62. The parallel between the virgin birth and the empty tomb plays an important part in Barth's explanation. In both events the accent is on "signs," namely "the virgin birth at the beginning and the empty tomb at the end of Jesus' life" (*K.D.* I, 2, 199). Cf., also on the empty tomb, his *Grundriss der Dogmatik.*

the problematics of sign — fact or form — contents, relationships, let alone with Barth's specific sign-concept of the function of the male in the world's events.[63] Yet it is quite evident that the sign-idea seems to appeal to many[64] because it does not lead to certain offensive conclusions. It contains no tendency to disqualify marriage,[65] nor does it prove Christ's sinlessness. Thus at present we find not only sharp criticism but also a more appreciative attitude which, sometimes hesitantly, sometimes emphatically, pleads for the maintenance of the Church's confession *natus ex virgine* as *indication, sign,* of God's sovereign grace: virgin birth over against the invasion of synergism, which so often triumphantly entered the doctrine of salvation.[66]

This sign-concept frequently results in a more relative consideration of the importance of the virgin birth. Though Barth

63. It is obvious that Barth's rather disconnected theory on the meaning of the sign (*Männergeschichte* — predominance of the man in history) may be conducive to strengthen the opposition to the virgin birth. See, for instance Kohnstamm, *De Heilige,* 1931, p. 173, "Seldom has male arrogancy over against the woman expressed itself more strongly than in the words just quoted in italics. A dogma must indeed be weak if it must be defended on such grounds!"
64. Not wholly but to a great extent under the influence of Barth's theory since 1927.
65. Cf. Kohnstamm's criticism (*Bijbel en Jeugd,* 1923, pp. 204ff. and *De Heilige,* 1931, p. 170ff.) who sees in the virgin birth the annihilation of marriage, a curse on fatherhood, and the opening of the way to monasticism. Cf. Y. Feenstra, *Het Apostolikum in de Twintigste Eeuw,* pp. 73-80.
66. The virgin birth is, also according to Korff, "a God-given sign" (*Christologie,* II, 311). He criticizes Barth's signification of the sign, but he accepts his idea of the sign-character, "a sign of the new beginning which God makes" (p. 312). When Korff writes (p. 313) that human power and human fatherhood are absent "to indicate that in the fulness of time it is not mankind that has reached the summit of its ability but that God sent his Son made of a woman" then it is very difficult to see a difference between him and Barth. Althaus, too, accentuates the sign-character, "a God-given *sign* to *show* us: here is the new man; God has made a new beginning" (*Die Chr. Wahrheit,* II, 1948, p. 219). Cf. A Köberle, "Even in a corporeal way in which this life began God wanted to indicate: now something new begins which is wholly a creative act and revelation of God's power" (A. Köberle, "Natus ex virgine Maria," in: *Deo Omnia Unum;* Festschr. für F. Heiler, 1942, p. 153). Finally we sometimes see the virgin birth as sign also emphasized in R.C. theology, for instance by M. Schmaus, *Kath. Dogmatik* II, 1949, p. 619, "Indication of the exclusive graciousness of the deliverance" and "sign of the singularity of the One so conceived and born."

greatly emphasized the inseparableness of sign and fact,[67] others abandon this close connection. The virgin birth is compared, for instance, with Christ's resurrection and the conclusion is drawn that there is a considerable difference in importance between the two.[68] Virgin birth and resurrection are not on the same level (*ibid.*, pp. 314ff.). The resurrection itself is revelation, but the virgin birth is "an accompanying sign of revelation." It is further removed from the center than the resurrection and is part "of the more secondary and indirect contents of the Christian faith" (*ibid.*, p. 314).

To be sure, this secondary character is defined by declaring that each part has *its own place* in the whole and thus its own greater or smaller "but inalienable value" in proportion to its place, but Korff is nevertheless of the opinion that the incorporation of the virgin birth in the creed, which only mentions the main points, does not accord with "the more modest position it occupies in the New Testament and consequently also in the contents of faith."[69]

We are of the opinion that approaching the confession of the virgin birth in this manner indicates a quantitative atomizing of the scriptural message. The old confession simply quoted what Scripture taught and connected the *natus ex virgine* immediately with the act of the Holy Spirit (conceived by the Holy Ghost), and this apparently involved no problem at all concerning the relationship of secondary with primary. Such a problem could come up only when the authority of Scripture was being questioned and doubt concerning certain concrete Scripture messages prevailed. In the same way a secondary character was attached to the message concerning the ascension on the basis of the statistical record of it in Scripture, just as with

67. In the thesis mentioned before (Thesis 22) Zuidema writes that Barth himself with various statements "crosses the line which he himself has drawn (this dogma confesses only one sign)."

68. Cf. Korff, *op. cit.*, II, 314ff.; cf. Althaus, *op. cit.*, II, 219: the *natus ex virgine* does not have "the rank of a soteriologic fact." "The church, therefore, may question it or have a different opinion about it." In "Fundamenten en Perspectieven" the virgin birth is not mentioned either. It only speaks of "an entirely original and sovereign act" by which God came to us in Christ and became man (art. 4).

69. However, Korff does not wish to correct the creed in this respect. "One does not tamper with classic documents like these." He is of the opinion, however, that the virgin birth is more in its place in Art. 18 of the Belgic Confession (II, 315).

respect to Christ's resurrection the question was asked whether "the empty tomb" really had been so central to the apostles. Such a questioning approach may lead to the most sceptical conclusions, of which no one gives such a clear example in our days as Emil Brunner.[70]

If Scripture does indeed point out the way of the *assumtio carnis,* then it is very difficult to see how one can speak of a "secondary" something without doing injustice to the mystery of Christ's birth. For the issue is not the respect for an isolated, miraculous, marvelous fact *as such* but the message of Scripture concerning the fulness of time. "Inalienable value" – these are Korff's words which we wish to underscore and to which we attach a greater significance than he does himself.

Whoever finds fault with the old creed on the basis of primary and secondary characters overestimates the human capability to judge the measure of importance of God's mysteries, which concern *the revelation of him who is the incarnated Word.*[71] We are deeply convinced that this sign-conception and the relativizing of this importance are closely related. Respect for the explicit, historically framed testimony of Scripture should caution us to proceed very carefully in drawing conclusions as to its "importance."

Relativizing the authority of Scripture creates a situation in which this "hierarchy of values" may start functioning in a simplistic manner. That is why a certain "shifting" is clearly noticeable.

In the earliest times the Church proceeded from the unanimous confession of and reverence for the testimony of Scripture to the consideration of the significance of the virgin birth. In our days – already in the nineteenth century – a shift is noticeable. Now it is just the *reverse.* First the meaning of the "sign" must be found, and when this is not evident the confession itself is questioned. Many still consider the earlier procedure, from acceptance to understanding, to be a suicide of the intellect (to quote Heinrich Vogel's expression). In 1892 the Eisenach Declaration was published, which dealt with the "deplorable

70. Brunner emphasizes that only Matthew and Luke mention the virgin birth. And in connection with original sin he argues, "In the N.T., yea even with Paul the story of Adam plays no role in connection with the doctrine of sin, excepting in Romans 5:12ff. and I Cor. 15:21" (*Der Mensch im Widerspruch,* 1937, p. 111).

71 Cf. Bornhäuser, *Die Geburts- und Kindheitsgeschichte Jesu,* 1930, p. 3.

confusion of conscience" which considered the virgin birth as one of the "fundamentals" of the Christian faith. Such a confusion was in flagrant contradiction with trusting faith, since revelation is neither concerned with "truth" or with the teaching of the virgin birth.

Over against this allegedly obscure concept of faith, either criticism or the primary search for the *meaning* of this sign was advocated. It is obvious that we are confronted here with a decisive methodological point, since a critical attitude towards the message of Scripture frequently shuts the door to a correct understanding of the significance of the virgin birth. Moreover, in our days it is quite evident that there is quite a difference of opinion as to its significance. One person considers the virgin birth to be in flagrant contradiction with the confession of the incarnation, while another sees it as a very illustrative sign of what the mystery of the incarnation implies. It is, therefore, absolutely incorrect to interpret the Church's confession as a legalistic misunderstanding of the message of Scripture.[72] It is our conviction that only by reverently listening to the message of Scripture is the door opened — and this is always the case — to a correct understanding of the meaning of the virgin birth.

Criticism of the virgin birth has often been extremely careless. For example, some have claimed to discover a necessary connection between the virgin birth and Roman Catholic Mariology. It was actually decreed by the Roman Church, in 1854, that the virgin birth implies the immaculate conception of Mary. The critics maintained that the doctrine of the virgin birth presupposes a misconception of the sanctity of marriage, and thus attempts to explain Christ's sinlessness by eliminating the normal relationship of marriage in order to avoid original sin.

It is indeed the case that historically the virgin birth has frequently been connected with certain other ideas which tend to distort its meaning. Not the doctrine itself, but its misleading interpretations tended to lead people astray. One example is its association with Mariology. How often has the virgin birth been made the *foundation* of Christ's sinlessness, which placed the divine institution of marriage in a questionable light![73] It

72. Cf. Haitjema's statement that Matt. and Luke "unequivocally incorporated the miraculous birth of Christ in the fact of the incarnation" (*De Heilsfeiten in het Geding-Kerk en Theologie,* 1950, p. 146).

73. However, we must be careful not to generalize with respect to R. C. theology. See, for instance, M. Schmaus, *Kath. Dogmatik,* II, (1949),

is possible to accept the virgin birth and still interpret it in such a way that it goes far beyond what Scripture teaches, thus making it a veritable stumbling stone. We see this already in the early Church, when the virgin birth was compared (apologetically!) with all kinds of marriages of the deities,[74] but it is found especially in those who find such a connection between the virgin birth and the transfer of original sin through the natural relationship of marriage that it is well-nigh impossible not to embrace the ideal of virginity and the "miracle of Mary." When Berdyaev was reading Brunner's *Mittler* and came under the spell of the pathos of his Christology, he also came across his rejection of the virgin birth, but then, he says, "it made me sad and the subject even annoyed me. It seemed to me that then we might as well cast everything overboard, since then everything else is worthless and useless."[75]

But Berdyaev's disappointment with Brunner's criticism has a peculiar background which is closely connected with his entire Mariology and conception of life.[76] And doubtless there are typical connections between the Roman Catholic Mariology and the virgin birth.[77]

For this reason it is so necessary to emphasize that this Romanizing process is *preceded* historically by the confession of the virgin birth. As far as the confession of the *Apostolicum* is concerned, it found its conclusive evidence in Scripture. And justice is done to this confession only if we ask first of all: Was its appeal to Scripture correct?

It must strike everybody who carefully reads the Scripture record concerning the virgin birth how simple and sober it is. Of those many theories woven around it later on, and on which the rejection of the virgin birth was based, we find not the

---

618, where the foundation in the elimination of marriage as being unworthy with respect to Christ is rejected. "Such representations could only be the result of gnostic influence which considers marriage an evil and a pollution. However, actually it is a divine institution."

74. An illustrative example – to our warning – may be found in Justin.
75. Barth, *K.D.* I, 2, 201; Kohnstamm, *De Heilige,* p. 177.
76. Cf., among others, Nikolai Berdyaev, *Von der Bestimmung des Menschen. Versuch einer personalen Ethik,* 1935, pp. 89-97. Barth, when agreeing ("Berdyaev's sigh is mine also") with Berdyaev's criticism, overlooks this element of the background (K. Barth, *K.D.* I, 2, 201).
77. Cf., e.g., the R.C. doctrine of the *virginitas in partu* and *post partum.*

slightest indication. One must, indeed, be very critically preoccupied to think that this account fits in beautifully with the heathenish imaginations of the Caesarean era.[78] In the text there is no trace of such indications, but only an account, in simple language, concerning the sovereign act of the Holy Spirit, "The Holy Spirit shall come upon thee, and the power of the Most High shall overshadow thee."[79]

The *power* of the Spirit is announced here; the overshadowing, a word which is also used in the account of the transfiguration on the mount: a cloud which overshadowed them.[80] The emphasis in this overshadowing is on the divine power by which the birth of Messiah is announced. When Barth remarked that the accent in this power of the Spirit over Mary was not on *generatio* but on *jussio* or *benedictio,* Kohnstamm raised the question how such a fine distinction could be preached and presented to heathen people as a missionary message.[81] But apparently this had been done since earliest times without for a moment impairing the unique character of this overshadowing. There is not a trace of justification for Kohnstamm's reference to a marriage of deities. This is, moreover, confirmed by Joseph's position in the Christmas account. The act of the Spirit is of a very special character and must indeed be described as *jussio* or *benedictio,* the supreme power in this unique event by which he, who is the Son of the Father, is born *as a man* of Mary. This limits all speculation. Whoever attempts to draw a parallel between this act of the Spirit and mythological relationships tries to give an explanation of that which finds its origin only in the power of God. This act of the Spirit, of which both Matthew and Luke testify points out the uniqueness of Christ's birth which can be known only by divine revelation.

78. Kohnstamm, *De Heilige,* p. 178. See for *contra*: G. Sevenster, *Christologie van het Nieuwe Testament,* pp. 138ff.
79. Luke 1:35. Büchsel, in *Der Geist Gottes im N.T.,* p. 197, points out that the account of the annunciation ends with Mary's words, "The point in this story is exactly these words by Mary and not the story of the conception." Cf., concerning the "veil of the mystery," Büchsel, *ibid.,* p. 191.
80. Luke 9:34; cf. Exod. 40:34, "Then the cloud covered the tent of meeting, and the *glory* of the Lord filled the tabernacle." Cf. Num. 9:15 and Exod. 40:34. The cloud is the revelation of the presence of the Lord.
81. *De Heilige,* p. 179.

The entire story has come to us in an explicitly historic entourage including Mary, Joseph, and the message of the angel.

Revelation alone can shed light on this story, not biological theories or historical speculations.[82] It bears no marks of human construction; it speaks only to the fulfillment of that which had been prophesied.[83] Every attempt to explain the birth account mythologically misses the context of the story.

It is quite natural that the controversy concerning the virgin birth should have involved, again and again, the exegesis of Isaiah 7:14, since Matthew writes after the story of the angel's message to Joseph, "Now all this is come to pass, that it might be fulfilled which was spoken by the Lord through the prophet, saying, Behold, the virgin shall be with child, and shall bring forth a son, and they shall call his name Immanuel; which is, being interpreted, God with us."[84] More than once this citation of Matthew was taken as further proof that the biblical foundation of the virgin birth is shaky, because in the original version of Isaiah 7:14 it says *alma* (young woman) and not *bethula* (virgin"), so that at the crucial point there would be no parallel between the *virgin* birth and Isaiah 7:14.[85]

Others, however, have pointed out that elsewhere in the Old

82. Cf. F. Kattenbusch, *Die Geburtsgeschichte Jesu als Haggada der Urchristologie. Theol. Stud. u. Krit.*, 1930, Vol. 102, pp. 454-474. Kattenbusch considers the entire birth story *haggada,* i.e., devotional retelling of historical events that are of religious significance. There was a desire to explain the "mystery" of Jesus, and the need was felt for a theoretical explanation of the fact that Jesus in such an incomprehensible manner belonged to God his "Father." In this way the *haggada* came into existence, which the Christian faith found confirmed by Isa. 7:14 which Hellenistic circles read from the Septuagint and which had in Isa. 7:14 παρθένος. According to Kattenbusch there was first the *haggada*: "once such haggada existed it called attention to Isa. 7:14" (p. 474). Thus the ἐκ παρθενου became the main thing in Gentile-Christian circles, whereas the Jewish Christians (soon to be called Ebionites) knew that *alma* and παρθένος were not identical. The Ebionites, as is known, deny the virgin birth.

83. Matt. 1:22, 23. Harnack, who criticized the virgin birth himself, rejected the religious-historical explanation on this basis.

84. Matt. 1:22, 23.

85. Cf. Gesenius, *Hebr. u. Aram. Hdw. Buch,* 1921, "The word [*alma*] means simply grown-up girl, not virgin." Already the Jews contested the virgin birth with reference to the word *alma*. Cf. Volkmar Herntrich, *Der Prophet Jesaja* (Das A. T. Deutsch), 1950, p. 127, "At this point the Jewish and old-Christian exegesis differ already."

Testament *alma* is used where "unmarried" is obviously meant, and attention was called to the fact that the Septuagint translated the *alma* of Isaiah 7:14 with παρθένος (virgin) whereas otherwise it has νεανις for *alma* (young woman) except in Genesis 24:43, where Rebekah is called παρθένος.[86]

Closely related to these problems is the other question concerning the character of the sign which is mentioned in Isaiah 7:14. The Lord will give a sign over against Ahaz' unbelief in the midst of the troubled conditions of his day. That sign is the belief of a young woman who will call the name of her child "Immanuel." The question now is whether the young woman's faith or the miraculous birth comprises the "sign." Undoubtedly the faith of this young woman plays a role in Isaiah's prophecy. The name she chooses for the child proves her victory over the pessimism of her day and reveals an implicit confidence in God who will give relief: Immanuel – *God with us.*

Some considered God's gift the sign and then, of course, the problem *alma-bethula* does not enter in at all, nor does the miracle of the birth. In that case the faith of the mother is the sign. This does not imply, however, that anyone who relates this act of faith to the sign wants to eliminate any possible relationships between Isaiah 7:14 and Matthew 1. H. N. Ridderbos, for instance, says that the prophet was not speaking of a miraculous birth – "the sign which he gave referred to something else"[87] – but that nevertheless the prophecy obtained its essential ful-

86. Cf. Gen. 24:16, "a virgin (*bethula*) neither had any man known her." That the Septuagint uses παρθένος proves, according to Zahn (*Comm. Matthew,* p. 85) "that to the unsuspecting reader of the Hebrew text the relationship expressed in this word was self-evident, even long before Christ." See also Zahn's other arguments in connection with Isa. 54:4, p. 85. See also D. Deden, *De Messiaanse Profetieën,* 1947, pp. 58ff.; Herntrich, *ibid.,* p. 128, "It [*alma*] is never used for 'married woman' "; and "*La Sainte Bible*" (A. Clamer) Tome VII on Isa. 7:14, p. 45.

87. H. N. Ridderbos, *Korte Verklaring* on Matt. I, 1952; cf. J. Ridderbos, *K.V.* on Isa. 7:14, who says that Isaiah 'at any rate does not wish to emphasize purity of virginity." "The sign which God gives to Ahaz commences with the giving of the name," p. 43. Cf. his *Het Godswoord der Profeten II* (Isaiah), 1932, pp. 204f.: it is not the miraculous birth that comprises the sign but his, "that a young mother shall name her son Immanuel and that, before the child will come to the years of discretion Judah will be rid of her enemies and this will be the confirmation of the faith expressed by the mother in the child's name."

fillment in Christ. For there is a "further implication"[88] which concerns the full reality of the Immanuel in Jesus Christ, and the *manner* in which Isaiah speaks of this faithfulness indicates the future virgin birth of Jesus.[89]

According to this exegesis (which, in my opinion, does far more justice to the all data than the one which reads the "virgin" of Isaiah 7:14 as "literally the virgin Mary,"[90] justice can also be done to the emphasis on the name "Immanuel" which is given in faith. Making this faith the "sign" does not, however, imply that Matthew does not consider Jesus Christ the fulfillment of this prophecy. He could write this immediately after the account of the angel's announcement to Joseph which told of the *virgin* birth. Thus the event in Mathew 1 (*this* birth) is not simply a "coming true" of an earlier prediction but a fulfillment which, on the one hand, is related to the faith in Ahaz' day and with the name "Immanuel,"[91] and which on the other hand, relates the mystery of Christ's virgin birth to that which was not yet central in Isaiah's prophecy. Whereas in Isaiah "Immanuel" was a *sign* of God's saving activity, in the fulfillment "Immanuel" himself came into full light. The name "Immanuel" is essentially the same as the name which at God's instruction will be given to Mary's child: Jesus. Those who believe that Matthew misquotes Isaiah misjudges the closeness of the relationship between prophecy and fulfillment. Those who explain the connection between Matthew and Isaiah by reference to a "miraculous" birth are not able to explain why, then, Isaiah did not use the word "virgin"

88. J. Ridderbos, *K.V.* on Isaiah, p. 44; *Godswoord der Profeten* II, p. 205. *De Messias-Koning in Jesaja's Profetie,* 1920, p. 20ff.
89. H. N. Ridderbos, *op. cit.,* p. 35, "Isaiah 7:14 is suitable to describe the exceedingly greater miracle of Christ's birth of the virgin Mary." J. Ridderbos in *Godswoord der Profeten* II, 205, puts the accent on the mentioning of the *mother*.
90. Cf. D. Deden, *op. cit.,* p. 63; cf. Edelkoort, *Christusverwachting,* p. 215, on Van der Born (*De Profetie*) who has the same opinion. See especially the counter-arguments of J. Ridderbos in connection with verse 16, "For before the child shall know to refuse the evil, and choose the good, the land whose two kings thou abhorrest shall be forsaken" (RSV: the land before whose two kings you are in dread).
91. "The blessed expectation contained in the name of the child of Isa. 7:14 is wholly fulfilled in the birth of Christ: God with us. In the Messiah God would not simply show that he is with his people but the Messiah himself is God-with-us," H. N. Ridderbos, *op. cit.,* p. 36.

(*bethula*).[92] If that were the main object in giving the sign; moreover, the fulfillment in connection with the name "Immanuel" must recede to the background.

It has been said, however, that an exegesis which concerns itself mainly with the faith-aspect of Isaiah 7:14 does not do justice to the connection with Matthew. Gresham Machen asks, "Why should an ordinary birth be regarded as a sign?"[93] We can appreciate this question in the light of the strong emphases which have been placed on the Immanuel prophecy in Isaiah. Those who limit the significance of Isaiah 7:14 to a young woman's confidence of faith certainly do an injustice to these emphases.[94] But this faith is not merely a subjective expression of trust which stands in contrast with Ahaz' unbelief, but a faith directed to God's saving activity and which in the context of Isaiah 7:14 cannot be separated from it. Hence the dilemma is not: either the sign of faith or the sign of God's dealings, because both are correlated and the significance of the prophecy lies in the confidence of faith which is not vain but *corresponds with God's dealings.* The prophecy may still be full of mystery,[95] yet "Immanuel" is not an idea, a hope, an expectation, but a reality of which this prophecy already testifies.[96] The point at issue is a sign which God himself will give (Isa. 7:14a), God's salvation, and only much later the full significance of this salvation will be comprehended when it is fulfilled. And when Matthew after his account of the annunciation writes, "Now all this was done, that it might be fulfilled . . . ." he indicates thereby the soteriological fulfillment of this Messianic prophecy. And he who thus fully focuses his attention on the name "Immanuel" will see in this relationship between Isaiah and Micah the fulfillment of Isaiah's mysterious statement, which to Matthew, too, finds its fulfillment in what takes place with Mary and Joseph and

92. Cf. also J. Ridderbos, *Godswoord der Profeten* II, p. 204, who says that Isaiah could have used another word (*bethula*) if he had meant to express that this mother would bring forth *as a virgin* and that the word he uses does not stress pure virginity. Cf. J. Ridderbos' remark regarding Prov. 30:19 (p. 204, footnote 2).
93. G. Machen, *The Virgin Birth,* p. 290.
94. Cf. Isa. 8:8 and Isa. 9:5.
95. Cf. Herntrich: "The unrequested sign which God now gives is draped with the veil of mystery" (*op. cit.,* p. 129).
96. Cf. Herntrich in connection with Isa. 8, "Immanuel is not an image of the realm of phantasy, not a King of no man's land" (*ibid.,* p. 145).

which he was allowed to describe.[97] Hence we are admonished not to go by our own ideas regarding the acceptability of the fact of the virgin birth, but to be filled with reverence for the witness in the context of Holy Scripture when examining the significance of this birth, which the Gospel clearly depicts as a birth of the virgin Mary.

The virgin birth is so much part of the message concerning the incarnation that we might ask whether we should not, out of reverence for this clear witness of Scripture, halt at this point, since this fact which tells us of the way of the Son of God in the flesh is known only by revelation. This question touches directly upon the *significance* of the *natus ex virgine.* If one rejects the sign-theory of the virgin birth, it is said, one must arrive at an "ontological" conception which usually affirms that the virgin birth was necessary to guarantee Christ's sinlessness, and this in turn implies a specific conception of marriage.

It can hardly be denied that such ideas have been entertained and advocated. Augustine, for instance writes, " . . . generated and conceived without any lust of carnal desire and therefore without original sin."[98] This, however, is too simplistic and general an explanation of the significance of the virgin birth to be advocated by the Church. It appears, at least, that in Reformed circles there was a consciousness of the dangers contained in such a presentation. Calvin opposed it, denying that the act of human generation implies sin and that thus Christ's sinlessness was founded *in* the virgin birth.[99]

97. Edelkoort (in *Christusverwachting,* p. 215) says that Bleeker is right in not following Ridderbos' accentuating the fact that only the mother is mentioned. In his book on Micah, p. 127, Edelkoort, when discussing Micah 5:3, "until the time that she which travaileth hath brought forth," refers to Isa. 7:14 and asks, "Would it not have a deeper significance that both Isaiah and Micah speak only of the mother of the Messiah? Could this – I ask it with diffidence – possibly indicate the divine birth of the Savior?" It is not clear how this can go together with Edelkoort's agreement with Bleeker's criticism of J. Ridderbos.
98. Augustine, *Enchiridion* (A. Sizoo – G. C. Berkouwer), p. 89. Latin text: "Nulla igitur voluptate carnalis concupiscentiae seminatus sive conceptus et ideo nullum peccatum originaliter trahens" (*Ench.,* XIII, 41).
99. Calvin, *Institutes* II, XIII, 4, writes, "We do not hold Christ to be free from all taint, merely because he was born of a woman unconnected with a man, but because he was sanctified by the Spirit that the generation was pure and spotless, such as it would have been before Adam's

Still, the relationship between virgin birth and sinlessness is a problem which has occupied the minds of many, be it often indirectly. For this particular problem is closely connected with the fact that the angel in his message to Mary announces the overshadowing by the Spirit and adds, "wherefore also the *holy thing* which is begotten shall be called the Son of God" (Luke 1:35).

This does explain the continual query concerning the relationship between the virgin birth and Christ's *holiness*, even though it does not necessarily mean that these theologians assume that either marriage or procreation implies the hereditary transmission of sin.

Bavinck, for one, says that the virgin birth "is not the *essential* ground and ultimate cause of Christ's sinlessness" and states that the virgin birth is "linked up not only with Christ's *deity* and *pre-existence* but also with his absolute sinlessness."[100] Similar expressions may be found everywhere,[101] and the question arises whether such reasoning does not come dangerously close to speculation. It strikes us that Bavinck mentions Christ's *deity, pre-existence* and *impeccability* beside each other.[102] In the first place he brings up the matter of Christ's deity and pre-exis-

---

fall." And he is still more opposed to the idea of those who say, "that if Christ is free from all taint, and was begotten of the seed of Mary, by the secret operation of the Spirit, it is not therefore the seed of the woman that is impure, but only that of the man" (*ibid.*). Polman agrees that the Christian Church frequently quite carelessly connected the elimination of the man with original sin as though this explained Christ's sinlessness, but "the best theologians have always denied this" (*Onze Nederlandse Geloofsbelijdenis*, II, 264). Bavinck, too, denies that the conception from the Holy Spirit is the essential ground and ultimate cause of Jesus' sinlessness and adds, "as so many contend" (*Dogmatiek*, III, 277), mentioning Rothe, Müller, and Ebrard. With respect to Ebrard we might question whether Bavinck is doing justice to him when reading the former's *Christliche Dogmatik* II^2, 1863, p. 5.

100. Bavinck, *Dogmatiek*, III, 272.

101. For instance in Luther's Larger Catechism: "Christus homo factus et a Spiritu Sancto ac Maria virgine *sine omni labe peccati* conceptus *et natus*, ut esset peccati dominus." See also the Catechism of Geneva (Müller, *Bekenntnisschriften*, 1903, p. 121) where is asked, "Cur id a Spiritu Sancto effectum est ac non potius communi usitataque generationis forma?" The answer is: "Quoniam penitus corruptum est humanum semen, in generatione filii Dei intercedere Spiritus Sancti opus decuit: ne hac contagione attingeretur, sed esset puritate perfectissima praeditus."

102. Note also the sequence.

tence. He considers the virgin birth the only way in which he, "who already existed as a person,"[103] could now also enter into the flesh in a human way and still remain what he was, namely the Son of God the Most High. The point of issue in Christ's birth is not an ordinary birth of a human being but the *incarnation,* i.e., his *assumtio naturae humanae.* His person is not the product of procreation, for the *Word* became flesh.[104] Bavinck sees the *uniqueness* of the mystery of the incarnation indicated by the reality of Christ's deity and pre-existence. Without this scriptural insight it is not clear how those who reject the virgin birth can escape *adoptianism* in their Christology.[105] In Jesus of Nazareth we are not dealing with a human child born of a father and mother and then in an unfathomable manner united with the Son of God, but with the incarnation of the Son of God, with his *being-sent* and his *coming* into this world.

In this connection it would be incorrect to explain the uniqueness of Christ's birth on the basis of certain *docetism,* as frequently is done. It is pointed out that the virgin birth is of a special nature, and hence the confession of this fact resulted from a desire to transfer this *special character* to Christ's origin and existence. Even the "ordinary" fact of being born is considered essential to the *reality* and *completeness* of Christ's human nature. But the starting-point of this reasoning is wrong. It would at least be wise to consider the possibility that the confession of the virgin birth has nothing to do with any form of docetism, but, on the contrary, is linked up with Christ's *pre-existence* and *deity.* This does not mean that we wish to deduce the virgin

103. Bavinck, *Gereformeerde Dogmatiek,* III, 277. James Orr speaks of the "inseparable relation" with "his sinlessness, his divine Sonship, the reality of his incarnation" (*The Virgin Birth of Christ,* 1907, p. 190).

104. Cf. Bavinck, *op. cit.,* p. 276, "Christ was Son of God from eternity; he was in the beginning with God. He is the first-born of all creatures. Thus he could not be procreated by the will of the man; he himself was the active subject who prepared himself, through the Holy Spirit, a body in Mary's womb."

105. Very positive in this respect is O. Noordmans (*Het Koninkrijk der Hemelen,* p. 113ff.) who – in my opinion in line with Bavinck's argument – deals with the Son's activity in his birth, by which his birth is *different* from any other birth. To apply the scalpel to the creed would be the same as mutilating the gospel, according to Noordmans (p. 114). This would make Jesus an adopted child and rob him of his eternal and natural Sonship. The Son himself takes on the flesh. If we remove this pillar, says Noordmans, much more would fall away and the preaching would become vain. Also Ebrard, *Dogmatik,* II, 5.

birth *a priori* and rationally *from* his deity and pre-existence (see note 110, below). Our objective is a scriptural witness which, however, may not be isolated from the rest of the witness concerning Christ. We do not wish to construe, but we must warn against such arguments as Brunner's, which considers the "natural procreation" absolutely necessary for the recognition of Christ's *human* nature and who for this reason considers the doctrine of the virgin birth a result of docetism.

That we are dealing with profound questions here becomes quite apparent from what Vollenhoven[106] says, namely that merely accepting and defending the miracle does not yet do full justice to it. He wants to draw further conclusions from the fact that "after the creation of Adam and Eve every human being originates from the seed of both father and mother." Consequently we are confronted with the dilemma: "either Christ is not completely man, or also with respect to him the fatherly factor may not be excluded. However, whereas the Mediator must be *completely man* it follows that here a new male seed was created." First of all we want to point out that there is a great difference between Brunner and Vollenhoven, because Brunner rejects whereas Vollenhoven accepts the confession of the virgin birth. But in one respect they agree: both proceed from the assumption that *structurally*, also with respect to its origin, the birth of the Mediator must be the same as any other birth. (Vollenhoven excludes only Adam and Eve, although they, too, were completely human). This causes Brunner to conclude to the presence of a "father" and Vollenhoven to a creative "fatherly factor." It must be agreed, however, if this is to prove the completeness of Christ's human nature, then only Brunner is consistent and we must accept a "father," not a "fatherly factor" (which, in my opinion, is an abstraction) and this again denies the virgin birth. Vollenhoven does not want to do this, but then he cannot maintain the creative "fatherly factor" in the place of a "father" in order to retain the completeness of Christ's human nature. He thus *weakens* his argument against Brunner's position (the "natural procreation") considerably. Certainly at this point we must beware of speculation and accept the uniqueness of the incarnation, the miracle of the *assumtio humanae naturae*,

106. D.H.Th. Vollenhoven, "De Visie op de Middelaar bij Kuyper en bij Ons," *Mededelingen van de Vereniging voor Calvinistische Wijsbegeerte*, September, 1952.

without detracting anything from the reality of Christ's human nature. Just because it is a miracle we cannot go any further than "simply acknowledging and defending" it, since any attempt at explaining it certainly does not contribute to a deeper understanding of the *natus ex virgine*. It is too long a step from the overshadowing by the power of the Most High to the fatherly factor. It is not true that in this way "a sharper than usual" distinction is made between the origin of Christ's human nature and the incarnation of the Word. It is not at all clear what is gained by doing so. Vollenhoven does not mean that "these two events" are separated *in time*, but according to him it still remains necessary "to distinguish sharply a twofold happening." But it is exactly this "twofold event" which we must deny because we cannot find any basis for it in Scripture, in addition to which it practically appears to be a duality: incarnation and the creation of the parental factor.[107] Brunner's irresponsible and unjustified criticism of the virgin birth can be effectively opposed only when the completeness of Christ's human nature is fully accepted and confessed over against any form of docetism, and also when no docetism is "discovered" where there is none.[108]

107. In this connection we refer to Lord's Day XIV of the Heidelberg Catechism, where we read that the Son of God (who is true and eternal God) took upon him the very nature of man of the flesh and blood of the virgin Mary, by the operation of the Holy Spirit. Notice the way in which the act of the *assumtio naturae* in connection with the working of the Holy Spirit is presented as an *act* of the Son.

108. In the December 1952 issue of *Mededelingen van de Vereniging voor Calvinistische Wijsbegeerte* Vollenhoven goes further into this matter and considers the question whether "the realization of the miracle could not also be approached in a different way, for instance, by assuming that God called forth the paternal seed from the maternal" (p. 3). Vollenhoven rejects this possibility because it easily reminds one of the Aristotelian relationship: "form — matter." It seems to me that this possibility must be rejected simply because of this "paternal factor" which, here again, is introduced and which places it on the same line with Vollenhoven's dilemma. He further answers the question whether his conception does not go beyond the limitations of our thinking: "We are indeed confronted with an unsearchable creative act of God. It is therefore safest not to go beyond a distinction between a divine act regarding Mary and the uniting of the two natures by the Son." To me it all depends what is meant by this "distinction" and whether the idea of the "fatherly factor" is absolutely excluded. I deem this of decisive importance in regard to the dogma of the virgin birth and only thus it is possible to fight on spiritual grounds, the multifarious criticism of the Church's confession.

The relationship between Christ's deity and pre-existence on the one hand and the virgin birth on the other contains a serious warning against presupposing all kinds of "possibilities"[109] which practically all lead to a certain form of adoptianism or – if this be avoided – to a flight into the mysterious.

Neither the consideration of the relationship between the deity and pre-existence of Christ and the virgin birth, nor the scriptural record, contains any disqualification or devaluation of marital relationship. On the contrary, this relationship is fully respected and left intact. For the procreation in this relationship implies the birth of *a living human being* and not simply an abstract "human nature." To be sure, this was not the way of the incarnation, but certainly not because it is an inferior way. Rather, it was because assuming human nature is something quite different from uniting a person who thus originates with the Son of God. The human procreation of a human life is not the way of incarnation. At the end of such a way we shall not find Jesus Christ. In analogy with what Jesus says concerning Abraham, we might summarize Bavinck's interpretation of the relationship with: before Joseph was, Christ is. This is no biological explanation (like Brunner's) nor does it eliminate the fatherhood (as does Kohnstamm), but it recognizes the *uniqueness* of this birth, which may also be described as a *coming into the world.*[110] Here

109. Cf. A Köberle, *Natus ex virgine Maria,* 1942, p. 153: "As far as Jesus' birth is concerned God could also have taken the natural way. He could, by means of his creative intervention in a pneumatically created miracle, have made a maritally procreated child to be the 'second Adam', the originator of a second mankind." We further mention in this connection the criticism of Bavinck by Korff, who contends "that there is no necessity for a virgin birth in Bavinck's creationistic thinking because creationism allows for the possibility that God can give a soul to a naturally procreated body and this soul could be Jesus' and the Logos could further unite himself with the human nature thus prepared." I am sure that Bavinck would have answered that he would not have been able to recognize such as the *assumtio naturae humanae* as *act* of the Logos and that he would have considered Korff's construction nothing but an "adoptional possibility" for which even Bavinck's "creationism" would not allow. To Bavinck *assumtio* is truly something different from *adoptio!*

110. This involves no speculation whatsoever. For this compare it with Anselm's line of reasoning in *Cur deus homo,* II, 8. He says that God can create man in four different ways: 1) de viro et femina; 2) nec de viro nec de femina (Adam); 3) de viro sine femina (Eve); and now comes the fourth way: "aut de femina sine viro, quod nondum fecit." So God, to show that he had power to employ this *modus* also chose this way

we are reminded of what Paul says, "The first man is of the earth, earthly: the second man is *of heaven*" (I Cor. 15:47). It is he who cometh down from heaven (John 3:31; cf. 6:32, 33, 38, 42, 50, 51, 58). Whoever considers this in relationship with Christ's birth *ex virgine Maria* is not speculating or making an attempt at fathoming the mystery, but is respecting the whole of Scripture. And whoever does accept the birth of Christ but rejects the virgin birth may be reminded that the attack upon the virgin birth coincided historically with doubt concerning Christ's *deity* and *pre-existence.* We recognize that this historical connection is not *a priori* but *a posteriori.* Nevertheless, in our opinion it can hardly be denied that this criticism coincided wth the renewal of *adoption* Christology in its nineteenth century form. It is the result of *anti-mythical* thinking, which did not really commence with Bultmann but which evolved from a deterministic limitation of God's activity and which was also applied to the *natus ex virgine.*[111] Ultimately this opposition cannot be due to difficulties in the *text,* which so clearly witnesses to the virgin birth, but to other circumstances. It became more and more impossible to the distorted nineteenth century Christology to discover any "sense" in the virgin birth, and so it

---

with respect to Christ's birth and "nihil convenientius, quam ut de femina sine viro assumat illum hominem quem quaerimus." It is hardly conceivable that Anselm makes Boso reply that this is an answer according to the desire of his heart. For this choice out of the different *modi* contains nothing biblical whatsoever. Cf. further Ignatius, *Ad Eph.* 18, 19 and Tertullian, *De carne Christi,* 18. An obvious repetition of Anselm's *modi* is found in Turretinus (as one of his arguments) in *Inst. Elenct. Pars* II, Geneva, 1689, p. 373: Adam, Eve, all those born afterwards, and then, "quartus modus ad admirabilem Dei sapientiam in hominum ortu conspiciendum, ut homo ex femina sine viro nasceretur, quod in solo Christo impletum." Turretinus refers here to Jer. 31:22. This line of reasoning is certainly different from Bavinck's and Noordmans'.

111. We do not mean to say that all criticism of the virgin birth is identical with a general rejection of miracles. Both Brunner and Kohnstamm assure that they are not motivated by a *rationalistic criticism of miracles.* Still, we believe that the general criticism of the virgin birth is closely related to the infection of the Christian faith by determinism, which influences also those who shy away from determinism in accepting the miracles. Cf., e.g., Hering, Z. *th. K.*, 1892, p. 61, who on the basis of the "evangelical" conception of Scripture writes, "No one can prevent us from not attaching any greater significance to it [the virgin birth] than to the miracle of the ax head which swam at Elisha's command (II Kings 6:6).

was considered an insurmountable stumblingblock for modern man to fully embrace the gospel.

Finally, we wish to consider why Bavinck not only relates the virgin birth to Christ's deity and pre-existence, but also to "Christ's absolute sinlessness." Does he not contradict himself, since he elsewhere says that the virgin birth is *not* the essential ground of Christ's sinlessness? Bavinck (and Reformed theology in general) have generally been interpreted as being careful not to make the virgin birth the ground of Christ's sinlessness, but when it comes to the test this is difficult to maintain, as Bavinck's "contradiction" shows. Korff says that the argument of the relationship between the virgin birth and Christ's sinlessness has been upheld for centuries both by Reformed and Lutheran theology (*ibid.,* II, 297). He counter-argues that it is not clear why the virgin birth should exclude original sin: "It is quite likely that Mary, too, had something to do with original sin!" But surely Korff is guilty of a serious misunderstanding. He creates the impression that anyone who mentions original sin in connection with the virgin birth automatically takes a position which Calvin certainly did not take, and that this is what Schleiermacher had in mind when he said that then Mary's sin must also be reasoned away.[112]

The problem becomes still more apparent when Korff considers it "extremely unfair" that Barth never advanced this argument.[113] We may confine ourselves to Bavinck, who himself sheds light on the "contradiction" when he explicitly mentions *original guilt*: "This elimination of the man in Christ's conception effected at the same time that Christ, as not being comprehended in the covenant of works, also remained free from original guilt and thus, in his human nature as well, he was preserved both before and after his birth from all pollution of sin" (*Gereformeerde Dogmatiek,* II, 277). It is evident that Bavinck considers this fact in connection with Christ's deity and pre-existence and that the emphasis is on him who was the Son of the Father, the One

112. Schleiermacher, *Glaubenslehre,* II, 63ff.
113. Barth in *K.D.* I, 2, 207, states that "the *ex virgine* is no technical basis for Christ's conquest of original sin" and says that the older dogmatics oftentimes denied this. Hence it is not clear what Korff means.

who had *come* and was *sent* into the world. Bavinck's problem is entirely different from what Korff takes it to be.[114]

Reformed theology is not in the least concerned with some sinful essence of marriage or procreation; nor with a still tendentious semi-Roman Catholic heresy, be it not quite as consistently developed as by Rome; nor yet with denying the statement made by Korff (with an exclamation mark!) that Mary, too, had something to do with original sin. The issue at stake is the problem of *original guilt.* Behind the argument concerning the virgin birth we see, besides the problem of adoptianism, the question concerning the reality of original guilt as a *judgment of God.* Only when this is fully realized can the Reformed confession of the *natus ex virgine* be judged fairly.

Elsewhere, particularly in the Roman Catholic Church, all kinds of Mariological speculations became associated with the *natus ex virgine.* These often gave this confession just as much a *Mariological* as a *Christological* character. A remarkable shifting of emphasis created specific Mariological dogmas, of which the perpetual virginity of Mary is the most striking.[115] Even though Scripture did not contain "clear indications" (B. Bartmann, *Dogmatik,* I, 427), yet this momentum was advanced as an essential matter. It is quite evident that certain motives played an important role here, as proven by the fact that also outside of the Roman Church a certain attention was paid to this perpetual virginity and that with Rome a corresponding interpretation was sought for the *brethren of the Lord.*[116] The

114. Cf. G. C. van Niftrik, "Original sin is not eliminated because there was no marital relationship between Joseph and Mary but because God deals graciously with Mary. If Jesus' sinlessness is connected with the absence of such a relationship then we must be consistent and, like the R. C. church, accept Mary's immaculate conception" (*Kleine Dogmatiek,* p. 104). Zuidema correctly writes that Van Niftrik's alternative either excludes or misinterprets the Reformed version (*Stellingen* 7).

115. "Virgo post partem semper virgo." Pope Paul IV (1555) made the clearest pronouncement against the Socinians: "semper in virginitatis integritate, *ante* partum scilicet, *in* partu et perpetuo *post* partum" (Denz, 993).

116. Cf. for the R.C. position, for example, *Dict. Theol. Cath.* VIII (I) s.v. Jesus Christ, pp. 1164 - 1172 and especially in still wider context (II) s.v. Joseph, in connection with his "virginity": "Purity, this is your triumph!" (Bossuet). "The complete and perpetual virginity" is concluded from the "sublimity of his mission" (p. 1519).

Articuli Smalkaldici,[117] for instance, speak of the *semper virgo,* and in Reformed circles Kuyper was frequently mentioned as one who entertained quite an outspoken opinion in this respect and who cautioned against any hasty judgment.[118] Generally speaking we may say that oftentimes improper motives have played a role in the consideration of the virgin birth and Christ's sinlessness. Indeed, there have been occasions when it was difficult to make a clear distinction between the Protestant and the Roman Catholic views with respect to the significance of the *natus ex virgine.*[119]

117. *Art. Smalk. Pars* I, IV: "Filius ita factus est homo, ut . . . ex Maria, pura, sancta sempervirgine nasceretur"; cf. also *Conf. Helv. Posterior,* 1562, Art. XI.

118. See especially *De Vleeswording des Woords* in which he, in connection with "the brethren of the Lord," speaks of indelicately defiling the graciousness and tenderness of Mary (p. 103). On pp. 131ff. Kuyper gives a further explanation after he has learned that his statement evoked questioning and declares that his standpoint as to Mary's perpetual virginity was neither Romish nor Lutheran but that this was the opinion of the best and most learned Reformed theologians "be it not a dogma" (p. 132) He further gives an exegesis of Matt. 1:25 and explains the difference from the fact that *formerly* people's feelings were far more *tender* and *delicate* and *holy* and lately they are much coarser in their judgment and inclined to deal with such delicate questions "quite the opposite way" (p. 134). In his Loci (*Locus de Christo,* p. 14) Kuyper refers to the R.C. appeal to Ezek. 44:2, which allegedly implies Mary's perpetual virginity (Vulgate: *haec porta clausa erit.* RSV: "This gate shall remain shut"). Kuyper wants to apply these words to Christ's birth only *per analogiam.* The conclusion to Mary's perpetual virginity Kuyper considers correct "and in agreement with Reformed theology." The neo-Kohlbruggians were, out of reaction against Rome, of a different opinion but "the more dedicated theologians" considered the brethren of the Lord differently. There is a pronounced element of *piety, sacredness,* and *tenderness* in Kuyper's argument *but it never becomes clear exactly what comprises this sacredness and why a different opinion would reveal more "coarseness"* (cf. Bavinck *Gereformeerde Dogmatiek,* III, 273 on Lutherans and Reformed). Kuyper mentions a reaction against Rome but such reaction is altogether justified because of the *apriorism* which makes the perpetuation of Mary's virginity an *essential* element and thus forces the Christologic dogma in a Mariologic direction. The exegesis concentrated especially on Matt. 1:25. See especially Hugo Koch, *Adhuc virgo. Mariens Jungfrauschaft und Ehe in der altkirchlichen Ueberlieferung bis zum Ende der* 4. *Jahrhunderts*, 1929, containing, among other things, important information on the question whether "the entire early church" was indeed unanimous in this respect (Zanchius on Kuyper's *Vleeswording,* p. 132).

119. The R. C. position is expressed by Bartmann, "Theology in agree-

In spite of this it has often been realized that basing Christ's sinlessness on the virgin birth creates a great problem and that Calvin at least pointed out how to refrain from doing so. We also see how frequently an attempt has been made to point out the connection between Christ's relationship to Adam and original guilt as God's judgment on mankind in Adam as the head of the covenant of works. In this way Bavinck mentions Christ's not being comprehended in the covenant of works.[120]

Usually it was asserted that it was exactly this kind of connection which contained a speculative element, so that an "ontological" significance had to be attributed to the virgin birth. But we must insist that historically the Church considered the scriptural testimony first and that afterwards – in the consideration – this testimony was seen in connection with the unique position of Christ as the head of the new mankind. It was exactly because the purely noetic explanation of the virgin birth was unsatisfactory that Scripture was searched for correct connections with the person of Christ. Usually this way could be taken without any danger of Mariological or ascetic consequences, especially because of the fact that the angel spoke of "that holy thing" which would be born of Mary. From this it was not concluded that the exclusion of Joseph *as such* caused this holiness, but this holiness became nevertheless a subject of intense consideration.

It was not primarily for the sake of dogmatic reasoning that Reformed theology spoke of Christ's *holiness* in connection with the virgin birth. Nevertheless, the fact that it did so speak of

---

ment with Augustine considers that the Christologic significance of the virgin birth is the exclusion of original sin." This places Augustine's statement, already quoted, beyond all doubt ("Generated and conceived without any lust of carnal desire and therefore without original sin"). Cf. A. Hering, "Die dogmatische Bedeutung und der religiöse Wert der übernatürlichen Geburt Christi," (*Z. f. Theol. u. K.*, 1895, p. 75).

120. Cf. also à Marck, *Compendium Theologiae Christianae didactico-elencticae*, Amsterdam, 1722, p. 375, where he, in connection with the "praeservatio ab omni labe," cautions against the conclusion that original guilt and pollution are passed on only by the *man*. Christ is free from original sin "ut supernaturali virtute ex lapsum secuta promissione tanquam alterius foederis caput natus, ratui Adamico per se non fuit subjectus, atque hinc massa seminis, a virginis persona ad filium constituendum segregata, absque omni merito gratiae antecedente, debuit a corruptionis poena, reatum solum consequente, eximi."

it in this connection resulted inevitably in misunderstanding, first, because it did not always make clear distinctions, and second, because it constantly *appeared* to be in agreement with that other view which emphasized *sin* in the marital relationship. The distinction, however, can be made; it is possible to show that the issue at stake here is the problem of original guilt as God's judgment and decree. It is not without reason that Bavinck points to several texts concerning the sanctification of Christ (*Gereformeerde Dogmatiek*, III, 275).

Possibly one of the reasons for the misunderstanding is that usually the word "sanctification" refers to the purification of sins personally committed and thus presupposes the *presence* of such sins. Scripture, however, speaks also of a different kind of sanctification. We not only learn that Christ is the Holy One of God, but he also says himself, "Say ye of him, whom the Father sanctified and sent into the world, Thou blasphemest?" (John 10:36).[121] It is remarkable that both his sanctification and the sending into the world are mentioned here in the same connection. We are not implying that Christ is speaking here of his birth of the virgin Mary, but unless the virgin birth is rejected *a priori* this word cannot be detached from that sanctification of which the angel speaks in the annunciation to Mary. "Jesus comes into the world *holy* and is therefore distinct from all men."[122]

This sanctification does not imply a change from a sinful to a holy state but a separation to a task, a sanctification to the service of the holy work of deliverance (*ibid.*, on John 10:36). The Father can sanctify Christ to the fulfillment of his office as the *second* Adam through the power of the Spirit and give him the Holy Spirit "not by measure" (John 3:34). Because of aprioristic-dogmatic motives the life of Christ has been far too often considered deistically as an already *defined* and *confined* life of the *man* Jesus of Nazareth. Scripture, however, speaks of the power of the Spirit over Christ in the weakness of the flesh. He is the Messiah anointed with the Holy Spirit (Isa. 61:1). And it is of great significance that Bavinck, following the testimony of Scripture, places the virgin birth in *this* connection: of his *coming*, his *office*, his *task*, his *holiness*, and his *Messiahship*.

121. Cf. John 17:19, where we read that Christ sanctified *himself* for his disciples.
122. Grosheide, *Commentary*.

When in the annunciation of Messiah's birth mention is made of his holiness, we see therein the preparation for the fulfillment of his office, his *Messianic* office, and his remaining in *this* obedience during the days of his flesh, in weakness and temptation. Here Christ is not a man who is subject to God's judgment, as are all other men who through their generation are contained in the covenant with Adam. He is the Son who himself takes the curse instead of passively becoming subject to it, because he enters a hell-bound and accursed world. Böhl makes a grievous mistake when he makes Christ subject to original guilt and considers it docetism to deny this (see my *The Person of Christ*). For that which Christ bears is not the terrifying result of mankind's fall in Adam, which descends on him like an unavoidable avalanche when he enters the world. On the contrary, his suffering and death will truly be a carrying and carrying away of the guilt which he *voluntarily* takes upon him. In so doing he is our brother, true man, like unto us in all things, sin excepted.

In confessing the virgin birth we do not attempt to exclude Christ from the original sin which supposedly would be derived from a human father, but rather from the original *guilt* of all who are born of *Adam.* Christ does not violate the *order* of God's judgment, but it does not include him. He subjects himself *voluntarily* to this judgment in an obedience unto death, yea unto the death of the cross. He, the man from heaven, does not originate *in* this world. He is not *by virtue of his birth* subject to the judgment which rests on mankind, but he will *vicariously* take it upon him. Here the light of holiness breaks through the shadows of judgment. For here is the fulfillment of the messianic longing: the Messiah, the man Jesus Christ, the bread from heaven given from above. He thus descends into the uttermost darkness. The guilt, the *alien* guilt, comes into *this* life only when he, the Son, God's holy child Jesus, takes it upon himself, and only thus he enters into judgment, forsakenness, and condemnation.[123]

123. In my opinion Lord's Day XIV of the Heid. Cat. points this out when it says of the *natus ex virgine*: "that he might also be the true seed of David, like unto his brethren in all things, sin excepted" and which describes the *profit* thereof as follows: "That he is our Mediator; and with his *innocence* and perfect *holiness,* covers in the sight of God my sins wherein I was conceived and brought forth." See also S.G. de Graaf, *Verbondsgeschiedenis,* II, 211.

When Church and theology mentioned the virgin birth again and again in connection with Christ's holiness, this was ultimately not the result of speculation. There was no "gnostic" motive to tear apart the "heavenly" and "earthly," and no low view of marriage which associated it particularly with the doom of life on earth. It was far more the realization of God's dealings with mankind's guilt in Adam, as Scripture pointed it out. No one was trying to construct an "ideal man" who actually has nothing to do with this earthly life. This is an idea which we so frequently discover in any gnostic-dualistically tinted conception which actually rejects a real birth from Mary. The mystery of Christ's birth is exactly this, that he enters the reality of this life as the Holy One. There *is* a profound relationship in what Bavinck calls the connection between Christ's virgin birth and his deity, pre-existence, and sinlessness. It is indeed possible and necessary to eliminate completely every devaluating thought with respect to human life on earth. Then it will also be possible to reject any "Mariological" inference from the confession of the virgin birth. For the object is not to glorify virginity, but to bring out the profound implication of God's judgment on all of mankind in Adam, as Calvin and others intuitively understood when they opposed the devaluation of marriage and procreation. The belief that Christ's virgin birth exempts him from God's judgment may not be ascribed to an inclination to docetism, nor to a denial of the incarnation of the Word. Rather the opposite is true.

The depth into which Christ descends does not show that he becomes subject to God's judgment, but rather it reveals a holy and marvelous *act* on Christ's part. In this taking the guilt upon himself he is God's beloved Son. *Therefore doth the Father love him.*[124] That which he experiences is far different from what mankind experiences under God's judgment.[125] His bearing the guilt is unique and incomparable with anything else.

Those who prefer to speak of a "sign" may say that in this Reformed view Christ's virgin birth also *signifies* something. But that is not what we are objecting to. The scriptural witness most certainly contains God's revelation concerning Christ's birth. But the situation becomes entirely different when "noetic"

124. John 10:17, "Therefore doth the Father love me, because I lay down my life, that I might take it again."
125. Cf. S. U. Zuidema, *op. cit.*, VIII.

is contrasted with "ontological" and thus, quite arbitrarily, the "sign" becomes the "form" as contrasted with the mysterious "contents." We do not dare[126] make such a distinction in the one act of God in the birth of Christ, in Christ's coming. In our opinion it is a construction which on the one hand attempts to stem the general tide of doubt and rejection of the virgin birth,[127] but on the other hand it is not free from criticism itself. The only way to get out of the impasse is to reject the distinction between "noetic" and "ontological" as an improper dilemma at this point, and further to speak of Christ's holiness in such a way that it opens our eyes to the power of his voluntary submission unto the depth of this sinful life in which he has been made to be sin for us (II Cor. 5:21).

Often a connection was seen between the virgin birth of Christ and those births of children in the Old Testament which revealed a new sovereign act of God. The question was raised whether these events did not indicate some obvious relationship. Stauffer remarks that the *idea* of the virgin birth was foreshadowed "by the accounts of the miraculous births of Isaac, Joseph, Samson, Samuel, and John the Baptist" (*Theol. des A. T.*, p. 98).

When we read these birth accounts, it always strikes us how God's activity is emphasized. The accent is on Rachel's barrenness, which God in answer to prayer terminates.[128] Sarah's barrenness is no less emphasized. Over against Abraham's self-willed sovereign doings (Hagar) God places the true sovereignty of his own dealings. Their impotence in connection with the promise is strongly brought out and is accentuated by Sarah's laughing after the annunciation of the birth of a son (Gen. 18:10-11). She mentions her own withered condition and Abraham's old age (vs. 12).

Her laughing corresponds with Abraham's unbelief at the previous annunication of this birth: he laughed and said in his heart, "Shall a child be born unto him that is a hundred years

126. Cf. Barth's statement, "That Jesus Christ is the incarnated Son of God stands or falls noetically with the truth of the *conceptio de Spiritu Sancto*. We cannot say, however, that the mystery of Christmas ontologically, as such, stands or falls with this dogma" (*K.D.* I, 2, 221).

127. Cf. as to this doubt H. de Vos, *Het Christelijk Geloof*, pp. 198f., and G. Sevenster, *Christology van het Nieuwe Testament*, pp. 133ff.; also O. C. Quick, *Doctrines of the Creed*, 1949, pp. 156ff.

128. Gen. 30:1, 2. See all of Gen. 30, which sharply contrasts the impotence of barrenness with God's deed in Rachel's life.

old? and shall Sarah, that is ninety years old, bear? (Gen. 17:17). God's miracle, announced in the answer after Sarah's laughing, "Is anything too hard for Jehovah?" (Gen. 18:14) and the birth of Isaac are described with great emphasis on God's activity, "And Jehovah *visited* Sarah as he had said, and Jehovah *did* unto Sarah as he had spoken. For Sarah conceived, and bare Abraham a son in his old age" (21:1, 2).

Samson's birth, too, is presented in the light of the miraculous over against the impotent barrenness of Manoah's wife (Judges 13:2). We also see the miracle of this new soteriological act expressed in the name of the angel of the Lord: "Wherefore askest thou after my name, seeing it is wonderful?" (vs. 18). Again, we read of Hannah's barrenness. The Lord had shut up her womb (I Sam. 1:5; cf. vss. 2, 8). Her prayer is answered, but it is expressly stated that Samuel is the child of Elkanah and Hannah (vs. 19). God's remembering her evidently does not eliminate the procreation, and Hannah sighs praises to God for his wonderful deeds (I Sam. 2, esp. vs. 5). Finally, we read of Elizabeth's barrenness on account of her old age (Luke 1:7). She, too, praises God's doings, "Thus hath the Lord dealt with me in the days wherein he looked upon me, to take away my reproach among men" (vs. 25).

When considering these data we may ask what Stauffer means by saying that the idea of the virgin birth is "prepared and pre-arranged" by all these events. He finds the same idea in Matthew and Luke, who, according to him, "wish to bring out that Christology reaches back into the grey past" and that the idea of the virgin birth "has been suggested by similar religious-historical representations." These Old Testament stories do not, however, explain the virgin birth. They illustrate God's grace and power in his dealings with his people, but the question of fatherhood plays no role at all. God's miracle shatters the curse of barrenness; but that is not the point with regard to Christ's birth. Elizabeth is even mentioned in the annunciation to Mary, ". . . in her old age; and this is the sixth month with her *who was called barren.* For no word from God shall be void of power."[129] But in Mary's case the situation is entirely

129. Luke 1:36, 37. Greijdanus summarizes the angel's word thus: "that which is said of Elizabeth and that *which is told you* is possible because God can do all things as he pleases" (*Comm. Luke,* I, 55). However, it is remarkable that mention is made in the annunciation of what God can do in *connection with Elizabeth.*

different. Christ's birth is entirely unique: it is the *mystery* of the incarnation.[130] We are not dealing with a general miraculous power which manifests itself in Mary's life and which is of the same nature as the other manifestations. The annunciations in the Old Testament birth accounts differ greatly from the annunciation of Christ's birth, and the reason for this difference lies in the nature of this mystery: the *Word* is become *flesh*.

As we have seen, the confession of Christ's virgin birth has been the object of criticism for about a century. To a certain extent this criticism was the result of theories and ideas which in the course of history had been developed with regard to the relationship between *this* birth and that which, according to Scripture, may and must be considered holy. This article was also criticized for another reason, namely that it seemed particularly to stress the "supernatural" as a reality by itself entering the "natural." But this was criticizing an article after it had been stripped of the personal character of what took place: the *coming* of the Son. The anti-mythical tendencies of this century and the preceding one apparently had no more use for this confession. And so the belief in the virgin birth was replaced by a respect either for the miracle (Brunner) or for the sanctity of matrimony. It will be up to the Church to show the way back to the scriptural witness, so that the incarnation may once more be adored not as a breathtaking "cosmological" event but as Christ's taking the way of poverty and forsakenness. Christ was not an ideal person who groped for the upward way, but the incarnated Word, who, as God's Messiah, was not subjected to God's curse in order that he might take this curse upon himself.

Noordmans says correctly that there is more at stake in the virgin birth than simply an incidental event which does not agree with the scientific mind, or which can become an in-

130. S. G. de Graaf, *Verbondsgeschiedenis* I³ (O.T.), 1952, says in connection with the birth of Isaac, "The birth of this child was a miracle. Thus it is a prophecy of the Lord Jesus Christ, whose birth would also be a miracle" (p. 93). In my opinion the difference has not sufficiently been brought out and the emphasis is too much on the general idea "miracle." It is remarkable that he does *not* relate God's act in Rachel's barrenness to the miraculous birth of Christ (p. 143). He does say of Samson's birth that it is a prophecy of the Redeemer, but he does not emphasize the miraculous (Christ "who would deliver his people not only from the hands of the Philistines but also from sin and from all their enemies"). Cf. on Elizabeth, *ibid.*, II, 205.

surmountable obstacle to those alienated from the Church. A veil must cover this indivisible mystery, and if the Church has any misgivings here she had better return quickly to the old story of the angels' song and the annunciation; the swaddling clothes and the adoration; the old story of *holiness* and *guilt*.

CHAPTER SIX

CHRIST'S SUFFERING

IMMEDIATELY after mentioning Christ's holy birth the Apostle's Creed passes on to his sufferings: "who was conceived by the Holy Ghost, born of the virgin Mary, *suffered*. . . ."[1] The Church did not mean thereby to mention the general human suffering in which Jesus Christ also participated. Connecting Christ's birth and suffering may remind us of the Buddhist view of life, that birth is suffering and life is suffering, but this has nothing to do with this confession of the Church, any more than the expression "dead," which follows, wishes to express the generality of death to which Jesus was also subject. It is far more a confession of *faith*. The confession wishes to bring out the *mystery* of the suffering which culminates in the "goodness" of that particular Friday. Neither was it the intention of the Church to refer to a mere historic event, nor to point especially to a dark phase in Christ's life, but to confess a redemptive-historical, gracious, and reconciling fact.

An often-used expression in the vocabulary of the Church is the "suffering and death" of Christ,[2] which suggests correctly that we do not understand his suffering according to the meaning of Scripture if we separate it from his death, although the creed has good reason for first of all calling our attention to his suffering. Again, it was not the Church's intention to point out how *undeserved* this suffering of Christ was or how exceptional it was compared to other suffering, which somehow was due

1. The original Creed had: "qui sub Pontio Pilato crucifixus est et sepultus." Later "passus" was added.
2. W. Michaelis, *Herkunft und Bedeutung des Ausdrucks "Leiden und Sterben Jesu Christi,"* 1945. He points out that this expression as such is nowhere to be found in Scripture (p. 5) but only in separate parts. However, his argument cannot prove that the Heidelberg Catechism is not supported by Scripture, because it emphasizes his suffering during all the time that he lived on earth – but especially at the end of his life (Q. 37).

to the sufferer's own fault. The Church indeed confessed Christ's sinlessness, innocence, or more positively, his *holiness,* but she never spoke of his innocence without immediately and in the same connection mentioning the *guilt* which he carried, and carried away, as the *Lamb of God* (John 1:29, 36). Christ's suffering is always connected with the fact that it was "for us," and the Church considered this the uniqueness of this suffering. His was a *fruitful, beneficial* suffering and death, the death of a grain of wheat that only by way of first dying bears much fruit. The message of the Church concerning his suffering is not tragedy or nihilism, but the message of the only sure foundation in a world of sin, suffering, and death. The message is not an individualization of Job's general lamentation, "Has not man a hard service upon earth?" (Job 7:1, RSV) but a specific, peculiar fact which was of such a nature that it could receive a place — and what a place! — in the Church's doxology and preaching.

We are not dealing with a tragic end of a still-young life or with the disillusion of a man with high ideals whose life had been made miserable by opposition and enmity, but with *sacrifice, self-surrender, ransom, reconciling suffering.* Instead of the suffering as such, the Church emphasized the significance thereof and expressed this in her preaching. This is not a speculative projection of the mind which tries to attach a meaning to something meaningless, but it is the full realization of the Word of the cross which is the power of God unto salvation (I Cor. 1:18). It is absolutely impossible to understand the preaching of Christ's suffering and death correctly, or even partly, if it is not realized that this confession does not emphasize innocence and pathos, nor does it re-confront us with the fathomless depth of human suffering; in short, if it is not understood in faith that his suffering is a matter of both *innocence* and *guilt.* This curious relationship between "innocence" and "guilt" includes everything the Church says concerning the suffering Christ, and his life's history can never be interpreted in terms of a general law of life or of suffering and death, neither can it be approached on the basis of antique or modern suffering theories, nor on the basis of a knowledge concerning the "meaning of suffering" which we derive elsewhere.[3]

3. Cf., e.g., M. Scheler, "Vom Sinn des Leidens" in *Moralia*, 1923, pp. 41-103, who says that the Christian concept of suffering is characterized

It strikes us that the accounts of Christ's suffering contain a manifold testimony to his *innocence.* So, for instance along the Via Dolorosa. We hear the cry of Judas that he has betrayed innocent blood (Matt. 27:4) and read of the intervention of Pilate's wife: "Have thou nothing to do with that righteous man" (Matt. 27:19). Pilate finds nothing in Christ worthy of punishment, and three times over he declares him innocent,[4] even quoting Herod for support (Luke 23:15). And finally we hear the centurion at the cross join in: "Certainly this was a righteous man" (Luke 23:47), while within the circle of the crucified the one thief testifies: "And we indeed justly; for we receive the due reward of our deeds: but this man hath done nothing amiss" (Luke 23:41). It strikes us that this last testimony concerning Christ's innocence is given in connection with the confession of the thief's own guilt and that he adds a fervent prayer which Christ answers by opening the gates of paradise. As far as the centurion is concerned we hear nothing further, but the other's witnessing to Christ's innocence proves to be fruitless.

No matter how unanimous this testimony is, it does not persuade the rest to participate in the blessings of Christ's innocence. Judas goes his own way, and Pilate, after having declared Jesus innocent, continues the procedure; "I will therefore chastise him, and release him" (Luke 23:16, 22; cf. vs. 25). The saddest thing in these attestations of innocence is that they reveal a consciousness of innocence but not of personal guilt. This reveals a pathetic misunderstanding of Christ's suffering. There is no eye for the *purpose* of this suffering, which carried Christ into the deepest shadows of death. They acknowledge Christ's innocence as did the daughters of Jerusalem, to whom Christ says, "weep *not* for me but weep for yourselves, and for your children" (Luke 23:28).

In sharp contrast with all these testimonies concerning Christ's innocence is the Church's confession of the *guilt* which caused this suffering. It is true, she confesses this in connection with the sinlessness of the immaculate Lamb of God, who takes away the sin, but the Church never approached Christ's suffering ex-

---

by an entirely different attitude towards suffering in that it does not ascribe a special significance to it (p. 97), in distinction from Buddhism, hedonism, heroism, etc.

4. Luke 23:14, 15, 22.

clusively from the standpoint of his innocence. For this reason none of the later attempts at a "judicial review" of Jesus' sentence will ever create more than a superficial interest from the side of the Church.[5] Such attempts are no better than the testimonies concerning Jesus' innocence during his trial. They express the desire to unmask Jesus' trial as a sham, and, by means of an exact historical examination, to reaffirm Christ's innocence; and it is considered of great importance to revise the verdict. "Condemning the innocent has far-reaching consequences. Rehabilitating them also has far-reaching consequences."[6]

In these pleas[7] we are confronted with a peculiar situation. It is beyond dispute whether Pilate justly delivered Christ over unto death. The Gospel, when depicting Pilate's hesitations and decisions, show only too clearly how warped his judgment was, for instance in his scourging Jesus after having attested to his innocence. The confessions, too, mention Pilate's condemning Jesus *innocently.*[8] What we must condemn in these pleas is the fact that they emphasize *rehabilitation.* It is all too typical of that particular evaluation of Christ which sees him as "the symbol and representative of mankind" and "the personification of goodness, justice, and truth."[9] The objective of such a rehabilitation is the "revival" of justice and morality, or the self-correction of the Jewish people or of mankind, and it is exactly for this reason that it misses the core of the gospel concerning the suffering of Jesus Christ. Its mistake is not that it points out the injustice in the trial[10] but that it disconnects Christ's innocence from the *guilt* which in the gospel is inseparably connected with this innocence.

All these declarations of Christ's innocence reveal a total blindness to the New Testament emphasis on significance of the

5. E.g., the action of a Jewish lawyer in Denver who wanted a meeting of the Sanhedrin in Jerusalem to reconsider Jesus' trial. In 1949 a Dutchman requested a revision by the new Jewish Supreme Court. See Frank J. Powell, *The Trial of Jesus Christ,* 1950.
6. N.G.H. Deen in his preface to Powell's book.
7. Cf. Powell, *op. cit.,* p. 148.
8. E.g., the Heidelberg Cat., Q. 38: "That he, being *innocent,* and yet condemned by a temporal judge . . . ." That which Kuyper once called a "judicial murder" Powell describes as "guilt, incompleteness and atrocious injustice."
9. Powell, *op. cit.,* p. 164.
10. Cf. K. Schilder on Jesus Christ as "exlex" in *Christ in His Suffering, passim.*

cross. They reveal a consciousness of the innocence but not of the guilt. God's action in and through this suffering and this bearing of the guilt is not seen. The early Church was never interested in rehabilitation, but she did incorporate Pontius Pilate's name and action in the Creed. This was not done to complain about the injustice done to Christ, but to show that therein and thereby *God's* wrath and condemnation descended upon him who, although innocent, but as the Mediator and the Lamb of God, was burdened with our guilt and thus condemned. Whoever does not see and acknowledge this when considering Christ's innocence misses the "gospel" of the cross and has become entangled in romanticism.

Every posthumous vindication contains a very unsatisfactory element, but this is particularly true in regard to Christ. It is moreover impossible, because his condemnation, suffering, and death are absolutely irrevocable. When Paul says, "Which [wisdom] none of the rulers of this world hath known: for had they known it, they would not have crucified the Lord of glory" (I Cor. 2:8), then he does not sound the call to correction and revision but to *faith* and *conversion*. For man's guilt and Pilate's injustice in the irrevocableness of this history is intercepted by God's action and grace: "Things which eye saw not, and ear heard not, and which entered not into the heart of man, whatsoever things God prepared for them that love him" (I Cor. 2:9). And all attempts to come to a revision – which would only strengthen man's self-confidence – will fail when the immeasurable proportions of both innocence and guilt are seen in the light of the cross, and as the word of the cross presents them. *This* history cannot be undone any more, not even *in abstracto*. The word of the cross is a power of God unto salvation unto everyone that believes. The only thing which can be done posthumously is not a human restoration but an act of God, namely, the resurrection of Jesus Christ from the dead.

This does not imply, however, that we may ignore the seriousness of action in Christ's suffering and death. On the contrary, scripture clearly teaches us that *men* paved the way to the cross. Christ, too, was fully conscious of this fact. When he announced his suffering he described in detail the part men would play therein – as, for instance, high priests, Pharisees, and others. He knew that he would be delivered into the hands of men (Mark 9:31, and concordant places) and to the Gentiles (Mark 10:33); and that he must suffer and be rejected (Mark 8:31);

be condemned to death (Mark 10:33); be killed (Mark 8:31); be mocked, scourged, and spat upon (Mark 10:34). He knew what some of his disciples would do: that he would be left, forsaken, denied, and betrayed by Judas; and that his own people would reject him (foretold in several parables; cf. John 1:11). In his answer to Pilate he made the distinction: "Therefore he that delivered me unto thee hath greater sin" (John 19:11), which shows that he was fully aware of the activities which were converging more and more upon him. Indeed, man's activity in Christ's suffering is so emphasized that at first glance we might come to think of it as the *primary* cause of Christ's suffering and death. We read about actions, plans, meetings, intrigues; even "power" – authority over Jesus (John 19:11) – the result of which is summed up in these words: "they crucified him" (Luke 23:33). It is one combined action leading to the cross. The way to the cross is paved by men, and at the end of this way is Christ, hanging on the cross between two malefactors. Their lives, too, are terminated by the activity of men. Suffering, death, and burial – were not all these things occasioned by *men*?

It is not surprising that the apostolic preaching emphasizes this activity, seeing that the Gospels do the same. Immediately after the outpouring of the Holy Spirit we see this human activity incorporated in the preaching. Christ has been nailed to the cross and slain by the hands of man.[11] Man's responsibility and guiltiness is underscored[12] by these words: "whom *ye* crucified" (Acts 2:36; 4:10). This human activity is strongly accentuated not just in a historical account but even in a prayer, when it is said that against thy holy Servant Jesus . . . "Herod and Pontius Pilate, with the Gentiles and the peoples of Israel, were *gathered together*" (Acts 4:27), which is seen as the fulfillment of the raging of the nations in Psalm 2 (Acts 4:25, 26). It combines the different activities into one, as is expressed in the phrase "gathered together against."

So we see that from the very beginning the apostolic preaching has been fully aware of the role men have played in connection with Christ's suffering. We might almost speak of "co-

11. Cf. the distinction made in regard to this activity by men in Acts 2:23: "Him . . . ye by the hand of lawless men did crucifiy and slay." Cf. I Cor. 2:8.

12. "And [you] killed the Prince of life" (Acts 3:15); "whom ye slew, hanging him on a tree" (5:30). Cf. Acts 10:39 and 13:28f.

operation," if we only realize that this activity, this "co-operation" is the absolute *opposite* of what Rome calls man's co-operation in his salvation. It is "co-operation" *in malam partem*, which is employed for the benefit of the world only by God's supreme power. This co-operation does not eliminate man's *full responsibility*. True, this responsibility is no obstacle to God's activity, but nevertheless it occupies a prominent place in Scripture. This, too, was part of all that befell Christ when he was kissed and betrayed, when he was killed and buried; and all this was as real as the piercing John mentions and which he considers the fulfillment of the Old Testament prophecy (Zech. 12:10, John 19:37), an act against Jesus Christ which is incorporated in the eschatological portrayal of Christ: "Behold, he cometh with the clouds; and every eye shall see him, *and they that pierced him*" (Rev. 1:7).

To think that this human activity sufficiently explains Christ's suffering and death would evidence simplistic hermeneutics. For it is clearly evident that Scripture, while not in the least minimizing the reality of human action, still points to another dimension in Christ's suffering. From the entire gospel it is apparent (and this *is* the gospel) that ultimately Christ in his suffering was not a victim of human arbitrariness and fathomless enmity. True, enmity and arbitrariness play an important role, but this arbitrariness does not have the decisive word. There is another line which *crosses* the line of human action, or, perhaps, *follows* it, or how shall we express this mystery? It is *God's hand* which holds the reigns throughout. This is evident not only in the limitation of human activitiy as we see it in the fulfillment of Scripture, "A bone of him shall not be broken,"[13] but also when men's action, apparently uninterrupted, proceeds until Christ's death on the cross. The light of God's action penetrates the darkness of man's action.[14] There is no dualism or dialecticism in the sense that the one activity excludes, cancels, or annihilates the other, but there is a historical proceeding in which faith, by the light of revelation, clearly discerns the nature of the divine action. This insight is clearly noticeable immediately after Pentecost. The eye of faith sees the one great event, which, however, has two aspects;

13. John 19:36 (cf. vv. 32, 33 and note the difference in treating Jesus and the other crucified ones).

14. Cf. Caiaphas' action in this divine light. See my *The Providence of God*.

Peter describes them when he says, "Him, being delivered up by the determinate counsel and foreknowledge of *God, ye* by the hands of lawless men did crucify and slay" (Acts 2:23). God's action does not commence with the resurrection of Christ from the dead, but "the crucifixion is already God's work, the *opus alienum* which he, through his enemies, accomplishes. So God's providence governs every step of Christ's way."[15] Man's action is not crowded out by God's *sole*-activity, but God's *all*-activity manifests itself in and through the human action. Christ's being delivered up by men through the act of Judas is at the same time his being delivered up by God.[16] Also the way Herod, Pilate, and others deal with Christ, as mentioned in Peter's prayer, must be seen in the light of God's action: they are gathered together "*to do* whatsoever thy hand and thy counsel foreordained to come to pass" (Acts 4:28). This "to do" does not express the purpose *they* had in mind, but what must be accomplished by means of their voluntary action. Grosheide speaks in connection with this prayer of the *language of faith,* which at once sees the hostile powers comprehended in the power of the Lord (*Comm.,* I, 146).

God's action does not run like a second line beside the line of man's action but is like an invisible, mysterious hand which rules and guides all human action from beginning to end. We are dealing here with the same relationship as we find expressed in Peter's epistle when he speaks of "a living stone, rejected indeed of men, but with God elect, precious" (I Pet. 2:4). Man's despising and rejecting Christ is a real, historical part in his suffering, but God accomplishes his good pleasure in and through this rejection. As human enmity it constitutes the "material," the form in which God's action becomes manifest, and Peter considers it the fulfillment of Psalm 118:22, "The stone which the builders reject is become the head of the corner. This is *Jehovah's doing;* it is *marvelous* in our eyes." Man's doing is clearly evident: the stone is rejected and refused

15. Stauffer, *Th. des N.T.,* p. 186. Cf. Grosheide, *Commentary* on Acts 2:23, who expresses this relationship thus: "That which men did was indeed their sin and trespassing of the law, but ultimately this was only secondary. They actually carried out God's plan." Grosheide speaks further of Peter's explanation of the crucifixion.

16. Cf. Rom. 8:32 (*παρέδωκεν*) and Mark 9:31 (*παραδίδοται*; John 19:11 (*ὁ παραδούς μέ*); Matt. 27 (*παρέδωκαν Πειλατῷ*); Mark 14:10 (*ἵνα αὐτὸν παραδοῖ αὐτοις*); Mark 15:1 (the Sanhedrin); Luke 23:25 (Pilate). Cf. Romans 4:25.

(I Pet. 2:4), but in and through this rejection God's control of events becomes manifest, just as Jesus himself saw the enmity of the leaders of his day in the light of the marvel of the rejested stone which, by God's good pleasure, becomes the head of the corner (Matt. 21:42; Luke 20:17). So God's wisdom and lovingkindness cross the arbitrariness of men, and the ugliness and injustice of Christ's suffering are placed in the light of the divine deliverance. The full realization of the relationship of these two aspects, rejection and God's good pleasure, gives the right conception of the meaning of the *passio Christi.*

Already Isaiah 53 clearly expresses God's action in and through the Messiah in the prophecy concerning the Man of Sorrows. Although it is true that this prophecy, too, points out very clearly what part man shall play in this process when it says that he was oppressed and afflicted (Isa. 53:7) and that he was numbered with the transgressors (vs. 12),[17] the emphasis is on the fact that it is the *Lord* who *has laid* on his servant the iniquity of us all (v. 6). It pleased the *Lord* to bruise him, *he* made him sick (v. 10, Dutch version). Whoever has an eye only for the suffering and scorn which men have caused the Man of Sorrows does not see the profound significance of this suffering.

It now becomes evident why Christ in his suffering reacts not only to the action of men, both friends and enemies, but also to *the Father.* Not only is he fully conscious that he has been sent by the Father, but he also sees God's activity in and through the suffering which men inflict upon him. When facing Pilate he acknowledges his power, but at the same time he knows that this power has been given Pilate "from above." In his suffering he knows that he is confronted with the cup and with the One who has given him this cup to drink, namely the Father (John 18:11); and in Gethsemane he speaks about this cup with the Father (Matt. 26:39, 42). The enemies are approaching and the disciples are sleeping, but to Christ Gethsemane is a place of prayer; he knows that his suffering is not only the result of what men are doing to him but that the *Father,* in and through their action, places the cup in his hand. On the cross Christ again speaks with the Father about the way of this forsakenness in ut-

17. Cf. how Christ applies these words to himself in Luke 22:37 and Mark 15:28; in Mark in connection with the crucifixion of the two malefactors and in Luke in connection with the announcement of the approaching end. Cf. Isa. 49:7 and 50:6 on the despising of the servant of the Lord.

most darkness; this too is an act of God. It is in these surroundings that the cry is heard: *It is finished!* The line of men's activity runs straight through to cross, death, and burial. But there is still another "end": the finished work before the face of the *Father*!

Thus far we have spoken of the two aspects, the two dimensions in Christ's suffering, namely, God's action and men's action, which must be considered in order to understand the uniqueness of this suffering. Now we must consider Christ's own activity in his suffering. The action of men which descends upon Christ is not a superior power which takes him by surprise. Christ in his suffering is not a passive, involuntary victim. On the contrary, from the beginning to the end of his suffering Christ was fully active and conscious, and even on the cross he refused the stupefying myrrh drink and took instead the sharpening vinegar (Mark 15:23, 36; cf. Matt. 27:48, Luke 23:37, and John 19:29f.). This illustrates Christ's full consciousness in which he finished his suffering. Already Isaiah 53:7 says that these things were not simply done *to* him (by God and men) but also that he *allowed* himself to be oppressed (Dutch version), and that he made himself an offering for sin (vs. 10, RSV); he *bore* the iniquities (vs. 11), he poured out his soul unto death and prayed for the transgressors (vs. 12).

These elements of strong and unremitting activity are also present in Christ's preaching. There is triumph in the words "after three days shall I rise again," which follows the announcement of his suffering. Even in the actions of men, *he* will be active when he "departs" (John 13:1); *he* commends his spirit into the hands of the Father (Luke 23:46). He came to *give* his life a ransom for many (Mark 10:45), and as the Good Shepherd he *gives* his life for the sheep (John 10:11, 15). Indeed, Christ left no trace of a doubt concerning his activity to the very end when he said, "Therefore doth the Father love me, because I lay down my life, that I might take it again. No man taketh it away from me, but I lay it down of myself. I have power to lay it down, and I have power to take it again. This commandment received I from my Father" (John 10:17, 18). This does not contradict his *being* crucified and his *being* delivered unto death. But the decision does not and cannot rest with men (*no man* taketh it from me), but *his* deed and willingness, his choice and consciousness will stay with him until he reaches the brink of death, yea, death itself.

When examining the scriptural witness concerning the suffering Christ, we soon notice that there is *progress* in his suffering. We are not dealing with a permanent experience of suffering in solitude, but with one long historical way of suffering amidst people and demons before the eyes of God. The Heidelberg Catechism says that he suffered "all the time that he lived on earth, but *especially* at the end of his life." It was not without reason that the Church spoke of the "*passio magna*," without wishing to minimize his suffering *before* the last days of his life. In the *passio magna* we see the final and utmost concentration of his suffering, and Scripture shows us that this distinction is not without reason, for Christ said to his disciples, "With desire I have desired to eat this passover with you before *I suffer*" (Luke 22:15).[18] Christ, too, is conscious of the fact that he has entered into a new phase of his suffering, as he had already foretold on several occasions. There is an inauguration of this suffering. There is a night of betrayal. There is an increased intensity in the *passio magna* which Christ has indicated as his time: "My time is at hand" (Matt. 26:18), the time when his people disown him, when he is betrayed, denied, bound and condemned, crucified and slain. At the beginning of this dark way he speaks of not yet being alone, but that the Father is with him (John 16:32) but on the cross the Father's name departs from his lips (Matt. 27:46). He learned obedience by the things which he suffered (Heb. 5:8) and accepted the way in which the cross loomed more and more as an unavoidable reality and in which he experienced utter forsakenness in the depths of his heart. Thus the evangelist can say that he *began* to be sorrowful and very heavy in Gethsemane (Matt. 26:37), and thus an

18. Michaelis' attempt to prove that the word "suffering" in the N.T. (also in Luke) means "dying" raises problems especially with respect to this text, and not only here, but also in the announcement of his suffering ("suffer many things" as in Luke 17:25). Michaelis refers in this connection to Isa. 53, but this does not solve the problem (*Herkunft und Bedeutung des Ausdrucks "Leiden und Sterben Jesu Christi,"* 1945, pp. 7-9). Michaelis, to whom suffering is identical with dying, deduces from this that Jesus' saving work concentrates in Christ's *death* on the cross and so all he can say about Jesus' life before his death (Gethsemane, trial, mockery, scourging) is, that this cannot be considered suffering in the same sense and to the same extent (p. 11). He incorrectly states that Stauffer's expression "passion before the Passion" is not based on the New Testament.

angel can appear in the garden to strengthen him to the heavy task which he has to accomplish (Luke 23:43).

Just as his suffering intensified, so did his isolation. First we see how his people repulse him more and more; then follows the betrayal, and after the betrayal the forsaking by the disciples, so that his solitude is absolute. Unrest, fear, fright, horror, agony seize him at various stages in his suffering until the moment arrives of utter forsakenness which the Church has always considered the utmost depth, because after that Christ again calls upon his *Father,* into whose hands he, dying, commends his spirit. Christ's suffering extends over days and hours. Each hour runs over with all the evil thereof and is, moreover, burdened with the anticipation and knowledge of even more to follow. But at every moment of each hour of agony there is always the same willingness *to give his life.*

In order to understand the meaning of this suffering we must note how Scripture again and again emphasizes its *necessity.* Scripture expresses this by saying that Christ *must* suffer. Through the mesh of human arbitrariness runs the thread of God's plan and action. That which is arbitrariness on the part of men such as Pilate and Herod (declaring him innocent, scourging, crucifying him) is subjected to a divine *must.* This "must" is by no means a forcing which eliminates men's free will and self-conscious activity, but points to God's plan and God's hand in this suffering. So Christ himself says to the disciples of Emmaus, "Behooved it not the Christ to suffer these things, and to enter into his glory?" (Luke 24:26).

There is a mysterious "must" in Christ's entire suffering. At times this is explicitly expressed, at other times implied by quoting certain passages of Scripture as being the fulfillment of certain incidents along the way of Christ's suffering. Thus we read that he *must* suffer (Luke 9:22; 17:25; 24:7, 26; Acts 17:3; Matt. 16:21; Mark 8:31; John 3:14 [so *must* the Son of man be lifted up]; cf. John 12:34; also Acts 9:16, where Paul's suffering for Christ is a divine *must*) and that "this which is written must be fulfilled in me, And he was reckoned with transgressors" (Luke 22:37). He not only relates the fact that the disciples will be offended to the prophecy concerning the shepherd who will be smitten and the sheep that will be scattered (Matt. 26: 31) but he also declares, "how then should the scriptures be fulfilled, that thus it must be" (Matt. 26:54) when he declines to pray to his Father for the more than twelve legions of angels. The fact that Jesus is taken is done "*that* the scriptures of the prophets might be fulfilled" (Matt. 26:56).

All the things which were written in the law of Moses, in the prophets, and in the psalms concerning Christ must be fulfilled Luke 24:44).[19] When the connection is seen between the scriptural prophecies and the "must" of the suffering, then it becomes clear that back of the Scripture witness is God's plan. This Scripture witness is so trustworthy that we may say that the Scriptures *must* be fulfilled. Kittel speaks in connection with this "must" of its "character of necessity and unavoidableness."[20] The quoted texts do not further indicate the *reason* for this "must," but it is quite evident that they refer to God's plan and counsel concerning Christ. Kittel's reference to an "expression of a necessity which originates in God's essence and being" contributes no further clarification. We can go no further than to speak of God's soteriological good pleasure manifesting itself in all of Christ's life but especially in his suffering. It has nothing to do with compulsion or determinism, neither with a *neutral* necessity, but with the *personal* "necessity" springing from God's will and Father-heart. This explains that Christ does not involuntarily subject himself to this "must" as to a *fatum,* but *willingly* surrenders to the holy will of the *Father.*[21]

In view of the fact that the Gospels are full of witness concerning Christ's way of the cross and the reality of his suffering and death, the question now is the correct *understanding* thereof. The age-old controversy concerning the significance of Christ's work has focused particularly upon the *meaning,* the *sense* and *significance* of his suffering. This is an alarming kind of controversy, for the very *purpose* of Christ's suffering is at stake. It

19. Cf. also the "must" in special circumstances of Christ's life: his being about his Father's business (Luke 2:49); his preaching (Luke 4:43); walking (Luke 13:33). Cf. also John 20:9: his disciples as yet knew not the Scripture, that he *must* rise again from the dead. Cf. Herman Ridderbos, *De Komst van het Koninkrijk,* pp. 150ff. Cf. I Cor. 15:4, Rev. 1 and 4, Mark 13:10 (the gospel *must* first be published among all nations), Mark 13:7, Matt. 17:10 (Elias), Matt. 24:10 (signs of the times). Cf. also Acts 1:16.

20. S.v. (δει).

21. Cf. H. Cremer, *Bibl. theol. Wörterb. des N.T. Gräcität,* 1893, s.v. (δεω) (p. 251) on "an unavoidable, enforcing or enforced 'must'."

is evident even from Scripture that his suffering may be misunderstood. Not only his disciples had a grave misconception of it, but also, and much more so, his enemies, who evidenced this in their bitter scorn. It is indeed possible to consider the cross the extermination of Christ, and to close one's eyes to the light in this darkness. Already Isaiah 53 makes mention of this misinterpretation. When it depicts the Man of Sorrows as bearing our griefs and afflictions, it also tells of Israel's interpretation to prove that it does *not* understand the deepest meaning thereof: "yet we did esteem him stricken, smitten of God, and afflicted" (Isa. 53:4).

That means: we (i.e. Israel) did not see the *actual* reason why he suffered.[22] It is possible to compare the Man of Sorrows with Pharaoh, who was plagued with great plagues (Gen. 12:17), but then the perspective of Christ's suffering is missed and the *mystery* it contains is not discovered. Then the phrase "no form nor comeliness"[23] is understood as the manifestations of God's anger[24] without our seeing what is involved in this wrath whereby all glory departs from the life of the Man of Sorrows.

It is evident that only by the light of revelation can a complete misunderstanding of Christ's suffering be avoided. Even the impressions which we receive when closely following Christ on his way of suffering are not able to give us a complete understanding. We are absolutely unable to give even a fairly complete analysis of Jesus' feelings and emotions, of his pain and forsakenness. The Gospels depict his suffering as a harsh reality. They do not romanticize, but are extremely sober compared with many songs originating from the passion-mysticism of later centuries, which often show a dissatisfaction with the sober Gospel accounts.[25] But even Christ's words, actions, and reactions during

22. Cf. Young: "we completely misunderstood the reason of the Servant's suffering" (E. J. Young, *Isaiah* 53, 1952, p. 44). Cf. J. Ridderbos, *K.V.-Jesaja.*

23. Isa. 53:2; cf. Isa. 52:14, "Like as many were astonished at thee (his visage was so marred more than any man, and his form more than the sons of men)."

24. Compare this with the explanation Job's friends gave of his suffering, which was too simplistic in spite of its "religious" character. Cf., in connection with Christ's suffering, the daughters of Jerusalem.

25. On this, see much material (also alarming material) in D. F. Bub, *Das Leiden Christi als Motiv im Deutschen Kirchenliede der Reformation und des Frühbarock,* 1951. He particularly points out the anti-

his suffering are very *sparse*. We cannot trace a clear line of emotions. There is intensification in his suffering, but after the fearful agony in Gethsemane we again hear words of strong self-consciousness and submission, while Christ's word on the cross concerning his forsakenness manifests anew the bitterness of his suffering. It is like a thunderstorm which for a moment seems to subside but later resumes with greater force. But who is able to give a "synthesis" of all these impressions, which, furthermore, are very limited, since it is not the intention of the Gospels to give us a complete account of all of Christ's reactions to his sufferings? We hear a few words of Christ relative to his suffering; we read of a particular look (Luke 22:61) or of an eloquent silence over against Pilate and Herod (Luke 23:9, Matt. 27:14). We read of his reaction to the manner in which he was taken: "Are ye come out as against a robber with swords and staves to seize me?" (Matt. 26:55), but further "the N.T. makes no mention of any reaction on the part of Jesus to the various humiliations, insinuations, mockeries and vilifications" (D. F. Bub, *ibid.*, p. 10), and also under the false accusations he remained silent (Mark 14:61, Matt. 27:12; cf. the picture of the sheep that is dumb before her shearers, in Isa. 53).

Obviously the Gospels have not the least intention of giving a complete and realistic picture of Christ's suffering and death. The description, however, is of such a nature that it clearly brings out that all this was not meaningless. The various accounts of the suffering are not independent and unrelated narratives, but together they are the introduction to the resurrection of Christ. Their objective is to depict the undeniable reality, even in its details, but not to portray the passion aspects as such, or isolated as an object of meditative-sympathetic interest. Christ's suffering is a prelude to the resurrection, albeit a real prelude, in all seriousness and grimness, in the shadows of death. The important question is now, What is the significance, the meaning — the transcendent meaning — of this immanent suffering till death?

---

naturalistic representation of Christ's suffering in the Lutheran church hymns. "The anti-naturalistic tendency remains until after 1600; possibly the most essential difference between the Lutheran and non-Lutheran (Catholic, Bohemian, Schwenckfeldian) treatment of the Passion" (p. 109). On Christ's passion cf. also J. Leipoldt, *Vom Jesusbilde der Gegenwart,* 1925, pp. 261ff.

The meaning of his suffering is understood only by the light of the whole Scripture. And if we wish to catch a glimpse of this revealing light, we should look to the frequently appearing words of Scripture: "for us." Scripture is not concerned with the mere pathetic death of the man Jesus of Nazareth, as if it were like every other death: "As for man, his days are as grass: as a flower of the field, so he flourisheth" (Ps. 103:15), but with the unique meaning, the *purpose* of and in Christ's agony and forsakenness.

Scripture presents and preaches Christ's suffering in connection with God's counsel and activity. *For us* – these words must always be kept in mind by the believers. Even Christ portrayed his suffering and death in this light when he said, "This is my body which is given *for you*: this do in remembrance of me" (Luke 22:19). This "for us" is often beautifully brought out in the hymns of the Church – also in the passion hymns, if they are scripturally pure. Because of this "for us" they have the character of psalms out of the deep and therefore they sound like songs of joy.

This "for us" contains a confession of guilt, which at the same time by no means neglects the historical facts. This we find beautifully expressed in Revius' passion hymn: "It is not the Jews, Lord Jesus, who crucified thee . . ." or in Heerman's song written in 1630:

> *But what can be the cause of such affliction?*
> *Alas! It is my sins, my malediction;*
> *The reason for this bitter agony,*
> *Lord Jesus, lies in me!*[26]

Since the entire Scripture so evidently emphasizes this "for you" in connection with Christ's suffering, and the hymns and creeds of the Church as well, it is amazing that throughout the centuries a vehement controversy has centered on precisely these words."[27] We might also put the issue, which is still with us, as follows: Why do we call it *Good* Friday?

In reaction, there has been another tendency to dismiss this

26. Cf. this and other passion songs with what Bub calls "Seitenwunderotiek" (*ibid.*, pp. 117, 123).
27. Cf. what Fiebig says on the cleansing blood: "It says only *that* it cleanses, not how" (P. Fiebig, *Jesu Blut ein Geheimnis*?, 1906, p. 11). Cf. also his ideas on the "λυτρον" and on the question to *whom* the ransom is given.

"battle" as a dispute among theologians; we ought, instead, to experience personally the depths of Christ's suffering. But this teaching only resulted in still another conception of the meaning and purpose of the *passio magna.* No matter how great the differences of opinion concerning this "for you" may be, they may never keep us from earnestly and continually seeking the light of Scripture so that we by faith and a true knowledge of Christ may know this "for you" as "for us."

It must be clear that we do not wish to isolate these words, "for you." Scripture indicates the reality of this same comfort by many other formulations. It speaks of the Good Shepherd who gives his life for his sheep (John 10:11, 15). His dying "for us" indicates that his suffering, like his entire life, is a beneficial reality whose purpose is "that they might have life" (John 10:10). His suffering cannot be isolated from his overall mission. Whoever separates his cup of suffering from his cup of joy, his death from his life, his foresakenness from his communion, has never sensed the meaning of Christ's suffering (cf. the Form for the Lord's Supper). Scripture teaches this in many different ways. When Christ, *knowing* that he was about to go to the Father, rose from supper to wash the disciples' feet, he spoke also in this connection of their *having part with him* (John 13:8). Having part with him does not mean that Christ's suffering depends for its efficacy on the disciples. On the contrary, Paul, who knows of a close bond with Christ and of being crucified with him (Rom. 6:6), appreciates the priority of the *blessing* above the *blessed* and says that Christ died *for us* while we were yet sinners (Rom. 5:8). *In due season* he died for the ungodly (5:6; cf. vs. 7, "For scarcely for a righteous man will one die"), and we are justified by his blood (vs. 9) and reconciled to God by his death (vs. 10).

The blood that cleanses from all sin (I John 1:7) is a source of unspeakable joy. It is the blood of the lamb without blemish and without spot (I Pet. 1:19) without which there is no remission (Heb. 9:22). By the shedding of his blood "now once at the end of the ages" he has put away sin (Heb. 9:26) and he was offered to bear the sins of many (vs. 28). Christ died *for* the nation (John 11:52f.) and gave his life a ransom for many (Mark 10:45, Matt. 20:28; cf. I Tim. 2:6, I Thess. 5:9, Eph. 5:2). The passover is sacrificed for us (I Cor. 5:7), and Christ has made peace through the blood of his cross (Col. 1:20; cf. Eph. 1:7 and 2:13, I Peter 1:2, Rev. 5:9).

By quoting all these Scripture references we do not mean to deny that they contain different shades of meaning, but even these nuances bring out the one great fact of the dying grain of wheat which brings forth much fruit. They all emphasize the one, great, beneficial purpose of Christ's suffering and death. The historicity of Christ's suffering and death manifests itself as a blessing and radically changes life in this world. "If therefore the Son shall make you free, ye shall be free indeed" (John 8:36).

Neither the purpose nor the fruitfulness of Jesus' life and death can be denied, but a controversy did arise as to the correct understanding of the words "for us." It is quite clear from the apostolic preaching that it is exactly this "for us" which constitutes *the* resurrection light that shines in this darkness. There is no indication that the apostles, out of disappointment, were merely trying to save the situation by attaching a deep significance to Christ's suffering. On the contrary, the apostolic preaching goes all out to call faith to witness that this significance is a reality which was prophesied already in the Old Testament, and that Christ's suffering must be understood thus and thus alone. We are confronted with this inescapable choice: either the preaching of the apostles did indeed point out the significance of Christ's suffering and death, or we are dealing with a theoretical construction of the young Church, resulting from disillusionment and disappointment, by which it tried to make Christ's life fit in with the Old Testament prophecies and thus manifest the divine "must." We may fully agree with Dibelius when he writes that it was also the gospels' objective "to preach that which under God's direction took place in the passion."[28]

But it is of decisive importance to know whether this preaching *creates* the meaning and significance of this suffering or whether it *finds* this by the light of revelation. If the latter, there is no doubt that this suffering becomes the subject of preaching *exactly because of its historic reality.* Only thus can the preaching become a witness to both the cross and the resurrection and consequently to God's activity in Christ's suffering and death.

28. This is true of both the original *Symbolum Romanum* and the later additions in the *textus receptus* (our 12 Articles of Faith). With respect to these additions we are especially referring to: *communio sanctorum, descensus ad inferos,* and *catholica.*

Only when Christ's suffering – in its historicity – is evaluated on the basis of God's activity and on what Scripture witnesses concerning him do we have the right conception of it. That is why Paul, when giving a resumé of the *historic* events: "died, buried, arisen" can add, "Christ died *for our sins according to the scriptures*" (I Cor. 15:3). He simply passes on what he first received himself. By this clarification, or rather *indication* of the meaning and significance contained in the historic reality, the message of the apostles has fully become "evangelical." This message is so penetrating and trustworthy, and so full of promise, that we must not tire of searching the Scriptures in order to retain responsibly the correct conception of the blessing of this suffering: "For God so loved the world, that he gave his only begotten Son, that whosoever believeth on him should not perish, but have eternal life" (John 3:16).

It is a remarkable fact that the Church clearly indicates the significance of Jesus Christ's *historic* life and death, not by way of an interesting biographical description, but as part of her *creed.* This clearly indicates that from the very beginning the Church understood by faith the significance of this history, namely, that it was *for us.* This point of view, as faith sees it, is expressed with special clarity in the explanation of the *Apostolicum* in the Heidelberg Catechism. We are not concerned with the complicated and difficult questions of the history of symbolism but with the viewpoint which sees Christ's life and death in a higher light, namely in the light of salvation. We wish to give a further explanation of this by considering this viewpoint of faith in connection with (1) Pontius Pilate, (2) the cross, and (3) Christ's death and descending into hell.

(1) The Church still confesses *sub Pontio Pilato* and by so doing she denotes a particular relationship between Christ and Pilate. His name, with Mary's, will travel along with the Church on her journey throughout the ages until the end. The question has often been raised why this is so, since the fact that he played a part in the Lord's suffering cannot be a sufficient explanation in itself. There were others who played at least as large a role. We are thinking, e.g., of Judas, whose name is continually mentioned in the Gospels in the clause "who also betrayed him" (Matt. 10:4; 26:25; 27:3; Mark 3:19; Luke 6:16; John 6:71; 12:4; 18:2, 5), and no one will deny that his

betrayal played a decisive role in the progress of Christ's suffering.

This is no less the case with Caiaphas the high priest, who in the impasse of hesitation finally and definitely organized the opposition by appealing to the Sanhedrin, "It is expedient for you that one man should die for the people, and that the whole nation perish not" (John 11:50ff.). What he says is very striking, the more so since his action must be seen in the light of divine revelation and providence: John adds immediately (vs. 51) that Caiaphas, being high priest that year, prophesied that Jesus should die for the nation. In spite of his importance – both historically as leader of the opposition and as instrument in God's hands – his name has not been incorporated in the creed of the Church. Neither was this the case with other figures associated with Christ's suffering, as, for instance, Herod, whose name is even mentioned in Acts when the believers reflected upon his part in Jesus' suffering (Acts 4:27).

It is remarkable that Jesus himself mentions only one figure of whom the Church in later centuries will speak. It is the woman who anoints him in the house of Simon: "Verily I say unto you, Wheresoever this gospel shall be preached in the whole world, that also which this woman hath done shall be spoken of for a memorial of her" (Matt. 26:13). But neither did the name of this woman find its way into the Creed. It is exclusively the name of Christ's judge that will forever be mentioned by the Church. The question often arose and still arises whether this selection from the many "stages" of the way to the cross is not rather "at random" and relatively incidental in comparison with, for instance, the name of Mary the mother of the Lord, or whether we are dealing here with an intuitive consciousness expressed in the confession, of which we still can say that it was a wise and good choice. It has been asked whether Pilate is mentioned in the Creed because he was, at any rate, the deciding authority who *delivered* Jesus unto death and thus, in his person, symbolizes the power of evil. But Christ himself prevents us from forming such an opinion of Pilate by what he says to the governor, "therefore he that delivered me unto thee hath greater sin" (John 19:11).

Pilate is not mentioned, then, because he is personally most guilty of Christ's suffering. The Creed does not mention the person who delivered Jesus unto Pilate, nor does it refer to Israel, which rejected Christ. Neither must we say that our present confession of *sub Pontio Pilato* is merely an attempt to preserve a formulation which was symbolically important to the early Church. The historical intentions behind some of the creedal phrases are sometimes impossible to discover with certainty;[28] at any rate, these intentions are beside the main point.

Even though the Church of more recent times is uncertain about the symbolic value of some early creedal phrases, it nevertheless rightly confesses Christ *according to the Scriptures* in the words of the Creed. The Church felt the necessity of basing its confession on the Holy Scriptures, and for this reason it could freely accept the wording of the Creed and so confess her faith, as also is done in the Heidelberg Catechism, Q. 38: "Why did he suffer under Pontius Pilate, as judge? That he, being innocent, and yet condemned by a temporal judge, might thereby free us from the severe judgment of God to which we were exposed." This explanation has become very familiar to us but it is, nevertheless, very remarkable, because here the historic factuality of Christ's suffering is seen in a very special light, namely, in the light of *salvation.* The Church, apparently, was not concerned with a biographic portrayal of a number of "stages" on the way to the cross, of which Christ's condemnation by Pilate was one, but with the *meaning,* the *significance* of this suffering: with the "for us." That is the place Pilate occupies in the Creed. That is what the early Church meant when it incorporated Pilate's name in the same series of short articles in which the forgiveness of sins and the life everlasting are mentioned. It was the *judge* Pilate, not the *man* Pilate, to whom the Church referred on the basis of Scripture.[29]

Pilate's name in the Creed has often been taken as an indication of time, to prove thereby that Christ's suffering was a real historical fact and to rule out any form of docetism. It is indeed possible that this, too, was partly the intention. We frequently come across this time element in the early Church; for instance, it is quite strong in Ignatius' attack upon docetism.[30] There, too, Pilate is mentioned. He says, for instance, that the resurrection took place during the governorship of Pontius Pilate (*Ad Magn.,* 11), elsewhere he mentions his name in connection with the cross (*Ad Smyrn.,* 1, 2), and in still another place the

29. Luke 13:1-5 mentions Pilate's name in connection with an atrocity which is being related to Christ. This gives Christ an occasion for a grave warning, but Pilate remains entirely in the background.

30. Cf. Ignatius against "ἀρνουντες τὸν θάνατον Χριστοῦ" (*Ad Magn.* 9, 1).

tetrarch Herod is mentioned (*Ad Smyrn.*, 1: και Ηερουδου τετραρχου). Mentioning historic figures often serves the same purpose as the usage of the word "truly," which we find so frequently in Ignatius.[31]

If this were the only reason for the Creed's mentioning Pilate's name, however, it could have chosen Herod's or Caiaphas' name as well. The Catechism, however, ignores this aspect entirely and emphasizes Pilate's function as *judge*. Without attempting to express a scientific and definite opinion as to the symbolic significance of the mention of Pilate's name in the Creed,[32] the Catechism simply relates it to its significance "for us." For this reason we are interested only in that interpretation of *sub Pontio Pilato* which sees this history in the light of God's activity and consequently in the soteriological light, as is so evidently done in the Heidelberg Catechism.[33]

When we perceive that the Catechism does not mention Pilate's name simply as an anti-docetic witness to the reality of Christ,[34] then we see at the same time that only the testimony of

31. Cf. Tacitus (*Annalen* XV, 44) on Christ's death: "Tiberio imperitante per procuratorem Pontium Pilatum supplicio affectus erat."
32. The uncertainty is also due to the fact that the original *Symbolum Romanum* had: "qui sub Pontio Pilato crucifixus est et sepultus" whereas the later *Apostolicum* reads: "passus sub Pontio Pilato, crucifixus, mortuus et sepultus." Cf., as background, I Cor. 15:4.
33. The Scriptural data concerning Pilate depict him in Acts 4:27, together with Herod, as instruments in the hands of God, who sovereignly rules all human activity connected with Christ's suffering. Further, in I Tim. 6:13, "I charge thee in the sight of God, who giveth life to all things, and of Christ Jesus, who *before Pontius Pilate* witnessed a good confession." It is therefore a false charge that the Creed arbitrarily incorporated the name of Pontius Pilate and that it is a construction of the human mind to emphasize his judgeship as is done in the Catechism. It is true, I Tim. 6:13 does not directly deal with the condemnation of Christ, but his confession is nevertheless a confession *before* Pontius Pilate and he is truly involved in a *lawsuit* so that Paul calls upon the believers in the world to also profess a good profession before *many witnesses*. The emphasis is on Christ's confession, but it is characterized by the fact that it was "before Pilate." Cf. R. Schippers, *Getuigen van Jezus Christus in het N.T.*, p. 152.
34. In connection with the contemporary anti-docetic interpretation see Barth's interpretation. He considers it an *indication of time*: "It thereby excludes and rejects a gnostic Christ-idealism" (*De Apostolische Geloofsbelijdenis*, 1935, p. 99). God's revelation is concrete and temporal "and can therefore be no less historically defined than, for instance, Pericles' reign in Athens" (p. 100). And therefore: *sub Pontio Pilato*. Yet, he is not entirely satisfied with this explanation, because he asks:

Scripture is the solid foundation of the confession of the Church, also with regard to *sub Pontio Pilato.* Scripture clearly states that Christ himself acknowledged Pilate's authority. When Pilate self-assuredly asks the silent Christ, "Knowest thou not that I have power to release thee, and have power to crucify thee?" (John 19:10) and thus proclaims the superior power of his "authority" by which Christ is in his hands, then Christ answers, "Thou wouldest have no power against me, *except it were given thee from above*" (vs. 11). Given from above — that is the reason why Christ acknowledges the authority (*exousia*) of Pilate on whom he is now dependent:[35] dependent in the hour of decision. This authority has been thus explained:

---

for what reason is this limitation of time given in connection with the *suffering* Christ? Barth's answer is that the time of the Roman governors is one of disorder and disobedience. It is a period which God in his forbearance tolerates, but nevertheless his wrath rests on it so that it is doomed to end in destruction (p. 100). It is the time in which the Son of God must *suffer*; it cannot be *anything but* a time of suffering for him; it is *our* time, the time of the *world.* Our aeon cannot but condemn Christ, as did Pilate, because Christ is the only innocent One in this aeon. Pilate is the *exponent of* the time of the world. Cf. G. C. van Niftrik, *De Belijdenis Aller Eeuwen,* 1949, pp. 104ff. In my opinion it would not be contrary to Barth's fundamental idea if he had shown that Caiaphas could have been mentioned just as well. The latter could have been presented as the representative of the religious body which sacrifices Christ and brings him to the cross. In 1952 Barth gave still another explanation of Pilate's name being in the Creed in "Christus und Adam nach Röm. 5" (*Theol. Stud.,* Heft 35, pp. 46-48). He does not just emphasize that Christ is being delivered into the hands of the Gentiles, but also makes mention of Pilate in connection with Rom. 5:20 ("grace did much more abound"). This refers also to the Gentiles, as is evident from the history of Christ's suffering. Pilate *represents* the Gentiles and therefore they participated in the abounding of sin, being the instruments in God's hands (p. 48) and thus also in the reconciliation. "From then on it can be said that the Gentiles who are without the law are no longer excusable on that account, but also — and this is far more important — that from then on there is no longer any accusation against them, neither is there any condemnation" (p. 48). He concludes: "Pontius Pilate does belong in the Creed. The pouring out of the Holy Spirit became objectively possible by that which was done by the guiltily-unguilty hands of this Pontius Pilate" (p. 48).

35. Cf. Karl Kastner, *Jesus vor Pilatus. Ein Beitrag zur Leidensgeschichte des Herrn* (N.T. Abhandl. IV. Band), 1912, p. 98, which speaks of the close relationship between Jesus' and Paul's pronouncement on the *exousia* of the powers ordained of God (Rom. 13:1).

Pilate can decide to crucify Jesus only by God's permission (*ibid.*, p. 98). The mystery of the crucifixion cannot, however, be approached in this way. This would make God a passive spectator in the suffering of the cross instead of the One who is *doing* something; remember the prayer after Pentecost! It is true, Pilate is doing something, but therein he is but the medium of God's sovereign, omnipotent activity.

God's action manifests itself in and through the judge Pilate even after he has declared Jesus innocent (John 19:4; cf. vss. 5 and 6) and before the final verdict (vss. 12-16). Pilate acts here as *persona publica* and thus he passes judicial sentence on the Son of man. That is the biblical background of the Catechism's explanation, which fully recognizes the arbitrariness in this verdict (he, being innocent, and yet condemned); nevertheless it does not detach this sentence from the given *exousia*. This reveals again – as in Caiaphas' prophecy – God's *crossing* the activity of man *in* the historical identity between Pilate's act in his capacity of a judge and God's act. That is why the Church always emphasizes the substitution, the aspect "for us" in the condemnation of the innocent Christ.[36]

In connection with Pilate's condemnation of Jesus we find a remarkable statement in John. When Pilate sought a way out of the impasse and for a moment considered the possibility of the Jews judging Jesus according to their law and they answered, "It is not lawful for us to put any man to death," then John adds, "That the word of Jesus might be fulfilled, which he spake, signifying what manner of death he should die" (John 18:32). Pilate's attempt to pass Jesus' activity off as a Jewish internal affair is unsuccessful. The Jews have already pointed out that they would not have delivered him up unto Pilate if he had not been a malefactor (John 18:30 κακὸν. ποιῶν). Now Jesus' case

36. Especially Kuyper accents this connection. He is of the opinion that the Church from the beginning considered *sub Pontio Pilato* not something incidental but profoundly *significant* (*E Voto*, I, 411). Christ's death is a judicial homicide by a temporal judge who was the bearer of God's majesty and whom the Lord had given "power" and authority. The verdict was not a human opinion but a judgment pronounced in the name of God. Even though the verdict is unjust it still is done in the name of the Lord. *Our* judgment is laid on the Immanuel. "If you cannot see God's judgment in that of Pilate, how on earth could it deliver you then?" (p. 416).

is no longer restricted to the scope of a purely Jewish controversy, and this John relates to Christ's own prophecy.

This is not incidental even though, humanly considered, the whole procedure is full of arbitrariness. But as far as Christ is concerned nothing incidental took place during this last phase of his suffering. There is a divine "must" also in the fact that not his own people[37] but a temporal judge condemned him. Christ's suffering could not remain restricted to the circle of his own people but must enter the realm of the temporal jurisdiction, that of the judge and the government; that is to say, of the judicial authority, which God himself has established there. *The Son of Man will be exalted also through the sentence Pilate passes on him.* He is rejected by his people, but in the world he is judicially condemned according to his own prophecy: "Behold, we go up to Jerusalem; and the Son of man shall be delivered unto the chief priests and the scribes; and they shall condemn him to death, *and shall deliver him unto the Gentiles* . . ." (Mark 10:33, 34; cf. K. Schilder, *Christ in His Suffering* [not a *casus judaicus,* but *oecumenicus*]). Christ's suffering under Pontius Pilate is thus part of God's plan, and his hand is active providentially in this phase as well. When the Church specifically mentions Pilate's name, then, she does not merely intend to guard against docetism. She points, rather, to the last stage of Christ's way to the cross, in which the final decision is made and the irrevocable verdict is given: the sentence of the judge. And so the Church confesses: "who suffered under Pontius Pilate." There is an unfathomable relationship between this verdict, this judgment, and the grace of God, the deliverance from judgment. For this reason Pilate's name will always call for special attention.

(2) In the Creed *sub Pontio Pilato* is followed by the Lord's *being crucified.* Again we are not concerned with a symbolic-historical analysis, but with the Church's overall viewpoint of Christ's suffering which the Creed depicts in its various historical

37. Cf. John 7:30, "They sought therefore to take him: and no man laid his hand on him, because his hour was not yet come"; cf. 8:20. This clearly evidences a divine prevention. See Grosheide, *Comm.* I, on John 7:30. It is different in Luke 22:53, "but this is your hour, and the power of darkness." *Their* hour coincides with *Christ's* hour: "Jesus knowing that his hour was come that he should depart out of this world" (John 13:1).

phases. The Heidelberg Catechism continues by asking immediately whether it is significant that Christ was crucified rather than dying a natural death (Q. 39). The Catechism does indeed refer to something historical, but it seeks to understand the *significance* of this history, namely of this kind of death which was the result of human decisions. The Catechism's answer points out again, as in the case of *sub Pontio Pilato,* that *God's* action crosses that of *man*: "Yes, there is; for thereby I am assured, that he took on him the curse which lay upon me; for the death of the cross was accursed of God." It appears that the Catechism is not concerned with an allegorical or semi-allegorical exegesis but with the understanding of faith, which speaks of the cross as a *comfort* and *assurance.*

The question must be asked whether this is simply a devotional intepretation or a correct scriptural interpretation of the cross, because this comfort is connected not only with Christ's death as such but with a specific kind of death, namely the death *of the cross.* This calls our attention to Philippians: "becoming obedient even unto death, *yea, the death of the cross*" (2:8). This verse not only points out how deeply Christ humbled himself but stresses particularly that his was the death *of the cross.*[38] It is evident that Scripture points out the special significance of the death of the cross because Paul sees a specific relationship between *cross* and *curse* and therefore it is such a comfort to the believers. He says: "Christ redeemed us from the curse of the law, having become a curse for us; for it is written, Cursed is every one that hangeth on a tree" (Gal. 3:13; cf. Deut. 21:23).[39] Paul considers it more than just incidental that the decision was made to crucify Jesus Christ. He sees a close connection with Deuteronomy which, to be sure, does not directly speak of crucifixion but at least of hanging. In this connection the law decrees that the body must be buried before sundown because: "he that is hanged is accursed of God; that thou defile not thy land which Jehovah thy God giveth thee for an inheritance" (Deut. 21:23). This judicial act after death implied, by its spectacular character, a special public degradation: "it meant that the intensifying of the capital punishment by this

38. Cf. Greijdanus, *Comm.,* p. 196: "*and that even* the death of the cross."
39. Gal. 3:13, Deut. 21:23. Cf. J. B. Lightfoot, *St. Paul's Epistle to the Galatians,* 1884, p. 153: "Again and again doubtless, as he argued in the synagogues, St. Paul must have had these words cast in his teeth."

additional hanging as an awe-inspiring spectacle must be considered as a direct divine judgment."[40]

This law is meant to prevent the defilement and desecration of the holy land, since this kind of punishment is a manifestation of God's dreadful judgment. Paul refers to these words when he says that Christ has become a curse *for us.* This very worst and very last thing happened to Christ, not as in Deuteronomy after his death, but in the one act of his crucifixion. Paul emphasizes the specific manner of Christ's death in a context which is wholly soteriological. He speaks of the curse which rests on transgressing the law. There is only one way to escape this curse and God's judgment: not by works but by faith in Christ, who redeemed us from the curse by becoming a curse himself and that *for us.*[41] His death occasioned a tremendous change: those who were under the curse are now redeemed. Here we see the radiant *light* of the cross: the delivering from the bondage of the curse.

Paul points out that Christ did not merely die, but that he died *in this manner* to show that God's curse was laid on him. And that is what the Jewish people wanted. The cross was the culmination point in the actions of men, the converging point of historical and psychological lines which seemingly were very arbitrarily drawn; but this arbitrariness is assimiliated by and made subservient to God's action. In all of Christ's suffering we plainly see the thread of God's providence. For crucifixion was not a Jewish form of punishment. Blasphemy was to be punished by stoning, not by hanging.[42] In their bitter opposition to Christ the Jews called upon the Romans to crucify Christ, a form of punishment which the Romans in turn had adopted from elsewhere. The Jewish people asked specifically for this heathenish punishment because they knew what "hanging on a tree" implied according to their law (Matt. 27:23, 26; John 19:6). Christ's *passio magna* is determined by the raging passion of the opposition. By demanding and inflicting this form of punishment it was not only Israel that got even with

40. E. König, *Das Deuteronomium,* 1917, p. 154. Cf. Josh. 10:26; II Sam. 4:12; I Sam. 31:10; Num. 25:4. LXX: "κεκατηραμενος ὑπο θεοῦ." Vulgate "maledictus a deo." Cf. Zahn: "As a warning" (*Comm.*, p. 156).
41. ἐξαγοράζειν. Cf. Zahn, p. 155.
42. "And he that blasphemeth the name of Jehovah, he shall surely be put to death; all the congregation shall certainly stone him" (Lev. 24:16).

Christ, but according to their religious concept also the God who made this law, and they gladly accepted the responsibility for this execution. They openly rendered Christ's whole Messianic dignity an absurdity. To Israel, Christ's death on the cross was their greatest victory.

But all these factors are, so to speak, only the "inside" of God's powerful doings which manifest, in the anti-messianic desire for Christ's crucifixion, the reality of the curse when this curse was laid on him whom God *made to be sin* (II Cor. 5:21) to reconcile the world unto God. But *in* this curse the *blessing* is revealed: "that upon the Gentiles might come the blessing of Abraham in Christ Jesus" (Gal. 3:14).

The explanation given by the Catechism is, therefore, wholly in harmony with Scripture. Like Paul, it denies that there is anything incidental in Christ's death.[43] God's activity manifests itself in this terror through everything that men do.[44] In

43. Cf. also John 18:32 concerning Pilate's advice to the Jews to judge him themselves and the Jews' refusal, "That the word of Jesus might be fulfilled, which he spake, signifying by what manner of death he should die." The transition from Jewish to Gentile jurisdiction is at the same time a transition from *stoning* to *crucifixion*. Cf. C. Bouma, *Korte Verklaring* on John, II, p. 163, and E. L. Smelik, *De Weg van het Woord,* p. 256: "there is a hidden power which drives Christ to the cross," and Grosheide, *Comm.,* II, p. 466. He points out that John mentions twice that Christ avoided stoning (John 8:59; 10:31). Cf. his announcing his suffering in Matt. 20:19.

44. It has always been considered remarkable that Paul writes that Christ became "a curse" for us (*κατάρα*) and that he does not write (in connection with Gal. 3:10, 13: cursed is every one . . .): "*κατάρατος ὑπὸ θεοῦ.*" According to Lightfoot, "St. Paul instinctively omits those words." Cf. Zahn (*Gal.,* pp. 156ff.) who, in my opinion, incorrectly concludes from the parallel "being made a curse" without being a sinner: "thus also as a curse, without being accursed by God" (p. 158). Zahn's exegesis is too much from a Jewish point of view. He further writes, "It was not necessary to point out to the Christian readers that Christ could be treated as a blasphemer and transgressor of the law only by violating the law and that he, being innocent, was not subject to the curse which God had placed on transgressing the law." Zahn does not fully see the close relationship between men's and God's actions in connection with the Mediator. Better is Büchsel in Kittel, TWNT, I, s.v. *ἀρά* (*κατάρα*) pp. 450, 451. Cf. Ch. de Beus, *Paulus, Apostel der Vrijheld,* 1952, p. 114, who refers to the Form for the Lord's Supper. Cf. Lightfoot, *op. cit.,* p. 140. The core of Zahn's argument is that the curse of the law (God's curse) could not strike the obedient Christ personally. Zahn's exegesis is based on this assumption.

this way Christ's death on the cross could become the occasion of a world-historical controversy between Jewry and Christendom, with both parties appealing to Scripture. There is such a close relationship between men's actions and interpretations on the one hand, and God's actions and viewpoint on the other, that Peter can write, "who his own self bare our sins in his own body upon the tree" (I Pet. 2:24). This close relationship results in still another: that between *stripes* and *healing* (I Pet. 2:24 and Isa. 53:5). That is what Paul, and the Church with him, clearly saw in Christ's suffering. The Catechism's answer, "Yes; for thereby I am assured" is the *echo* of what Paul says about salvation. This does not thereby make Christ's historic death on the cross merely subjective, but it is the *acknowledgment* of the reconciliation, the exchange, the substitution. The historicity of the cross does not make it coldly objective, for the cross is God's marvelous way of *redeeming the world.*

As we have seen, both the Heidelberg Catechism and Reformed theology when explaining the Creed strongly emphasize the intertwining of God's and man's activity in the work of reconciliation. It is important to note that this emphasis is based on Scripture as a whole, not on a few isolated texts. In particular, the Old Testament provides a necessary background for the understanding of the cross. Christ himself was conscious of God's activity in and through men's actions when he recalled the Old Testament psalms and prophecies concerning his suffering; for instance, Psalm 22 (Matt. 27:46, Mark 15:34 [not in Luke and John]).[45] And the Gospel writers are reminded of this psalm when they see how his clothes are being divided and he is the object of scorn (Ps. 22:6-8, 28-30).[46] These and many other references reveal that Christ's whole suffering was not something arbitrary, and therefore that it was God's doing.

Some have concluded from these elements in the suffering accounts that they were legendary stories, since they allegedly resemble Paul's interpretation in Galatians 3, and that these stories have no historical foundation. Bertram, for one, holds that the cross was a mystery to the infant Church at first, and that gradually it added other features which originated from

45. Psalm 22:1; cf. Mark 14:27, "All ye shall be offended: for it is written, I shall smite the shepherd, and the sheep shall be scattered" (cf. Zech. 13); Matt. 26:15 and Zech. 11:12.

46. Mark 15:46 and John 19:24 with explicit reference to Ps. 22:18, "They part my garments among them, and cast lots upon my vesture."

a *cultic* interest. "The Old Testament prophecy was read into the account and from this again more tradition originated, so that finally the entire drama of the cross was seen as a whole series of fulfilled prophecies and the question even arose whether something had possibly been still overlooked."[47] He concludes "that we can attach very little historical value to it all." Much of it is uncertain "since it is either burdened with Old Testament prophecy or obscured by attached legends" (p. 79). The few known facts were supplemented with what was found in prophecy, which was necessary because "the uncertainty of the past could not be confirmed any more."[48]

Bertram arbitrarily corrupts and tampers with the suffering accounts when he speaks of the fulfillment and its implications as reconstructed history arising from a cultic consciousness."[49] That which evoked the Church's adoration — God's activity in cross and resurrection — is explained as a construction originating from a Christ-cult. "The story concerning Christ's suffering is actually a cult story of Christendom" (*ibid.*, p. 96). Such an approach leads to fatal consequences if applied to other episodes of history which Bertram accepts simply as a matter of course. He excludes *a priori* the possibility of a real connection between the Old and New Testaments, between the curse of the law and Christ's becoming a curse, between betrayal among Israel and Judas' betrayal (Acts 1:20 and Ps. 69:25; 109:8), between the psalms of suffering and Christ's *passio magna*, between the prophecy concerning Christ's bones not being broken and the fact that they were not broken.[50] According to him, the Church resorted to the "prophetic proof" to offset the *skandalon* of the death of the cross.[51]

47. G. Bertram, *Die Leidensgeschichte Jesu und der Christuscult. Eine formgeschichtliche Untersuchung*, 1922, pp. 74, 75.
48. *Ibid.*, p. 79. "Umbildung" — a reconstruction — e.g., the drink which Christ was offered (p. 80).
49. *Ibid.*, p. 84. For instance the ἐμπαιζειν (p. 85) the non-breaking of his bones and the spear thrust: "This representation belongs to the realm of phantasy" (p. 85); cf. also "the legendary story of the two thieves" (p. 89) and the "contrast motif."
50. John 19:33, 36; Ps. 34:20. Cf. the motivation in John 19:33 (and saw that he was dead already) and Exod. 12:46 with regard to the passover lamb: "neither shall ye break a bone thereof."
51. Behind Bertram's method is his opinion that history and religion are incompatible (p. 79). Cf. the criticism of rendering the accounts legendary in J. Schniewind, *Das Ev. nach Markus*, p. 199.

This view is diametrically opposed to the confession of the Church. To her the *skandalon* of the cross is not removed *by way of an interpretation* which places the dark cross in a "higher" light; rather, she sees the cross as an act of God by which the word of the cross becomes the word of salvation to anyone who believes.

Dibelius correctly points out that, given the Old Testament data, no one could possibly deny that Christ was a historic person.[52] It is moreover true that to the Church this connection with the Old Testament is of great importance[53] and that the Word of God has kept many from stumbling over the *skandalon,* but the question is: *is* there really such a connection, or was it simply created by the Church in order to get out of an impasse concerning Christ's suffering and death? We have here either God's soteriological activity or the *a posteriori* creation of the primitive Church. Everything depends on

52. M. Dibelius, *Die Formgeschichte des Evangeliums,* 1933², p. 189.
53. "Jesus' suffering was found to be pre-portrayed in certain O.T. texts – Ps. 22, 31, 69; Isa. 53" and these O.T. references were then quoted. It had been . . . foretold, and "all that was done to Jesus – capture, mistreatment, parting of raiments, revilement – was then sanctioned in the history of salvation, so that all of it was according to the will of God" (*ibid.,* p. 185). Compare, in this connection, Bultmann's article on "Prophecy and Fulfillment" in *Glauben und Verstehen,* II (1952), 162-186, which deals with the various texts that had been fulfilled. He speaks of "the impossibility of the N.T. and traditional conceptions" in many instances, e.g., Isa. 7:14 – Matt. 1:23; Jer. 31:15 – Matt. 2:17; Isa. 53:4 – Matt. 8:17; Zech. 11:12f. – Matt. 27:9f., etc. The N.T. authors are simply "reading into" the text what they already know (p. 167). According to Bultmann the connection between "prophecy" and "fulfillment" consists simply in this: the O.T. Jewish prophecy *is* fulfilled in the N.T. Church but "it is such in its contradiction, in its failures" (p. 183). How easily Bultmann ignores the connection as it is expressed in the N.T. is evident especially when he, to mention just one thing, writes concerning Isa. 53:4 and Matt. 8:17, "The Servant of the Lord in Isa. 53:4 is loaded down with afflictions and does not remove them as does the healing Jesus (Matt 8:17)" (p. 165). This evidences an *a priori* obstacle to seeing a connection. When Bultmann searches for the *kriterium,* then he indeed touches upon an important question which urges to caution in pointing out *signa divinae providentiae.* Cf. E. Fascher, "Das Weib des Pilatus," *Theol. Lit. Zeitung,* 1947, pp. 201-204. That the problem of demythologizing Claudia Procula is not as simple as Fascher supposes seems to me obvious on the basis of the entire story of Jesus' suffering. (Cf. F. W. Grosheide, H. N. Ridderbos, and K. Schilder.)

this, because the meaning, the *divine meaning* of Christ's suffering is at stake.

The Church has always believed that the main question with respect to the cross was not a matter of an interpretation of the *skandalon* outside of a true foundation in history itself, but the relationship between the divine and human activity, in other words, the fulfillment of the promise in the reality of the Messiah. The New Testament often shows this connection clearly and in various ways, but then again only by simply stating the facts. It does so, however, in such a way that from the context it is evident that God has his hand in all that men do, even if it is not expressly stated.[54] God's activity is particularly evident in the cross, according to the Scriptures, so that it is no wonder that the Church has always *gloried* in the cross.

Although we are not called upon to give a historical analysis of the Church's creed and what she originally meant by it, we still want to point out that the Creed mentions the cross without speaking of its meaning in this article. Kattenbusch considers it remarkable, this "absence of every indication as to the object or the meaning of the death on the cross."[55] This, however, is not so remarkable because it is true also with respect to *sub Pontio Pilato,* the "death" and the "burial." The answer is that *credo* – "I believe" – prefaces the entire creed. This indicates that the *Church's* object is not to memorize some more or less important facts, but to set forth a vision of faith regarding the *meaning* of the cross. Moreover, Kattenbusch gives the answer himself when he writes, "It must have been immediately clear what it implied to believe in a 'crucified' Messiah."[56] I believe ". . . in Jesus Christ, who was crucified." With these words the Church of all ages speaks of the meaning of this darkness, the curse and forsakenness. It is for this reason

54. Cf. Christ's crucifixion on Golgotha outside the city (John 19:17f.; cf. C. Bouma, *Korte Verklaring* on John, II, 176), whereas later on it is said (Heb. 12:12) that Jesus's death without the gate has great significance.
55. F. Kattenbusch, *Das Apostolische Symbol,* II (1900), 631.
56. *Ibid.,* p. 631: "It is remarkable that mention is made of [Christ's] crucifixion and not of [his] death. Hence this peculiar manner of death must have specific significance for the belief in his Messianic κυριότης." In the light of the testimony of the New Testament *crucifixus* is by no means strange and remarkable (cf. I Cor. 15:3-4).

that she in faith commemorates the Man of Sorrows in his humiliation unto death, yea, the death of the cross.

(3) It is quite remarkable that the Apostolic Creed adds "dead" after "crucified," the more so since the original *Apostolicum* had only "buried" after *crucifixus.* Historically speaking it remains a difficult question why "dead" should have been added later.[57] After the Heidelberg Catechism has dealt with the significance of the cross, it follows the sequence of the *textus receptus* of the Creed and continues: "Why was it necessary for Christ to humble himself even unto death?" Obviously the Catechism is not interested in a scientific-historical answer but in a confession of faith, even though this will simply confirm the faith of the Church of all ages. Even the question implies that it is a humiliating death. Christ's historical death is at once conceived of as part of his humiliation in connection with Philippians 2. After having called specific attention to the fact that Christ's end was occasioned by "even the death of the cross," the Catechism further adds the answer of faith: that Christ had to humiliate himself unto death. Expressing this necessity already in the question indicates how much the Catechism wants to emphasize the aspect of *confession.* It is not interested in an explanation of the word *mortuus* in the old Creed, but in what the Church of all ages has to confess *according to the Scriptures* concerning Christ's death. As with respect to the expression *sub Pontio Pilato,* so with regard to the term *crucifixus,* it emphasizes Christ's substitutionary suffering *for us* and thus its soteriological aspect. Again a historical fact — Christ's death — is seen in the light of God's activity. The Catechism clearly emphasizes the relation between the death of Christ and the believers' life. Christ's death is seen in the light of God's justice. It cannot be explained in terms of the tragedy of life or the general transitoriness of man's existence, but only as his standing before the face of the Father. We are dealing with history, to be sure, but what kind of history!

A neutral approach to this death results in nothing but a drama of the man Jesus of Nazareth who considers himself the Messiah and who is being delivered by his people to the heathen judge who condemns him to death. Faith, however, sees in it the fulfillment of prophecy and the realization of the Messiah. We are dealing with the history of salvation and grace and with the dying wheat that bears fruit.

The Catechism accentuates this in the question: "Why must we also die, since Christ died for us?" Christ's dying for us (Q. 42) proves to be a further interpretation of the satisfaction for our sins mentioned in Question 40. This is a pertinent question: Why must we still die? Has that not become superfluous?

The answer to this question can hardly be called exact. This is quite remarkable, since the Catechism usually answers its questions very much to the point. Question 42 does not give an explanation of our still having to die, but instead, it offers the comfort of Christ's death over against the transiency of our existence. "Our death is not a satisfaction for our sins, but only an abolishing of sin, and a passing into eternal life."

The meaning of this answer is clear. It pictures death – our death – as being exempted from the sentence expressed in Question 40, namely the satisfaction of the justice and truth of God, and is now only a passing into eternal life. This answer is backed by the testimony of Scripture. There can be joy in our heart because we are able to die without having to pay the penalty, and without judgment. There is indeed a close connection between this comfort for the believers and what Paul writes in I Corinthians 15:54: "Death is swallowed up in victory." This is an eschatological word which will be realized as soon as "this corruptible shall have put on incorruption, and this mortal shall have put on immortality." Nevertheless this is still the most challenging word ever spoken by a human being – "O death, where is thy victory? O death, where is thy sting?" (I Cor. 15:55).

The reason Paul can speak thus is contained in what follows: "The sting of death is sin; and the power of sin is the law" (vs. 56). Death derives its real power from sin and it is this sin for which Christ has atoned.[57] That accounts for the change in evaluating death as we encounter it in I Corinthians 15 and the echo thereof in Lord's Day XVI. Christ's death, which is the propitiation for sin, is placed as a bright light illuminating the gloom of the believers' death. That is the way the Church sees Christ's death – as the dying grain of wheat.

After "dead" follows "buried." We again proceed from the explanation given by the Catechism. The explanation of *sepultus* contains a remarkable aspect. Whereas in considering the phrases *sub Pontio Pilato,* "crucified," "dead," and afterwards

57. Cf. Kittel, TWNT, s.v., κέντρον, and Rom. 5:12.

also the phrase "descended into hell," the Catechism immediately places the aspect of satisfaction in the foreground, now, all of a sudden, this approach is abandoned. There is a marked interruption in the explanation of the Creed. The question why Christ was buried is answered thus: "To prove thereby that he was really dead." This approaches the subject from an entirely different angle. No mention is made whatsoever that this was "for us" or that it had any bearing on our salvation. Christ's burial is simply seen as an historical fact and as a proof that he truly died. This explanation could be called an anti-docetic interpretation. It need not surprise us that this part of the Catechism has often been criticized. It has been pointed out that the explanation the Catechism gives in Lord's Day XVI, even though not incorrect, is far from complete.

This criticism is motivated by the conviction that Christ's burial means far more than just a sign that he was really dead. Kuyper considered this explanation too short, "and thereby causing misunderstanding."[58] It was also "too shallow." Convincing proof, of Christ's death, according to Kuyper, is furnished by the piercing spear as recorded in the Gospel: "And he that hath seen hath borne witness, and his witness is true: and he knoweth that he saith true, that ye also may believe" (John 19:35). But "nowhere is the burial itself mentioned as proof for his death." According to Kuyper, Ursinus himself sensed the weakness of the Catechism in this respect when he further described the object of Jesus' burial as (1) the proof of his death; (2) a deep humiliation unto the shame of the grave; (3) a sanctification of our graves.

Thus we see that Reformed theologians such as, for instance, Kuyper interpret *sepultus* in the same manner as the Catechism explains the surrounding articles. Kuyper considers it in immediate connection with the results of sin. The grave is the sinner's deepest humiliation. According to Kuyper, Christ would not be a complete Savior for us if he had not descended into the grave.[59] Kuyper particularly opposes the idea, current also among Reformed theologians, that the grave was part of the Lord's exaltation. According to this viewpoint, Christ's humiliation ended with his death on the cross and the "it is finished" of his mediatorial work. Kuyper considers this untenable be-

58. A. Kuyper, *E Voto,* I, 438.
59. *Ibid.,* p. 440.

cause "it is finished" indicates only that Christ was approaching the end, and, moreover, scripture always considers the grave as part of the curse. Kuyper takes great pains to picture this concretely: "Lying in the grave, he felt, fathomed, bore the anxiety, notwithstanding the fact that his separated human spirit was in paradise. And when on the third morning he arises, then this is not an awakening without knowing what had happened to him during those three days, but it is a conscious proceeding from the bowels of the earth, as Jonah proceeded from the belly of the fish." So Kuyper definitely considers Christ's burial and state of death part of his state of humiliation. Just as the Catechism points out the relationship between Pilate's judgment and our acquittal, between the cross and our being freed from the curse, between Christ's death and our passing into eternal life, so does Kuyper with respect to the connection between Christ's grave and ours.

Bavinck, too, without referring to the Catechism, thinks along the same lines. Christ's burial has "a specific meaning. It is not only proof that he really died and therefore also rose from the dead, but its specific significance is that Christ, although committing his spirit into the hands of his Father, who received him into paradise, was for three days subject to the state of death and belonged to the realm of death and thus bore the punishmen of sin."[60]

Junius speaks of Christ's *duplex obedientia*: "*vel potius duae partes*: *obedientia vitae et mortis seu obedientia ante mortem et in morte*."[61] Rivetus in the Synopsis XXVII and IV speaks of those stages in the state of humiliation as *passio magna,* among which he also counts Christ's burial, while in Synopsis XXII he deals with the *sepultura* in which "*significata est*: *corporis peccati mortificatio et abolitio*." At this time – *triduum mortis* – Christ "*velut in potestate ac vinculis mortis versatus est Dei filius, quasi devictus et exanimis jacens, cum tamen mortem vinceret et eius vincula disrumperet*" (Synopsis XVII, XV).

But especially Calvin points out elements different from those expressed by the Catechism. When dealing with the phrase "dead and buried" he says, "This shows again how in every respect he took our place to pay the price of our salvation"

60. H. Bavinck, *Gereformeerde Dogmatiek*, III, 401f. Cf. H. Bastingius, *Verclaringe van de Catechismus der Christelijke religie* (ed. Rutgers, 1893), p. 161, who also mentions the sanctification of our graves.
61. Junius, *Opera Theologica Selecta* (ed. Kuyper), p. 198.

(*Institutes*, II, XVI, 7). Christ surrendered himself to the power of death in our stead in order to deliver us from it. He tasted death for everyone, and that took place *by the grace of God* (Heb. 2:9), which made this death of significance and value to others.[62] That is to say, by his death he destroyed him who had the power of death – the devil – and delivered all who through fear of death were all their lifetime subject to bondage (Heb. 2:14-15). Calvin says in connection with Hebrews 2:9 that Christ's death offers a double benefit: the deliverance from death to which we were subjected, and the mortification of our flesh.

Calvin refers also to our being buried with him, as mentioned in Paul's epistle to the Romans, and so he sees further consequences than does the Catechism, which does not mention these elements at all. In fact, all of Reformed theology considers Christ's burial part of his vicarious suffering and death. It is considered the decisive final phase of his sin-bearing, and as the wages of sin unto death.

It is true, we shall never be able to fathom the state of Christ's death since it is part of the mystery of his person – *vere Deus, vere homo* – and Scripture certainly nowhere gives us an analysis by which we can synthesize clearly "paradise" and the state of death (cf. Luke 23:43). The Church, however, understood clearly that she could incorporate Christ's death and burial into her message of God's grace by which we are delivered from the fear of death. In this way the Church both confessed and preached Christ's death and burial (I Cor. 15:4). It is thus that his life ended in the way of humiliation. We still see men's activity even in his burial and the watch at his grave. In the garden of Joseph of Arimathaea the way of humiliation is still visible, even though we can only stammer with respect to Christ's *status mortis*, as does the Belgic Confession in Article 19 in which the oneness of Christ's person is confessed in these words: "Therefore that which he, when dying, commended into the hands of his Father, was a real human spirit, departing from his body. But in the meantime the divine nature always remained united with the human, even when he lay in the grave."

It is clear that here we reach the limits of our understanding

62. Grosheide; cf. Van Oyen: "Through the grace of God by his death he removed the sentence of death."

and that we must simply accept the comfort of this ultimate humiliation, which is terminated only by an act of God and transformed into exaltation.

Scripture sheds some light on this burial of Christ. Already in Isaiah 53 we read that the Servant of the Lord – the Man of Sorrows – is cut off out of the land of the living. "And they made his grave with the wicked, and with a rich man in his death; because [KJV] he had done no violence, neither was any deceit in his mouth" (Isa. 53:9). Isaiah speaks of this grave with the wicked in connection with the judgment executed upon the Man of Sorrows, for it is preceded by the words: "for the transgression of my people to whom the stroke was due." Isaiah wants to bring out the deep humiliation of the Man of Sorrows, and this humiliation means also that he is made like unto the wicked who are subject to the condemnation of the judge. This mysterious equation with the wicked sends the Servant of the Lord to his death.

Isaiah adds immediately, however, that he made his grave with the *rich* in his death, *because* he had done no violence, neither was any deceit in his mouth. Every attempt has been made to explain the connection in verse 9. One of these explanations is that the word "rich" forms a parallel with "wicked." However, for one who cannot see any basis for such a presentation the question remains what, then, this contrast means. The meaning becomes clear only when the humiliation of the Servant of the Lord is seen as the fulfillment of prophecy. We read in Matthew 27 that Joseph of Arimathaea took the body of Christ and wrapped it in clean linen and laid it in his new tomb which he had hewn out of the rock. This is the fulfillment of Isaiah's prophecy. Here, as in other occurrences, it is God's providence and good pleasure that direct this equation. On the cross and in his death Christ has been put on a level with the malefactors, but at his burial there is an unexpected new element: the burial by Joseph of Arimathaea. While it is true that Christ is still in humiliation because the burial takes place, nevertheless this places the last phase of the humiliation in a different light. We can already discern a glimmering of God's favor, just as God's signs at the cross point to the great significance of this utmost humiliation. Isaiah sees a connection between the grave of the Man of Sorrows and Christ's innocence.

The cross represents not innocence but guilt, which is born by the Lamb of God. Schilder leaves the question whether there is a connection between Isaiah 53 and Christ's burial in Joseph's tomb unanswered. He says – correctly – that the New Testament does not thus quote Isaiah 53.[63] However, when we see how often connections are pointed out between the Old and the New Testaments in the light of fulfilled prophecy, we must agree with J. Ridderbos and Young that this element was also contained already in the prophecy concerning the Man of Sorrows. This light, however, does not elevate the burial as such to exaltation. Christ himself spoke of this burial when he announced his suffering, and when he spoke of what the adulteress in Simon's house had done as a preparation for his burial (Matt. 26:12). To the scribes and Pharisees he mentioned the sign of Jonah: "For as Jonah was three days and three nights in the belly of the whale; so shall the Son of man be three days and three nights in the heart of the earth" (Matt. 12:40; Luke 11:30). In the apostolic preaching, too, mention is made of Christ's sepulchre, not only in a historical connection but also in connection with the state of Christ's death (Acts 13:29). After Christ's crucifixion and death have been pictured as acts of men, the resurrection is called a divine act: "having loosed the pangs of death: because it was not possible that he should be holden of it" (Acts 2:24). This "not possible" was from the beginning the reflection of God's good pleasure and also of the power of Christ's suffering and death, which were full of the fruit of his satisfaction. The definite action of men (three days and three nights)[64] is enveloped by the definite action of God which becomes gloriously manifest precisely in what men do.

Peter quotes Psalm 16 here, which, essentially does not refer to David but to Christ: "Because thou wilt not leave my soul unto Hades, Neither wilt thou give thy Holy One to see corruption" (Acts 2:27). Peter sees Christ's resurrection as the fulfillment of the phrase: "his soul was not left in hell" (Acts 2:31). The reality of death and burial contains God's *new beginning*, and thus the humiliation borders on the exaltation. We may not indulge in all kinds of prying questions, as has so often been done, which evidence more interest in the anthropology than in the soteriology in this humiliation. We could, by analogy, raise the same curious questions with respect to Lazarus' death,

63. K. Schilder, *op. cit.*, III, 538. Bavinck, however, mentions Isa. 53:9 in connection with Christ's burial.
64. H. N. Ridderbos, *Mattheus,* I, on Matt. 12:40.

and his return to life, and the time in between, but Scripture simply ignores such questions and calls our attention only to the power of Christ's suffering, evident already then and there, and which does not halt before the gates of death. Scripture points out only the categories of God's justice and the wages of sin resulting in Christ's utter isolation – his being cut off out of the land of the living. So the Church confesses: "who suffered . . . ; was crucified, dead, *and buried.*" After that follows the exaltation – the resurrection. And this exalted Lord says: "I was dead, and am alive" (Rev. 2:8; cf. Col. 1:18, Rev. 1:5, "the first begotten of the dead"). "I was *dead*" is a word from his own holy mouth. Before his resurrection there is nothing but an interminable road of suffering which extends into the inner chambers of death. It was, perhaps, bold language which Kuyper used when he spoke of Christ's "feeling, fathoming, bearing the pangs of death," but it is at least closer to our heart than the description of the state of his death as "a vague nothingness." Christ's burial, confirmed and sealed his death, and it was only God's activity unto salvation in this death that vanquished the pangs of death.

It is therefore consistent with Lord's Day XVI of the Catechism to thank and praise him also for this isolation, because now we may, as a result, appropriate the comfort of Psalm 23: "Though I walk through the valley of the shadow of death, I will fear no evil; for thou art with me; thy rod and thy staff, they comfort me."

Finally we wish to examine the meaning of the confession of Christ's *descent into hell.* We realize that we are touching upon profound questions here, and that it is necessary to know exactly what we confess with these words, which also meant to convey a message to the world. There is, however, great difference of opinion concerning the interpretation of this article of the Creed. This is partly because the word *descensus* was not in the Creed originally but was added later.[65]

65. It is not even certain when this addition entered the Creed. According to Rufinus (410) the confession of the church of Aquileja contained the clause *descendit ad inferna,* while in any case it was in the confessions of Sirmium, 359; Nice, 359; and Constantinople, 360 (*eis ta katachthonta kathelthonta*). Concerning the meaning Rufinus says that it seems to be the same as of the word *sepultus.* In that case the

Obviously, we must make a clear distinction between the symbolic-historical and the dogmatic problem, because the symbolic-historical question concerning the original meaning of *descensus* in the Creed cannot be decisive with respect to the dogmatical consideration of the *passio magna*. We are not interested in a historical conclusion but in the meaning of this clause in connection with the teachings of Scripture. It is not always easy, however, to see clearly the distinction between the different theories and ideas concerning Christ's descent into hell.

It makes quite a difference whether we confess, as Rome does, that this *descensus* was a local descent[66] or whether we deny this. Moreover, time and again the question was raised whether the *descensus* must be considered as a phase of Christ's humiliation or of his exaltation. The *Catechismus Romanus* teaches that the object of Christ's descent into hell was to announce to the demons the delivery of the fathers from the *limbus patrum*. Roman Catholic theologians in particular speak of the glorious and mighty revelation of Christ's saving power in the nether regions.[67] Thomas Aquinas considered it fitting that Christ descended into hell (*Summa Theol.*, Pt. III, Q. 52, 1). As it was fitting that Christ died in order to save us from death, so it was fitting that he descended into hell in order to save us from such a descent (*conveniens*). He also speaks of the *descensus* as the liberation of the prisoners, so that we find elements in his conception of both the humiliation and the exaltation. In Lutheran theology we meet the same tension, with the emphasis on triumph.[68]

---

descensus would not be a new article but a further clarification. However, there was a general consciousness of the curiousness that *descensus* had been added.

66. E.g., against Abelard at the Concilium Senonense (1140-41). His position is condemned as one of the *Errores Petri Abelard*: "Quod anima Christi per se non descendit ad inferos, sed per potentiam tantum." Pope Innocent II confirmed this condemnation at the 4th Lateran Council in 1215: "descendit ad inferos, resurrexit a mortuis, sed descendit in anima et resurrexit in carne."
67. B. Bartmann, *Lehrbuch der Dogmatik,* I, 409ff.
68. For the position of the Greek Church see Gass, *Symboliek der Griekse Kerk,* p. 179. The object is: triumph and delivery.

From the discussions in the 16th century it becomes evident that there was also a tension between the *descensus* being humiliation or exaltation, which occasioned an official pronouncement in the *Formula Concordiae.* The controversy centered particularly around Aepinus and

We are not interested, however, in finding the precise interpretation of the *descensus* in the Creed. We are now dealing with Christ's suffering, and we wish only to point out that in the interpretation of Christ's descent, his humiliation has been emphasized.

This is particularly true in Reformed theology. Already Calvin, who connects the dogmatic solution with the historic interpretation, rejects the idea that the clause *descensus ad inferos* states something new, because in that case a clear statement ("buried") would be explained by a less clear one. He considers the *descensus* in connection with Christ's suffering. Nothing would have been accomplished (finished) if Christ had only died. He had to undergo the severity of the divine wrath and therefore he had to battle the hosts of hell and the terror of eternal death. It is in the *descensus* that Christ bore this death.[69] He not only paid the price for our deliverance with his body, but also in his soul he bore the fearsome torments of a lost sinner. That is why Peter says that he has borne the pangs of death. Not just death, but he was wrapped in the sorrows and pangs of death which ensued from the curse and wrath of God and which culminated, according to Calvin, in the terrible forsakenness on the cross.[70]

Parsimonius. The former in his commentary on Ps. 16 considered the *descensus* part of the satisfaction and as *ultimus gradus* of the humiliation (*extrema pars obedientiae et satisfactionis*). The valuable ideas of Aepinus were attacked on the basis of Christ's word: It is finished. It was a battle between *Consummatists* and *Infernalists*. The *Formula Concordia* admonished to simplicity of faith and referred to the well-known Easter sermon of Luther in which he said that we must believe "quod tota persona, Deus et homo, post sepulturam ad inferos descenderit, Satan devicerit, potestatem inferorum eveerterit et diabolo omnem vim et potentiam eripuirit" (F.C.P., II, Art. IX). Loofs thinks that this statement of the Formula Concordia "dogmatizes one of Luther's explanations, which Luther did not mean to be dogmatic at all but simply illustrative" (Loofs, *D.G.*, p. 924) because he stated in the same sermon expressly that he used metaphors and that the descent "did not take place bodily because he remained in the grave during those three days."

69. To hinge one's argument in favor of Christ's exaltation on the fact that in the Creed the *descensus* follows the burial Calvin considers ridiculous, because after the Creed has explained what Christ had to suffer publicly, it now adds the invisible and incomprehensible judgment which he underwent before God. Obviously this does not prove that the Creed indeed meant to imply that.

70. Bavinck has still another interpretation of the Creed by way of a "supplement and enlargement" of Calvin's explanation, which he bases on

The most striking explanation, however, is the one given by the Catechism and which, in essence, is similar to Calvin's. The Catechism puts this in a peculiar form. The answer to the question: Why is there added, "he descended into hell?" does not just give an objective presentation of the *descensus* but accenuates the comfort contained in the depth of Christ's suffering. "That in my greatest temptations I may be assured, and wholly comfort myself in this, that my Lord Jesus Christ, by his inexpressible anguish, pains, terrors, and hellish agonies, in which he was plunged during all his sufferings, but especially on the cross, hath delivered me from the anguish and torments of hell."

This language of faith is entirely in line with the explanation of the Creed in the preceding Lord's Days – excepting that of the burial – and points out unmistakably the element of satisfaction in Christ's suffering. It is remarkable that the Catechism here speaks very personally of "me" instead of the usual plural "us." This "I" does not indicate a tendency toward individualism, but emphasizes the personal comfort which is the portion of the believer in the greatest temptations. This obviously refers to the forsakenness on the cross. The depth of this suffering is called here the "inexpressible anguish and pains" into which Christ was "plunged," whereby the Catechism refers to Matthew 26:38 (Christ's soul being exceedingly sorrowful, even unto death) and Matthew 27:46 (fourth saying on the cross). The language of the Catechism reminds us here of Calvin's, and Christ's historic suffering is seen in its comforting significance.

Gerard Brom does not agree with this viewpoint at all, nor with the wording of the Catechism: that Christ was subjected to *hellish anguish*. He calls the latter "a most dismal representation" (*Gesprek over de eenheid van de kerk,* 1946, pp. 79, 80), and contends that this disrupts the unity of the divine-human

---

the *place* of the *descensus* in the Creed and on Acts 2:27, 31; Rom. 10:7 and Eph. 4:9. He considers it the *state of death* in which Christ was between death and resurrection in order to bear the punishment of sin until the end and to deliver us from it (*Gereformeerde Dogmatiek,* III, 409). Cf. the Westminster Confession, Q. 50. The Synopsis explains the "state of death" in the same way as does the Catechism, with emphasis on the *status mortis,* but it does not reject the conception of the *descensus* as "inferni dolores et irae Dei gravitas." Conclusion: "nec inconveniens est, hos duos descensus, quod nonnulli faciunt, conjungere" (*Disp. de statu humil.,* XXVII).

person.[71] But why, then, was that not the case with all of Christ's suffering, and how must we understand Christ's question "Why hast thou forsaken me?" Both Calvin and the Catechism wish to bring out the seriousness of this saying, since between the first and last saying the Father's name departs from Christ's lips. Again and again there has been a tendency in the Church not to take Christ's forsakenness seriously enough.[72] Neither Calvin nor the Catechism, however, could see this simply as a *feeling* of forsakenness but as a real forsakenness on Christ's part, by which he as the Mediator bore the guilt of sin. And this affords the greatest comfort in the greatest temptations, also the temptation that this particular suffering and loneliness might not have been for us. This particular suffering of Christ, too, is a *substitutionary* suffering.

Calvin believed that this was the correct interpretation — historically — of the Creed. We are not so sure any more, in view of the fact that the descent was not made an article of faith until later on.[73] It would be correct, however, to say that Reformed theology and confessions have accepted Christ's de-

71. In my *Conflict with Rome,* I refer not only to Brom but to Guardini, who does far more justice to the depth of Christ's suffering.
72. Already Calvin had to defend himself against those who attacked his viewpoint. See *Institutes,* II, XVI, 12, over against those who are of the opinion that he does a "grave injustice" to Christ. Calvin, however, does not shrink back from this criticism and speaks particularly of the terror and anxiety of Christ "which is so evidently taught by the Gospel writers." The question as to why this extensive discussion is given (compared with the *Institutes* of 1536) need not be discussed here. For this see the interesting article by Paul Althaus, "Calvins Kampf um seine Lehre von Leiden Christi" in *Theol. Blätter.* Vol. 21, 1942, pp. 132-36. From this it will become clear how serious Calvin considered this matters, as is also evident from his sermons on the Man of Sorrows which he preached in 1558. Althaus quotes from these sermons: "Jesus descended into the abysses of fear and terror." Cf. the expression "terrible anxieties" which he uses against his opponents (Althaus, p. 135). We wish only to add that Althaus is quite sure that he can prove that Calvin's defense was directed against the attacks from theologians who had been influenced by Zwingli.
73. Regarding the symbolic-historic question we further refer to the series of articles by H. H. Kuyper in *De Heraut,* 1909, in which he correctly says: "It must be left up to one's personal conviction, both on historical and exegetical grounds, as to how to interpret Christ's burial and state under the dominion of death." It seems to me that the only objection one could have against Lord's Day XVI is the answer as given there.

scent without thinking of a *local* descent.[74] The object was to confess the hellish forsakenness of Christ as the Mediator between God and man, and thus an interpretation was given which was perhaps historically uncertain but nevertheless according to the Scriptures, which depict the Man of Sorrows as subject to the justice and wrath of God, being made a curse for us. When the Church continues to interpret Christ's descent as the source of comfort in our greatest temptations, she is not guilty of establishing an *Umdeuting* (reinterpretation, or forced interpretation) which is in conflict with Scripture, but her sole objective is to confess the fulness of salvation as the divine comfort resulting from Christ's sorrows and forsakenness, just as it is expressed in the Form for the Lord's Supper: "He hath humbled himself unto the deepest reproach and pains of hell, both in body and soul, on the tree of the cross, when he cried out with a loud voice, 'My God, my God! why hast thou forsaken me?' that we might be accepted of God and never be forsaken of him." Here the Church does not detract anything from the greatness of Christ's suffering nor from the mystery of his saying "My God" instead of "My Father," thus giving all who believe in him the right to pray freely and without hesitation: "Our Father, who art in heaven."

Finally, we must realize that Christ's descent is not a powerless, inactive humiliation. The great turning point in Christ's life lies between humiliation and exaltation. Yet his humiliation is full of the power of his death. Hence the signs accompanying Christ's death must also be seen in that light. All of Christ's suffering was at the same time a battle with Satan (see our last chapter). He came to annihilate the works of Satan, but the glorious victory begins already in the depths of his humiliation.

This is why the Church always speaks of Christ's suffering from the viewpoint of victory, delivery, and comfort. But all this was brought about by his humiliation, his reconciliation.

74. It has often been pointed out that the so-called *Repetitio Anhaltina* and the *Colloquium Lipsiense* have been considered Reformed confessions, as, for instance, by Niemeijer who ranks them among the Reformed Symbols. Müller, however, in his *Bek. Schriften,* 1903, omits them, since he does not consider them Reformed confessions. According to him the *Repetitio* of 1579 is not a confession, and "certainly not a Reformed one" but a personal thesis of the Philippist Wolfgang Amling. And the *Colloquium* is simply a compromise between the Lutherans and the Reformed in order to come to a merger.

Our liberation is the result of his condemnation, our life of his death. Our delivery is accomplished by his anguish, and our victory in temptations by his descent into hell. God is a God, according to Amos, who "turneth the shadow of death into the morning" (Amos 5:8). These words aptly describe the meaning of Christ's suffering. When the darkness of God's judgment surrounds him who in his humiliation called himself the Light of the world, then it is this light which breaks through this darkness. Then the meaning of his life and death becomes manifest, because "he that followeth me shall not walk in the darkness, but shall have the light of life" (John 8:12).

CHAPTER SEVEN

THE RESURRECTION OF CHRIST

WHEN discussing Christ's suffering we were mainly concerned with the meaning and significance of this historical suffering as it is so clearly depicted in the Scriptures. They clearly indicate that his suffering was not senseless, tragic, or hopeless. This becomes especially manifest in the historical fact of his passage from humiliation to exaltation, Jesus Christ's resurrection from the dead. It is impossible to separate the fact from the significance of the resurrection, as though the main thing were the idea rather than the historical reality of the resurrection. The Scriptures present the message of Christ's resurrection as being of essential and decisive significance. Again and again the apostolic message calls our attention to both the crucifixion *and* the resurrection. The fact of the cross is followed by the "but" of the fact of the resurrection. This "but" expresses the joy and superior power of God's activity in the glorification of the Son of man (Acts 2:23; 3:11f.; 4:10; 13:29).

It is God who raised Jesus from the dead (Rom. 4:24; 8:11, 34; 10:9; I Cor. 15:4, 12; II Cor. 5:15) and his resurrection was wrought through the glory of the Father (Rom. 6:4). Thus death has no more dominion over Christ, and he dies no more (Rom. 6:9). Christ's resurrection has far-reaching consequences. It is a historical fact which must be believed with the heart (Rom. 10:9). Christ's resurrection is not just one isolated fact among other unrelated facts but opens up wide perspectives because of the relationship between Christ's and our resurrection (I Cor. 6:14; II Cor. 4:14; Rom. 6:4ff.). Christ's resurrection must be held in remembrance (I Tim. 2:18) since it has a very real bearing upon the future (I Thess. 1:10). Its import is so absolute that without it our faith would be fruitless and vain and we would still be in our sins (I Cor. 15:17); if Christ be not risen then they also who are fallen asleep in Christ are lost (I Cor. 15:18) and vain would be both preaching and faith (I Cor. 15:14; cf. Kittel, s.v. κενός). To Paul everything depends upon this soteriological fact. Had not Christ truly arisen we would be "false witnesses of God; because we witnessed of God that he raised up Christ" (I Cor. 15:15).

From all these testimonies it becomes evident that the Church has always vigorously defended the historical reality of Christ's resurrection over against those who misrepresented it. Especially during the last century the wonder, and consequently the fact, of the resurrection has been considered an impossibility on rationalistic and deterministic grounds, and the Church's belief in it has been explained as a projection of the mind on the part of believing souls. This controversy focuses more and more on *the empty tomb*, not because the Church was more concerned with the historical circumstances than with her living Lord, but because the empty tomb had been *denied*. There were others who still maintained that Easter had special significance and insisted on "objective" events centered around the Lord, but who nevertheless did not see any significance in the empty grave. They considered it a certain "realism" not compatible with the nature of the Christian faith, which, according to them, should not be made dependent upon this historical fact. Paul in particular, it was said, attacked this so-called "realism" where he speaks of the historical reality of the resurrection in the most existential categories, namely, salvation and condemnation, the meaning of human life, and the life of the deceased.[1] The apostolic emphasis is in the first place on God's activity in Christ's resurrection after his humiliation, and also on the activity of Christ himself, since he had said of his resurrection:

1. Frequently it is argued that Paul does not know of the idea of the empty tomb, which, presumably, is evident from I Cor. 15, where he does not mention it at all. But this argument is untenable since it is an argument from silence. It proceeds from the assumption that Paul should have mentioned it expressly if he had adhered to it. This argument does not hold because the empty grave is not another soteriological fact besides that of the resurrection, but it is the accompanying historical aspect of it, as the angel specifically points out in his message to the women.

   The apostolic message testifies to the soteriological fact of the resurrection. That the empty tomb is not mentioned does not imply that it was denied. Cf. P. Althaus, *Die Wahrheit des kirchlichen Osterglaubens – Einspruch gegen E. Hirsch*, 1940, pp. 21ff. and W. Künneth, *Theologie der Auferstehung*, 1934, pp. 75ff., who says that the conviction concerning the empty tomb was "a self-evident element of the belief in Jesus' resurrection." Cf. also S. Greijdanus, *De Opwekking van Christus*, pp. 28ff.

"Destroy this temple, and in three days *I* will raise it up" (John 2:19; cf. John 10:17-18).

We are dealing with an event that took place without the disciples' having expected it at all and of which they, after much doubting, had to be convinced – quite the opposite of a projection! – and only then did they begin to witness to it in the world. It is the testimony concerning the real victory over death, of which the angel spoke in the resurrection announcement. There we find it presented in the historical sequence of events, when the angel told the women (bearing the sweet spices) that Jesus, who was crucified, was not there, and he pointed out to them the place where he had lain.[2] He who had arisen from the dead was going before them into Galilee. None of the resurrection accounts contains any projections or constructions of the mind whatsoever. On the contrary, they rather reveal that the disciples were fettered by the chains of unbelief and perplexity, without any expectation of the great fact (Mark 16:8; Matt. 28:8; see for their doubt: Matt. 28:17; Mark 16:5; their unbelief: Mark 16:11, 13). When Mary Magdalene brought the tidings to the mourning disciples, they did not believe her (Mark 16:13). These stories connect the resurrection with unbelief rather than with wishful imagination. The ones who remember Christ's statement "after three days" are not the disciples but the high priests and Pharisees who are discussing the words of this "deceiver" (Matt. 27:63) and hence ask for a guard at the grave. Christ himself upbraids the eleven for their unbelief and hardness of heart because they believed not them which had seen him after he was risen (Mark 16:14; cf. for their perplexity Luke 24:38). Instead of a subjective projection, we find that unbelief and hesitation are only gradually removed by the real presence of the risen Lord. (See, for the disciples on their way to Emmaus, Luke 24; and, for Thomas' unbelief, John 20.)

John writes concerning the reaction on the part of the disciples: "For as yet they knew not the scripture, that he must rise again from the dead" (John 20:9). Neither Scripture nor Christ's own words had made their hearts receptive to the fact which had now become reality. After the overwhelming reality of the

2. Matt. 28:5; cf. especially John 20:6, 7: Simon Peter therefore also cometh, following him, and entered into the tomb; and he beholdeth the linen cloths lying, and the napkin, that was upon his head, not lying with the linen cloths, but rolled up in a place by itself."

cross there was nothing left in their hearts but a black memory of the anguish of his suffering, the victory of the enemies, the burial as the confirmation of the end, his now silent voice, and the loss of his encouraging and glorious presence. Only Christ himself could remove their doubt and unbelief, their hopelessness and sorrow. The empty tomb is inseparably linked with his appearance. Only in communion with the living Lord were the obstacles removed and the way paved for their apostolate.

It is hardly imaginable that anyone should speak of the living Lord without attaching any significance to the empty tomb. It has often been alleged that the Church made a *proof* out of the empty tomb in order to make the resurrection acceptable. This is, however, not the case. True, even the angel mentioned the empty grave, but it is evident that this was not meant as a rational or historical proof for Christ's resurrection. After all, it is possible to interpret the empty grave differently and say with Mary Magdalene: "They have taken away the Lord out of the tomb, and we know not where they have laid him" (John 20:2), or, as the watchmen interpreted it, as the result of the disciples' theft of the body of Jesus (Matt. 28:13). But all these different possibilities do not abrogate the significance of the empty tomb, because it signifies the absolute-historical character of Christ's resurrection. Not the empty grave but the resurrection of Christ is the great soteriological fact, but as such the resurrection is inseparably connected with the empty tomb and unthinkable without it. It is absolutely contrary to Scripture to eliminate the message of the empty tomb and still speak of the living Lord. The Gospels picture his resurrection in connection with historical data, moments, and places of his appearance. Scripture nowhere supports the idea of his living on independently of a corporeal resurrection and an empty tomb. That the idea of Christ's "living on" is in conflict with the New Testament testimony becomes apparent, for instance, when Heering, in *De Opstanding van Christus* (1946, p. 54), says that the story of the keepers of the grave is the most difficult one to maintain.

One must arrive at such conclusions when one proceeds from the biblically foreign contrast between "pneumatic" and "historic." Those who give the pneumatic aspect priority over the historic can hardly read the Gospels without prejudice and without applying a drastic selection.[3] Thus the historical aspect

3. Heering, *op. cit.*, p. 205: "the biblical accounts are not concerned with the question of reality and truth."

in the Gospels is considered of little consequence, and so the question is raised: "Even if Christ's resurrection was but a purely subjective, sudden insight, a final penetrating recognition of their Master, why could God not use this long-delayed insight to achieve his objective, soteriologic end?"[4] Heering's object, evidently, is to bring out the contrast between the "realistic" resurrection and the "pneumatic" living on, and so it does not surprise us any longer that even supposed parapsychological appearances are brought in to support this peculiar conception of the resurrection event.[5] Thus we arrive at the objective vision, not the subjective (*ibid.*, pp. 168, 165), in which the empty grave plays no role, but in which the bodily risen Christ is displaced by a Christ who "lives on." Yet it is the Christ whom the angels called the crucified one who no longer lives "here" in the grave, the Christ who shows his hands and feet to the doubting Thomas. We shall always have to choose between an idealism which considers the historical empty tomb of no consequence, and the testimony of Scripture, which calls our attention to the gracious work of God in the person of the crucified One.

We may consider the parapsychological interpretation of the resurrection accounts a border case, but there are also other views which try to reconcile the idea of the living Lord with a denial of the historicity of the resurrection from the dead and of the empty tomb. So Banning, for instance, believes that the New Testament is interwoven with ideas prevailing at the time it was written. These ideas must be analysed and removed in order to recover the religious truth (W. Banning, *De Evangelische Boodschap,* 1946, p. 74). This procedure is generally followed with respect to eschatology, but to a large extent it has not been applied to "the realistic conception of the corporeal resurrection" (*ibid.*, p. 74). But Banning believes that there are

4. *Ibid.*, p. 166. The joy of the belief in the resurrection, says Heering, did not diminish when God removed their fear and remorse by the vision of his Son who was dead and is now living.
5. Cf. also G. Zorab, *Het Opstandingsverhaal in het Licht der Parapsychologie,* 1949, who is of the opinion that the accent in the resurrection account is on *the appearance of the deceased Lord.* To him, as to Heering, the empty tomb is of secondary importance over against the primary character of the "appearances" (with the same criticism of the story of the keepers). Everything which does not fit with the appearance-theory is rejected as "later additions." (For instance, Zorab, *op. cit.*, pp. 48ff.)

insurmountable *religious* objections (italics are his) to the latter view. Just as Christ's birth as the Light of the world is not dependent upon the realistic-biological conception of the virgin birth, "no more do we consider the fact that the Christian church is guided in her faith by an ever-present, active Lord, dependent upon the realistic-materialistic conception that the same body which died on the tree of the cross after three days in the grave began to function again" (*ibid.*, p. 74).

Even without these "ideas" (compare Bultmann's "demythologizing") the religious truth remains unaltered, according to Banning. It is the truth of a living Lord, ever present in the midst of the Church. The dogma of the corporeal resurrection of Christ never afforded more *comfort* and *light* than "the belief in the unfathomable love of God" (*ibid.*, p. 75). It is impossible to be committed to the "materialistic interpretation of the resurrection" (*ibid.*). Even without such an interpretation it is possible to believe that in Christ the love of God came to us historically and personally in order, among other things, to break the power of sin. And "the victory over death and sin, manifested in the resurrection, is real to us in the communion in faith with the living Lord" (*ibid.*, p. 76; cf. also Banning, *Het Vrijzinnig* [liberal] *Protestantisme op de Tweesprong* [crossroads], 1945, p. 71). It is thus that we share in Christ's promise: "I am with you even unto the end of the world" (*ibid*).

The cross as the sign of God's love (Banning, *De Evangelische Boodschap,* p. 76) is God's way to the victory over Satan and the breaking of the power of sin (Banning, *Het Vrijzinnig Protestantisme,* p. 77), and by this cross life is "vitalized and directed by Christ's eternal light" (*ibid.*). Christ is the center of world history, the great, burning heart effulging the new life, God's eternal life (*ibid.*, p. 75). He uses nearly every predicate and title which the Church has applied to her living Lord, but he boldly asserts that these may be applied without accepting the corporeal resurrection.[6] It is noteworthy that in describing the

6. Cf. G. Horreüs de Haas, *Moderne Theologie. Beginselen en Problemen,* 1940, pp. 145ff. Several attempts have been made at explaining the resurrection accounts in the Gospels, e.g., as the subjective and the objective vision. In support of the latter an appeal has been made to Paul, who after mentioning a number of "witnesses" of the resurrection, continues: "And last of all he was seen of me also, as one born out of due time" (I Cor. 15:8). From this it is inferred that Christ's "appearances" were of the same nature as Christ's appearance to Paul on the road to Damascus. However, this inference is untenable since

confession of the corporeal resurrection he constantly uses the words "realistic" and "materialistic." This creates the impression that the Church in her confession means *more* than that Christ really rose from the dead. Realism and materialism suggest a one-sided interest in the corporeal, as though everything depended upon that, against which Banning and others speak of the pneumatic character of the living Lord. It is obvious that the gospel is beset by no such dilemma and that, when speaking of the body and the historical corporeal state of Christ, it is by no means "realistic" though very real. This simplistic criticism of the confession of the corporeal resurrection frequently betrays a gross underestimation of the body!

The Gospels themselves show us the significance of the corporality in the resurrected Lord's appearances to his disciples. when meeting Thomas he showed his pierced hands. He ate and drank with the disciples, and they, because of unbelief, were allowed to touch him.[7] There is a touch of the irony of history in the fact that in a day in which so much effort is put forth to "demythologize" the presentation of the New Testament, the attempt is being made at the same time to get rid of dualism

---

Paul's objective is to present "witnesses" of the living, resurrected Lord. As such Paul is the *very last* in the line of witnesses. It has been pointed out, and correctly so, that Paul, according to this expression (last of all) only knows "a limited number of resurrection appearances and witnesses." He is the last one *in this number* (Althaus, *op. cit.*, p. 17). To these do not belong "the visions and revelations of the Lord" of which Paul speaks in II Cor. 12:1. Cf. also Acts 22:18. The word ἔκτρωμα clearly points in the same direction.

7. Cf. Künneth, *op. cit.*, p. 67. "The reference to the corporeality of the resurrected Lord bars any spiritualizing etherealization of the event as a psychic phenomenon or a pneumatic experience." The Gospels speak the way they do (Künneth calls it "realistic-impressively") because of "an inner and foremost interest in the corporeal reality of the resurrected One." This does not mean that the appearances may not and must not be seen as the bodily appearance of the *glorified* Lord. Now and then the Gospels reveal something of Christ's glory, e.g., when speaking of the eyes of the disciples on the way to Emmaus which were holden that they should not know him (Luke 24:16) and which were opened later on (vs. 32); and of Christ's sudden appearance in the midst of the disciples (vs. 36, cf. John 20:14); and of his refusal to be touched, at least in John 20:17; cf. vs. 19. We cannot, when speaking of Christ's glorified body, deny the mysterious element in these appearances. Indeed, the crucified One *is* the resurrected One and the Scriptures emphasize the bodily resurrection to bring out the identity, which is the foundation of our salvation. (Cf. Künneth, *op. cit.*, pp. 68ff.)

by coming to a clearer understanding of the significance of the "body." In this light we must view the criticism of the realistic or materialistic confession of Christ's resurrection.[8] Such criticism fails, *a fortiori* in this modern day, to make any impression and sounds much like an accusation from the nineteenth century when idealism had its heyday.[9]

There is no reason whatsoever to speak of a one-sided interest in the bodily resurrection. This confession definitely concerns the living, ever-present, and conquering *Lord*, but this living Lord is only known in the way Scripture depicts him and his resurrection. The question may be asked, What right has the liberal to speak of the "living-on" Christ, that is, what *biblical* right? We reject the parapsychological explanation (the "appearance of one deceased") which points out a "way" in which the real Christ may appear. Neither can we agree with the unwarranted presentation of a *living* and nonetheless *present* Lord. This is practically the same as the idea that the cross is the sign of God's love. It is then no longer a matter of the bodily resurrection but of the breaking of the power of sin, which takes place in the love of God of which the cross is the symbol. Hence nothing further is necessary, neither in time nor in history. The corporeal resurrection cannot be an event, let alone a *new* event, with particular significance for the breaking of the power of sin. So to Heering the cross is "an act of the utmost power of reconciliation" which fells all self-righteousness and assumed innocence. In the cross "Christ spreads in mercy his arms out as if to say: Even this very last, this utmost thing I am doing for you, in perfect harmony with the will of the Father, in order to open your eyes at last according to his saving intent, and to convince you of his love, to draw you, to you ir-

8. As, for instance, G. J. Heering: "We do not conceive of Christ's resurrection, ascension, and return in a realistic sense (hence not corporeal), not in the sense as a person "ascends" and "returns," but yet they are real: as resurrection, glorification, and victory of the living Christ, in God's power and according to his will" (*Geloof en Openbaring* II, 1937, p. 381; cf. also p. 133).

9. How different is the way Scripture speaks of the body in the words of Paul: "But the body is not for fornication, but for the Lord; and the Lord for the body," and further, in connection with Christ's resurrection: "And God both raised the Lord, and will raise up us through his power" (I Cor. 6:13-14). Cf. also what follows in verses 15-20, to which Schniewind correctly refers in this connection (*Kerygma und Mythos,* I, 109).

resistibly even in spite of all your resistance, to the Father, and to make you kneel down before his mercy" (*Geloof en Openbaring*, II, 175). Thus Heering pictures the function of the cross. It is the sign of God's love, the sacrifice which broke man's resistance and led to repentance and thanksgiving. "Only Christ preaches God's love with his word, his life, and especially his death" (*ibid.*). By his sacrifice he has, in principle, broken the sinful, blind resistance of men. On the basis thereof *no new event* of a resurrection is *necessary*. Heering does write, "The crucified One is the *resurrected* and *risen* One" (*ibid.*, p. 133), but he does not mean this in the sense of a bodily resurrection, as Paul describes it. Not only must this realistic interpretation of Christ's living presence be rejected, but it is, moreover, superfluous. The cross takes the place of the bodily resurrection. Heering's idea concerning the relationship between cross and resurrection comes very close to that of Bultmann, particularly in respect to his presentation of the cross as a historical fact and his rejection of the reality of the resurrection.[10] Thus the significance of the corporeal resurrection becomes entirely illusory, on the basis of both the modern world-view and the significance of the cross.

At times one might get the impression that the controversy concerning the corporeal resurrection (and the empty tomb) is simply an argument about the actual facts of history. But it is not; at stake is the very nature of divine redemption, of which the resurrection is an integral part. That is why the Church, in keeping with its earliest apostolic witness, cannot concede.

On the basis of their position neither Heering nor Bultmann can see any significance in a corporeal resurrection. Bultmann is interested exclusively in the resurrection *faith* which emphasizes the significance of the *cross*. There is a great deal to be said for this emphasis, but the Church has never preached the

10. This explains why Heering, although criticizing Bultmann in his latest book, agrees with him in this respect and is of the opinion that Bultmann in his anti-mythologic viewpoint has a strong case against Schniewind, who unquestioningly accepts the empty tomb, the bodily appearances and the resurrection on the third day. "Bultmann is right: this mythological representation based on uncertain and contradictory accounts in the New Testament, wholly in line with the old world-view, yet entirely contrary to ours, can only be considered as a human interpretation of divine activity" (*De Verwachting van het Koninkrijk Gods*, 1952, p. 121).

cross *at the expense of* the resurrection. On the contrary, in the apostolic preaching — the background of the Church's confession — cross and resurrection are inseparably linked. Paul, for instance, says that Christ has redeemed us from the curse of the law, being made a curse for us on the cross (Gal. 3:13), and at the same time he sees Christ's resurrection as the absolute *conditio sine qua non* of our salvation, without which, therefore, our whole salvation is in jeopardy (I Cor. 15:14, 17). To him there is evidently no contradiction between the significance of the cross and the subsequent resurrection from the dead. The reason lies in the historical character of his message, a message that has nothing in common with the present-day *timeless* idealism which attaches greater importance to the idea than to history and which, because it conceives of the cross as a *symbol* or *idea* of the love of God, is not further interested in the resurrection of Christ. Paul says that Christ died "for our sins according to the scriptures" (I Cor. 15:3), but he immediately adds that he rose again, also "according to the scriptures" (vs. 4) To him there is apparently a profound connection between the two, and he sees them as one complete, *progressive* act of God in Jesus Christ. No matter how he emphasizes the significance of the cross, without Christ's resurrection there would still be condemnation because sin would still be supreme. Hence Paul's greatest concern is not so much whether or not the resurrection is recognized as a historical fact but whether the soteriological significance of this new, historical miracle is understood.

With this word "new" we touch the core of the matter. When we unhesitatingly apply this word exactly at this point we do not mean "new" in the sense of just another new event which has no connection whatsoever with what took place on the cross. We do imply, however, that this was a *new* act of God in history, namely, the resurrection of Jesus Christ from the dead. From all of the apostolic witness it is more than clear that the resurrection of Christ is not merely a symbolic and therefore noetic (knowable) *verification* of the significance of the cross in the accomplished work of Christ, but an actual, divine activity which makes the immeasurable power of Christ's reconciling suffering and death a historical and effective reality. According to Paul's pronouncement "we are false witnesses of God" if we, on the basis of a misconception of the cross, misinterpret the significance of the resurrection. Then there is no use preaching the cross, because we are simply false witnesses. Paul considers what God actually did of extreme importance, and he is not concerned with an *illustration* or *sign* of what took place in the cross. If that were the case we certainly would not have the right to speak of a *new* act of God. Then the resurrection would be only a noetic illustration, an indication of what the historical reality of our salvation as such, and by itself, would be.[11]

According to this "noetic" view all of I Corinthians 15, in its tremendous earnestness and wide, even eschatologic, perspectives can no longer be understood. Bultmann says that Paul's enumeration of eye-witnesses is a "fatal" argumentation. But Paul is not concerned with the "miracle" but with the reality, the new reality of the resurrection, and consequently with the witnesses of the resurrection (cf. R. Schippers, *Getuigen van Jezus Christus*). Whoever considers the resurrection exclusively as "revealing" the meaning of the cross lines up with Bultmann, who substitutes the resurrection *faith* for the resurrection *fact.* Berkhof points out correctly that this viewpoint "does not create an inherent Easter-kerygma" (*ibid.*, p. 182; cf. what follows: "or, rather, the kerygmatic content of this resurrection idea has already been worked out and exhausted with respect to his suffering").

It is noteworthy that Berkhof points out that this conception as such is not unscriptural, referring to Paul's statement: "declared to be the Son of God with power, according to the spirit of holiness, by the resurrection from the dead" (Rom. 1:4). It is indeed true that the significance of the cross is revealed in the resurrection of Christ. But this revelation does not say that the resurrection is *only* an illustration which demonstrates the significance of the cross. It is far more a matter of the power of Christ's suffering and death becoming effective in the reality of salvation. The point at issue is not the illustration of an idea but the power and blessing of Christ's finished work in the victory over death.

11. Cf. Dr. H. Berkhof, who correctly emphasizes the "new" element in the resurrection and who describes the "current interpretation" thus: "But we understand it to mean that it does not accept a new element in our relationship to God, but it brings to light the new situation which resulted from [Christ's] reconciliatory suffering. Thus it has no actual, but a demonstrative significance; not for our life, but for the knowledge of our life; not ontic, but noetic" ("De prediking in de Paastijd" in *Handboek voor de prediking*, I, 1948, p. 181).

Berkhof has pointed out that the Western Church often has difficulty in understanding the uniqueness of the resurrection joy, because of its conception that the resurrection reveals the significance of the cross. In contrast, he points out that the Eastern Church suffers from no such uncertainty, but rather experiences a jubilant liturgical joyousness (*ibid.*, p. 182). The Eastern Church indeed emphasizes the aspect of victory in the resurrection. Here Easter, as the celebration of Christ's victory, is "the heart of the entire ecclesiastical year."[12] We are not now interested in examining the depth of this Eastern resurrection joy, nor its motivations and consequences, but the question for us is — whether or not in response to these victory aspects — if we sense something of the *new* element in Christ's exaltation, in the *victory* over death. Without in the least underestimating the dangers contained in this Eastern, frequently exuberant enthusiasm,[13] we cannot deny that the apostolic witness sounds the note of joy about the resurrection as a new act of God. We cannot dodge this question by pointing out that the Eastern Church puts the accent on the deliverance from transitoriness and death, whereas the Western Church emphasizes the removal of guilt. When we clearly see Christ's work as that of the Lamb of God which taketh away the sins of the world, we can and must have an eye for the victory over death which, by the removal of guilt, leads to the riches of salvation, to eternal life, now and in the future as an eschatological reality. Thus it is impossible to devaluate either the cross on the basis of the resurrection or the resurrection on the basis of the cross. In the gospel both the *revelation* and *progress* of God's saving activity are shown in both the cross and the resurrection. For this reason we can speak of the *new* act of God in the resurrection. Here we see no illustration of an "idea" but rather the grain

12. P. Hendrix, *Het schone Pascha. Indrukken over het Russisch-orthodoxe Paasfeest,* 1940, p. 33. See especially Chapter 1: "The Easter joy in Russian orthodoxy."

13. Hendrix, *op. cit.*, p. 39: "This all-effulging Easter joy, the certainty that death is swallowed up, and that the believer is potentially already partaking of deification is the key-note of all theology, of all mysticism, of the entire liturgic cult in the orthodoxy." Cf. Archimandriet Dionissios, *Russische orthodoxie,* 1947, pp. 140ff. on Easter. He calls it the "festivity of festivities, the festivity of the great, heavenly joy." S. Zankow, *Die orthod. Kirche des Ostens in ökumenischer Sicht,* 1946, p. 50 (*Kirche der Auferstehung*) and *Das orthodoxe Christentum des Ostens,* 1929, p. 52.

of wheat bearing fruit. It would be deplorable indeed if the Western Church would experience less of this "primitive-Christian" joy than the Eastern Church and that she would explain this by pointing out that she emphasizes the removal of guilt! Already in the New Testament this joy is everywhere evident. It sings the praises of God, "who according to his great mercy begat us again unto a living hope by the resurrection of Jesus Christ from the dead" (I Pet. 1:3), "the God of peace, who brought again from the dead the great shepherd of the sheep with the blood of an eternal covenant even our Lord Jesus" (Heb. 13:20). There is not the slightest indication that either the cross or the resurrection is of lesser value: "*Grace* be with you all" (Heb. 13:25).

Christ's victory over death was not a spectacular event in order to convince Jerusalem and the whole world of its undeniable truth and reality, but to reveal its saving power. There is no arbitrariness in the progress from cross to resurrection. All arbitrariness has been taken out of it by the essence of what took place in Christ's suffering and death. When the Lamb of God was nailed and killed on the cross "by wicked hands" it was God who raised him up and who loosed the pains of death, not arbitrarily, but in accordance with the reconciling power of this holy suffering and death "because it was not possible that he should be holden of it" (Acts 2:24). These words "not possible" presage and imply the *progress* from cross to resurrection. They, too, show that God's activity was *new* and yet not arbitrary, just as Paul says when he writes that Christ died for us when we were yet sinners, adding : "while we were enemies, we were reconciled to God through the death of his Son, *much more,* being reconciled, we shall be saved by his life" (Rom. 5:10). By saying "much more" Paul does not minimize the significance of Christ's death, judging by the ring of joy, thanksgiving, and adoration in the words "in due time . . . for the ungodly" (Rom. 5:6). "Much more" is a pre-eminently *historical* indication, pointing out the power and fruit of the suffering and death of Christ in whose resurrection our eternal life is safeguarded. Indeed, this Christ is "declared to be the Son of God *with power,* according to the spirit of holiness, by the resurrection of the dead" (Rom. 1:4), but this resurrection is not an illustration of a timeless idea, not a revelation of a general truth, but the historical actuality of Christ's victory by the majesty of the Father. The resurrection is more than a sign of the significance of the cross; it is a historical reality which itself becomes the sign, the pledge of our absolute victory over death in the resurrection of the body (Lord's Day XVII, Heidelberg Catechism). It is a pledge, but at the same time the foundation, and therefore the guarantee of our faith. The angel said on the resurrection morning: "*Fear not* ye: for I know that ye seek Jesus, which was crucified." This proved that guilt had been removed. And that fact is the basis of primitive-Christian joy, in which there is no dilemma between the removal of guilt and the delivery from death and corruption,[14] a joy which rests on the unity of Christ's reconciling work. The dilemma disappears in the certainty of his promise: "He that believeth on the Son hath everlasting life."[15]

The Church may not, simply out of opposition to the Easter joy of the Russian Orthodox Church, overemphasize the removal of guilt as the main implication of Christ's resurrection if she does not at the same time see the glorious perspectives of life eternal and the resurrection of our bodies. She must avoid an unbalanced emphasis, and she must have an eye for the full light of Christ's work, which penetrates the grave and the inner chambers of death. Both glorious facts are implied, as is clear from what Paul says: "But alive unto God in Christ Jesus" (Rom. 6:11). To Paul the connection between Christ's resurrection and ours is so inseparable that the one stands or falls with the other: "But if there is no resurrection of the dead, neither hath Christ been raised" (I Cor. 15:13; cf. also vss. 15b, 16). In Corinth there was a group that denied the resurrection of the body. Paul, therefore, points out the significance of Christ's resurrection. The latter was not an isolated historical fact. It was a glorious indication of far-reaching consequences. It affects the future of the believers, as Paul declares elsewhere: "And God both raised

14. Berkhof says (*op. cit.*, p. 185) that according to Paul the reconciliation is not our whole salvation, "but only half of it." In my opinion this is not a true interpretation of what the apostle says, nor is what follows: "By the removal of guilt and punishment the negative relationship between God and man changes into a neutral one. But only in the resurrection God creates a positive relationship between Himself and the sinner." In my opinion this representation is too abstract and misinterprets the scriptural teaching concerning reconciliation.

15. Cf. John 11:25-26: 'I am the resurrection, and the life: he that believeth in me, though he die, yet shall he live; and whosoever liveth and believeth on me shall never die."

the Lord, and will raise up us through his power" (I Cor. 6:14; cf. Rom. 8:11; II Cor. 4:14; I Thess. 4:14; I Cor. 15:57; also Col. 3:4). On the basis of the power of Christ's resurrection as the power unto reconciliation Paul can call the unbelief of these Corinthians absurd. Paul is not interested in "proving" Christ's resurrection. To him it is an undoubted fact which many eyewitnesses have confirmed (I Cor. 15:5f.). But this historical fact has, by its very nature, such far-reaching consequences that Paul can say that if the dead are not raised then Christ is not raised either (I Cor. 15:15). Hence it is incorrect to say that Paul actually reverses the order and proceeds from the resurrection of our bodies. This argument is amply refuted by the many instances in which Paul proceeds from Christ's resurrection and in that connection also speaks of ours (cf. K. Barth's exegesis in *Die Auferstehung der Toten,* 1924, e.g., pp. 85ff., and especially p. 88). But against the Corinthians' outright denial of any resurrection he reverses the order for the purpose of bringing out the close connection between Christ's resurrection and ours. "But now *hath* Christ been raised from the dead, the firstfruits of them that are asleep" (15:20).

The very fact that Christ is the "firstfruits" signifies what his resurrection implies. It is not just an isolated, remarkable event, but a beginning, a foundation, a pledge, and a guarantee. It could be preached and had to be preached in order to bring out its implications, so that it would provide a solid foundation for the hope and expectation of a blessed future. Is not Christ the *first*born from the dead?[16] He, who is the first, will be followed by others: "But each in in his own order: Christ the firstfruits; then they that are Christ's, at his coming" (15:23). The glorious resurrection light beams forth in all directions. It is the light of victory and of comfort. The dying grain of wheat has borne fruit. The death of the believers means *gain* – to be present with the Lord (II Cor. 5:8).

Just as the Heidelberg Catechism, when discussing Christ's suffering, brings out the comfort it contains for the Church, so it points out the profit, the benefit, and blessing contained in Christ's resurrection on the third day (Q. 45). It had previously mentioned something about the benefit of Christ's sacrifice

16. Col. 1:18. It reads here πρωτότοκος. I Cor. 15 has "firstfruits" – ἀπαρχή (vss. 20, 23), firstborn; cf. Rev. 1:5 and Acts 26:23 – Πρῶτος.

and death on the cross (Q. 43). When we compare both answers we find that this benefit is described as the crucifixion, mortification, and burial of our *old* man *with* him by his *power*. The benefit of his resurrection is presented as the victory over death, the resurrection by his power unto a new life, and finally as a sure pledge of our own bodily resurrection.

These are not two different kinds of blessings. In both instances mention is made of Christ's power in connection with the old man and the new life. There is, however, one remarkable distinction. With respect to the significance of the resurrection of Christ, the Catechism mentions first of all the victory over death "that he might make us partakers of that righteousness which he had purchased." Thus the Catechism tries to bring out the progress from suffering to glory. Neither those that make a separation between cross and resurrection nor those that consider the resurrection as an illustration of the cross do justice to the apostolic testimony, which preaches the crucified and resurrected Savior and which comforts the believers with the power unto reconciliation contained in Christ's historical resurrection with the words: "For ye died, and your life is hid with Christ in God" (Col. 3:3).

Only those who view Christ's resurrection in the above light are able to grasp something of what the Scriptures relate concerning the forty days between resurrection and ascension. These accounts describe the many appearances of Christ and give us a clear impression of their significance. During those forty days Christ did not triumphantly declare his victory before the forum of either Pilate or Herod, nor to the people of Israel. In many theories on the descent into hell an element of revenge plays an important role, but it is exactly this element which cannot be found in Scripture at all. Scripture speaks only of the relationship between the resurrected One and those that are his, to whom he has returned as the Good Shepherd.

These appearances have a unique character. Christ's primary purpose was not to bring personal and individual comfort and encouragement to each one of the small group of disciples.[17] This short historical period is closely connected with the uni-

17. Naturally, we do not mean to deny that these appearances contained personal comfort, nor do we underestimate this comfort. However, this aspect was subservient to the far greater object which reached far beyond this small circle. Cf. Berkhof, *op. cit.*, p. 193.

versality of that great event which found its climax in the cross and the resurrection. The disciples will have to bear witness of that event in the world. To be sure, they had already gone out into the land with the commission to preach the Kingdom of Heaven, to heal the sick and to cast out devils,[18] but their apostolate was not fully complete until they had received their commission *after* Christ's resurrection when it was confirmed and sealed (see H. N. Ridderbos, *De Komst van het Koninkrijk*, p. 323). Luke begins his book of the Acts of the Apostles by saying that Christ after his suffering "showed himself alive after his passion by many proofs, appearing unto them by the space of forty days, and speaking the things concerning the kingdom of God" (Acts 1:3). In this same connection we read that Christ commanded them that they should not depart from Jerusalem, but wait for the promise of the Father (vs. 4, cf. Luke 24:49) and for the baptism with the Holy Spirit, after which he indicated that they should be witnesses unto the uttermost parts of the earth (vs. 8). Their personal joy and gratitude on account of Christ's resurrection is, so to speak, the arrow on the bow pointing towards the universal object – the witness in the world. This new task corresponds with Christ's historical progress from suffering to glory, and the consciousness of this new, definite progress is silhouetted against the background of the apostolic message: "and he was seen for many days of them that came up with him from Galilee to Jerusalem, who are now his witnesses unto the people (Acts 13:31). Peter is speaking here of the resurrection and says, "Him God raised up the third day, and gave him to be made manifest, not to all the people, but unto witnesses that were chosen before God, even to us, who ate and drank with him after he rose from the dead. And he charged us to preach unto the people, and to testify that this is he who is ordained of God to be Judge of the living and the dead" (Acts 10:40-42; cf. vs. 39). This witness refers back to that which had irrevocably and undeniably taken place, which is

18. See Matt. 10:1f. (unclean spirits, sicknesses); Mark 6:7f. – unclean spirits; preaching ("And whosoever shall not receive you, nor hear you . . .") and Luke 9:2 – "And he sent them to preach the kingdom of God, and to heal the sick." Cf. v. 6 – "preaching the gospel . . . every where." See H. N. Ridderbos on the temporary character of their first mission, in *De Komst van het Koninkrijk*, p. 321, and Kittel, TWNT, I, s.v. ἀπόστολος, p. 431, in connection with "the primitive-Christian apostolate as gift from the resurrected One."

evident also from the fact that after the ascension Peter looks for men "that have companied with us all the time that the Lord Jesus went in and went out among us, beginning from the baptism of John, unto that same day that he was received up from us" (Acts 1:21-22), one of whom will then become "witness with us of his resurrection." That which the disciples experienced and witnessed during those forty days related to their future apostolate. "Soteriologically, these appearances place the disciples in a unique position because of their involvement, a position unattainable by other people either then or thereafter."[19]

It is clearly evident that Christ's activity during these forty days points up the unique and universal import of his cross and resurrection. History will be full of this message unto the utmost ends of the earth, the message of the decisive salvation of God's Kingdom and of that one Name: "And it shall be, that whosoever shall call on the name of the Lord shall be saved" (Acts 2:21). The important message of these forty days is: the Kingdom of God *in* Christ. The message concerning the historical events — through suffering to glory — from then on enters kerygmatically into the history of the entire world.

This message will be a *skandalon* in the world, and the followers of this religion will be branded as the sect of the Nazarenes (Acts 24:5; cf. 24:14) who go about profaning the temple, a joint accusation by both Jews and Gentiles (Acts 24:9). The gospel of the resurrection is interpreted as a blasphemy against Moses and God (Acts 6:11, 13) and as a changing of the customs (vs. 14). But in all these things the Lord Jesus' followers, whose life is hid with Christ in God, will be part of the *ecclesia crucis*, persecuted in everything, of whom the world is not worthy (Heb. 11:38), but seized by the power of Christ's resurrection, a power which, also in their lives, manifests itself graciously and irresistibly.

By this way of the proclamation, the way of the apostolate, the

19. Künneth, *Theologie der Auferstehung*, p. 71. Cf. Paul as one of the apostles, Acts 22:15 — "For thou shalt be a witness for him unto all men of what thou hast seen and heard." Grosheide mentions the little that Paul had seen and heard as yet, but at the same time the fundamental import of Christ's appearance on the road to Damascus, by which fact Paul was ranked among the first apostles (*Comm.* II, 291). Cf. also Acts 26:16 and R. Schippers, *Getuigen van Jesus Christus in het Nieuwe Testament*, pp. 114ff., and Kittel, TWNT, p. 438.

Church will be gathered from among every tribe and language and people and nation (Rev. 5:9). The new song brings praises to the Lamb that was slain "and hast redeemed us to God by [his] blood" (Rev. 5:9, KJV). The cross of Christ is the focal point of all the ages. The apostles know nothing but Jesus Christ and him crucified (I Cor. 2:2). And for this reason the resurrection is preached, for the message of the cross is the message of the spotless Lamb, "who was foreknown indeed before the foundation of the world, but was manifested at the end of the times for your sake, who through him are believers in God, that raised him up from the dead, and gave him glory; so that your faith and hope might be in God" (I Pet. 1:20-21).

The sign of this salvation is the sacrament of baptism that will be administered along with the proclamation of the gospel.[20] The preaching of the gospel and the administration of baptism is backed by the King's word: "All authority hath been given unto me in heaven and on earth" (Matt. 28:18). The disciples' commission is solidly based on Christ's authority, which is a resurrection authority. Not only their preaching but also the added sign of baptism will always refer back to what took place, to the death and resurrection of Christ. "Or are ye ignorant that all we who were baptized into Jesus Christ were baptized into his death?" (Rom. 6:3). Christ's progress from death to resurrection is not *repeated* in baptism, but it does become powerful and effective if this baptism is administered and received with the objective that we "also might walk in newness of life" (Rom. 6:4; cf. Rom. 7:4).

Thus, when the believer battles against the power of sin and death in his life, he may hear the word of preaching and experience the strength of the sign accompanying this preaching. In these last days he will be able to resist the temptation no longer to keep in remembrance Christ's cross (Luke 22:19 – "this do in remembrance of me") and resurrection (II Tim. 2:8 – "Remember Jesus Christ, risen from the dead"). Without this twofold remembrance, which essentially is one, God's reconciling act is denied and the "old" life is strengthened against the "new" life in Christ. The New Testament solemnly warns against apostasy – after having tasted the power of the world to come

20. Cf. John 20:21 – "As the Father hath sent me, even so send I you." See Kittel, TWNT, I, 403f. on πέμπειν and ἀποστέλλειν.

(Heb. 6:5).[21] For such is it impossible to come again to repentance, seeing they crucify to themselves the Son of God *afresh* (Heb. 6:6). Such persons fall back into a life of estrangement, with all the catastrophic results of such a reversal: thorns and briars and the curse of God – the opposite of his blessing (Heb. 6:7-8). This clearly depicts the contrast between "old" and "new," *death* and *life*.

Christ's resurrection preaches the transition from death to life. This is not a matter of an "existential" eschatology pitted against a dramatic, futuristic eschatology, as, for instance, posited by Bultmann, who, on the basis of John 5 speaks of the "situation of decision" and the (κρισις) in Christ ("Die Eschatologie des Johannes-evangeliums," *Zwischen den Zeiten*, 1929). Those who attempt to force such a dilemma onto us must simply ignore the *futurum* elements in John 6 as non-original and non-essential, as Bultmann actually and unblushingly does.[22] On the other hand, Bultman's extreme view should not drive us to the opposite mistake, namely, to underestimate the decisive importance of the transition from death to life *in* Jesus Christ.[23] It is the transition which is brought about by him who has said: "I am the resurrection, and the life" (John 11:25). This and

21. By this "remembrance" the New Testament does not mean a formal, psychological remembering but a purposeful remembrance corresponding to the historical work of Christ "once for all." Cf. the noteworthy remarks by Michel in Kittel, TWNT, IV, s.v. μιμνησκομαι, e.g., on p. 681 ("not meant in a historical, intellectualistic sense"). Cf. II Pet. 3:1-3 and the role of the Holy Spirit in this remembrance (John 14:26). That the "remembrance" plays such a prominent role in the New Testament is not incidental. It is the opposite of timeless idealism, which does not need remembrance. "Whoever remembers the church proclaims thereby the gospel; whoever remembers himself subjects himself thereby to Jesus' word" (Michel, p. 682). Cf. N. Dahl, *Anamnesis. Stud. Theol. Lund.* 1948, pp. 69-96.

22. Bultmann, quoted article, p. 4, where he says of John 5:28 ("all that are in the tombs shall hear his voice, and shall come forth"; cf. 5:25) and John 6:54 ("I will raise him up at the last day") that these statements are "obviously only eschatological in a dramatic sense of the word" and are strongly to be suspected of being the result of later editing. See also R. Bultmann, "Zur eschatologischen Verkündigung Jesu" (*Theol. Lit. Zeitung*, 1947, pp. 271-274).

23. Especially John 5:24 – "I say unto you, He that heareth my word, and believeth him that sent me, hath eternal life, and cometh not into judgment"; cf. 5:25 – "The hour cometh and now is"; John 8:51 – "I say unto you, If a man keep my word, he shall never see death"; and John 11:25ff.

the clear emphasis of the Gospel of John do not eliminate the historic *futurum,* they do not substitute a "vertical" eschatology for the horizontal, but they do give a solid foundation to the *futurum* in what took place. The significance of Christ's work does not shrivel up and fade out in a "moment of decision" but is presented to us in the New Testament in the full riches of its soteriological implications. When Martha, in connection with Lazarus' death, reflects on the future and "knows" that he will rise again in the resurrection at the last day, after Christ has said: "Thy brother shall rise again" (John 11:23-24), then Christ does not deny this *futurum* (cf. Matt. 22:23-33) but he does call her attention away from it and unto himself, the Resurrection and the Life. And he asks her: "Believest thou this?" (John 11:26). Life is immanent in him (cf. also I John 3:14 – "We know that we have passed out of death into life"); it is made inviolable by the power of reconciliation and is the foundation of the lively hope which does not put to shame (cf. I Pet. 1:3). In him the Church sees the Shepherd of his sheep, the great Shepherd, brought again from the dead through the blood of the everlasting covenant (Heb. 13:20). Believing in him is unconditionally identical with having *life* in *his* name.[24]

24. "But these are written, that ye may believe that Jesus is the Christ, the Son of God; and that believing ye may have life in his name" (John 20:31).

CHAPTER EIGHT

CHRIST'S ASCENSION

THE NEXT STEP of Christ's exaltation following his resurrection is, in the words of the Apostles' Creed: "He ascended into heaven." Those acquainted with the heated controversy concerning the reality of Christ's corporeal resurrection will not be surprised to learn that this same battle has also involved the confession of Christ's ascension ever since the nineteenth century. Bultmann, for one, considers it among those elements, those formulations of the *kerygma,* which certainly are subject to "demythologization." Hence we must ask whether the ascension is real and what its significance is.

The Reformed confessions adhere to the scriptural teachings concerning the ascension. The Heidelberg Catechism, for instance, states that Christ ascended from the earth before the eyes of his disciples and was taken up into heaven. Lord's Day XVIII deals specifically with the meaning and significance of the ascension. Actually, it is mainly a refutation of the Lutheran position regarding Christ's ascension (cf. A. Kuyper, *E Voto,* on this Lord's Day.)

Lately, however, it has been frequently pointed out that Scripture is not very explicit on the fact of the ascension. Neither Matthew nor John mentions it. Mark does mention it, but that part of his Gospel is controversial material and has been subjected to textual criticism. We read there: "So then the Lord Jesus, after he had spoken unto them, was received up into heaven, and sat down at the right hand of God" (16:19 cf. Luke 24:51; see also S. Greijdanus, *Comm.* II, *ad loc.*). Luke is the one who gives a historical account, both in his Gospel and in the Acts. There we sense a historical atmosphere, when we read that Jesus led his disciples to Bethany, where he lifted up his hands and blessed them. "And it came to pass, while he blessed them, he parted from them" (Luke 24:51). Acts says that the disciples *beheld,* and it mentions a cloud which received him out of their sight, so that they gazed toward heaven as he went up. The angels said that "this Jesus, who was received up from you into heaven, shall so come in like manner as ye beheld him going into heaven" (Acts 1:11). This message caused great joy, so that they returned to Jerusalem with gladness in their hearts (Luke 24:51). Then began the period of waiting, which they spent singing praises to God (Luke 24: 53). It was a joyful period of waiting, which was apparently related closely to the separation brought about by Christ's ascension.

But the scriptural witness to Christ's ascension is by no means limited to Luke. Everywhere in Scripture we find direct or indirect references to this fact. Christ himself speaks not only of his resurrection on the third day but also, in a special sense, of his "going away." He knows when his hour has come that he must go to the Father (John 13:3; 14:28; 14:2). He says to the disciples: "Whither I go, ye cannot come" (John 13:33) and to the Jews: "Ye shall seek me, and shall not find me; and where I am, ye cannot come" (John 7:34, 36; 8:21f.). His going away is of the greatest import to the disciples (John 16:7 – "It is expedient for you that I go away"). It means the preparation of a place for them (John 14:2) and the sending of the Comforter (John 16:7-10). Hence his references to his going away contain more than simply an indication of his approaching death, even though he does not explicitly mention his ascension into heaven. His separation from them is closely related to his exaltation and glorification. When the Greeks desire to see Christ, he says: "The hour is come, that the Son of man should be glorified" (John 12:23). When the multitude reminds him of the fact that the Christ "abideth for ever" (John 12:34) Jesus answers by referring to his departure: "Yet a little while is the light among you. Walk while ye have the light, that darkness overtake you not" (vs. 35). All these statements indicate an approaching great event, that itself will also mean separation (cf. John 12: 8 – "For the poor ye have always with you; but me ye have not always") but a separation that is filled with God's mercy and goodness. His going away means glorification, and is a blessing and beneficial reality. True, Christ's references to his going away are too vague and general to say that they clearly indicate the ascension of which Luke writes, but they do point to a soteriological historical progress which finds its realization in this event. His going away to the Father becomes a fact when he ascends.[1]

In this connection we also mention Luke 9:51, which speaks of his being received up: "And it came to pass, when the days were well-nigh come that he should be received up, he stedfastly set his face to go to Jerusalem." The same expression "received up" is also used in Mark 16:19, Acts 1:2, 11, 12, and I Timothy 3:16, to designate his ascension, and Luke is definitely referring to an event of which the ascension is a part. Zahn calls attention to the fact that Luke in this text speaks of "days," whereas in Acts the singular form "day" is used. This can be explained by the consideration that Luke is not referring to the isolated fact of the ascension but to "Jesus' passing from the terrestrial to the celestial life without going into details as to how this process took place."[2] There is a connection between the days that he must be "received up" and his decease at Jerusalem (ἔξοδος Luke 9:31). At one time Christ uses the expression "me ye have not always" (John 12:8), and at another time "the bridegroom shall be taken away from them" (Luke 5:35), referring on both occasions not simply to the end of his life but to his being taken up *to the Father* (Acts 1:2ff.). Hence we find that Scripture often indirectly refers to the ascension without mentioning the fact as such. Only seldom do we find it described as the day in which he was taken up, as in Acts 1:2, after the forty days in which he showed himself alive to his disciples. The references to Christ's ascension are sometimes direct and at other times indirect, but in the *kerygma* they are always used to bring out the soteriological implications. We never find an isolation of a historical fact. We may say that the historical aspects in the Gospel of Luke and in the Acts are assimilated into the gospel message, as, moreover, in Luke they are always presented in connection with Christ's blessing and *parousia.* It is also evident that the apostles bring out the close connection between Christ's ascension and his sitting at the right hand of God. Peter in his sermon on Pentecost points out that Christ's resurrection is inseparably connected

1. Cf. John 20:17 – "Touch me not; for I am not yet ascended unto the Father: but go unto my brethren, and say unto them, I ascend unto my Father and your Father, and my God and your God."
2. Zahn, *Comm.* Luke, p. 398. Cf. C. Stam, *De Hemelvaart des Heren in de Godsopenbaring van het Nieuwe Testament,* 1950, p. 18, and Delling, Kittel, TWNT, III, 7.

with his ascension when he is speaking of Christ's exaltation on the right hand of God as the fulfillment of Psalm 110 (Acts 2:34ff.).

In a few sentences Peter summarizes Christ's resurrection (Acts 2:32), his exaltation by the right hand of God (vs. 33), and the pouring forth of the Holy Spirit (vs. 33). He particularly accentuates Christ's ascension, as is shown by the fact that he quotes Psalm 110 and then points out that this psalm had not been fulfilled in David, "For David ascended not into the heavens" (vs. 34) – the same kind of argument he had used shortly before in connection with the resurrection of Christ (vs. 29).[3] Whoever destroys this harmony obscures at once the true insight into the Messianic glory which, according to the apostolic testimony, has become a reality in Christ's resurrection and ascension.[4] Bavinck says correctly: "Beyond a doubt, Christ's ascension, as well as his resurrection, has from the very beginning been a part of the faith of the Church" (*Gereformeerde Dogmatiek,* III, 439). Not until long afterwards, when there was no longer an unconditional faith in the Holy Scriptures, was there a tendency to tear apart the things which had always been one in the Church's preaching and belief. This concerns not just a few isolated texts which, quantitatively, are considered an insignificant witness to Christ's ascension, but it concerns all of what the New Testament says concerning Christ's "going to the Father," his going into heaven (I Pet. 3:22), his ascension up on high (Eph. 4:8), his being received up into glory (I Tim. 3:16), and all this in connection with his sitting on the right hand of God as the exalted Messiah. When Bavinck says that "to him who, with the entire Church and on the basis of the apostolic testimony, believes in Christ's resurrection, the ascension is but the natural and logical sequence," then Bavinck does not mean to say that the ascension is only the logical consequence of the resurrection, but the consequence of accepting all that Scripture says concerning Christ's progress to the right hand of God, which also includes the historicity of the ascension and all that it implies for our salvation.[5]

3. "I may say unto you freely of the patriarch David, that he both died and was buried, and his tomb is with us unto this day."
4. Cf. also Eph. 4:9f., where the ascension of Christ is seen as the fulfillment of Psalm 68, but here also in close connection with his incarnation. See vs. 10.
5. In this connection Bavinck could write: "That is why the ascension as such, as an event on the fortieth day after the resurrection, is seldom

Only severe Bible criticism can lead one to a denial of the ascension and even to its complete elimination from the original apostolic *kerygma*. Frequent attempts have been made to prove that neither the ascension nor the resurrection were originally part of the apostolic preaching. Some claim, for instance, that the apostles originally believed and taught that Christ ascended to heaven from the cross.[6] According to this idea the Church was at first not concerned with the contrast between Christ's death and *resurrection*, but between his death and *exaltation*. The message concerning Christ was eschatological. He is the eschatological Christ. Over against Christ's weak human appearance stood his exaltation, as is also apparent from his word to the thief and his last word to the Father. Paul, too, "seems to presume Christ's ascension from the cross" because in Philippians 2 he contrasts Christ's humiliation with his exaltation, "without mentioning his burial and resurrection."[7] Bertram says that the original gospel message contained no reference to a burial or an empty tomb. "At the outset Christ's appearances do not call attention to either a burial or an empty tomb. But the Church soon accepted these ideas as historical facts and finally the vision-legends receive their physical character via the story of the empty tomb" (*ibid.*, p. 199).

One must indeed have very little confidence in the trustworthiness of the Gospels and epistles in order to arrive at the conclusion: "It is most congruent with the New Testament idea to identify the resurrection with the ascension" (*ibid.*, p. 204). In Bertram's opinion the Gospel of John also excludes both grave and resurrection (p. 210) and . . . "on the other hand, it makes no difference that the gospel of John mentions Jesus' resurrection occasionally or follows the synoptic way of representation with regard to the later events." From the fact that John links Christ's death so closely with his exaltation and calls his death "the

---

placed on the foreground but is linked with the resurrection" (*op. cit.*, p. 439). Hence it is incorrect to speak in this connection of a hierarchy or order of values, as though the ascension were less important than the resurrection. Such an approach is not only atomistic but also, fundamentally, unhistorical. Cf. A. A. van Ruler, *De Vervulling der Wet*, 1947, p. 193.

6. G. Bertram, "Die Himmelfahrt Jesu vom Kreuze aus und der Glaube an die Auferstehung Jesu," in *Festschrift für Deissmann*, 1927.
7. *Ibid.*, p. 197. He also points out the "contrast" in Rom. 5:10 and Luke 24:26.

hour of his transfiguration," Bertram deduces that for John there is no time-problem and in his account the one motif is predominant: the Crucified One is the Exalted One. Even to Bertram it must remain an unsolved problem why John still follows the synoptics with regard to the resurrection stories. On the basis of such an arbitrary misrepresentation he sees everything distorted: "The finale of the exaltation transcends the historical, while the resurrection legends attempt to translate the superhistorical into time-dimensional presentations" (p. 212).

Again, in Hebrews "no mention is made of Jesus' resurrection" (p. 213) except once, namely Hebrews 13:20, which has an Old Testament connotation (p. 214). This epistle "in general disregards the actual history" (p. 214). The fundamental idea is: Jesus' exaltation from the cross to heaven (p. 215). Only later on this motif was changed and the cross had to stand aside for the resurrection (p. 216).

Thus the *kerygma* of cross and resurrection is done away with, as well as the resurrection itself. The period of forty days loses all significance. As soon as a biblical author does not explicitly mention the resurrection or the ascension, the conclusion is drawn that he was not aware of them. Hence it becomes evident that the meaning of Scripture can be understood only in its fulness, unity, and harmony. If we appreciate this harmony we can see why in a certain instance only one central idea is stressed, without doing injustice to what is taught elsewhere in the apostolic preaching.

This is most clearly illustrated in the letter to the Hebrews. It is quite obvious why Bertram eliminates the section that deals with Christ's resurrection: it upsets his theory about this letter. But anyone who chooses not to follow Bertram understands already from this single word concerning the shepherd of the sheep whom God brought again from the dead (13:20), that the resurrection of Jesus Christ resounds throughout the entire letter and that it is part of the glory of Christ on the right hand of God of which this letter gives such a circumstantial description.[8] However we may look at it, whenever the New

8. We call attention to the context in Heb. 13:20 where it is said that God has brought back again from the dead the shepherd of the sheep *by the blood of an external covenant*. Hence, at the conclusion of this letter the author sees Christ's glory in heaven connected with his suffering and resurrection. Cf. Grosheide, *op. cit.*, p. 387: "possibly the

Testament mentions Christ's glory it always mentions at the same time the way which led to this glory. That is at once evident with regard to the resurrection, and that also explains the fact that Hebrews does not simply discuss Christ's glory as such, but that this glory is historically related, as is evident from that part which deals with Christ's being crowned with glory and honor (Heb. 2:7, 9) and his sitting down on the right hand of the Majesty on high (1:3). See also Hebrews 10:12: "But he, when he had offered one sacrifice for sins for ever, sat down on the right hand of God." Bertram can use this text only if he proceeds as follows: the glory of Christ in Hebrews minus Hebrews 13:20 equals the ascension "from the cross."

He who eliminates all these and similar statements from the whole of the scriptural witness misunderstands the character of Scripture and simply considers it an arbitrary collection of writings. Our attention is called to the high priest who as a forerunner has entered for us (Heb. 6:19), who passed into the heavens (4:14) and who is made higher than the heavens (7:26). The specific statement by the author that Christ entered into heaven itself (9:24) may never be taken as referring to an ascension from the cross, because the harmony of Scripture indicates that these aspects of the letter to the Hebrews must be seen in connection with cross, resurrection, and ascension. Only in this connection do they form a logical unit.[9] Hebrews emphasizes Christ's glory, but this must be seen as part of the soteriological whole of the work of Christ. This glorified Christ is also the captain of salvation (2:10) and the author and finisher of faith (12:2). Part of the consolation derived from God's faithfulness is the hope we have, which is as an anchor of the soul, both sure and stedfast "and entering into that which is within the veil; whither as a forerunner Jesus en-

---

clause 'brought again from the dead' refers also to the ascension." In any case it evidences a redemptive-historical, organic outlook on the work of Christ.

9. Cf. Grosheide, *Commentary on Hebrews,* p. 51, on the "principal idea" of our letter. Cf. also pp. 69-70: ". . . that the author passes on from Christ's death to his sitting on the right hand of God is done because the object of his argument requires such" (p. 70). When Grosheide says that resurrection and ascension are only of secondary importance to the objective of the argument in Hebrews then he does by no means mean to say that they are unimportant with respect to the foundation of our salvation.

tered for us" (6:19, 20). This is beautifully worked out in Grosheide's commentary: "Just as a captain casts his anchor, so the soul of the believer casts his anchor, and just as the captain does not put his ultimate trust in his anchor but in the anchor ground, so the believer does not first of all put his trust in his hope but in the ground of his hope, namely the promises of God which have been fulfilled by the forerunner and which will still be fulfilled" (*op. cit.*, p. 187).

Here the anchor ground is not the sea, but heaven. The anchor holds there securely because Christ entered there as our forerunner. For this reason Hebrews' mentioning of the glory of Christ who entered into heaven is not a speculation of the Church but the assurance of the reality and inviolability of the reconciliation "for us" as the result of Christ's suffering and death. Hebrews contains no mythical reconstruction of the life of Jesus. but rather preaches his redemptive suffering and death which reach into heaven. Here the believer may rest the anchor of his soul, even when he stands amidst numerous perils.[10]

In this light we may now ask concerning the significance of the ascension. The Apostles' Creed does not attempt to give a biographical explanation of Jesus' life, but it *confesses* Christ's ascension. Hence the question is justified, What is the meaning and object of this confession? Are we indeed dealing with a *new* soteriological fact, distinct from the reality of Christ's resurrection? Is there still more implied – to quote Lord's Day XVII – in saying that Christ has overcome death by his resurrection? And if so, does that not devaluate the great and universal resurrection power and its eschatological import? Clearly, we discover no trace of such a devaluation in Scripture nor in the apostolic *kerygma*. To be sure, there is indeed a redemptive-historical progress of the salvation of God in Christ. In Christ's ascension as well as in his resurrection we are confronted with an absolute decision between timeless idealism and gospel. Timeless idealism, which is uninterested in important historical progress and decision, will never be able to understand the significance of Christ's resurrection and ascension, nor of Christ's promise concerning the coming of another Comforter.

To idealism everything is timeless and eternally true; nothing

10. H. van Oyen, *Christus de Hogepriester,* pp. 112, 113.

actually new can ever take place. This is diametrically opposed to what God's Word teaches. God's activity under the Old Covenant pointed already to new things to come (cf. Isa. 42:9; 48:6; 65:17; 66:22; Jer. 31:22). Just as the promised Comforter will not devaluate Christ's work, but instead will make it fully effective historically,[11] so the ascension does not minimize the power and glory of the resurrection. On the contrary, the ascension drives home the message that our hope may fully rest in the anchorage of Christ's reconciliation. The new event which takes place in the ascension does not render the old event (the resurrection) valueless or relative, but it is the historical revelation of everything Christ's work embodied. That it is *better* that he depart can never be understood from the viewpoint of idealism, but only from the biblical viewpoint. God's salvation in and through the progress of Christ's messianic work is presented and established as inviolable salvation.

This viewpoint is obscured by many because of their quantitative approach to the scriptural witness. Thus they lose sight of the unity which Paul set forth when he described God's salvation not quantitatively but qualitatively historically with respect to the living, personal Lord: this is the mystery of godliness: "He who was manifested in the flesh, Justified in the spirit, Seen of angels, preached among the nations, Believed on in the world, Received up in glory" (I Tim. 3:16).

Those who fail to see the resurrection in the letter to the Hebrews must search for Christ's suffering and death and resurrection in Paul's letters. Such people, however, do not understand the liberty which the Spirit employs with respect to the explicitness and implicitness of his message, now here, now there, as, for instance, when in this text six facts are enumerated including Christ's being preached and believed. The unity

11. A clear sample of this depreciation of the historical perspective may be found in Bultmann when he writes concerning the idea of the Paraclete: "This Paraclete must apparently be considered as an idea, since its manifestation is not exclusively concentrated in one historical bearer but is divided among several consecutive messengers, or is repeated in them" (Exkurs: "Der Paraklet," in *Commentary on John,* p. 437). Cf. G. Bornkamm's criticism in "Der Paraklet im Johannesevangelium," in *Festschrift R. Bultmann,* 1949, p. 13. Bornkamm's own conclusion, that the Paraclete "fundamentally is no one else" than the exalted Christ, is, however, no more in agreement with the redemptive-historical data of the New Testament than Bultmann's position (Bornkamm, *op. cit.,* pp. 28, 35).

of faith and the history on which this faith is based become fully evident here. It is impossible to introduce a hierarchy of values here which inevitably paves the way to a denial of the *historical* aspect in God's activity.[12] Both in Scripture and in the apostolic preaching, Christ's life and work, his humiliation and exaltation, are circumstantially described. Every single message can be understood only against the background of the whole of the witness concerning the living Lord. When seen in that light there can be no doubt that the message concerning Christ's salvation of the world embraces also the preaching of his ascension.

When considering the significance of the ascension in the sum total of God's activity in Christ Jesus, and the meaning of his being taken up, and his active ascension, we clearly receive the impression from Scripture that it speaks of a departure, a separation. He was parted (διέστη) from them (Luke 24: 51). How, now, must we understand this separation? We read: "a cloud received him out of their sight" (Acts 1:9). There is suddenly a radical change in the relationship between Christ and his disciples. Before his death there was the daily communion and companionship on the terrestrial plane of the historical life in Palestine. The disciples touched him, ate with him, heard his words, and looked upon his face. Christ himself had mentioned several times that this kind of companionship could not last. In fact, it would be very short. The day would come that they would no longer see him (John 16:10). He would not speak *much* with them any more (John 14:30). He is the bridegroom who will be taken away. When the disciples were accused of eating and drinking – unlike those of John – Jesus defended them by placing their manner of living under the protecting light of his presence: "Can ye make the sons of the bridechamber fast, while the bridegroom is with them?" (Luke 5:34). They cannot fast (Mark 2:19). They were living in the time of salvation, the messianic time, during which the joy of the coming messianic kingdom fills their hearts.[13] It is

12. Cf. C. Bouma, *Commentary* on I Tim. 3:16, concerning this enumeration as not being chronological.

13. "The Messiah's presence, the time of salvation which has arrived, means joy" (Kittel, TWNT, s.v. νῆστις, IV, 933).

a unique relationship which began with Christ's coming.[14] But instead of the bridegroom's presence Christ announces that different days are ahead: "But the days will come; and when the bridegroom shall be taken away from them, then will they fast in those days" (Luke 5:35). Then, indeed, sadness and sorrow will fill the hearts of his followers as Christ has predicted: "Verily, verily, I say unto you, that ye shall weep and lament, but the world shall rejoice" (John 16:20). All this indicates that a road of suffering lies ahead of him. In the story of the anointing at Bethany we read that the disciples will not have Christ always with them, and his burial is also mentioned (John 12:7-8).

It will be a separation in the way of suffering and death. But this separation does not imply a severing of the bonds of communion. After Christ mentioned their weeping and lamenting he added, "Ye shall be sorrowful, but your sorrow shall be turned into joy" (John 16:20). He uses a parable in order to bring out the temporary character of their sorrow: "A woman when she is in travail hath sorrow, because her hour is come: but when she is delivered of the child, she remembereth no more the anguish, for the joy that a man is born into the world" (vs. 21). The announcement of sorrow contains at the same time a message of indefeasible joy: "And ye therefore now have sorrow: but I will see you again, and your heart shall rejoice, and your joy no one taketh away from you" (vs. 22). Their joy, interrupted by a period of suffering, will return, and it must be noted that the period of suffering will be replaced permanently by the messianic joy which will be given to the Church through this suffering. It actually makes no difference whether we apply this joy to Christ's resurrection and appearances or to the coming of the Spirit.[15] In any case their joy returns again at Christ's resurrection. Their fears are removed by the risen Lord. Joy returns and this joy remains even after the ascension. Here again is proven that "your joy no man taketh from you." And it is striking that the apostles return with joy to Jerusalem after the message from the angels on Mt. Olivet.

14. Cf. Matt. 13:17 – "For verily I say unto you, That many prophets and righteous men desired to see the things which ye see, and saw them not; and to hear the things which ye hear, and heard them not"; cf. Luke 10:23, 24 (many prophets and kings). Cf. H. N. Ridderbos, *De Komst van het Koninkrijk*, p. 266, on the messianic time of joy.

15. So Grosheide in his commentary on John 20 and 22. C. Bouma in *Korte Verklaring* applies it to the resurrection.

All this must be taken into consideration before designating the ascension as a *separation.* At any rate the ascension may not be identified as the time of fasting which would follow the period of joy during Jesus' earthly life. The ascension occasions no decline in their joy. Their sorrowful fasting may not be attributed to Christ's ascension; it is rather associated with the period of suffering in the lives of the disciples who, with horror and dismay, have seen the Messiah carrying his cross. After their temporary sorrow has passed the joy of faith bursts forth. That is a very important aspect when we reflect upon the significance of the ascension.

Van Ruler has said that Reformed theology has justly emphasized the element of separation.[16] Quite logically the question may be asked whether this is indeed the case. Although Reformed theology does speak of the "separation," in my opinion it is not particularly emphasized. This may be clearly seen from two examples: Calvin and the Heidelberg Catechism. Calvin says that Christ's departure was of greater benefit to us than his presence would be (*Institutes,* II, XVI, 14). He speaks of Christ's promise that he would not leave his disciples comfortless (John 14:18, Dutch version: "I will not leave you behind as orphans"). Though his bodily presence is withheld from their view, still Christ does not cease to be near, and Calvin speaks of an "even more present power" by which he governs heaven and earth.[17] He keeps his promise to be with us even unto the end of the world,[18] and as far as the presence of his majesty is con-

16. See A. A. van Ruler on the ascension in *Religie en Politiek,* 1945, p. 138; *De Vervulling der Wet,* 1947, especially pp. 103ff.; *Verhuld Bestaan,* 1949, pp. 144ff.; *De Betekenis van de Hemelvaart.* (*Onder Eigen Vaandel,* XVII.)

17. "Ut praesentiore virtute et coelum et terram regeret" (*Inst.* II, XVI, 14). This corresponds to the greater abundance of the Spirit which he then poured out ("quanto maiorem Spiritus sui abundantiam tum effuderit"). Note Calvin's use of comparatives when he speaks of the more glorious furtherance of his kingdom and the greater power manifested by him.

18. Cf. Calvin on Matt. 28:20 – "I am with you alway. . ." (ed. Tholuck): "Modus autem presentiae, quam Dominus suis promittet, spiritualiter intelligi debet: quia ut nobis auxilietur, non opus est e coelo descendere, quum Spiritus sui gratia, quasi extenta manu e coelo juvare nos possit." It is true, there is a separation "qui secundum corpus immenso locorum spatio a nobis distat") but "non modo per totum mundum Spiritus sui efficaciam diffundit, sed in nobis quoque vere habitat." Calvin is concerned with "arcano modo Christum mirabiliter operari." Cf. also Cal-

cerned we have Christ always with us even though he said to the disciples that with respect to his presence in the flesh: "Me ye have not always." For he gives his own "no uncertain proofs of his very present power" (*Inst.* II, XVI, 17).[19] Commenting on Acts 1:9 Calvin takes issue with Rome and accentuates the ascension and the separation.[20] There he is speaking of the corporeal presence, but this separation does not eliminate a continued communication.[21]

The Heidelberg Catechism points in the same direction. Even though it is said that with respect to his human nature he is no more on earth, "with respect to his Godhead, majesty, grace and spirit he is at no time absent from us" (Q. 47). He is in heaven "for our interest" (Q. 46) as our Paraclete[22] and sends us his Spirit as a surety. It is a separation, but a fruitful one and

---

vin on Acts 1:9, where he writes that when we wish to have Christ bodily with us we remain on that account far removed from him ("longius subinde ab eo abscedet").

19. "Separatio a mundo" (Acts 1:11). True, Christ's Kingdom is, on account of the lowliness of the flesh, more or less concealed on earth (*Inst.*, II, XVI, 17) and the Church is not free from tribulation, but faith is sure of his presence and looks forward to the "visibilis praesentia, quam supremo die manifestabit."

20. "Revocare volunt Angeli discipulos a carnalis praesentiae desiderio" (on Acts 1:11). The fact that Christ – according to the angels' word – will return indicates "ne frustra ante venturum expectent. Quis non videt, iisdem verbis corporis eius absentiam e mundo exprimi?"

21. In this connection Calvin says – as so often elsewhere – "Fateor praeterea, et verbo et sacramentis eum nobis adesse. Neque vero dubitandum est, quin vere participes fiant carnis et sanguinis ipsius, qui illorum symbola fide recipiant" (on Acts 1:11).

22. Heidelberg Catechism, Q. 49. In connection with this confession we are logically reminded of the significance Rome attaches to Mary's ascension into heaven, which was made a dogma of the Church in 1950 (*Munificentissimus Deus;* Nov. 1) in the pronouncement: "That it is a God-revealed dogma that the immaculate mother of God, ever virgin, Mary, after the completion of her earthly course has been taken up in the heavenly glory both with body and soul." We cannot now discuss the motives and backgrounds of this dogma. We just call attention to the triumph of Mary *with* Christ which is confessed in this dogma ("complete triumph over sin and its consequences"). Hence she is able *with* Christ to apply the fruits of salvation unto us. Just as Christ's resurrection was the triumphal finale of Christ's victory, so Mary had to be crowned with her glorification. In the theological explanation of this new dogma the emphasis is on its *comfort,* as we find that especially in A. H. Maltha's *De Tenhemelopneming van Maria,* 1950, p. 62: "She is our pure, human bridgehead in heaven; stronger yet, she is the first successful troop-

full of blessing,[23] so that our communion with him is not disturbed.

It can hardly be maintained that Reformed theology accentuates the aspect of separation. The record shows rather that this separation is placed in the light of the new *modus* of Christ's presence and that the blessing and joy of Christ's ascension are emphasized in accordance with Scripture. The accent is just as much on the expectation and the guarantee which are contained in his ascension as on his physical separation from us.

This involves a correct conception of the progress, the consolidation and the proclamation of the power of Christ's work in the days of his humiliation. For that is what Scripture teaches when it says that the Kingdom Christ founded consists in righteousness and joy in the Holy Spirit (Rom. 14:17; cf. 15:13 [all joy] and Phil. 2:8, 4:4), and when Peter says to the believers: "Whom having not seen ye love; on whom, though now ye see him not, yet believing, ye rejoice greatly with joy unspeakable and full of glory" (I Pet. 1:8). There is a longing for the future, as John writes, "We shall see him as he is" (I John 3:2), but those who have not seen and yet have believed are also pronounced blessed (John 20:29). We might even say that the joy of faith and communion are *dependent* on this separation, so that in this unique redemptive-historical progress the "separation" can never be used as the dominant motif without doing injustice to the significance of the ascension. The secret of this "separation," to faith, is precisely that it effects the communion, and the solution of this secret is to be found in the Comforter whom Christ sent. The communion with the living Lord is experienced as a great reality by means of the gift of the Spirit. The messianic joy is not the portion of the Church *in*

---

landing over the bridgehead which is Christ. We shall follow." According to the dogmatic bull Mary is an exception to the general rule that the righteous do not receive the complete fruit of the victory until the end of time (p. 27). Thus the *ascensio Mariae* becomes a sign and symbol of "the value of a human life when it is completely dedicated to the execution of the will of the Heavenly Father and to the happiness of all men" (p. 51) and at the same time a protest against materialism (p. 52) and, finally, a strengthening of our faith "in our own resurrection" (p. 52).

23. The fruits of the ascension are accentuated again and again in Reformed theology. They are "multi ac magni" (*Synopsis Disp.* XXVIII, XX); cf. "spes futurae nostrae haereditatis in capite nostro plenissime confirmata" (*ibid.*). Cf. Heppe. *Dogmatik,* 1861, pp. 363-64.

spite of but *because* of Christ's ascension. Hence Van Ruler says correctly that we may not attach too much significance to the word "concealment." "Its significance is limited if we wish to describe the significance of the ascension with regard to God's Kingdom."[24]

Again and again the attempt has been made to describe the significance of the ascension in one striking word. Van Ruler speaks of the ascension in terms of separation, concealment, and expectation, and admits that its essential meaning is still not exhausted by these descriptions. Hence he speaks of exaltation (accession), concealment (which does not imply separation), and expectation as the aspects of the ascension, and these three aspects are, so to speak, united in the fulfillment (*ibid.*, p. 108). That is, according to him, "the most essential description of the soteriological fact of the ascension." How difficult it is to express its significance in one word becomes evident when Van Ruler says that the fulfillment is still more than these three aspects together. "Over and above the other three the word 'fulfillment' contains an incomparable *plus*" (*ibid.*, p. 115). Calvin, too, speaks of this aspect of fulfillment: Christ has been taken up in order to fulfill all things (*Comm.* on Acts 1:11). Naturally, it is quite important to know what is meant by this fulfillment.

According to Van Ruler the fulfillment means full reality and true presence (p. 112). In the ascension Christ's power penetrates all things. They have an inward iridescence and become transparent. After the ascension we are standing in a glittering world. The reality has become messianic (p. 113). Christ's presence is not, as in the Lutheran conception, a bodily presence but it is the power of his finished work (p. 112). This messianic reality gives meaning and significance to all things. "The Messiah bears the reality" (p. 114). This fulfillment, however, is not yet the eschatological fulfillment, but there are already "fragments, flashes, prophecies, and guarantees of his coming again" (p. 114). Christ's Kingdom, he himself, penetrates and fulfills all things (p. 110). We are confronted with the messianic activity by which reality is emptied of every demonic depth and burden; and it is the ascension which presents this messianic reality.

Van Ruler does not, however, imply a "realized eschatology."

24. A. A. van Ruler, *De Vervulling der Wet,* 1947, p. 106.

The eschatological fulfillment will be the *real* fulfillment. Christ's Kingdom has eschatological limits, also with respect to the fulfillment. Within these limits the messianic work reaches above and beyond itself (p. 110, with reference to Eph. 1:9), which is due to the difference between Christ's Kingdom and God's Kingdom (p. 135). The two are not separated because Christ's Kingdom *is* God's Kingdom, namely "in the manner of the concealment in the flesh" (p. 135) as a *modality* of the Kingdom of God ("which cannot be understood but as a modality of the *regnum Dei*," p. 108). In the future there will be a new and unique act of God "when the messiahship of Christ will cease and even the incarnation will be terminated" (p. 135). The same is true of the outpouring of the Holy Spirit, which is also a modality of God's Kingdom (p. 137). According to Van Ruler we must proceed carefully in concluding that the gift of the Holy Spirit is the initial realization of the Kingdom of God (pp. 142, 157, 159), for the gift of the Spirit is also surrounded by an eschatological border and the period of the Spirit is just as much an "interim" as is that of the messianic reality.[25]

According to Van Ruler the gift of the Holy Spirit is not the initial realization of the Kingdom of God, and hence he also rejects the viewpoint which considers the gift of the Spirit in connection with the Messiah. The work of the Holy Spirit must be considered in connection with the Kingdom and is relatively independent of the gift and work of the Messiah.[26] We do not

25. There will come a moment that the Son will put off the cloak of the flesh. "Thus also the Spirit. When the flesh is done away with then also the outpouring and the indwelling (of the Spirit) will be terminated. When the eternal light of the Kingdom of glory rises over the entire creation, then the illumination of the Spirit (in his outpouring and indwelling) will be extinguished. This eschatologic viewpoint does not imply that now we simply live in expectation. There is more, namely expectation *and* enjoyment" (p. 160). But exactly in this way we understand "that we are not able in any present existence-form to receive, preserve, and portray this abundance of salvation in its all-surpassing glory" (p. 160). There are certain existence-forms which are chosen and sanctified in order that we may receive this salvation, but these are scanty and poor, such as prayer, experience, sacraments, liturgy. Cf. on the signs and the Spirit himself as *the great sign* of the coming Kingdom, p. 161.

26. Van Ruler, *op. cit.*, p. 159: "Since the Spirit is neither the Kingdom itself nor even the initial realization of the Kingdom, there still remains the full expectation of the Kingdom even after the Spirit has been poured out."

have here a relationship between *objective* (work of Christ) and *subjective* (work of the Holy Spirit). It is not the case that the objective revelation is terminated and that the work of Christ from now on needs only to be applied subjectively (pp. 168, 188). In the temporal messianic-pneumatic presence of God in the flesh there is indeed a close connection between Christ and the Spirit, but the work of the Spirit includes more than the work of Christ. The Spirit's work creates the *regnum Christi* in the scope of history: "The Christian centuries come into vision. Also the Christianizing of culture, the theocratizing of the state. In a word: the baptism and the instruction of the nations, and the course of the gospel of the Kingdom in the earth. That is what the gift of the Spirit includes above the gift of the Messiah" (pp. 186-87; cf. 192-93, 197). This viewpoint of Van Ruler possibly confronts us with the core of his theology: the relationship between Christ and the Spirit. The Spirit extends the sacrifice of reconciliation into a Christian existence (p. 187). The gift of the Spirit is incorporated into the Kingdom of Christ, and at the same time it affords this Kingdom "an enormous expansion."[27] In connection with our subject we are mainly concerned with the relatively independent nature of the work of the Spirit as distinguished from that of the Messiah. We cannot see how Van Ruler can maintain this viewpoint if he wants to do justice to the connection, so clearly indicated by Scripture, between the ascension and the outpouring of the Holy Spirit. Why, then, does Scripture say that the Spirit is poured out *in the last days*? One who maintains that this is precisely the beginning of the one fulfillment will hardly be able to explain why the outpouring of the Spirit is a fruit of the ascension when he holds to a sharp differentiation between the Kingdom of God and the Kingdom of Christ, and between the messianic and the superior pneumatological aspects.

We may indeed speak of a redemptive-historical progress in Christ's ascension and thus also of the "more" of the period after

27. Still, the work of the Spirit remains temporary. The gift of the Spirit is something outside his true orbit ("is er in de vreemdheid, het erbijkomende, in de verborgenheid van de gave des Geestes," p. 189). It will ultimately come to an end. This is, according to Van Ruler, a very important viewpoint. The ascension accentuates this concealment unmistakably (p. 191). The gift of the Spirit is not yet a turning from the concealment to the revelation of God's activity, but participates in the concealment of Christ's Kingdom.

Pentecost, but we may not make this the basis for rejecting the gift of the Spirit as an initial realization of the Kingdom of God, nor for rejecting the "objective-subjective" distinction, as Van Ruler does. It seems to me that his objections to the "initial realization" are based on certain strong ideas ("*sterke reactie-momenten*"), a fact which becomes quite evident when he says here that eschatology is endangered. It is exactly here that the significance of the ascension comes into focus. Nor can the connection be established by the notion of "signs." Van Ruler does, indeed, maintain that the "sign" or the "signs" link the Kingdom of God with the Kingdom of Christ, and the theocracy with the Kingdom of God: moreover, the signs imply more than a formal "indication, because they are 'actual' signs" (p. 161). According to Van Ruler, in these signs the harvest has begun (p. 151). But on the other hand, there is evidence of duality in his statement that "the harvest itself," namely "that which will take place with regard to the world," is God's secret (p. 151). It is difficult to see how Van Ruler can maintain an eschatological distinction between the harvest which has begun and the harvest proper on the basis of an objection to the "initial realization" of God's Kingdom. The latter, if interpreted correctly and not in an optimistic, evolutionistic sense, may be identified with the fruit of the work of Christ in this earthly dispensation. The firstfruits of the Spirit do not jeopardize eschatology, but rather, according to Paul, stimulate our expectation. We may speak of "the harvest" in an eschatological sense, but Van Ruler also speaks of it in connection with the messianic and pneumatic reality of this temporary intention when he says that messianically and pneumatically man stands in the fulness of salvation, in the harvest of the world (p. 151). If this is taken with full seriousness it is difficult to understand how Van Ruler can object to the "initial realization," the more so when he maintains that the *regnum Christi is* a modality of the Kingdom of God and the latter is concentrated in the gift and the work of the Messiah and the Spirit, "and especially as such it is present on earth as historical reality."[28] He who maintains this may emphasize the initial and temporal aspects and say that the Kingdom of God "in its real eschatological essence transcends and exceeds it" (cf.

28. Van Ruler, *Het Koninkrijk Gods en de Geschiedenis,* 1947, p. 8. Cf. the Kingdom, which, to be sure, is eschatological, but which descends upon us out of the future in an overwhelming manner and thus creates history (p. 9) as "God's dealings with this reality of ours" (p. 8).

De Vervulling der Wet, pp. 165, 193), but in so doing he agrees rather than disagrees with the idea of "initial realization."

It seems to me that in Van Ruler's discussion we see a clear reflection of today's heated arguments concerning eschatology. We are reminded of Cullmann, Dodd, and Barth, who move and attack each other within the same conception. The increasing opposition to Barth's Christomonism has led many to embrace the conception of the messianic "interim,"[29] which opposition is based on the differentiation between the Kingdom of Christ and the Kingdom of God[30] and on the relative independence of the work of the Spirit. To me it is not just coincidental that Van Ruler hesitantly mentions the "filioque" in the *Nicaeno-Constantinopolitanum* and that he calls the incorporation of this word in the Creed "mostly a cutting of the Gordian knot."[31]

Finally we wish to point out that Van Ruler's idea that the gift of the Spirit includes "more" cannot be proven by the existence of Christian culture and the teaching of the nations. For Christ's commission to his disciples before the ascension fully includes both the nations and their baptism. The "enormous increase" in the work of the Spirit is fully included in the power of reconciliation and of Christ's resurrection. Those who place the messianic and the pneumatological realities side by side,

29. Cf. R. Schippers, "Het Messiaanse Intermezzo bij Van Ruler" in *Bezinning,* Oct., 1950.

30. Van Ruler follows Cullmann here. The latter, however, must admit that the New Testament does not logically carry this differentiation through. Cf. Van Ruler on Cullmann, *Het Koninkrijk Gods en de Geschiedenis,* p. 21. Cf. also, H. N. Ridderbos, *De Komst van het Koninkrijk*: "At least the gospel does not teach this differentiation, neither the term nor the matter itself (p. 101).

31. Van Ruler, *De Vervulling der Wet,* p. 166. He first of all points out that the Church long hesitated. "In fact, she still hesitates," and neither the basis nor the motive for this decision have ever become clear to her, according to Van Ruler (p. 166). Historically it seems to me incorrect to speak of hesitation, and the motive of this decision certainly had to do with the problem of subordinationism (cf. Haitjema, *Dogmatiek als Apologie,* 1948, pp. 272ff.). Van Ruler, although he is of the opinion that there is no sense in going back on the Church's decision, still maintains: "But neither must we attach too much importance to it." Van Ruler's hesitation with respect to the "filioque" is evidently connected with his viewpoint regarding the "relative independence" of the gift and the work of the Spirit compared with the gift and work of the Messiah (p. 167). Cf. his article on "the Experience" in *Kerk en Theologie,* April, 1950.

and then explain their relationship as being "relatively independent," cannot in my opinion do justice to their basic unity, nor to the fact that the Holy Spirit in the last days will take everything of Christ. We surely may not interpret God's redemptive-historical, progressive activity with such a pneumatic "plus" that it jeopardizes the "filioque." This, it seems to me, explains Van Ruler's idea of the "messianic interim," which in its special form is connected with his view of the *regnum Christi* and of the eschatological perspectives of I Corinthians 15. This interim-character culminates in the abrogation of the *unio personalis,"* which is hardly consistent with the Creed of Chalcedon, nor, more importantly, with the Scriptures themselves.[32]

In my opinion, those who consider the pneumatic "plus" to be even slightly independent of the work of Christ fail to recognize the absolutely theocentric character of the entire messianic work. This work was wholly official, and therefore can be linked with the Spirit only by asserting that Christ's work goes forth as a historical power *through* the Holy Spirit. This is implied in the close connection between Christ's ascension and Pentecost. Characteristic of the dispensation of the Spirit is that it concerns the only name, the name of the crucified and resurrected One; and the relationship between Christ and the Spirit is so close that the Scriptures preach the historic correlation of the work of the Holy Spirit with the reconciliation in Christ rather than making a clear distinction between the work of Christ and the

32. Cf. on these questions S. Greijdanus, *Menschwording en Vernedering,* 1903, pp. 197-98. Greijdanus is here dealing with Marcellus of Ancyra, who taught that Jesus Christ would again lay aside his human nature. Cf. Wolfgang Gerricke, *Marcell von Ancyra. De Logos-Christologe und Biblizist. Sein Verhältnis zur antiochenischen Theologie und zum Neuen Testament,* 1940, pp. 142ff. It is not possible to go into all the details. We simply point out the relationship between Marcellus' viewpoint and Sabellianism, and the problem of this interim which engaged especially Kuyper's attention when he opposed the *Vermittlungs*-theology of the 19th century, which theory on the basis of the *idea* of the "God-man-nature" naturally had no use for an interim. Kuyper's fierce opposition against this kind of "incarnation" did not entice him to embrace Marcellus' position, however. See, *Locus de Christo,* III, 196 and I, 96 (on the "cessante causa cessat effectus" in connection with Christ's mediatorship of salvation). Cf. Greijdanus, *op. cit.,* p. 198: "The idea of such an abolition finds no support in I Cor. 15:28 whatsoever, but is definitely contradicted by it." Cf. R. Schippers, "Het Messiaanse Intermezzo bij Van Ruler" in *Bezinning,* 1950, e.g., on Calvin.

work of the Holy Spirit. Paul says, "Wherefore I make known unto you, that no man speaking in the Spirit of God saith, Jesus is anathema; and no man can say, Jesus is Lord, but in the Holy Spirit" (I Cor. 12:3). We read of this Spirit that he says with the bride, "Come" (Rev. 22:17). In the context of this invocation the exalted Lord says of himself that he is the root and the offspring of David, and the bright and morning star (Rev. 22:16). Here, too, the invitation is given to take freely the water of life (vs. 17), of which the Son of Man in his humiliation had spoken as the well of water springing up into everlasting life (John 4:14).

It is inconceivable why the broadness of life, the wideness of the world of nations, and the expansion of the apostolate should lead to the idea of a "plus" which should be more than and relatively independent of the messianic reality. There is every reason not only to confess, with the Church, the ontological trinity with the *filioque,* but also to confess the "economic" trinity and the ascension of Jesus Christ.

A consideral amount of theorizing has taken place in connection with the cloud which took Christ away from the view of the disciples. Questions have been raised in connection with the ancient and modern world-pictures in order to make the reality of this ascension somewhat more intelligible.

We may subscribe to Oepke's characterization of the scriptural account, "which respectfully keeps the secret."[33] To faith, the ascended Christ is the same person who will return on the clouds of heaven (see Matt. 24:30; cf. 26:64). The Church needs to understand nothing but the connection between the cloud which took him out of sight and his return on the clouds of heaven; between the separation and the joy; between the ascension and Pentecost. Many words are heard in the proclamation of the ascension: separation, being with us, preparation of a place, responsibility, calling, victory and expectation, fulfillment and longing.

But all these words express the same faith in Him who remains the same in all eternity, and who in the power of his reconciliation sends the other Comforter (John 14:16) in order thus to be with us until the end of the ages.

33. Kittel, TWNT, s.v. νεφελη (IV, 911).

CHAPTER NINE

"SITTING AT THE RIGHT HAND OF GOD"

PASSING on now to this new phase of Christ's exaltation which is called his sitting at the right hand of God, we first of all face the question whether we should make such a distinction, especially with respect to the ascension. Since Ascension Day is actually the last of the Christian Commemoration Days, should not Christ's *sessio* be dealt with when discussing his ascension?

It is indeed clear that there is a very close connection between Christ's *ascensio* and his *sessio*. This connection is even closer than between the resurrection and the ascension, since a period of forty days separates the two latter events. At first sight *ascensio* and *sessio* seem to be two phases of the same event, in the sense that the fact of the ascension results immediately in the fact of the session. Obviously referring to the ascension, Scripture says that Christ "when he had made purification of sins, sat down on the right hand of the Majesty on high" (Heb. 1:3). Why, then, does the Creed make such a clear distinction between the ascension and the *sessio?* This question is the more pertinent when we compare Lord's Day XVIII with XIX of the Heidelberg Catechism, which stresses the connection between the ascension and the *sessio* very strongly. The answer to the question concerning the significance of the ascension refers to Christ's presence in heaven where he is our advocate (Q. 49), and this same idea is expressed in connection with the *sessio*. The same answer mentions the seeking of the things which are above "where Christ sitteth on the right hand of God" (A. 49). On the other hand, in Lord's Day XIX the ascension is brought up again (Q. 50), which was discussed in the preceding section, while both sections speak of the gift of the Holy Spirit. This connection is brought out most clearly when the *sessio* is thus explained: "Because Christ is ascended into heaven for this end, that he might appear as head of his church, by whom the Father governs all things." Hence it is impossible to treat the ascension as an isolated fact, apart from him who – ascended into heaven – is sitting there at the right hand of God.

Yet it is remarkable that not only in the Creed but also centuries later a distinction was made between the ascension and the *sessio.* Bavinck realizes this when he says that the *sessio* is closely connected with the resurrection and the ascension but yet clearly distinct from them, according to Scripture (*Gereformeerde Dogmatiek,* III, 439). Kuyper also sees a marked distinction: the *sessio* concerns "an entirely different matter" and is a stage all by itself in Christ's exaltation,[1] which, according to him, is often, out of exceeding carelessness and ignorance, overlooked in praying as well as in preaching and speaking. Nevertheless Kuyper's reasoning must still seem weak when he says that Jesus would still have ascended to heaven even if he had not been set at the right hand of God. Such a separation is incompatible with the unity of Christ's office and of his entire life's work.

The supposition that Christ could have ascended to heaven as Mediator in order to bear his sacrifice into the sanctuary, but still not be clothed with the special power of the *sessio,* is simply impossible. Nevertheless, we must with Bavinck on the basis of Scripture make a distinction between the ascension and the *sessio.* The act of the ascension expresses the end of Christ's earthly sojourn, with all the inherent aspects of his messianic work, in his passing into glory. The *sessio* is full of this glory and calls our attention to it, namely, to the reality of Christ's power and glory at the right hand of the Father. Scripture is replete with proofs of this. We are confronted with the high and impressive actuality of the messianic ascent. Because the historical progression is one uninterrupted unity, there is a variety of description. Peter, for instance, says that Christ is exalted at the right hand of God[2] immediately after he has said that God has raised him up, while in his epistle he speaks of the resurrection of Jesus Christ, "who is on the right hand of God, having gone into heaven" (I Pet. 3:22).

There is an indissoluble connection between resurrection, as-

1. Kuyper, *E Voto,* II, 31. Cf. p. 32: "Hence both stages of exaltation ought to be clearly kept apart. The glory of his ascension is one thing, the glory of his sitting at the right hand of God quite another."
2. Acts 2:33; cf., indirectly on the ascension, 2:34. In Rom. 8:34 Paul writes, "It is Christ Jesus that died, yea, rather, that was raised from the dead, who is at the right hand of God." Cf. Col. 3:1, Heb. 8:1.

cension, and *sessio*; and for this reason the New Testament — hence also the Church's confession — can speak of the *sessio* as the finale, as we might call it, of the ascension, as the way to the Father,[3] and consequently can speak of the *sessio* as the definite confirmation of Christ's power which he, on the basis of the completion of his messianic office, has received. He is crowned with honor and glory. Stephen saw him standing on the right hand of God (Acts 7:56). Christ already during his suffering prophesied concerning this glory: "Henceforth ye shall see the Son of man sitting at the right hand of Power, and coming on the clouds of heaven" (Matt. 26:64). This statement to the Jewish Sanhedrin links his suffering with the glory which he will receive and with his *parousia*. In his suffering he is not the counterpart of the Messiah, but just then he is the Messiah as prophecy has pictured him.[4]

Christ's sitting at the right hand of God certainly evidences his power. During the state of his humiliation he had been tempted to accept this power without his suffering, but this he rejected (Matt. 4:9). At the end of his suffering, however, his power is no longer contrary to his messianic office, but its expression and realization. Power, in the struggle for it, is often conceived as brutish and arbitrary force, but in Christ's glory we have an example of what pure and holy power means. It has nothing to do with arbitrariness whatsoever, but is in full harmony with God's justice and love, which are glorified in this power. Of this glory the Catechism says that Christ by his power defends and preserves us against all enemies (Q. 51). The power of his final victory, in the reconciliation of guilt, becomes manifest. Hence the confession of the *sessio* does not by any means reduce the significance of the resurrection and the ascension, but rather emphasizes them (cf. Heb. 8:1, 10:12, 12:2). Christ's work was not a well-intended but powerless work which did not obtain its objective. That seemed so during his suffering, which is evident from the complaint of the disciples of Emmaus: "But we hoped that it was he who should redeem Israel" (Luke 24:21). But Christ showed them that they had been deceived by appearances, and that he would soon enter into his glory (24:26). He is the *Kurios*, the Lord, and it is the power of the Spirit which

3. Here again we see its twofold aspect: Christ's activity (he sat down on the right hand of God, Heb. 1:3) and God's activity which set him at his own right hand in the heavenly places (Eph. 1:20).

4. Cf. Dan. 7:13. Cf. H. N. Ridderbos, *Korte Verklaring, Matt.*, II, 211.

leads to the acknowledgment: "Jesus is Lord."[5] All the New Testament joy converges in this one glorious prospect as the annihilation of all that terrifies. This indicates a universal prospect: it is an absolute dominion, which also implies that Christ is an advocate with the Father (I John 2:1, cf. Rom. 8:34), who by his power and authority keeps us forever.

Hence the Church does not consist of a group of individual believers who are united by the same "conviction," but she has her Lord, her Head in heaven (Col. 1:18, Eph. 1:22, 4:15, 5:23). Without this relationship the Church can never be understood. She is not merely a cultural phenomenon, for her relationship to Christ manifests her true essence. All gifts and powers and the protection of the Church derive their reality only from the Lord in heaven, as does her growth: ". . . may grow up in all things into him, who is the head, even Christ" (Eph. 4:15). In the *sessio* we are dealing with Christ's power, the power of his holy sacrifice by which our salvation is established in heavenly inviolability. Here heaven is not the antithesis of terrestrial life, as though the latter were of no significance any more. On the contrary, just because of the Lord in heaven, earthly life becomes meaningful, since in him it is freed from arbitrariness and the threat of chaos inherent in the power of sin. Separation from Christ is made impossible by the love of Christ, our Lord (Rom. 8:39). Neither length nor breadth, height nor depth, are able to overwhelm this power now that the man-child has been caught up unto God and to his throne (Rev. 12:5-6). To be sure, the Church must carry on through the darkness of oppression and persecution — the woman flees into the wilderness — but her deliverance is sure in his power, which assures her of his keeping and protection. In the midst of the darkness of her trials (Heb. 11:36-40) shines the light of his promises, and she is admonished not to fail of the grace of God (Heb. 12:15), to lift up the hands which hang down and the feeble knees (Heb. 12:12, cf. II Cor. 3:1ff.). To be apprehended of

5. I Cor. 12:3. Cf. Phil. 2:11. Cf. Kittel, TWNT, III, s.v. *κύριος*. Note the profound connection between humiliation and exaltation relative to Christ's Lordship. In Rom. 1:4 we read in connection with the resurrection "Jesus Christ, our Lord" (cf. Acts 2:36) and in John 13:13 Christ says, "Ye call me, Teacher and, Lord: and ye say well; for so I am." Yet his Lordship is linked up with his washing the disciples' feet: "Know ye what I have done to you" (vs. 12). Cf. vs. 14: "If I then, the Lord and the Teacher, have washed your feet . . . ."

Christ means to reach forth unto those things which are before and to press toward the mark of the prize of the high calling of God in Christ Jesus (Phil. 3:13-14, cf. vs. 20). The *sessio* is not an abstract theme resulting from the Church's idea of the Lord; instead, it is the foundation of her doxology: "Blessed be the God and Father of our Lord Jesus Christ, who hath blessed us with every spiritual blessing in the heavenly places in Christ" (Eph. 1:3). Indeed, God "hath raised us up with him, and made us to sit with him in the heavenly places, in Christ Jesus" (Eph. 2:6).

This is not escapism, for the New Testament does not speak dualistically but historically. Again and again it stresses the reality of the *kerygma* in Christ Jesus, who does not call us out of the world but rather tells us how to live in the world. A practical, concrete example is seen in Paul's admonition to slave owners: "And, ye masters, do the same things unto them, and forbear threatening: knowing that he who is both their Master and yours is in heaven, and there is no respect of persons with him" (Eph. 6:9. cf. also Col. 4:1 where we find the same master-slave relationship). The hope which is laid up in heaven (Col. 1:5) does not turn its back upon life on earth but directs it toward communion with the living Lord.

We wish to emphasize that the *sessio Christi* can be confessed only in faith. It is not a conclusion from our analysis of reality, for by faith alone can we recognize Christ crowned with all power in heaven and on earth, the head of his Church. In these days there is much confusion both in the world and in the Church; it is easy to lose sight of Christ's scepter, and of the light that emanates from his once-for-all work of redemption. That work places Christ in the very center of the cosmos; He is the Light of the *world*.

It is in this connection that the Church speaks of the significance of the *sessio Christi*. History does not follow its own course. When John on Patmos weeps because no one is worthy to open the book in the right hand of him who sat on the throne, then the encouraging answer is: "Weep not; behold, the Lion that is of the tribe of Judah, the Root of David, hath overcome to open the book and the seven seals thereof" (Rev. 5:5). John sees the Lamb there, *standing* as it had been *slain* (vs. 6). It is as though a window is opened upon the full dynamic of history, and we are vividly reminded of all that took place. The entire chapter centers around what the Lamb of God accomplished in the historical fulfillment of prophecy (cf. Rev. 5:5, Gen. 49:9-10, Isa. 11:1, Rev. 22:10; see also Rev. 5:9, 12, 13) and especially around Christ's victory. Christ's decisive work definitely concerns the world and history. In Revelation he is called "Lord of lords and King of kings" (17:14).

Hence it is easy to understand why many have explored the connection between Christ's sitting at the right hand of God and the history of the world, particularly the "powers" ruling the world. It has been recognized generally that Christ possesses supreme power, but many have asked whether the fact that Christ came to his glory by way of the cross has any specific significance and what the consequences thereof are for the world. Thus the confession of the *sessio Christi* has become a focal point in the contemporary theological discussions.[6] It has been pointed out that the glory of Christ could not be merely a matter of saving sinners, but that it must also concern the cosmic aspects of his work.[7] Visser 't Hooft declares that traditional Protestantism has well developed the idea of Christ's prophetic and priestly office, but that it has not done so with his kingly office (*Het Koningschap van Christus,* 1947, p. 12). In his opinion the Reformers showed a reserved attitude toward Christ's kingship, more so than with regard to his other offices, and this shows, according to him, that they lacked eschatological insight. This criticism surprises us, since at least Calvin was of the opinion that Christ "is called Messiah especially on account of his kingship" (*Inst.*, II, XV, 2; discussed in detail in II, XV, 3ff.), even though he also does justice to Christ's prophetic and priestly offices. Since Visser 't Hooft's criticism includes Calvin too, it is evident that he is referring to a certain kind of evaluation of Christ's kingship. Protestant tradition, he says, has related Christ's dominion too much to the realm of his Church without determining "in which respect and in what manner Christ is King of the world" (*op. cit.*, p. 16; cf. "no clear

6. This is discussed in greater detail in my *The Providence of God,* Chapter IV.
7. Such a condition usually calls forth dangerous dilemmas, for instance, cosmic-soteriological. Werner Elert correctly criticizes Erich Schaeder, who wrote in *Theozentrische Theologie*: "World missions is essentially not a matter of saving people or souls, but the establishment of Christ's Kingdom in the world." Truly a strange "not – but"! See W. Elert, "Regnum Christi" in *Zwischen Gnade und Ungnade,* 1948, pp. 74-75.

explanation concerning Christ's dominion in society"). Here we are touching upon the core of this particular criticism, which proves to be closely related to the current theory that the state has a Christological basis.

The point is not whether Christ's royal dominion is accepted or denied, but what the nature and significance of this dominion are. Hence it is quite questionable whether Visser 't Hooft does justice to history when he states that Christ's kingship has been rediscovered in the twentieth century after it had been totally denied by Schleiermacher and neglected by the Reformers before him.[8] This is equating the positions of Luther, Calvin, and Schleiermacher, whereas there is a profound difference between Calvin's viewpoint and that of Schleiermacher.[9] In Calvin there is no trace of a non-cosmic, subjective conception of Christ's kingship, nor do we find any such in Q. 50 of the Heidelberg Catechism.[10] What Visser 't Hooft does not find in Calvin and others is obviously a particular conception of the *regnum Christi*, which today is inseparably connected with the idea that the state has an eschatological foundation and which finds its ultimate development in the well-known analogy-conception.

Like Barth, Visser 't Hooft attempts by means of the analogy-idea to explain how the truth by which the Church lives is significant for human society.[11] "The actions and decisions of the church in the world attempt by way of analogy to express what the church is and what she confesses"; in this way Christ's

8. Visser 't Hooft finds evidences of this rediscovery especially in the period between the first and second world wars, and particularly in the later development of the dialectic theology (chapter 2). In his foreword he also mentions Kuyper, who nearly half a century before (in Princeton, where Visser 't Hooft held his lectures) in his Stone Lectures "in a penetrating manner spoke of these world-embracing perspectives of the gospel."

9. Cf. Schleiermacher's statement: "Consequently Christ's rule extends only over the church's implanted, inherent powers of salvation," in *Der Christliche Glaube,* 1884[7], p. 144, par. 105.

10. Cf., among others, K. Fröhlich, *Die Reichgottesidee Calvins,* 1922, pp. 27ff. on Calvin's ideas: "the *regnum Christi* looms before us in its grandeur" (p. 28). Indeed, "the concept of Christ's Kingdom is the keystone in the mighty structure of the Calvinistic Christology." For the difference between Calvin and Schleiermacher see Calvin's commentary on Matt. 28:19.

11. He compares his idea with the Calvinistic doctrine of common grace (*op. cit.,* p. 127). How this can be compatible with what he writes of Kuyper (see note 8, above) is not shown.

kingship is manifested concretely. The Church knows and confesses the Light of the world in Christ, which by analogy has political implications (Barth, "Christengemeinde und Bürgergemeinde" *Theol. Stud.*, No. 20, 1946, p. 22), for instance "that the church is the declared enemy of all secret politics and secret diplomacy."[12] We are dealing with analogies, *Entsprechungen* of the Kingdom of God as it is believed and preached in the Christian community, in the realm of the external, relatively tentative problems of the human society (p. 33), and hence with Christian, spiritual, prophetic knowledge. We are dealing with "politics" on the basis of the *sessio Christi.* That is supposed to be the meaning of the expression in the Catechism that the Father governs all things by Christ, even though Barth's "examples" show some uncertainty.[13] The state is said to have a Christological basis; the work of Christ places its imprint on the state, so that all political decisions (indeed, why not all?) are to be made on the basis of the cross. The reign of Christ supposedly refers to this structuring of political decisions, to this imprint on the state.[14]

This discussion is therefore not concerned with maintaining Christ's *regnum* over against its denial, but with a certain con-

12. Barth gives still more illustrations. For instance, because of the ecumenical character of the Church she is, in politics, necessarily opposed to all "abstract local-regional and national interests" (p. 32); and because of the grace of God conceived of after the analogy of politics, she stays away from "solving conflicts in society by means of violence" (p. 32). We cannot, however, see why Barth considers such "solutions" (with his analogy-idea) to be possible and legitimate in special instances, especially if the analogy-idea is applied to the perfection of the Heavenly Father and the politics of peace on earth (p. 33).
13. According to Barth we are not dealing with a system (p. 34) and "it is in the nature of the mentioned or still to mention points of comparison or crises that the transitions from the one realm to the other in their details will always be debatable, always more or less plausible, and that whatever we add to this is not of such a nature that we can call them final proofs" (*op. cit.*, p. 34). Cf. also what Barth writes concerning the "striking inclination" – on account of the gospel – to democracy (p. 36).
14. Brunner sharply criticizes Visser 't Hooft's book precisely with regard to this matter of "analogy" in *Dogmatik, II,* 1950, pp. 371-75, where he says that Visser t' Hooft does not even produce a semblance of a criterion by which to distinguish good from bad laws (p. 374) and that he confuses the *regnum Christi* with the state. Cf. on Barth's "new principle" (the analogy), which according to Brunner originates from Barth's uncertain attempt to deduce concrete norms for the state from Christology (p. 374).

ception of the relationship between Church and state which has absolutely no basis either in Scripture or in any confession. To proceed from Christ's supremacy over all things to the application of the analogy-principle is to exceed the limits of our understanding; it will ultimately pave the way for the weakening of the power of the dominion of Christ, an unavoidable result when the structural basis of the state is misinterpreted and the political decisions in the state are said to derive from the cross of Christ. This theory, instead of acknowledging the "concealment" of the dominion of Christ, wants to penetrate this mystery before his coming. Scripture indeed emphatically teaches Christ's power, and especially the confession of the *sessio Christi* emphasizes it, but this does not by any means imply that the cross becomes the basic principle for all political decisions. On the other hand, it does not mean that the cross has nothing to do with the state and politics either. Every secularization of the state and politics and every form of absolutism or deification of the state is the result of the denial of God's sovereignty, which in the cross of Christ becomes manifest as a blessing to the world. It is this Christ who is the King of kings and the Lord of lords (Rev. 17:14). But the acknowledgment of his power unto salvation and his dominion has nothing to do with the analogy-principle.[15] Whoever adheres to the analogy-principle must come to the conclusion that Paul held an "abstract" sovereignty idea when in Romans 13 he acknowledges God's ordinances concerning the state without deducing them from analogies.

We do not know the structure and stability of the world by way of the cross, but our service in this world becomes possible again on the basis of our communion with the living Lord. Whoever attempts to deduce the structure of all political decisions from the cross Christologizes history.

It seems to us that this turn of contemporary theological thought concerning the *regnum Dei* is closely related to a bent

15. In my opinion due to a misunderstanding, Van Ruler remarks that Herman Ridderbos (*De Komst van het Koninkrijk,* p. 326) "curiously enough" follows entirely the line of Barth's thinking (A. A. van Ruler, *Bijzonder en Algemeen Ambt*, 1952, p. 14). However, Barth's analogy-idea is missing in H. N. Ridderbos, so that his quoting Barth on p. 326 by no means implies this "analogy" as, moreover, is perfectly clear from Ridderbos' lecture at the Social Congress, 1952 (*De Bijbelse Boodschap en de Sociale Verhoudingen*).

toward irrationalism which wishes to preach Christ in a chaotic, disconnected world. In this line of thinking Christ does not merely restore *service* by his reconciliation, but he establishes stability out of chaos. Scripture, however, furnishes no basis for such a theory. To hold that the state is Christologically founded is to contradict Scripture and the confession of the trinity; nor is there any scriptural proof for a sharp distinction between *regnum Christi* and *regnum Dei.*

Scripture does indeed speak of the *sessio Christi* in connection with God's dominion over all things, but it is *God* who rules and who in Christ blesses and protects life and guides it to the fulness of the Kingdom of God. It goes without saying that God's activity in Christ can call our special attention to the dangers of wickedness in state and politics. He who understands the *sessio Christi* knows the arrogance and pride behind the lust for power by which some imagine that their lives are preserved. This "misconception" was brought to light historically by God himself when he disarmed the earthly powers and revealed the unity of his love and his justice. Already Mary in her song mentions this when she warns against filling one's life outside of God without obedience to him. But the position that the state has a Christological structure and is Christologically founded is invulnerable to such "unmasking" as Mary's song speaks of. According to this theory the state must be considered in conjunction with the Church and the cross, and the essential meaning of the state must be based on the assumption that it is the cross which puts order into its chaos.

Bavinck, when speaking of Christ's kingship, points out that in the New Testament Christ is particularly called the head of the Church (*Gereformeerde Dogmatiek*, III, 479). Therefore, he says, Christ's kingship is entirely different from that of the rulers of the earth.

But Bavinck by no means denies Christ's kingly power. This power has been given to him for the gathering together of his Church and for her protection against all enemies. In this connection he writes that the various Scriptures which speak of the power given to Christ do not imply "that the world is positively ruled by Christ, they do imply that it is under his dominion and subject to him and that one day, be it involuntarily, it will acknowledge and honor him as Lord."

It is not very well possible to make a distinction between "to rule positively" and "to be under his dominion" since the one includes the other. His dominion, however, refers to the concealed form of Christ's kingdom, so that only by faith we know of this dominion.

Hebrews 2, with reference to Psalm 8, calls our attention to the fact that we see not yet all things put under him (man) but, the author continues, "we behold . . . Jesus . . . crowned with glory and honor" (vss. 8-9). It is a glory and honor resulting from his sacrifice, and thus, by the power of this sacrifice, he governs the world with power. By his victory he dethroned the powers, made them a public spectacle, and conquered them. Scripture emphatically ridicules the powers which boast and resist the cross. In the *sessio* we observe something of the laughter of the holy, divine irony: "He that sitteth in the heavens will laugh: the Lord will have them in derision" (Ps. 2:4). This divine laughter is also heard with respect to his decree (vs. 7) and throughout history. Christ's *sessio* is the tentative finale of his earthly course. Every power which refuses to be a *serving* power becomes subject to the justice of Christ's glory.

Christ's sitting at the right hand of God is the fulfillment of Psalm 110: "Sit thou at my right hand, Until I make thine enemies thy footstool" (vs. 1, cf. Kittel, s.v. κύριος). The New Testament Church doubted not in the least the reality of Christ's sitting at the right hand of God. Later the question arose how, since Christ is *vere deus, vere homo,* his being in heaven must be understood. Such questions played an important role in the sixteenth-century controversy between Lutheran and Reformed believers. They agreed that Christ had ascended but disagreed sharply about the nature of Christ's presence in heaven. This difference of conception, however, has nothing to do with the still later criticism of the preaching of the ascension, which criticism is based on the modern conception that the universe cannot have a "heaven" above the earth. The latter criticism makes it impossible to believe in the ascension at all. Consequently the ascension and also Christ's sitting at the right hand of God in heaven are said to require "demythologizing." Noordmans, for instance, declares that this stumblingblock no longer has the significance it used to have (Noordmans, *op. cit.,* p. 164). "The conflict does not concern the natural but the revealed religion." But precisely because it concerns God's revelation, the reality of Christ in heaven is at stake now as much as in the preceding century. Hence it is truly not a natural-scientific conflict but a religious one, because what is at stake in the confession of the Church is precisely this: the historical perspectives, Christ's intercession, his preservation of the saints, and his coming again.

All this is at stake in "demythologizing," and it is the duty of the Church to make this clear by means of a living faith, without her assuming the right to give a scientific explanation concerning "heaven" as the place where Christ is sitting at the right hand of God. After Bavinck has stated that Scripture definitely teaches the *sessio Christi* he very carefully adds, "Whether the right hand of God in turn indicates a particular place in heaven we cannot say with any degree of certainty" (*Geref. Dog.*, III, 440). It is surely not incorrect to speak of the right hand of God, but still it is a metaphorical expression. "The Christian church has always realized this and has refrained from further defining the place of Christ's exaltation." Bavinck wants to bring out the power and glory of Christ in heaven as implied in his *sessio.* Such confession is by no means a scientific one but a soteriological confession of faith. To the Church it has always been a source of comfort to know that Christ is in heaven with the Father. And over against the denial of both the *ascensio* and *sessio* as being contrary to the "modern world conception," the Church may continue on the basis of Holy Scripture to speak of these facts in simplicity of faith.

In this connection we finally wish to call attention to the remarkable controversy between Lutheran and Reformed believers concerning Christ's being in heaven. For a correct understanding of this controversy it is best to take Question 47 of the Heidelberg Catechism as our starting point. After the discussion of the article which deals with Christ's ascension the question is considered whether Christ is not then with us even unto the end of the world as he has promised (cf. Matt. 28:20).

This promise of Christ has always been the starting point of the Church's reflection on our communion with Christ between his ascension and the *parousia.* The Catechism refers back to the person of Christ — *vere deus, vere homo* — and continues, "With respect to his human nature, he is no more on earth; but with respect to his Godhead, majesty, grace, and spirit, he is at no time absent from us." It has often been alleged that Reformed theology evidences Nestorian tendencies in this answer of the

Catechism because it makes a distinction between the human and the divine natures of Christ, so that the question could be posed whether the Catechism really does agree with what the *Chalcedonense* says of the two natures' being "undivided and unseparated." Now it is true that Reformed theology has always strongly opposed those who violated the terms "unmixed and unchanged" of the *Chalcedonense,* because there were evidences – especially in Lutheran theology – that some were imparting divine attributes to the human nature of Christ, contrary to the teaching of the *Chalcedonense.* The question remains, however, whether Reformed theology was guilty of an opposite tendency toward Nestorianism, since Question 47 seems to point in that direction.

In our opinion it must be insisted that Reformed theology was fully aware of the danger both of monophysitism and of Nestorianism, as is fully evident from the answer to this question. In a forthright manner it poses the objection in the question: "But if his human nature is not present wherever his Godhead is, are not these two natures in Christ separated from one another?" The answer is: "Not at all," because, even allowing for the so-called *Extra-Calvinisticum* it is by no means denied that the Godhead is also present in Christ's human nature and remains personally united to it. Hence when the Catechism speaks of "with respect to his human nature" and "with respect to his Godhead," it does not mean to separate the two natures but to do justice to Christ's ascension, his no longer being with us bodily, as Scripture so clearly emphasizes.[16] The Catechism intends to bring out this scriptural teaching – the element of *separation* in the ascension – when it says that Christ, with respect to his human nature, is no more on earth. It speaks not the language of science but the simple language of faith when it explains, in connection Christ's promise in Matthew 28, that he, with respect to his Godhead, majesty, grace and spirit, is at no time absent from us. It is at once evident that when the Catechism says "with respect to his human nature" and "with respect to his divine nature" it does not separate these, but immediately relates

16. The proof texts furnished with Question 47 clearly indicate this, namely Heb. 8:4, ". . . if he were on earth . . ."; Matt. 26:11, "For ye have the poor always with you; but me ye have not always"; John 16:28, ". . . again, I leave the world, and go to the Father"; John 17:11, "And now I am no more in the world . . ."; and Acts 3:21, "whom the heavens must receive until the times of restoration of all things. . . ."

Christ's presence with us to the power of his Godhead, majesty, grace and Spirit, correctly referring to John 14:18: "I will not leave you comfortless." Hence the Catechism does not separate the two natures but tries to do justice to the mystery of Christ's person and to express the nature of Christ's presence now, which is different from his presence when he was still on earth. Reformed theology acknowledges, indeed, the element of separation in so far as it refuses to deduce Christ's promised presence from a sort of *communicatio idiomatum* which would result in an omnipresence of Jesus Christ in his *human* nature.

It is precisely at this juncture that we touch upon the core of the well-known controversy between Lutheran and Reformed theology. A typical representative of the Lutheran dogmatical position is Gerhard, who also comments on Christ's promise that he will not leave us comfortless. Gerhard says, "The God-man is speaking here, and promises his presence not only with respect to his divine but also his human nature."[17] We cannot speak of a presence of Christ if his *humanitas* is excluded.[18] That would mean that his promise is void of all comfort.[19] Gerhard applies this idea to Christ's ascension and his sitting at the right hand of God. There is a great difference between the ascension of Enoch and Elijah and Christ's, because the former are no longer on earth, but Christ's position is entirely different.

He is exalted at the right hand of God, which does not imply a limited place but the infinite power of God and his majesty over heaven and earth by which God rules the world (*ibid.*, p. 558). By his ascension and *sessio* Christ partakes of this dominion also with respect to his human nature. According to Gerhard there is no element of limitation or local nature connected with Christ's *sessio*.[20] By virtue of the *unio personalis*

17. Johannis Gerhardi, *Loci Theologici* (ed. Frank Tom), I, 1885, p. 557 (with reference also to Matt. 18:20 and 28:20). "Pronomen *ego* est totius personae nomen. Ergo enim totius personae secundum utramque naturam praesentiam infert," directed against those who interpret this promise "de sola deitate" (among others, against Piscator and Keckermann).

18. *Ibid.*, p. 557: "Ubicunque non est humana Christi natura, ibi etiam Christus non est homo, nisi quis dicere velit, Christum alicubi absque humana natura esse hominem."

19. "Quae igitur consolatio ex illa promissione hauriri possit?" Cf. also p. 514.

20. ". . . ergo Dextra Dei non est aliquis finitus ac circumscriptus in coelo locus."

Jesus Christ is omnipresent.[21] The right hand of God is interpreted as God's omnipresence, to which Christ's human nature is exalted. Hence the *Calviniani* are wrong when they maintain that Christ's body is only in heaven until the day of the final judgment (*ibid.*, p. 562).

The Lutherans were obviously convinced that the Reformed viewpoint evidenced a Nestorian separation of Christ's natures, no matter how emphatically the Reformed claimed that they, also in this regard, wished to maintain the *unio personalis* inviolable.[22] But the Lutherans could not very well defend themselves against the accusation from the Reformed that the Lutherans contradicted the *Chalcedonense* by attributing the divine omnipresence to Christ's human nature. The Reformed, on the basis of Scripture, refused to allow their human Brother to become lost in the omnipresence of God. They, no more than the Lutherans, could fathom the relationship between the divine and human natures, whether in the *ascensio* or in the *sessio,* but they preferred simply to stammer concerning the double *vere* with the *Chalcedonense* rather than to fall into the abysses of monophysitism and docetism. We may admit that Reformed theology had to guard itself against Nestorianism, but it is quite evident from this whole controversy with the Lutherans that the Reformed were fully aware of this danger. With respect to the inseparable *unio personalis* they went as far as they could on the basis of Scripture.

The Reformed objection to the Lutheran interpretation of

21. Concerning the difficulty with respect to the Lord's supper see especially p. 562, where Gerhard defends his position over against Bellarminus, who said, "Ubiquitatem pugnare cum sacramento eucharistiae . . . . Nam si caro Christi est ubique, certe non egemus eucharistia, cum domi habeamus in pane et vino et aliis omnibus cibis corpus Christi." Gerhard's reply is weak when he says that Bellarminus confuses the *praesentia sacramentalis* and the *praesentia majestatica.* This poses the problem of Lutheran Christology and the doctrine concerning the Lord's supper. Lutheran theology distinguishes between *praesentia majestatica* and *praesentia sacramentalis,* which is dependent "a Christi institutione et voluntate" (p. 562).

22. Gerhard himself furnishes striking examples of this from Beza and especially from Zanchius (*ibid.*, p. 563), for instance when he cites Zanchius' "Ego certe non contradixero, et ita omnes docti ac pii concedunt, humanam Christi naturam *personaliter* esse omnipotentem, ubique praesentem" (p. 563). Gerhard considers this a concession and comments: "quod una manu dederunt, altera iterum eripiunt," even though he discusses these things as arguments "ex adversariis."

Christ's *sessio* ran parallel with another objection, namely to the Lutheran doctrine of consubstantiation. Both, according to the Reformed, denied Christ's true humanity. The Reformed did not wish to deny Christ's *praesentia realis* in the Lord's supper, but did insist upon the scriptural doctrine that Christ is both really present and also absent. They were not interested in explaining this with a speculative dimensional theory, nor did they deny the anthropomorphic character of "the right hand of God," but they did wish to confess the true humanity of Christ. This humanity should not be dissolved in a general *omnipraesentia Dei,* for Christ was and is our Advocate with the Father.

Barth correctly points out that the Reformed theologians sharply discerned the weak spot in the Lutheran *sessio* doctrine.[23] He adds, however, that there is a weak point in the Reformed argument as well, namely in the statement that, although Christ departed from us as far as his body is concerned, he yet remains with us with his Godhead, Spirit, power, activity, and majesty. Does that then leave "a humanity deprived of its Godhead" (*K.D.* II, 1, 550). And are Answers 47 and 48 of the Heidelberg Catechism insufficient? If the Lutherans were to ask whether we are now dealing with the entire Christ, "then these answers must, in spite of all their correct elements, be considered insufficient if not evasive" (*ibid.*). We cannot now pursue the solution which Barth proposes in order to bring the controversy between Lutherans and Reformed to a higher level. He does so by proceeding from his own idea concerning God's omnipresence,[24] on the basis of which, according to him, it becomes possible to do justice to both the Lutheran and Reformed motives.

23. K. Barth, *Kirchliche Dogmatik,* II, 1, 549: "She [Reformed theology] opposed the application of the *ubique* to Christ's human nature and hence to his corporeality as such." The Reformed viewpoint adheres to Christ's "concrete, non-problematic humanity."

24. This conception, which is peculiarly in line with Barth's entire dogmatics, is not concerned with the general background of the omnipresence of God by which the special presence is a special application thereof. On the contrary, the general truth is included and implied in the special. According to this viewpoint "God's omnipresence is not only more or less noetically [for our perception] but also ontically [in its reality] connected with his peculiar presence exactly in his revelatory and reconciliatory activity" (*K.D.* II, 1, 538). This is the decisive aspect on the basis of which Barth tries to circumvent the controversy between Lutherans and Reformed, which came to a dead end because it could not be solved on the 16th century level (see especially pp. 550-51).

We only wish to point out that in our opinion the core of this controversy was the Lutheran inclination to elevate and overestimate the human nature in the *unio personalis*. That is what the Reformed justly contested, and when Barth, on the basis of his solution, wishes with the Lutherans to emphasize Christ's real presence, then it may be pointed out that this is an element which the Reformed have always emphatically taught — so emphatically, indeed, that Gerhard derives an argument from it to defend his own conception of the *sessio!* Consequently when we, contrary to Barth, hold that this problem was in principle solved on a scriptural basis in the sixteenth century, then we are by no means implying that this was a *rational solution,* any more than Chalcedon's defense against two different heresies was a rational explanation of the *vere deus, vere homo.* Neither did the Reformed confession concerning the *sessio* point in that direction. This controversy was prompted by religious motives because they were scriptural. In my opinion, the clearest solution may be found in Calvin, who paved the way for all of Reformed theology. He vigorously rejects the invisible, corporeal presence of Christ, because he says that we have the *man* Jesus Christ as an Advocate in heaven, our flesh and blood, and nothing may be added to or subtracted from the concreteness of this statement.

This does not mean that Calvin assumes the liberty to rationalize Christ's exaltation or that he pretends to have a clear conception of Christ in heaven. He says that Christ's body is exalted above all the heavens (*Inst.* II, XVI, 14), He is sitting at the right hand of God. According to Calvin this means that he rules in the power and majesty and glory of the Father (*Inst.* IV, XVII, 18). This kingdom "is not limited by any intervals of space nor circumscribed by any dimensions. Christ can exert his energy wherever he pleases, in earth and heaven, can manifest his presence by the exercise of his power, can always be present with his people, breathing into them his own life, can live in them, sustain, confirm and invigorate them, and preserve them safe, just as if he were with them in the body."[25] Calvin

25. *Ibid.*, ". . . non secus acsi corpore adesset." Compare the Lutheran standpoint regarding the "place" in heaven with what Calvin says: ". . . hoc regnum nec ullis locorum spatiis limitatum, nec ullis dimensionibus circumscriptum." Against the Lutheran Westphal, Calvin remarks: "Quid, an nos inter medias sphaeras Christum locamus? Vel tugurium ei extruimus inter planetas?" He answers: "Coelum est magnificum Dei palatium, toto mundo opificio superius" (in W. Niesel, *Calvins Lehre vom Abendmahl,* 1930, p. 77).

can say as much as the Lutherans concerning the blessing and power of Christ, but he rejects the ubiquity as an assault upon Christ's true humanity, which is our pledge in heaven. To be sure, Calvin points out the inconsistencies in the Lutheran doctrine, but his main motive is soteriological in character. The most striking aspect of this whole controversy is the fact that both parties wanted to defend vigorously Christ's salvation. The Lutherans, too, are concerned with the comfort of the believers. But for the sake of that salvation and this comfort the *man* Christ must be "*capax infinitae potentiae*," as Brenz puts it.[26] If Christ were not omnipresent then his soteriological work would be devoid of all comfort, and therefore everything depends upon Christ's corporeal omnipresence. Here is where the decision must be made in the controversy between Lutherans and Calvinists. In the light of the ecumenical confession of the Church in the Chalcedon Creed, this decision will have to be in favor of the Reformed confession — not because she has fully fathomed the mystery but because she has refused to go even one step toward the deification of Christ's human nature, a tendency which has been a constant temptation in the history of the Church and of which there are indications also in Lutheran Christology.

In the light of this decision we may point out the problems resulting from this Lutheran doctrine, problems which not only jeopardize the reality of Christ's humanity in the *sessio*, but in Christ's earthly life as well. On the basis of the Lutheran doctrine of the *communicatio idiomatum* it cannot be said that Christ's bodily presence in Bethlehem, Bethsaida, or Gethsemane was confined to these places, either. But Scripture leaves no doubt in this matter, and Lutheran doctrine has restored in turn to the explanation that Christ either laid down his divine attributes or did not make use of them in order to do justice to the concreteness of his terrestrial life. It is no wonder that precisely this matter was the source of a long-lasting controversy, which was one of the factors that occasioned that strange *kenosis* doctrine of the nineteenth century which was nothing but a departure from the original Lutheran Christology and from Chalcedon.

26. Cf. Otto Fricke, *Die Christologie des Johann Brenz,* 1927, p. 198; cf. also W. Köhler, *Dogmengeschichte. Das Zeitaler der Reformation,* 1951, pp. 228ff.; H. Schmid, *Die Dogmatik der ev. luth. Kirche,* 1893[7], pp. 292f.

Calvin, on the other hand, did not have to resort to these artificial solutions which are characteristic of the Lutheran position. For one thing, he avoided the difficulty of not being able to speak concretely of Christ's life on earth and of having to consider Christ's human nature after his exaltation as participating in the attributes of the divine nature. He rejected the ubiquity of the human nature, while at the same time he emphasized Christ's unfathomable personal presence in accordance with his sitting at the right hand of God.

It is quite obvious that the character of Christ's second coming is closely connected with these problems. Niesel says correctly: "We must finally remark that the Lutheran assertion that Christ is invisibly present draws our attention away from eschatological realities."[27] Niesel is referring to the supposed invisible presence of Christ's body, and points out that Calvin was fully conscious of these dangers. Hence he admonished the believers to look in faith to heaven. It is the same language which we encounter in the Reformed Form for the Lord's Supper, in which the believers are admonished to lift their hearts up on high "where Christ Jesus is our Advocate at the right hand of his heavenly Father." Again, this is not spiritualism or escapism, for the New Testament conception of heaven is not that of an *idea*. It is indeed possible to lift one's heart on high to heaven, in the sense in which the New Testament speaks of Christ's heaven in historical and end-historical perspectives and by which one's ordinary life under the scepter of this Lord is filled with a burning expectation of his new presence.

27. Niesel, *op. cit.*, p. 81. Cf. Bavinck, *Geref. Dog.*, IV, 672.

CHAPTER TEN

CHRIST AND THE FUTURE

NOW THAT we have considered Christ's resurrection, ascension, and session at the right hand of God, our attention is suddenly turned in a different direction as the Apostles' Creed proceeds with the discussion of the expectation of Christ's return. When we discussed Christ's way to exaltation, our attention was again and again called to the past, to what had taken place. There we were, in the full sense of the word, dealing with the *facts* of salvation, with God's activity in all those events which reveal clearly the fruits of Christ's suffering and death.

But now our gaze is directed to the future, to that which is "not yet." *Faith* is required in a very obvious sense, even though faith is also required to confess the resurrection, ascension, and *sessio.* Indeed, the unity and continuity of the Creed at this point makes especially clear the fact that Christ's work of salvation is radically *historical,* passing from the past *into the future.*

Reformed dogmatics distinguishes sometimes three, sometimes four, stages in Christ's exaltation. The Synopsis mentions only the resurrection, ascension, and *sessio,* while others, following the Creed, add a fourth, Christ's return. The difference is not crucial as long as the close connection is seen between the reality of Christ in heaven and his coming on the clouds of heaven. This coming is presented in Scripture as a new event which is still to be expected, and for that very reason it is connected with Christ's glory and power at the right hand of God. It is not our intention here to bring up the eschatological problems and the eschatological confession of the Church, but we must consider the fact that the work of Christ, also in his exaltation, is eschatologically oriented. The confession of the *sessio Christi* is not a confession which suddenly stops short, gazing into infinite distances. The disciples who were doing this were sent back into the world by the angels with the message of Christ's return (Acts 1:9). True faith possesses in Christ's *sessio* wide open windows looking out on His return. The *sessio* is not the ultimate goal of God's ways, and hence the Church may, in the midst of all changing perspectives (past, present, and future), proceed immediately with the words of the Creed: "From thence he shall come to judge the quick and the dead." Scripture teaches that Christ's *sessio* has its limits because he will ultimately return.

It has been said that the New Testament contains a certain tension between Christ's *being* in heaven and his *coming*, because it seems to emphasize his coming more than his presence in heaven. "He is not presented as *being* but principally as *coming*." Whenever the New Testament does speak of his being in heaven as a "situation," then this is explained as a sign that the expectation of his coming has been reduced in vigor.[1] But this view has absolutely no foundation in the New Testament. Christ's power and glory, preservation and intercession, rule and scepter, and his dominion as the *Kurios* in heaven are not contrary to the expectation of his coming but are, on the contrary, oriented eschatologically in the revealed progress of God's activity. This fully agrees with what we read in Acts 3:21: "Whom the heavens must receive until the times of restoration of all things." The same Church which knew that her Lord was in heaven and which in her relationships on earth was constantly reminded of this fact as an all-decisive reality (think of the slaves!) was also expecting him from heaven in his second coming. Paul speaks of a turning from the idols to God "to serve the living and true God, and to wait for his Son from heaven."[2] The Church's joy about the *sessio Christi* is essentially identical with her expectation of his coming. Whenever these two diverge in the life of faith, the Church becomes either secularized (the abiding city) or entangled in nervous tensions and apocalyptic sentiments. To be sure, we may speak of Christ's *being* in heaven, but this may not be placed as some-

1. Cf., e.g., in Kittel, TWNT, s.v. *οὐρανος*, p. 524, where it is said that the admonition to the masters concerning their slaves in connection with the Lord in heaven could only be given "when this power and intensity subsided and therewith the matter of a well-regulated life in this world came up," so that the phrase "in heaven" may not be taken as a "pregnant Christian formulation." This argument criticizes certain passages in the New Testament which are expressions of a deep faith, as e.g., Rom. 8:34 (*sessio* and the love of Christ). Cf. also Col. 3:1 and Heb. 8:1.
2. I Thess. 1:9, 10. Cf. also Phil. 3:20, "whence we also wait for a Saviour, the Lord Jesus Christ"; Tit. 2:13; I Thess. 4:16; II Thess. 1:7.

thing static over against the dynamic of history and the future. The *sessio* of the living, personal Lord in heaven implies a looking forward to the fulness of God's Kingdom, to the great day which is coming.

The Church has indeed always realized that the work of Christ was not just an important historic event which because of its great significance would exert an influence on generations to come. Christ's work cannot be honored by merely calling it something "classic," nor can it be justly approached through the category of "historical" influence or creativity. This separates his work from his person, and so changes the nature of his work grossly. Indeed, there is no doctrine which reveals the inseparability of Christ's work from his person more clearly than the doctrine that he will return at the end of history. The whole of his mediatorial work, in the *ascensio* and *sessio* as well, was directed by a purpose; and in the *parousia* this purpose will become fully manifest. It is true that Christ's deeds in history already brought the Kingdom very near (by the finger of God he cast out demons), but all these deeds were eschatologically oriented. That is why the apostolic teaching is very much concerned with the *directedness* of Christ's work, the final objective which alone gives it significance. Hence, also, the Church's expectation is not a vague longing for some future earthly kingdom of peace, but an expectation of *the* Kingdom; of the day of the Lord, when the immeasurable power of Christ's work will be fully revealed; of the *parousia,* Christ's being present again and "our gathering together unto him (II Thess. 2:1; cf. I Cor. 1:8).

There is a direct relationship between Christ's coming again and the life of the Church under the power and blessing of Christ *in heaven.* This blessing became full reality in the Church when the Holy Spirit was poured out, which pointed the Church to the coming again of Christ. Because of Christ's dominion the believers are admonished to strengthen their hearts and to be unblamable in holiness before God at the coming of Christ (I Thess. 3:13; cf. I Thess. 5:23).

The Church must in all holy conversation and expectation hasten unto the coming of the day of the Lord (II Pet. 3:11, 12). The strong connection between the *sessio Christi* and the *parousia* is evident from Paul's admonition to "seek the things that are above, where Christ is, seated on the right hand of God." In this connection Paul speaks of Christ who "shall be manifested" (Col. 3:1-4). The time prior to his coming is still filled with grief and temptations, but that time must be seen in the light of the future, and the genuineness of faith will prove to be "unto praise and glory and honor at the revelation of Jesus Christ" (I Pet. 1:7).

Faith, sanctification, and hope are connected with the ultimate presence of Christ. Faith and love are the characteristics of the Church, even though she has not seen Christ and does not see him now (I Pet. 1:8), but that is why she looks forward to the grace which is to be brought at the revelation of Jesus Christ (I Pet. 1:13) and at the appearance of the chief Shepherd (I Pet. 5:5; cf. Christ's remark concerning his being not ashamed of those who are not ashamed of him and his words, Mark 8:38). Because his followers expect him in faith, love, and a holy walk of life, they will not be ashamed of him at his coming (I John 2:28) but will have boldness and confidence. They will not be ashamed, because their life was already hid with him in God (Col. 3:3); they were not unfamiliar with his glory, which was as yet concealed. For they were sealed with that Holy Spirit of promise by the power of their exalted Lord (Eph. 1:13), sealed unto the day of redemption (Eph. 4:30). It is a sealing with the Spirit of Christ as an earnest in our hearts (II Cor. 1:22), and thus it is an establishment in the Anointed One (II Cor. 1:21). Hence there is only one central admonition to the Church during the ages when she has to wait: "Grieve not the holy Spirit of God" (Eph. 4:30). It is the time of sanctification and of expectation, the time of the Spirit, and therefore the time of hope and of prayer. "And the Spirit and the bride say, Come. And he that heareth, let him say, Come" (Rev. 22:17). All the glory of the communion with the exalted Lord does not exclude but includes the prayer for the fulness of the Kingdom in the presence of the Lord. In I Corinthians 16:23 the blessing: "The grace of the Lord Jesus Christ be with you" follows immediately after the cry for Christ's return: "Maranatha." It is the prayer in answer to which the Lord in heaven says: "Yea: I come quickly. Amen" (Rev. 22:20; cf. Kittel. TWNT, IV, s.v. μαρανα θά).

The Church's orientation will always be decisive in her pilgrimage between Pentecost and the *parousia*. The question may be asked: Is the Church facing toward the past or the future?

This is a well-known dilemma which presents itself in various areas of life. It is the dilemma between the more conservative and the more progressive attitude in life, between the appreciation of tradition and the desire to march with history in its dynamically ever-unfolding drive toward the future. Whoever understands somewhat the relation between *sessio* and *parousia* will come to the conclusion that this dilemma does not obtain with respect to the orientation of the Church. To be sure, a Church may deviate in either way: she may be guilty of a traditionalism incompatible with her dignity, or she may ignore history and longingly look forward to "the eternal Kingdom."

A church may even – in times of spiritual inertia – be well-nigh exclusively oriented toward the present and have no eye for either the historical or the eschatological. That is the condition when she is secularized, when she thinks that she has here an abiding city, notwithstanding the emphatic apostolic teaching to the contrary (Heb. 13:14; cf. 11:10, 14-16). She has then lost sight of the motivating principles by which alone she can live.[3] She no longer looks for the city which has foundations, whose builder and maker is God (Heb. 11:10), but substitutes her own "now" for the "now" of Scripture which preaches God's salvation. Her redemptive-historic consciousness has then succumbed to the temptation, and her expectation has faded. She loses her orientation toward the *parousia* as well as the *sessio,* and grieves the Holy Spirit. Because the message concerning Christ in *heaven* no longer penetrates its heart, the true "Maranatha" is no longer heard. Then, since the interrelations of salvation are inseparable, the secularized church finds that its

3. We see something of this controversy in the discussions concerning "The First Report of the Advisory Commission on the Theme of the Second Assembly of the World Council of Churches" (July 1951; see *The Ecumenical Review,* Oct., 1951, pp. 71-81, and further discussions, Jan. 1952, pp. 161-73. Cf. the second report, Oct. 1952, pp. 73-98). The core of all these discussions, it seems to me, lies in the relation between *sessio* and *parousia.* Cf. Horton, who attacks "a *purely* futuristic and *purely* eternalistic version of the Christian hope (*ibid.,* 1952, p. 162); Pierre Maury on "the true content of eschatology," namely the cross of Christ (*ibid.,* p. 168); Hartenstein, who is of the opinion that the first report "overstresses the realized eschatology" (p. 169). The second report (participants, among others, John Baillie, K. Barth, H. Kraemer, C. H. Dodd, etc.) again particularly deals with the relation between *sessio* and *parousia* and on the basis of the relation between cross and resurrection criticizes the "false eschatology" (*ibid.,* pp. 81ff.). This second report is not the final one but the introduction to the third (Aug. 1953).

Lord's Supper, too, inevitably deteriorates into nothing but a traditional institution, and the prayer in the *didache,* in which the "Maranatha" is connected with the Lord's Supper, becomes incomprehensible.

The questions which arise in connection with the above-mentioned dilemma are far-reaching. It is very important for the Church to understand that her life can never be understood on the basis of this dilemma. The impossibility of this dilemma becomes manifest in the inseparable connection between *sessio* and *parousia.*

It is undeniable that the expectation of the Church is unique. This is because the message concerning Christ's coming links the past with the future, as is shown in the doctrine of the *sessio,* which both refers back to the redemptive-historic past and points forward to the future. Scripture never depreciates the past when it deals with the future. In the Revelation of John the apocalyptic visions are replete with references to him who is the first begotten of the dead (Rev. 1:5) and who washed us from our sins in his own blood (Rev. 1:5). Christ is in the midst of the seven candlesticks as one like unto the Son of man (Rev. 1:13). He is the Lion of the tribe of Judah (5:5) who is worthy to open and to read the book of history, the Lamb who receives the adoration: "Thou wast slain, and hast redeemed us to God by thy blood" (5:9, KJV; cf. 5:8, 12, 13, 7:10, 14, 17; cf. also 11:8; 12:11; 13:8). The eschatological imagery is replete with holy memories of the past, and everything is presented in the light of that which took place – the battle which was crowned with victory (12:5, 7ff.; 17:14), the following of the Lamb (14:4), the testimony of Jesus Christ (12:17), the song of the Lamb (15:3), the faith of Jesus (14:12), the marriage of the Lamb (19:7), the bride of the Lamb (21:9), the apostles of the Lamb (21:14), and the Lamb's book of life (21:27). Here the expectation of a glorious future is permanently safeguarded against the threat of a vague ahistoric longing for a better world. This expectation is deeply rooted in history and derives its strength from what became historic reality in the cross and resurrection of Jesus Christ.

Here we have the real touchstone of all Christian expectation. This expectation derives its content from the act of God in Jesus Christ and is, in the holy dynamics of God's activity, its historic and final-historic consequence. The holy remembrance in the Lord's supper ("ye proclaim the Lord's death till he come,"

I Cor. 11:26; "this do in remembrance of me," Luke 22:19) is connected with the expectation of the marriage feast of the Lamb (Luke 22:16); and the admonition to remember that Jesus Christ is risen from the dead is connected with the testimony of the Lord from heaven: "These things saith the first and the last, who was dead, and lived again" (Rev. 2:8; cf. 1:17, 18).

This connection between past and present is of the greatest significance for understanding the future expectation of the Church. Twentieth-century eschatological thinking has emphasized more and more the actual *karakteristicum* of the New Testament expectation, namely, its "immediate expectation." Especially Albert Schweitzer, together with the so-called *consistent* eschatology, proceeded from the assumption that *the* characteristic of the New Testament expectation was that it looked for the immediate consummation of the Kingdom of God. Schweitzer, and in our day especially Martin Werner and Fritz Buri, insist on this and link this with the problem of the so-called tarrying of the *parousia,* in other words, the non-fulfillment of this expectation, which is *the* problem of the New Testament Church and of the Church of all ages, the vacuum of the end-time which was expected but which did not come. Particularly Oscar Cullmann raised his voice in protest against this conception of the New Testament eschatology. He believes that the New Testament is not so much concerned with what is to come as, in the first place, with Him who already has come.[4] The question concerning the future cannot occupy the Church in the same way as it did the Jews, "since another date is recognized as decisive." To be sure, the question concerning the future, the "when," is still voiced (Acts 1:6), but the resurrected Christ "refuses to answer this question and speaks instead of the coming of the Holy Spirit which will be the result of what had taken place."

That is the new content of faith which Christ gave to the young Church, namely, "that since Easter the focal point lies no longer in the future for the believing Christian," which is a fundamental insight and a revolutionary thesis "accepted by the entire primitive Christian Church, namely, that "the central event has already taken place." It is true that there will be a

4. O. Cullmann, *Christus und die Zeit,* 1946, pp. 70, 77, 122-24, 134. The "immediate expectation" has its roots "in the belief in the redemptive occurrence which had already been ushered in and completed." This belief is "the basis of the immediate expectation" (p. 77).

"consummation" in the future, but this refers back to history. Cullmann employs the simile of V-day of World War II. The battle is not yet finished but the decisive victory has already been gained. By the fulfillment of Psalm 110 in history – Messiah on his throne – eschatology, too, is absolutely determined and governed. Not the future, but the past – Christ – is the most important thing for the Church, so that the fundamental thesis of consistent eschatology," which considers the eschatological future as the main object of the primitive Church's interests," must be considered incorrect.[5]

It is striking that Cullmann again and again speaks of that which was of the greatest interest to the New Testament Church. In justified criticism of the consistent eschatology of Schweitzer, *et al.*, he points to the fundamental significance of God's redemptive-historical activity in Jesus Christ.[6] Whoever detaches this from the expectation does injustice to the primitive Christian expectation, and Cullmann has correctly pointed out the lack of insight on the part of those who are forever occupied with the problem of the "immediate expectation." But, as is so often the case with strong reaction, Cullmann in his criticism overemphasizes the significance of the present and future, and thus he fails to do justice to the full significance of the expectation for the future. A typical example of this may be found in his remark that whenever a short resume of the content of faith is given there "is as yet no mention of the future."[7] In this con-

5. *Ibid.*, pp. 134, 207. In opposition to the "consistent eschatology" Cullmann writes, for instance, that in Paul's expectation "the center, the immovable point of orientation does not lie in the future, but in the past, hence in a fact which cannot be shaken by a tarrying of the *parousia*" (p. 77).
6. This also influences Cullmann's understanding of Jesus' statement concerning the Church, because he attacks the criticism that Jesus on the basis of his eschatological expectation cannot have spoken of a Church. Hence, he again develops his thesis of the present, of the "anticipation of the Kingdom of God," in which the decision has already been made. "Whoever considers only his prophecies to be decisive, should then ask what the difference is between Jesus and the rest of the prophets. All prophets spoke concerning the future, also concerning a near future. But with Jesus we find this new aspect, that there is also fulfillment" (O. Cullmann, *Petrus, Jünger-Apostel-Martyrer*, 1952, pp. 217ff.) This also explains Christ's statement concerning the Church.
7. Cullmann, *Christus und die Zeit*, p. 134. Elsewhere Cullmann points out that this does not imply an elimination of the coming again of Christ, but "that the hope for the coming again of Christ is implied in the certainty of His resurrection and His exaltation at the right hand of

nection he further states that the Christian hope has lost nothing of its intensity, but "it expresses itself only in prayer, not in a confession." It is obvious that we meet here with a certain shifting of emphasis, because the prayer for Christ's coming cannot be detached from the content of faith but, on the contrary, this content of faith becomes strongly evident in this prayer (cf. Rev. 22:17). Hence, Cullmann in the same connection must acknowledge the fervor of the New Testament expectation. It is not a dilemma of "either primary or secondary," but what took place determines the nature of the expectation. The expectation is not an eager reaching for the future as though nothing had happened yet, but the expectation of him who did come and who one day, in a new act, will be present again.

We may, indeed, on the basis of the New Testament, oppose all one-sided interest in an immediate expectation which, moreover, is mostly understood as a historical end-phase, but we may never on the basis of the history of salvation make the expectation relative. Hence Cullmann in his analysis of this apostolic message must inevitably return to the "not yet." The resurrection of the dead is "the object of the hope for the future."[8] Cullmann avoids the one-sidedness of the "main interest" when he emphasizes the connection between the history of salvation and the future. The Gospel of John, too, which places the emphasis on the presence of salvation, leaves room for a specific eschatological event. Even though the believer possesses life eternal, the resurrection of the body takes place only at the end of time, and in opposition to Bultmann, Cullmann does not consider eliminating this *futurum*, which is an essential part of the New Testament teaching. There is in the New Testament no dilemma of past versus future, because the connection between past and future is, in Christ Jesus, absolutely unique. That is why the eschatological expectation does not violate the remembrance of faith; and Paul, for example, can connect the resurrection of the body with Christ's resurrection.

The nature of Christ's *sessio* is such that it cannot be the last thing the Church looks forward to, but it is the stimulant to the very last expectation, of Christ's "sitting at the right hand

---

God which is already a fact" (*Die ersten Christlichen Glaubensbekenntnisse,* 1943, p. 51, and *Königsherrschaft Christi und Kirche im N.T.,* 1941).

8. Cullmann, *Christus und die Zeit,* p. 211.

of God, from whence he shall come to judge the living and the dead."[9] The Apostles' Creed, which verbally quotes these words from Scripture, links Christ's new presence with his judging the living and the dead. It thereby refers back, as does Paul, to the profound connection between the past and future which is an essential part of the Christian expectation of the future. Christ's judgment is not isolated from the past as if it were a new and dark aspect of the picture of the future, but it is based on the power which is given to the Lord of heaven, and thus it is directly connected with his finished work.

Christ's judgment reveals the connection with the past because it is given to Jesus Christ as the crucified and resurrected One. God himself, says Paul, has appointed a day "in the which he will judge the world in righteousness by the man whom he hath ordained; whereof he hath given assurance unto all men, in that he hath raised him from the dead" (Acts 17:31). It is the Father who has given him the judgment (cf. John 5:22). He has the power, the authority to sit in judgment, "because he is a son of man" (John 5:27).

It is obvious that in this text no contrast or separation is intended between the Father and the Son, but nevertheless in the sharp formulation of John 5:22 it is clear according to what norms this judgment will be passed on the living and the dead. It clearly reveals that the nature of Christ's coming judgment is determined by his resurrection, his humiliation, and his exaltation. On our way toward this future we can have no peace and safety except in communion with the Lord in heaven, who sits at the right hand of the Father. His coming again is indeed a new event, but it is not a dark uncertainty without any connection with the present or the past. For the throne from which this judgment will be executed is nothing less than the throne of God and of the Lamb (Rev. 22:1, 3; cf. 3:21; 7:10, 17). That is how inseparably *sessio* and *parousia* are related. "Jesus Christ is the same yesterday and to-day, yea and for ever" (Heb. 13:8). This Judge, who is "at hand" (Phil 4:5) and who "standeth before the doors" (Jas. 5:9), is the same as the Mediator who prays

9. In II Tim. 4:1 Paul speaks of the living and the dead whom Christ will judge, and he charges Timothy to preach the word with an appeal to both Christ's appearing and kingdom. This is remarkable because it reveals a strongly eschatological thought, but it also speaks of Christ's kingship in connection with his appearing. Moreover, Paul emphasizes Timothy's responsibility over against him who will judge.

for us and who is the secret of the song of assurance that triumphs over the senseless accusations (Rom. 8:33) in the superior power of the love of God in Christ Jesus (Rom. 8:35, 39). He who in faith understands the *sessio Christi* in daily perseverance and rejection of all temptation will one day recognize this Judge and not be afraid. "Fear not; I am the first and the last, and the Living one; and I was dead and behold, I am alive for evermore, and I have the keys of death and of Hades" (Rev. 1:17, 18).

We have discussed his humiliation and exaltation, what took place and was accomplished once at the end of the ages, God's dealings in and through and in spite of man's activity, and Christ's suffering and glory afterwards. The one single work unfolds in overwhelming majesty and opens windows upon the future on every hand, windows from the cross to the throne of the Lamb, from the supper of the Lamb to the marriage feast of the Lamb, from Christ's resurrection to the resurrection of the body, from our struggle to his victory, from our sin and guilt which he bore on the cross to the robes washed white in the blood of the Lamb (Rev. 7:14), and from the stricken conscience to the Judge of the living and the dead.

The cry "Maranatha" has often been very feeble in the history of the Church. At times it can hardly be heard at all. The saying of the Spirit and the bride, "Come, Lord Jesus," often seems to be a word of Scripture that finds no realization in the life of the Church. There can be only one reason for the languishing and fading longing of the Church, namely an obscuring of insight into the wealth and riches of the work of Christ. This insight of faith disappears and fades away in the face of many dangers and temptations. It is *the* temptation of the Church and *the* motive of the power of darkness: the incessant battle against *the holy remembrance.*

The only remedy for the Church is to pray in this struggle: "Deliver us from the evil one!" For in this prayer — also a prayer for remembrance — the Church may reach for the exaltation which implies the certainty of God's hearing and answering: "For *thine* is the kingdom, and the power, and the glory, for ever."

CHAPTER ELEVEN

ASPECTS OF THE WORK OF CHRIST

WHEN PAUL, in Ephesians 3:14-21, bends his knees unto the Father in a fervent intercession for the Church of Jesus Christ, then his prayer and ensuing admonition are full of the glory of Christ. He speaks of the indwelling of Christ in the hearts of the believers and prays that the Church – "with all the saints" – will be able to apprehend "what is the breadth and length and height and depth, and to know the love of Christ which passeth knowledge" (vss. 17:19). The Church should yearn to be filled with the fulness of God, by coming to *know* the love of Christ (vss. 18, 19). Elsewhere, Paul warns against egocentric and puffed-up knowledge, but the kind of knowledge mentioned here is free of intellectualism because those who have it are rooted and grounded in love (vs. 17); theirs is the knowledge of the love of Christ which passeth knowledge (vs. 19). Paul is not concerned with the general outlines of a speculative theory, but with those outlines which become manifest in the knowledge of the love of Christ.[1] Hence his prayer and admonition turn into a doxology which embraces the ages (vss. 20, 21). This doxology is inseparably connected with the unsearchable riches of Christ (vs. 8) and with the mystery which from the beginning of the world hath been hid (vs. 9). Unsearchable . . . Paul does not retract this word when he speaks of the knowledge of the love of Christ.[2] The words "unsearchable riches" belong together by virtue of the nature of this knowl-

1. Cf. S. F. H. J. Berkelbach van der Sprenkel, *De Brief aan de Efeziërs*, 1941, p. 52.
2. The same word is also found in Rom. 11:33, "how unsearchable are his judgments, and his ways past tracing out." Cf. "O the depth of the riches" of Rom. 11:33 with the "unsearchable riches" of Eph. 3:8. Delling writes that when Paul in Rom. 11:33 conjoins "unsearchable" with "past finding out," he means also that his answer to the question concerning the meaning of the judgment upon Israel cannot claim absolute validity. This conclusion, it seems to me, has nothing to do with what Paul means to say; cf. Rom. 11:25 (Kittel, TWNT, I, 359).

edge. Paul does not condemn reflection in general, but he does warn against sterile theorizing which violates the approach of faith and love.

We realize to some extent the unsearchability of these riches when we note how Scripture speaks of the work of Christ. Already in Chapter I we saw the multiplicity of aspects of Christ's work which Scripture brings to our attention. These "aspects" are not speculative abstractions, but elements of the one reality of Christ's work, and their presence in Scripture can be explained, at least in part, by the so-called "organic" doctrine of inspiration. The revelation concerning the Word become flesh utilizes *human means* in all their variety. Scripture is not formulated like a systematic treatise; rather, it resembles a mountain stream which pours its waters into the valleys. It shows us history and witnesses to Christ, but always according to the language and historical environment of this or that human witness. There are words in Scripture referring to Christ's work which appear only a few times, while others appear again and again. These variations in language can be seen, for example, when we compare the Epistle to the Hebrews with the other epistles. But whatever the terminology, the message is the same. The aspect of the "for us" is brought out in many different ways. We will try to catch some glimpses of the light which Scripture sheds on Christ's work by discussing its teaching under the following headings: (a) Reconciliation; (b) Sacrifice; (c) Obedience; (d) Victory. We will not understand the secret of the work of Christ until we discover that it is not composed of separate parts, but is one inseparable mighty work.[3]

A. RECONCILIATION

It is beyond dispute that Holy Scripture summarizes the work of Christ under the aspect of reconciliation. To be sure, there are various ways in which this word is used, for instance in the writings of Paul and a few times in those of John and in other books of both the Old and New Testaments, but wherever it is discussed it is evident that this matter lies at the heart of

3. We refer once more to Eph. 3:14ff., where Paul recapitulates everything in "the love of Christ." This love is the unity of all the aspects of the work of Christ as the unsearchable riches which derive from his poverty as a historical reality. Cf. Eph. 3:8, 19 with II Cor. 8:9.

the gospel. We are, according to Paul, "reconciled to God by the death of his Son . . . through whom we have now received the reconciliation" (Rom. 5:10, 11), and elsewhere he says that "God was in Christ reconciling the world unto himself, not reckoning unto them their trespasses" (II Cor. 5:19). That, to Paul, is the great, marvelous, and astonishing event which is full of the riches and comfort of grace. This reconciliation may and must be preached: "God . . . gave unto us the ministry of reconciliation" (II Cor. 5:18). Paul sees the joy of this reconciliation in connection with justification and the peace which we have with God (Rom. 5:1). The reconciliation is the direct opposite of the previous enmity (Rom. 5:10) and comes to pass through the death of Christ (Rom. 5:10), through the love of Christ who died for all (II Cor. 5:14, 15) and was made to be sin for us, who knew no sin (II Cor. 5:21). It is evident that Paul has the same thing in mind even when he does not specifiically use the word "reconciliation," for instance when he writes, "But now in Christ Jesus ye that once were far off are made nigh in the blood of Christ" (Eph. 2:13). Here again we sense the atmosphere of peace after enmity, community after separation: "For he is our peace, who made both one, and brake down the middle wall of partition" (Eph. 2:14). When describing this peace Paul again speaks of reconciliation: that he "might reconcile them both in one body unto God through the cross" (Eph. 2:16). There the enmity has been slain (*ibid.*) and peace has come whereby we have access unto the Father (vs. 18).

The joy of this reconciliation occupies such a central place in Paul's preaching that we know it is not a minor part of salvation but *all* of salvation, for it concerns God's activity in Christ. For this reconciliation, however, Paul uses two words, namely, *katallagē* and *hilasmos*. When he speaks of *katallagē* he always refers to the relationship of peace which is brought about by the death of Christ, to the communion in contrast with the previous enmity, to the reconciliation as the removal of all obstacles, to the access to the Father.[4] Access and boldness, peace and trust are of the essence of the *katallagē*. The eye is directed to the reality which was effected in Christ and which is the fulness of the eternal salvation. That is why reconciliation

4. Cf. also Eph. 3:12, Rom. 5:2. K. L. Schmidt in this connection points to the access which is none else but Christ as the Door (John 10). Cf. I Pet. 3:18, "Because Christ also suffered for sins once, the righteous for the unrighteous, that he might bring us to God."

is closely related to justification. Both result in the same peace, which takes the place of the darkness of guilt and enmity. Peace implies the unity of both, because these two words imply the same reality of salvation, as is evident especially from Romans 5.[5] In fact, when Paul deals extensively with reconciliation his message ends with the statement: "that we might become the righteousness of God in him" (II Cor. 5:21).

Paul's other word for reconciliation, *hilasmos,* is also used by John when he writes, "and he is the propitiation for our sins" (I John 2:2, 4:10).

Usually *hilasmos* as *expiatio* is distinguished from *katallagē* as *reconciliatio.*[6] *Hilasmos* refers more to the means of reconciliation, to that which effects the reconciliation. Significant is Paul's statement that "God hath set forth [Christ Jesus] to be a propitiation,[7] through faith, in his blood, to show his righteousness because of the passing over of the sins done aforetime" (Rom. 3:25; cf. Heb. 9:5). This obviously has reference to the putting away of sin. *Hilasmos* and *hilasterion* never imply the opposite of the *katallagē;* rather, the *katallagē,* the new relationship of peace after the enmity, is directly connected with the *hilasmos,* the taking away of sins. Paul's word *hilasterion* (Heb. 9:5) refers back to the mercy seat of the Old Testament, over which the cherubim spread their wings (Exod. 25:20). There in the cloud upon the mercy seat God would appear and visit his people (Lev. 16:2). Here Aaron could not enter in without due preparation. The blood of the sin offering must be sprinkled upon the mercy seat (Lev. 16:14). Thus "he shall make an atonement for the holy place, because of the uncleanness of the children of Israel, and because of their transgressions, even all their sins" (Lev. 16:16; cf. vss. 18ff.). It is the reconciliation "to cleanse you . . . from all your sins . . . before Jehovah" (Lev. 16:30).

Now when Paul sees Christ as the *hilasterion,* he points out

5. Cf. Kittel, TWNT, I, 255. Cf. also p. 258, where Büchsel says that being reconciled may not be reduced to being justified because the former implies "the awakening of love," which is not the case with the latter. It seems to me that this does not explain the difference. Justification is not an abstract, formal act of a Judge but the revelation of God's love (Rom. 5:8), namely the love which is shed abroad in our hearts (vs. 5). Justification cannot be distinguished from reconciliation by determining whether or not love has been awakened, but by the specific judicial act of God which, however, may by no means be isolated from his love.
6. Cf. Bavinck, *Gereformeerde Dogmatiek,* III, 441ff.
7. Cf. A. Nygren, *Der Römerbrief,* 1951, pp. 118ff.

the means of reconciliation as the way which leads to the great peace, the communion, the full riches of the *katallagē*. Similarly we read in Hebrews that Christ is a merciful and faithful High Priest in things pertaining to God "to make propitiation for the sins of the people" (Heb. 2:17), that is, to make them inactive, meaningless before God. Reconciliation corresponds to the German word *Sühne,* to the cleansing of sins; the putting away of the obstacle to effect the *katallagē.* Thus John, too, sees Christ as the *hilasmos* for our sins. Hence the *hilasmos* is not the opposite of the *katallagē* but is part of the one act of God. Whereas Paul writes that God was in Christ reconciling the world unto himself, John says that herein is love, that God sent his Son to be the propitiation for our sins (I John 4:10). It is the blood of Jesus Christ that cleanses us from all sin (I John 1:7).[8] Hence we may, if we wish, distinguish *katallagē* as *reconciliatio* from *hilasmos* as *expiatio.*

In the past, theological controversy concerning the reconciliation has always centered upon the *expiatio.* It was generally admitted that the apostles taught the *katallagē,* the relationship of peace after the enmity, but a vehement debate ensued, and continues still, concerning the *way* to this peace. What is the meaning of the "cleansing blood," of the blood sprinkled on the mercy seat, and of the putting away of unrighteousnesses? All these questions finally converge on the one central and dominating question which returns again and again, namely, *Who* is the object of reconciliation? Is it God, or man? Is God reconciled to the world, or the world to God? Again and again we notice that the theology of reconciliation almost invariably proceeds from this dilemma. We also notice an almost unanimous preference for the idea that *man* is exclusively the object of reconciliation, and that Scripture nowhere says that God himself is reconciled. The latter idea has recently come to be called the *Umstimmung Gottes,* meaning that God, on account of the work of Jesus Christ, is *umgestimmt*: he changes his mind so that the *katallagē* can be effected. According to this idea the Father essentially and originally was not inclined to bestow love and reconciliation, but was moved to do so by Christ on the basis of his act, his sacrifice, his cleansing of sins. The criticism of

8. It is, therefore, not clear why Büchsel says that it deserves attention that John neither in I John 2:2, nor in 4:10, speaks of Jesus' death but of His "Gesamtsendung (Kittel, *op. cit.,* p. 318). Nevertheless Büchsel himself refers to John 5:6; 3:16; 1:7.

this *Umstimmung Gottes* is quite unanimous and attacks the alleged opposition between the Father's disposition and that of his Son Jesus Christ. The *Umstimmung* is said to deny the trinitarian character of reconciliation in the one activity of God, and to contradict the *locus classicus* in Paul's writings, namely, "God was in Christ reconciling the world unto himself" (II Cor. 5:9). On the basis of this and many other statements it seems to be incontestable that it is not God but man who is reconciled, and that God is the subject of the reconciliation in the sense that the initiative originates in his heart. He did not need to be moved, but rather, eternal love moved him in the divine apriority of the initiative to reconciliation. However the *hilasmos* should be understood, at any rate it is not a changing of God's mind from the outside, influencing him to turn from wrath to love and from enmity to reconciliation.

We should ask, first, whether the dilemma sketched above is actual and inescapable. This is the more necessary because our problem is not merely a theoretical one, but also involves several confessions of faith. Especially the Reformed confessions contain several expressions to which, according to many, the same criticism applies as has been brought against the *Umstimmung*. We refer particularly to such statements as seem to speak of a turning of God from wrath to grace, a turning effected by Christ's sacrifice. We mention in particular Article 21 of the Belgic Confession which speaks of the satisfaction of Christ in these words: "that He has presented Himself in our behalf before the Father, to appease His wrath by His full satisfaction, by offering Himself on the tree of the cross." And the Canons of Dort assert in equally strong terms that the believers are saved from the wrath of God by Christ and that they "may again experience the favor of a reconciled God" (V, 7; cf. I, 4). But also in other Reformed Confessions such expressions are by no means exceptions but appear frequently in connection with the death of Christ.[9] From the context in which the wrath of God is mentioned in these confessions, namely, where they deal with the believer's being reconciled by Christ, it has often been said that

9. Further examples are the Catechism of Geneva (1545) and the Westminster Confession (1647), which says in Art. VIII, 5: "The Lord Jesus by his perfect obedience and sacrifice of himself, which he through the eternal Spirit once offered up unto God, hath fully satisfied the Justice of God." Cf. also the Heidelberg Catechism, Q. 11, 12, 14, 16, 17, and Canons of Dort, II, 1, 2, 3 and Rejection of Errors II, 7.

the confessions advance a theory in which God is not the subject but the object of reconciliation. They seem to state that God the Father was induced to the reconciliation by the satisfaction, the sacrifice, of Christ, and hence not by the unfathomable love of his Father heart.

It ought to be observed, however, that the Confessions apparently do not proceed from the above-mentioned dilemma, because if there is such a dilemma then the Confessions do not eliminate it one bit. On the one hand they speak freely of the quenching of the wrath of God, and on the other, without any consciousness of apparently contradicting themselves, of God's initiative in his reconciling activity. The same Belgic Confession that speaks of the quenching of God's wrath says that the Father has appointed the Mediator between himself and us, and that it has pleased God to give us his own Son as an Advocate (Art. 26); while the Canons of Dort, which deal with God's wrath and his being reconciled, remind us also of the love of God revealed in the giving of his only-begotten Son (I, 2). Hence, according to the Canons, the initiative to our reconciliation proceeds from God and . . . "God mercifully sends the messengers of these most joyful tidings" (I, 3). To be sure, they teach that we are delivered from the wrath of God by a true and living faith (I, 4), but while they acknowledge the wrath of God they do not overlook the fact that God took the initiative in our reconciliation. On the contrary, they confess that by ourselves we cannot satisfy the justice of God, that we cannot deliver ourselves from the wrath of God, and that therefore God out of infinite mercy sent his only-begotten Son as our Mediator.[10] Hence, on the one hand they fully confess the reconciliation on the basis of God's election and mercy, while on the other they emphasize that this reconciliation is by Christ and they reject the errors of those who teach "that Christ neither could die, nor

10. Cf. especially Canons I, 7 in connection with election as "the unchangeable purpose of God, whereby, before the foundation of the world, He has out of mere grace, according to the sovereign good pleasure of His own will, chosen from the whole human race, which had fallen through their own fault . . . to redemption in Christ, whom He from eternity appointed the Mediator and Head of the elect and the foundation of salvation." Cf. also Belgic Confession, Art. 20, "We believe that God . . . sent His Son . . . . God therefore manifested His justice against His Son . . . and poured forth His mercy and goodness on us." Cf. also the Form for the Lord's Supper, specifically the prayer of thanksgiving after the Supper on God's giving us his Son for a Mediator.

needed to die, and also did not die, for those whom God loved in the highest degree and elected to eternal life, since these do not need the death of Christ" (Rej. of Errors, II, 7; cf. Canons II, 9 concerning the Church, "the foundation of which is laid in the blood of Christ").

At any rate, we find no mention here of the dilemma, and we must be careful not to consider these confessional statements concerning the divine initiative (especially in the Canons when they deal with election) as secondary and traditional elements which, although derived from Scripture, are allegedly beside the point. If we did, we could indeed build up a confessional reconciliation theory entirely on the basis of the *placatio,* the silencing of God's wrath, but such an interpretation is through and through untenable. It is possible, however, to find a solution which transcends this dilemma, and we are of the opinion that the Reformed Confessions have successfully done so.[11] These Confessions have done justice to the biblical teaching on the wrath of God, and their statements on this subject are much to the point. According to the Confessions, apparently, it is impossible to pose a sharp dilemma between the divine initiative and a (vaguely defined) *Umstimmung* without thereby failing to do justice to God's wrath.

Those who agree with Ritschl that the wrath of God is a misconception on our part which is removed by Christ in the reconciliation, naturally have no reason to express themselves in the manner of the Reformed Confessions. But those who recognize that the wrath of God is part of the biblical teaching cannot avoid asking what Scripture means by saying that Christ delivered us from the wrath to come (I Thess. 1:10). The basic error of the dilemma is this: it misrepresents the Church's teaching concerning the quenching of the wrath of God, and thereby creates a problem where none had existed. It is assumed rashly, that the Church taught the *Umstimmung,* namely, a doctrine of reconciliation according to which the Father, who was not in-

11. Cf. H. N. Ridderbos, "De Christologie van het Nieuwe Testament" in *Gereformeerd Theologisch Tidschrift,* 47th ed., 1947, p. 58, who speaks of a false dilemma, and correctly writes concerning the criticism by Sevenster on the idea of God being the object of reconciliation: "Apparently he can visualize the idea that God is the object of reconciliation only as a pagan idea of sacrificing." He further correctly says that the argument "that the initiative of reconciliation proceeds from God Himself" is hardly convincing here.

clined to reconciliation, *changed his mind* because of the Son's intervention.[12] Of course, on the basis of II Corinthians 5 it is not difficult to refute such a misrepresentation, and it must be admitted that the doctrine of the Church did full justice to the clear teaching of this passage. Besides, it was not only this Scripture which showed the Church the right way. Everywhere in the Bible this divine initiative to reconciliation is taught. For Scripture clearly speaks of the love of the Father in giving his Son (John 3:16), and in the Son of Zacharias (Luke 1:78) of the tender mercy of our God whereby the dayspring from on high has visited us. That is why the general and not sharply analyzed term *Umstimmung* often suggests much that is unfair, unreasonable, and unsatisfactory.

Umstimmung suggests and implies things which neither the Bible nor the Confessions ever taught. Hence we must proceed to a more careful analysis by saying that any idea of *Umstimmung* which does not do full justice to what we, on the basis of Scripture, called the divine initiative to reconciliation, misinterprets and minimizes the mystery of Christ's reconciling work. Only then can we ask the pivotal question whether there can be harmony between the place the wrath of God occupies in the Confessions and all those references in Scripture which are so pregnantly summarized in the words of Paul: "But all things are of God, who reconciled us to himself through Christ, and gave unto us the ministry of reconciliation; to wit, that God was in Christ reconciling the world unto himself" (II Cor. 5:18-19).

Modern theology is willing to concede that the idea of God as author of reconciliation has not been entirely neglected in the Church and in theology.[13] But at the same time it points out that the Church's emphasis on the *placatio* flagrantly contradicts this idea. Korff, for instance, refers to many statements by Luther, Calvin, and Bavinck which, according to him, show this

12. Cf. the rejection of this caricature by K. Schilder, *Commentary on the Heidelberg Catchism*, II, 167.

13. Brunner in *Der Mittler*, p. 427, correctly points out that the Church's doctrine of reconciliation is often attacked after it has first been presented as a caricature and he adds, "Neither Paul nor the Epistle to the Hebrews nor any of the great theologians nor any of the classic Confessions have advocated this absurd idea of an *Umstimmung* of God, because it is more than clear in the New Testament that it is God who by his love provides the reconcilation of the world." Brunner also rejects an unavoidable choice between the subjectivistic doctrine of reconciliation and the idea of *Umstimmung*.

one-sided emphasis. Did not Luther say that Christ offered himself up to placate God and to change him from an angry judge to a merciful God? And has not Calvin said that Christ reconciles us to God and makes him favorably disposed toward us? And did not Bavinck emphatically state that not only must man be reconciled with God but also God with man? According to Korff all these theologians do indeed recognize and acknowledge God's activity in salvation, but why then do they use all these unfortunate expressions which inevitably create the impression of an *Umstimmung* and which suggest the terrible and blasphemous idea that God is a person against whom we must be protected by Christ? Why, then, do they speak of *placatio*, of a silencing of the wrath of God? It is not God but man who must be reconciled. That which takes place in reconciliation is a divine act which in Christ is directed toward us. Hence Korff's object is to substitute his unilateral conception for the dual idea which he detects in theology, namely the duality of the divine initiative to reconciliation and the placating of his wrath, his *being* reconciled. With this conflict we touch upon the basic questions concerning the doctrine of reconciliation.

When theology deals with the *placatio*, it always and emphatically speaks of God as object of reconciliation; hence it is obvious why the critics urge that this *placatio* eliminates or at least obscures the divine activity in reconciliation.[14] Some critics, such as Bolkestein, for instance, who says that the Confessions present reconciliation as an act of God and do not teach an *Umstimmung*, are even willing to interpret the manner of expression of the Confessions with a certain benignity. He is familiar with the criticized expressions of the Confessions, such as "God is reconciled" and the "quenching of His wrath," but he views these as figurative expressions. He adds, however, that any revised confession should state more clearly that God is the sub-

14. Cf., among others, G. Sevenster, who in *Christology* insists that the reconciling activity originates in God and that the idea that God's wrath must be placated does not agree in the least with the biblical teaching." "Hence, it is not God who must be reconciled; on the contrary, the object of reconciliation is always man. In none of the texts is it shown that reconciliation is a reconciliation of God." Cf. also M. H. Bolkestein, *De Verzoening*, 1945, p. 111: "In this reconciliation God is not the receiving but the giving One."

ject of reconciliation, to avoid misunderstanding.[15] The existing confessions, he says, create the impression that "God's mind has been changed by an achievement of Christ so that he now is gracious whereas he was not before." It cannot be denied, however, that the existing confessions emphasize the activity of God, and therefore the problem cannot be solved by formulating a revised confession. For precisely this so-called "figurative way of expression" touches the central question of the doctrine of reconciliation, namely how, according to Scripture, the wrath of God is removed and how we through Christ are delivered from it. We are confronted with this question, for instance, in the polemics between Bolkestein and Korff. Bolkestein criticizes Korff's denial "that the forgiveness lies in the dimension which we cannot see, in the dimension between Jesus and God."[16]

According to Bolkestein, the reality of reconciliation affects not only the relation between Christ and us, but also between Christ and the Father.[17] How must we interpret this? The answer to this question is of great significance for the correct understanding of the doctrine of reconciliation. Bolkestein's answer is this: as far as the dimension between Christ and the Father is concerned, the reconciliation is the divine solution to the problem of sin and guilt. According to the biblical teaching man's sin is irreparable and his relationship to God is objectively disturbed. "Sin not only changes us and our relationship with God, but also God and his relationship with us." God's wrath is a real thing; it is his "No" over against sin which gives the sinner over to destruction. This wrath-situation can only be changed by God himself.

It is quite evident that at this point Bolkestein must come to a decision and that here he must deal with the "figurative manner of expression" in the Confessions. His solution is that God has placed himself in our condition and life. Bolkestein, in his criti-

15. Bolkestein, *op. cit.*, pp. 111-115. For criticism on this idea of an "figurative way of expressing" see A. F. N. Lekkerkerker in *Gesprek over de Verzoening*, 1949, p. 111.

16. Bolkestein, *op. cit.*, p. 116; cf. his reply to Lekkerkerker, particularly concerning the difference between him and Korff.

17. In a counter-article Lekkerkerker says that the differences between Bolkestein and Korff are "only seemingly so," since Bolkestein does not clarify his position concerning the "manner" of reconciliation and he "leaves that which takes place between the Father and the Son in the twilight of mystery to such an extent that it is entirely overshadowed by that which takes place between the Son and man."

cism of the idea of the quenching of God's wrath, attempts to remove the dualism it poses between Christ and God as though Christ brings about a change in God, and in this connection Bolkestein brings up the subject of patripassianism. "To be sure, patripassianism is a heresy, but nevertheless we shall have to go as far as approaching the border of this heresy." This simile is none too clear but Bolkestein adds: "We shall have to say: it was God himself who in his Son took our flesh and blood and descended into our miserable condition; it was God himself who in his Son made himself subject to our condition." Again and again this type of solution emphasizes "God himself." It was God who in his Son took our flesh upon himself; our life and destiny became his; he identified himself with our condition. God is "the subject of reconciliation, the hidden subject of the person of Jesus Christ." God's solution to the conflict between himself and us was "to bear it in himself." That is the mystery of reconciliation in the dimension between God and Christ.

At this point Bolkestein differs from Korff, defining his position very sharply in his concern to go as far as he can toward patripassianism. He approaches the view of Barth, who says that God's own heart suffered on the cross. It is not clear, however, why Bolkestein mentions patripassianism and not theopaschitism (which says that God suffered in Christ). This same question had arisen previously when Blink Kramer, for example, wrote: "Christ's heart broke, that is to say, God's heart broke under our misery," and, "in Christ God himself bears our sin and misery"; a little white later he adds in a further explanation: "We are not defending . . . patripassianism, which teaches that the Father suffered in Jesus Christ."[18] He was referring, rather, to theopaschitism (the suffering God),[19] and when both Kramer and Bolkestein reject patripassianism as heresy this does not mean that they are rejecting theopaschitism at the same time. And today the latter has become more and more *the* problem of the doctrine of reconciliation. To be sure, we cannot say that

18. A. Blink Kramer, *Verzoening*, 1918, pp. 38, 81.

19. Concerning patripassianism see, e.g., Tertullian, *Adverus Praxean*, introduction, pp. iii-xxiv; this concerns modalism in the doctrine of the Trinity, so that *patripassianism* is indeed the correct name. Patripassianism and theopaschitism indeed touch many of the same questions, but must nevertheless be distinguished from each other. Cf. the theopaschitic controversy in the sixth century in the textbooks of the history of dogmatics.

theopaschitism is now generally accepted without hesitation, but there are unmistakable signs of it in theology.[20] Its adherents thereby wish to refute the idea that God was unconcerned; they wish to include and involve him in the history and misery of this world because these concern him very much.

The idea of the suffering of God returns now and then even at the periphery of the Church, and was strongly emphasized in English theology after World War I in the expression "the suffering God."[21] In our day this idea is also strongly advocated on the Continent. According to this theology God does not keep himself removed from the world, coldly unconcerned about our condition and tensions, but he takes our guilt upon himself (in Christ) and in utmost divine self-denial surrenders himself to the judgment. In this way salvation is said to originate in the heart of God, and is based upon the sacrifice of unfathomable and incomprehensible mercy, the sacrifice of God himself, who takes everything upon himself. Roscam Abbing, for instance, also rejects patripassianism,[22] but the theopaschitic problem still remains quite evident when he speaks of God who directs his judgment upon the sinner at himself. God battles the conflict within his own heart. "God made the misery, the suffering, the guilt and sin of man his own." God maintains himself by giving himself. What Bolkestein calls the dimension between God and Christ Roscam Abbing describes thus: "In heaven, in the heart of God, justice triumphs because God denies himself and directs the judgment at himself and thus makes it valid."[23] A. E. Loen gives a still stronger formulation of this idea when he say: "God

20. For example, Blink Kramer writes that God "denies himself in Christ" (*op. cit.*, p. 38), nevertheless we must proceed carefully, "lest we transfer God himself and his revelation in Jesus Christ to the world" (*ibid.*, p. 82). His solution is that the Father remains outside the world, but "suffers with" the Son, since he [the Son] is the essence of God's essence."

21. Cf., among others, J. K. Mozley, *The Impassibility of God,* 1926, and O. C. Quick, *Doctrines of the Creed,* 1949, pp. 184-87. Cf. G. Aulén, *Het Christelijke Godsbeeld,* 1927, who mentions the partiality of many for the idea of the suffering God. "This theme exists in many variations. At times it is uncertain and hesitant, then again it is very strong." See also what Aulén says concerning Söderblom, William Temple, and W. R. Inge.

22. P. J. Roscam Abbing, *Diakonia,* 1950, p. 35.

23. *Ibid.,* p. 129. Hence there is "a suffering and struggling, a losing and winning both of God's love and of his judgment, both in God's heart and on Golgotha."

willed to bear death and damnation for us; that which God took upon himself can no longer fall upon us."[24] We find the same emphasis upon "God himself" in Karl Barth, particularly when he deals with the perfect attributes of God.[25]

It becomes more and more evident that the background of the doctrine of reconciliation is the doctrine of the attributes of God. That is the issue at stake in Bolkestein's idea of the "dimension," which he maintains in opposition to Korff.[26] These theologians are concerned with presenting the true image of God over against the idea of an unconcerned, aloof God, and therefore they emphasize the love and mercy of God which are revealed in the fact that God himself in the stead of the sinner bears the judgment. They see the mystery of reconciliation in the light of a trinitarian love-drama (as the background and content of the *cur deus homo?*), and it is quite evident that thus they seek to transcend the problems connected with the orthodox doctrine of reconciliation by means of a higher divine synthesis in which reconciliation in Christ follows only one line, namely, from above to below. Thereby it is not necessary to introduce the idea of

24. A. E. Loen, *De Vaste Grond,* 1946, p. 55. Cf.: "God for our sake made himself vulnerable and had to bear the burden of this judgment and damnation." Hence, reconciliation is something that took place in God himself, an inner motivation of God, but in this reconciliation he also enters time. "The eternal God became man, bore our condemnation and entered death. The suffering of Christ is God's suffering on account of our sins" (p. 58). Cf. the expression: "the suffering and the love of a tri-une God" See, on these ideas of Loen, S. U. Zuidema in *De Mens als Historie,* 1948. Cf. Loen on the "*cur deus homo?*" in *De Vaste Grond,* p. 56.

25. Barth, *K.D.* II, 1, 446ff., where he again and again speaks of Jesus Christ who on the cross took upon himself the wrath of God: "No one else but God's own Son, and hence the eternal God himself in his oneness with the human nature which he in free grace had taken upon himself." And in connection with Gal. 4:4 ("made under the law") he says: "That applies to God's Son, to God himself." See also his *De Apostolische Geloofsbelijdenis,* 1935, on God's self-sacrifice in Christ's suffering and death (p. 112): "If God himself suffers in Christ the curse which we have incurred, then this implies that he, the Other, has sacrificed his existence for us" (p. 114). God has, without ceasing to be God, entered in Jesus Christ in the utmost temptation and agony."

26. Lekkerkerker does not consider the difference between Bolkestein and Korff to be very great. The question is whether he does not overlooked the fact that in Bolkestein the problematics of theopaschitism plays a decisive part, whereas in Korff this is definitely not the case.

"satisfaction" at all, which would change the direction of the line, or which would at least interrupt it and make it a broken line. They want to do justice to the reality of God's wrath and avoid the position of Ritschl, who considers this wrath a misconception on our part. But they place the experiencing of this wrath in God himself. From their various formulations and from their desire to avoid patripassianism it is evident that they cannot explain God's experiencing and undergoing his own wrath, but that proves to them that reconciliation is a mystery. Thus the new theopaschitic doctrine of reconciliation becomes the great counterpart of the orthodox doctrine of satisfaction, after the latter has first been interpreted as a primitive *Umstimmung*. The new doctrine places the wrath element at the top of the line which runs downward, and thus the wrath-conflict is projected into God himself, which he solves divinely by undergoing and overcoming the judgment and by surrendering himself in mercy.

It cannot be denied that these recent ideas are the result of an attempt to present an image of God which, especially in times of oppression and misery, can be understood as a *mysterium fascinans*. Rather than accepting (their caricature of) a doctrine of satisfaction which presents God as a God who must be placated, these theologians prefer to accept the idea of a wrath-conflict in God and of the motives of impotence in him (the impotence of his self-surrender and of his love) instead of the features of his majesty and divine sovereignty. Moreover, these theologians attempt to supply their theory of the wrath-conflict with a dogmatic foundation by referring to the incarnation of Christ. Precisely because "God was in Christ," the wrath-conflict receives depth and meaning and rids itself of the abstract aspects of "that which took place" in God in the stillness of eternity. It indeed concerns a process in the heart of God, but this heart beat visibly and audibly on Golgotha. Hence they view the orthodox doctrine of reconciliation with its satisfaction-aspect as a misrepresentation of the deep significance of the incarnation, and therefore also as a Nestorian separation of the two natures of Jesus Christ.

We should not suppose that these are new questions. They were discussed already in the days of the Reformation, for instance, in connection with the monophysitic aspects of Lutheran theology and especially because Scripture is very specific about reconciliation. It is remarkable that many of the disputed expressions which appear in the Confessions are also found in the writings of Calvin, who also occupied himself with the "dimension" idea which now is the chief topic of discussion. We already noted that Korff, in his criticism of the *Umstimmung*, also mentioned Calvin. Korff says that he cannot discover unity in Calvin's position because it shifts from God's wrath to his love and from love to wrath.[27] Thus, Korff says, it seems that there are two opposing principles in God, and the New Testament teaching compels Korff to differ from Calvin. He refers particularly to Calvin's statement that Christ reconciles us to God and makes him favorable and kind to us. Calvin indeed says that Christ is the Mediator who by His own holiness procures the favor of God for us.

A deserved curse obstructs the entrance, and God in his character of Judge is hostile to us, expiation must necessarily intervene in order that as a priest employed to appease the wrath of God, he may reinstate us in his favor. For even under the law of the priesthood it was forbidden to enter the sanctuary without blood, to teach the worshipper that however the priest might interpose to deprecate, God could not be propitiated without the expiation of sin. But Christ by the sacrifice of His death wiped away our guilt and made satisfaction for sin. Christ has removed the enmity between God and us, and purchased a righteousness for us which made God favorable and kind to us (*Inst.* II, XV, 6; XVI, 5). God could be appeased by Christ in no other way.

At first glance we might conclude that here Calvin does indeed simply teach an *Umstimmung*, without realizing the tremendous problems which are involved. But the remarkable thing is that Calvin also declares that when we treat of the merit of Christ, we do not place the beginning in him, but we ascend to the ordination of God as the primary cause. Hence it is incorrect, according to Calvin, to oppose the merit of Christ to the mercy of God, because both are involved.[28] "For Christ could not merit anything save by the good pleasure of God, but only inasmuch as he was destined to appease the wrath of God by his sacrifice, and wipe away our transgressions by his obedience." Calvin quotes John 3:16 at this point and says; "We see that the first place is assigned to the love of God as the chief cause

27. Korff, *Christologie,* II, 192, 193, 195.
28. Korff refers to this statement in connection with the *Umstimmung,* but for this reason Calvin's whole argument becomes the more interesting (Korff, *op. cit.,* p. 192, note 4). See *Inst.* II, XVII, 1.

or origin" (*Inst.* II, XVII, 1, 2).[29] He speaks of the mystery of reconciliation in these remarkable words: "that God in order to remove any obstacle to his love towards us, appointed the method of reconciliation in Christ. There is great force in this word *propitiation;* for in a manner which cannot be expressed, God, at the very time when he loved us, was hostile to us until reconciled in Christ" (*Inst.* II, XVII, 2),[30] while in this context he cites II Corinthians 5:19, which is so often quoted to refute the *Umstimmung*.[31]

This sufficiently proves that Calvin cannot be grouped with those who accept a simplistic *Umstimmung*-idea, that he far transcends the dilemma, Is it God or man who is being reconciled?, and that he looks for a different solution in order to do justice to the biblical teaching of the reality of the wrath of God. Calvin sensed that at that point he might be accused of inconsistency and contradiction, so he says, "As there thus arises some appearance of contradiction, I will explain the difficulty," and he answers the question how it can be said that God, who prevents us with his mercy, was our enemy until he was reconciled to us by Christ. It is remarkable that Calvin does not attempt here to arrive at a rational and speculative synthesis, but remains throughout fully conscious of the *ineffabili modo,* the mode in which the Spirit usually speaks in Scripture. He offers a solution which is in accordance with the teaching of Scripture and which does justice to both God's justice and his love. Calvin's object in these seemingly paradoxical statements is to respect the limits which Scripture imposes. These limits comprise the biblical testimony regarding both God's love and his justice, his wrath and his mercy, man's sin and his deliverance from God's wrath, and regarding Christ as the Lamb of God who has borne the wrath of God.

Within these limits Calvin is conscious of the fact that he can only stammer when speaking of both God's love and his wrath. He is conscious of God's eternal love of his eternal decree of salvation, of Christ's being appointed as Mediator from eternity, but at the same time he is conscious of the historical signifi-

29. Cf. Calvin's commentary on Rom. 3:25. There again he refers to John 3:16.

30. Cf. also *Inst.* II, XVI, 4, where he quotes Augustine, "Incomprehensible and immutable is the love of God. [He was] loving, though at enmity with us because of sin."

31. Cf. Calvin's commentary on II Cor. 5:18.

cance of the work of Christ for the expiation of our guilt and sin. He is not concerned with finding a solution to the abstract problem of time and eternity, but he is very sure of the eternal God who himself, in history, opens a way of full reconciliation and who does so in Christ, who carries away the sin and guilt and who thus is the Revelation – in history – of both God's justice and mercy.[32] Therefore, for Calvin, God's wrath and love are not to be explained as an intertrinitarian dialectic which is settled in "God Himself," but rather, these are revealed in the harmony of God's activity in history.

Calvin deals with the very same problems which again and again presented themselves in the history of the Church and theology and which also play an important part in the doctrine of reconciliation. They are the problems of the "eternalization" of salvation, which blinds men to the significance and necessity of Christ's work, and the "historization" of salvation, which detaches the importance of Christ's work from the love of God and which thus leads to a one-sided *Umstimmung* concept in the doctrine of reconciliation. Calvin obviously wishes to avoid both, and he does so by respecting the entire scriptural message. What Korff designates as Calvin's shifting from God's wrath to his love and from his love to his wrath is indeed present, but this is nothing but Calvin's recognition of God's love from before the foundation of the world and of the significance of history. We may, if we wish, use the word "synthesis" to describe Calvin's position, but only insofar as he, relative to the problems concerning God's eternal love and the historical work of reconciliation, reminds us of Ephesians 1:4, "even as he chose us in him before the foundation of the world."[33]

As we have seen, the dilemma of subject versus object does not apply to the Reformed confessions and theology regarding reconciliation. Reformed theology does not teach an *Umstimmung* which violates God's initiative.[34] Rather, it attempts to

32. See especially Calvin's extensive commentary on II Cor. 5:19, which gives much information on his position. Again and again he goes into the matter of the seeming contradiction.
33. Cf. Calvin's exegesis of Eph. 1:4 and of Rom. 3:25.
34. Cf. H. Bavinck, *Gereformeerde Dogmatiek*, III, 353. He says that we must be reconciled with God, but at the same time that Christ in his entire person and work is a revelation of the love of God. Already the Old Testament taught that God is righteous and holy, jealous of his honor and full of wrath against sin, but he is also merciful and willing to forgive. He is just as loving, merciful, and willing to

transcend the dilemma and emphasizes the divine initiative to reconciliation and the love of God. It sees this taught so explicitly both in the Old and the New Testament that it could hardly ignore this revelation. Scripture constantly speaks of the love of God as the foundation of the salvation of the world. It does not speak of a divine love which had to be called forth from the outside and which did not proceed originally from his own heart. Rather, Scripture teaches that God's sending his Son was the result and evidence of this primary love. God loved the world and therefore he sent his Son (John 3:16, I John 3:10). It is the tender mercy of God which visited us (Luke 1:78; cf. vs. 50, Song of Mary). It is the grace of God that brings salvation (Tit. 2:11). God is rich in mercy (Eph. 2:4) and this mercy is revealed in Christ. II Corinthians 5:18 teaches very emphatically that all these things are of God, and everywhere in Scripture we find this illustrated and confirmed. When the New Testament unfolds the ways of Christ's sacrifice it does not by any means blur the divine initiative. On the contrary, exactly at this point it brings out and emphasizes the love and sovereignty of God's activity. Indeed, Christ is the propitiation, but it is God who has set him forth to be a propitiation (Rom. 3:25).

Already under the Old Covenant this way of working on the part of God is clearly evident. The sacrificial mode by no means proved that reconciliation does not originate in God. Even though it is clear that forgiveness is closely linked with this sacrificial rite, it is nevertheless apparent that God himself has

---

forgive as Christ. "Hence, Christ has not by His work moved the Father to love and mercy, but the love of the Father precedes and is revealed in Christ who is a gift of God's love" (p. 353). The God of Revelation is therefore "no heathen god whose wrath and hatred against mankind must be averted," a position which Bavinck very critically considers a gnostic contrast between the Father and the Son (p. 354, cf. also p. 384). Heppe, too points out that Reformed theology did not identify the doctrine of satisfaction with a primitive *Umstimmung*. "Meanwhile, Christ's satisfaction must not be understood as though God were first moved or forced to let mercy take place of justice, or as though he thereby were changed from an angry into a reconciling God; much rather, Christ's reconciling work was based on God's eternal decree and on the ensuing mandate which was given to Christ" (p. 343). Cf. on Luther concerning the same matter, W. Köhler, *Dogmengeschichte. Das Zeitalter der Reformation,* 1951, pp. 236-39. Cf. Kuyper, *Loci,* III, 100ff. There is an overwhelming number of examples in the history of the Church that show that the simplistic designation *Umstimmung* is not accurate.

instituted it, and this reveals his manner of working: "For . . . I have given it [the blood] to you upon the altar to make atonement for your souls" (Lev. 17:11).

The gift offered to God is not an isolated thing with value in itself, given to God from the outside in order to change his mind. The sacrifice is never a thing that goes contrary to the divine initiative of reconciliation; on the contrary, it is the meaningful expression of this initiative.[35] It is God himself who appears in the cloud upon the mercy seat (Lev. 16:2), and in this manner of reconciliation God reveals his covenant and his love. This is the way in which the Lord leads the people he has chosen, "because Jehovah loveth you" (Deut. 7:8; cf. Amos 3:2; Hos. 11:1, 4; Deut. 9:4f.; 23:5 – Balaam's curse turning into a blessing "because Jehovah thy God loved thee").

Since, then, Scripture speaks so clearly of the love of God, and that it is God who brings about reconciliation, what, then, can be the meaning and significance of Christ's work, and how must we view the reality of God's wrath? If the primary cause is indeed the reconciling, merciful, and loving inclination of God, what, then, can be the meaning of the price of reconciliation, of Christ's reconciling work, of his cleansing blood? Does not Christ's mediatorial work inadvertently but nevertheless quite obviously push the Divine initiative into the background, and does it not evoke the idea of an *Umstimmung?*

When we read the Scripture we see time and again what importance it attaches to the phrase "through Christ." This refers to the blood of the covenant that is shed for many (Mark 14:14, Matt. 26:28), and in heaven a song is sung in which the redeemed sing of the blood of the Lamb that brought them unto God (Rev. 5:9). Why and how are we redeemed "with the precious blood of Christ, as of a lamb without blemish and without spot"? Why do we still need a High Priest, in spite of the divine initiative, who opens the way "that we might obtain mercy and find grace to help in the time of need"? What is the connection between the inner mercy of God and the way of suffering and shame of the Lamb, the Lamb of *God?* We are not raising these questions anew, because they have once and for all been answered by the testimony of Scripture to the justice and love, the holiness and mercy of God which in this Lamb, in this great suffering, in this *passio magna* come to expression.

35. Cf. H. Mandel, *Christliche Versöhnungslehre,* 1916, p. 157.

But we ask these questions in connection with the confession of the Church and the ever-recurring questions concerning the necessity of this dark way of suffering unto death, yea the death of the cross, on the part of Jesus.

This matter has been considered from every angle, and various theories have been given. One is the so-called subjective doctrine of reconciliation, which views the suffering of Christ as a sign of the love of God which aims at evoking love in return and thus to realize reconciliation. This theory attempts to "reveal" the love of God, but it does not make clear why this revelation of an inviolable fact had to be in the form of Christ's death on the cross. This theory has been advocated in one form or another ever since Abelard. Its characteristic feature is that it eliminates every element of the wrath and righteousness of God in the process of reconciliation. It makes the cross the sign and principle by which to recognize the love of God. Another idea is that the cross is also the sign of the absolute seriousness of sin which is revealed in the cross.[36] Such sign-theories not only contradict the confession of the Church but also the plain teaching of Scripture, which presents the cross of Christ not as a sign, an illustration, a revelation, but as a historical event, a historical act which takes away sin. The entire Scripture emphasizes the seriousness of this event, and therefore we read, "apart from shedding of blood is no remission" (Heb. 9:22), and find the comparison with the testator who must of necessity be dead before the testament can be of force (Heb. 9:16, 17). Scripture does not picture Christ's blood as a noetic sign of God's mercy. Indeed, the death of Christ does manifest the love of God, but not as a rather arbitrary sign or illustration but as a happening, a coming to pass of forgiveness.[37] In the subjective doctrine of reconciliation nothing takes place. There is no appreciation for the historical work of Christ, but an ignoring of its tremendous proportions which defy all imagination. Why else do we read in Scripture of the communion of the blood of Christ (I Cor. 10:16) and of being made nigh, after having been far off, by the blood of Christ (Eph. 2:13), of the purging of the conscience by the blood of Christ (Heb. 9:14; cf. I John 1:7, I Pet. 1:2), of the robes washed white in the blood of the Lamb (Rev. 7:14), and of the victory

36. So H. Grotius, *Defensio fidei catholica de Satisfactione Christi,* 1617.
37. Cf. Grosheide in his *Commentary* on Heb. 9:20.

by the blood of the Lamb (Rev. 12:11)? These passages do not speak *merely* of a revealing function of the cross, but of God's love in harmony with his holiness and righteousness. This love becomes manifest in the *passio magna*, when Christ in the encounter with the Father takes our sin upon himself and carries it away (John 1:29).

The error of the noetic, subjective doctrine of reconciliation is that it denatures the love of God to an affectionless, unconcerned sentiment which is incapable of being insulted or injured, a love which needs only to be unveiled, without suffering and without sacrifice and without an act in history. This "unveiling" takes the place of the wrath of God, which must be eliminated as a human distortion of the concept of God. The entire teaching of the Scripture shrivels to naught; there is no appreciation of why the suffering of Christ was a "must," why such a High Priest became us (Heb. 7:26), who once at the end of the ages has appeared to put away sin by the sacrifice of himself (Heb. 9:26). These texts speak not only of the publishing of the fact of God's love, but of the revelation as it was executed in history. It matters not that the Church, in her indicating of the mystery of reconciliation, hardly proceeds beyond a stammering, as did Augustine and Calvin when they spoke of both God's wrath and his love. The Church must sound forth her emphatic "No" to the superficial noetic doctrine of reconciliation, for it fails to recognize the teaching of Scripture.

Neither can the Church recognize Heering's interpretation of Scripture, who describes the meaning of the cross in these words: "Christ with a divine gesture spreads his arms out and says: Also this last, this very last thing I did for you, in complete unanimity with the Father, according to his gracious and saving intent, in order to open your eyes at last, to convince you of his love, to draw you irresistibly, in spite of all your opposition, to the Father, and to make you bow down under his mercy."[38] According to Heering, Christ preaches "God's love by means of his word, but especially by his death." In the cross he reveals the love of God. To be sure, Heering also mentions the "sin-crushing and liberating power of the cross," but these effects are implied in Christ's preaching, which publishes the love of God.

38. G. J. Heering, *Geloof en Openbaring*, II, 175, 176 (1937). Cf., the truest proof of love, also of God's love, is the sacrifice. Heering considers the idea that the cross is the satisfaction of the wrath of God too "anthropopathic" and as payment too juridical and legalistic.

For that reason the cross, for Heering, is a sign in protest against the teaching of the Confessions, which connect the death of Christ with the wrath of God. In addition, Heering alleges that the formulations of the Confessions give the reconciliation an "anthropopathic" character. With this word and the words "juridical" and "Anselmian," the adherents of the noetic viewpoint attack the clear teaching of Scripture concerning the divine activity in reconciliation, which is realized in Christ in his bearing the wrath of God. The conflict truly concerns not simply a few scattered expressions of the Confessions but the testimony of Paul, who constantly sings the praise of the Resurrected One, of Jesus "who delivereth us from the wrath to come" (I Thess. 1:10).

The battle over the dilemma concerns essentially the love of God. From every side we hear the accusation that when reconciliation is presented as a satisfaction, a placation, or a propitiation of the wrath of God, it ascribes traits to God which obscure his love. For that reason the Church in her defense has always pointed out the harmony of God's attributes, the unity between his holiness and love in the actuality of the historical reconciliation.

Korff has rejected both the idea of an *Umstimmung* and of a conflict between God's mercy and his righteousness. The possibility that this latter idea could exist in the Church is not imaginary. Precisely when we reject the above-mentioned dilemma, when we consider the message of the truly divine reconciliation not to be in conflict with the reality of his wrath, we must be on our guard against this danger. One might, in reaction to Ritschl's criticism of the idea of God's wrath, speak with Lekkerkerker of "something of a conflict between the Son and the Father, between God and God," to designate what happens "in the dimension between Jesus and God."[39] It must be realized, however, that Korff has warned beforehand against this idea of a conflict, because he wishes to emphasize that it is *we* who must be reconciled. He rejects the idea that the real mystery takes place between Father and Son because this presupposes a duality in God, a battle within God himself, as Luther teaches.[40] Korff says that the New Testament offers no ground for such an idea. Brunner, for instance, says that the central mystery of

39. Lekkerkerker, *Gesprek,* p. 77.
40. Korff, *op. cit.,* pp. 187-197.

Christ is that God's love conquers his wrath, but Korff declares that he has found no trace of evidence for such an "alleged central mystery" in the New Testament. He indeed speaks with some reservations about a "conflict" between the Son incarnate and the Father when Christ utters his fourth word on the cross, but this is no evidence whatsoever of a duality within God. Although we agree with Korff that the word "conflict" is very carelessly used, it is nevertheless clear that his sharp criticism is connected with his rejection of the doctrine of satisfaction, which, according to him, implies that grace can become active only "after justice has first been satisfied." This, he thinks, robs God of the initiative to grace and reconciliation. Since God is the subject of reconciliation, the sentence cannot be pronounced beforehand because then the initiative of reconciliation does not lie with God.

Again we touch upon the core of the doctrine of reconciliation. Korff, of course, is too well acquainted with the teaching of the Bible to eliminate the aspect of justice from reconciliation. There is indeed a connection between justice and love which is of decisive importance in reconciliation. But it lies in the one dimension, from God to us. God does not forgive "just like that," and cannot forgive at the expense of moral seriousness. Korff rejects the subjective doctrine of reconciliation. "The demand of justice must in any event be fulfilled in us." That is Korff's conclusion regarding reconciliation. God through Christ fulfills the demand of the law in the believers, who become different people. In other words, grace fulfills the demand of justice *afterwards*. This viewpoint differs from the doctrine of satisfaction because the latter emphasizes the order of justice. In the New Testament *grace* occupies the dominant place. "Grace takes the place of the order of justice, and behold, afterwards it appears that exactly thus, by grace and in the way of grace, the order of justice has been satisfied." Indeed, "the order of justice is abolished, but nevertheless its objective is reached."

Thus, however, there is still an element of competition in the relation between justice and love, and love prevails. In spite of his statement that the requirement of justice — after its elimination — is filled after all, Korff nevertheless emphasizes the aspect of grace, and in this connection he complains that "theology in general has little emphasized the love of God, let alone doing it full justice." The criticism becomes quite sharp when Korff agrees with Harnack that the orthodox satisfaction-doctrine ascribes to God "the horrible privilege not to be in a position to forgive out of love." This citation is quite in line with Harnack's liberal theology, but it is rather out of place with Korff since the latter realizes better than Harnack that this presentation is nothing but a caricature. This citation creates the impression that according to the Confessions the demand of God's justice is satisfied in history before God's love comes to expression. But this is a misrepresentation of what the Church teaches, because she speaks of both God's love and his wrath, of both his mercy and his justice, as we have pointed out before.

Those who follow Harnack's thinking do not understand that behind the doctrine of reconciliation is God's love, and they interpret divine justice after the analogy of human justice, which must succumb to love. When, therefore, Korff agrees with Harnack, the question may be asked whether he, when talking about the elimination of the judicial order, means the same thing by the justice of God as Scripture does. The fact that he presupposes an "order" between justice and grace indicates already that he belittles God's justice, as though it were comparable to our human administration of justice, which can be very faulty and corrupt. Moreover, it is difficult to see why Korff, in agreement with Brunner, says that God's love overcomes his wrath. They thus make a caricature of the doctrine of satisfaction, as though the satisfaction supplies only the means for the atonement for sin. This is contrary to the very idea of forgiveness, according to Korff. That which we as human beings do, or must do, namely, forgive each other freely, must not God do so himself? Satisfaction and mercy are mutually exclusive.

The reason that Korff so emphatically rejects the idea of satisfaction is, no doubt, that he thinks of it as *Umstimmung* in the primitive sense. It is fortunate, however, that the Church has always realized otherwise. It is completely untrue to Scripture to begin with a general idea of satisfaction and then apply it to God's work of reconciliation in Jesus Christ. The mystery of reconciliation is such that we cannot approach it by saying that God's justice was satisfied *beforehand* in order that the doors of grace might be opened; rather, there is a mysterious harmony between God's love *from eternity* and Christ, whom he appointed as the means of reconciliation. We cannot begin with a human concept of love, then try to connect it with the concept of "justice." In the cross of Christ God's justice and love are *simultaneously* revealed, so that we can speak of his love only in connection with this reality of the cross. For this reason we speak of a mystery: not a mystery in general, but the mystery of reconciliation.

At this point we can agree with Korff that the mystery lies in the words "for us." "The rest we can let go, as long as we maintain the mystery which is a mystery of salvation." But that is exactly what the Church in her Confessions intended. The Church did not mean to explain rationally the words "for us" by using familiar concepts like paying and satisfaction, though Korff suggests otherwise by his statement "that various Protestant confessions indeed contain a certain theory concerning the suffering of Christ." According to him the Confessions do not emphasize the "for us" aspect enough, but that is exactly what the Confessions are doing. In the face of the many distortions and misrepresentations of the mystery of reconciliation, all we can do is describe the meaning of the words "for us" on the basis of what Scripture teaches. It is the Church's duty to emphasize the reality of the cross of Christ over against those who teach that reconciliation is only a sign or symbol. And when Korff describes "for us" as *expiatio,* as an expiation of the guilt of sin, then he proves that one can say more than "for us" without saying anything differently.

This reminds us of a statement by Brunner, who says: "We may not seize the word 'mystery' as a cover for our ignorance, as a retreat for our irrationalistic arbitrarinesses and mystic exuberances. For the gospel gives us a very clear message concerning the cross. It does not speak of 'something mysterious' but of a very definite mystery."[41]

That applies also to the words "for us." Those who wish to *transcend* this mystery merely grope in an unreconciled reality. Those, however, who *describe* it, do a service to the Church and to its preaching as long as they remain open to the teaching of Scripture, which everywhere connects "for us" with all of God's attributes, with his eternal love in Christ, and hence also with

41. Brunner, *Der Mittler,* 1927, p. 393. And example of an unwarranted use of the word "mystery" may be found in H. van Oyen when he writes: "Every attempt at an juridical satisfaction-theory is an argument, a form of reflection which attempts to penetrate analytically the unfathomable mystery of reconciliation, and which thus desecrates the mystery of God's love" ("Liefde, Gerechtigheid, en Recht" in *Nederlands Theologisch Tijdschrift,* 1st ed., 1946, p. 34). Note especially the word "thus." We might ask why, then, Paul in Romans 3 is not guilty of the same thing.

his holiness and his wrath. "Delivered from the wrath to come. . . ." When Paul expresses his great joy in these words, he is not thinking of a gnostic contrast between justice and love, corresponding to God and Christ, but he is referring to one and the same act of God. He does not solve the mystery of God's love in a synthesis, but he lives out of it in faith as the historical reality in which Christ was the sacrifice and as such is the revelation of the love of God.

Even though we shall never be able to fathom God nor the fulness of his loving and holy activity in Jesus Christ, nevertheless the message concerning his love can be heard and understood in faith. This message does indeed concern the love of God, but it has nothing to do with a priority of his love over his holiness. Those who try to prove such a priority by appealing to I John 4:8 and 16, "God is love," must then accept a hierarchy of attributes in God. But in John no such hierarchy can be found. John's statement is not comparative or antithetic but thetic, and thus the Church may confess God's love. But she may not pretend to understand the depths of this love apart from the whole of revelation. John says, "Herein was the love of God manifested in us, that God hath sent his only begotten Son into the world . . . to be the propitiation for our sins" (I John 4:9, 10). We know the love of God in the way wherein Jesus Christ finishes his work even unto death. In this manifestation of God's love we perceive that we cannot apply our limited human standards to the love of God. This love is not indifferent to sin and to the consequent disruption of the world and man's life. Hence Scripture presents the wrath of God not in tension with, but in harmony with his love. Only thus can it be explained that in the cross of Christ we behold simultaneously God's justice and his love, and that "Zion shall be redeemed with justice" (Isa. 1:27).

Christ was fully aware of this as he walked the way of God's justice and love to the very end. Hence, also, we must object seriously to the idea of a conflict in God as this is entertained in the new doctrine of reconciliation. For this conflict in its theopaschitic form, although it upholds the deity of Christ,[42] nevertheless it is in essence a mutilation of the mystery of the trinity.[43]

42. Cf. H. Vogel, *Gott in Christo,* 1951, pp. 655ff.
43. That is what I called theopaschitism by way of a brief description in my book *The Person of Christ,* 1952, pp. 310f.

The Church's opposition to theopaschitism was not the same as its rejection of the gnostics, according to whom the unity between the human Jesus and the divine *aeon* was broken before the cross because God cannot suffer. The Church objected to theopaschitism because it kept speaking of "God himself," whereas Scripture speaks of Jesus Christ, the Word incarnate. The Church did not thereby attack Christ's deity, but she emphasized "that [Christ is] not the divine nature as such, but definitely the person of the Son became man."[44] The Church was convinced that according to Scripture it was the Son who suffered, Jesus Christ, who was both true God and true man, and that God's wrath and curse were directed against him. It is very striking that the biblical terminology regarding reconciliation never speaks theopaschitically, but always points to the relation of the Word Incarnate to the Father. Precisely where the phrase "God in Christ" appears in connection with reconciliation, it is said that God has made Christ to be sin for us (II Cor. 5:19ff.).

For this reason the theopaschitic tendency in the new doctrine of reconciliation, the new doctrine of "substitution," is a human attempt to present the trinitarian background of the incarnation in a logical synthesis. But in so doing it oversteps the limits of speculation, because this new doctrine is not concerned with the mercy, the concern, the initiative of God,[45] of which the Confessions of the Church are full, but it speaks of God's abandoning himself, of God's taking upon himself the misery and sin of the world, so that it brings in a separate concept, namely, the suffering of God, although it immediately adds: "in Christ." The Church, however, has always viewed Jesus Christ — *vere*

44. H. Bavinck, *Gereformeerde Dogmatiek*, III, 255. Bavinck mentions here only patripassianism, of which he (correctly, I think) says that in this form it no longer exists. He further mentions only the pantheistic systems, in which the divine permeates the physical world and in which the history of revelation is the history of the suffering of God. When Bavinck mentions that there is an element of truth in this idea, he obviously makes no concession to theopaschitism, as is quite evident from what he says further.

45. No Scriptural basis can be found for theopaschitism even in those places where God's "affections" are mentioned, such as Gen. 6:6, "And it repented Jehovah that he had made man on the earth, and it *grieved* him at his heart," and Isa. 63:9. "In all their affliction he was afflicted." From the depth of these anthropomorphic words (anthropomorphic does not imply a devaluation of their meaning!) we cannot deduce theopaschitism, because the latter involves a specific incarnation problem.

Deus et homo – as the Man of Sorrows,[46] and on the basis of Scripture she refuses to explain the relation of God to Jesus Christ in a manner which ultimately can hardly be distinguished from modalism. It is true, the reality of reconciliation – "a propitiation . . . to show his righteousness" (Rom. 3:25) – confronts us with an unfathomable mystery, but it is exactly this mystery which the Church in her Confessions wishes to honor.

I agree that oftentimes the word "satisfaction" is used in such a way that it seems to mean *Umstimmung,* and that it seems to interpret the "conflict" between God and Christ as a "gnostic" conflict rather than as a mediatorial relationship. The Church must also realize, in connection with the necessity of reconsidering the new doctrine of reconciliation, that she may not react to the emphasis on II Corinthians 5:19 (the divine initiative) by detracting from the full, biblical message that herein the love of God is manifest, that he sent his Son into the world. It is, moreover, easily shown that the doctrine of "reconciliation through satisfaction" did not originate from such a reaction, but from the desire to do full justice to the message of Scripture and the love of God as well as his righteous wrath. And since its formulation precludes, on the one hand, the subjectivizing of reconciliation, and on the other hand, precludes theopaschitism, it deserves more appreciation than it has often received as the "orthodox" doctrine of reconciliation.[47]

46. Lord's Day VI, Q. 17 says concerning the Godhead of Christ that Christ "by the power of His Godhead . . . might bear in His human nature the burden of God's wrath." There is no trace of Nestorianism to be found here, any more than in Q. 47, because the Catechism wishes to say that divine power was necessary for the man Jesus Christ in order to be able to bear the wrath of God. Moreover, the idea of mediation is clearly behind these words. The Catechism is not speaking of an abstract, isolated human nature, but of the one, unique Person of Jesus Christ. Cf. K. Schilder's *Commentary on the Heidelberg Catechism,* II, 184ff.

47. It is difficult to see why our position regarding reconciliation is "dialectic" (A. F. N. Lekkerkerker, "Dialectisch Spreken Over de Verzoening" in *Nieuw Theologisch Tijschrift,* 1st ed., 1940, pp. 214ff.). Apart from the general difficulty in defining this dialectic, it is, in my opinion, evident that Lekkerkerker's treatment of reconciliation is by no means similar to the dialectical theology of Karl Barth. In spite of the fact that the former often appeals to Barth, there are, it seems to me, considerable differences. No doubt all the words whereby the Church attempts to describe the mystery of reconciliation will bear the characteristics of the thing confessed, that is to say, of the message of the

It is evident that the question concerning the object of reconciliation – God or man[48] – is a vain attempt to force an entrance into the mystery of reconciliation. Proceeding from II Cor. 5:19, "God was in Christ reconciling the world unto himself," this question has often been asked and answered simplistically. The problem of the "pinnacle of reconciliation" is supposedly solved by saying that reconciliation is a divine act resembling an uninterrupted straight line proceeding from above.

This exegesis does contain some worthy criticism of an un-Christian concept of God. We certainly may not minimize the perspective of II Corinthians, for the correctness of the doctrine of reconciliation depends upon it. "With respect to the *katallagē* God and man are by no means equals," and Paul certainly means to say that God through Christ's work "places man in a reconciled relationship to himself." The point at issue is "an act of God," and the confession of the Church clearly emphasizes this act.[49] But at the same time we see that this reconciliation is effected in history by the death of Christ, who became a curse for us (Gal. 3:13). Then, therefore, Church and theology use words in the doctrine of reconciliation such as "paying," "buying," and "satisfaction" of the justice of God, its purpose is not to detach the work of Christ from the reconciling activity of God. The love of God was not separated from the curse which Christ bore, nor was the work of Christ separated from the reconciliation of God. The word "satisfaction" was not introduced after the analogy of human self-assertion, as though God has a distorted sense of honor and greatness. Of course, any doctrine of reconciliation can be analyzed in such a way that the unity of God's activity in the cross of Christ is fragmented, but it is utterly incorrect thus to interpret the Church's teaching. When she spoke

---

love of God as well as of the way in which this love manifests itself. Nowhere is this done more clearly and convincingly than in the words of Calvin which we cited earlier.

48. E.g., "God is in the entire context [viz., of Rom. 3:25] seen only as subject, not as object, which is entirely in line with the Pauline doctrine of reconciliation" (Kittel, *TWNT*, III, 321). Cf. also I, 255: "God reconciles us, that is to say, the world, unto himself. II Cor. 5:18f. He is not reconciled."

49. F. W. Grosheide, *Commentary* on II Cor. 5:19.

of the *satisfactio vicaria,*[50] she wished thereby to emphasize the love of Christ.

Van Oyen gives this interpretation of Christ's satisfaction: "He [God] must at all costs remain true to himself: with inexorable severity and without respect for persons he must maintain justice; mercy and grace are here *corpora aliena.*"[51] This is nothing but a caricature, on which no theology can be built. As if this were the Church's interpretation of God's justice and holiness! Now, over against this caricature of the orthodox doctrine of reconciliation, Van Oyen places the marvel of God's mercy, "which remains the same; and especially in his wrath, in his grief, God does not seek Himself and does not strive after his own interest, but after the covenant with his people." "Does not seek Himself" . . . hereby Van Oyen antithetically imposes human egoism upon God, as if thus the glory and holiness of God and his wrath can be shown![52] Van Oyen himself admits that Scripture emphatically speaks of God's wrath and justice. This shows how weak the criticism of the orthodox doctrine of reconciliation is in the light of Scripture. Such criticism must ultimately resort to hiding God's wrath behind his love, or even, with Ritschl, denying the reality of his wrath altogether. And since neither option has any basis in Scripture, we must try to understand the harmony of the scriptural witness ever more fully, speaking with Paul of the reconciliation received at the same moment that Christ appears as the means of reconciliation. And on the basis of this means of reconciliation and the curse upon Christ's life, we will be able to say, "But God commendeth

50. Cf. J. Rivière, "Satisfactio vicaria" in *Revue des Sciences Religieuses,* XXVI (1952), 221-57, who says that the doctrine is much older than the term (Anselm uses only *satisfactio*). Rivière mentions further Heidegger and Turrentinus. In Roman Catholic circles the term became accepted after it was used in the Vatican Council. The reason why it became accepted at such a late date was apparently that of a reaction to the special content it received during the Reformation. After the Vatican Council the expression was first felt to be a neologism, but soon it became generally accepted as a theological term.

51. H. van Oyen, "Liefde, Gerechtigheid en Recht" in *Nieuw Theologisch Tijdschrift,* I, 39, 33, 40 (1946).

52. Lekkerkerker called Van Oyen's attention to the word of the Lord: "Thus saith the Lord Jehovah: I do not this for your sake, O house of Israel, but for my holy name which ye have profaned among the nations, whither ye went" (Ezek. 36:22). *Nieuw Theologisch Tijdschrift,* 1st ed., 1946, p. 220.

his own love toward us, in that, while we were yet sinners, Christ died for us" (Rom. 5:8).

We prefer, therefore, to remain with the language of the Confessions regarding the unfathomableness of God's eternal love in Christ, rather than breaking apart the wrath and love of God so that the cross of Christ becomes only a terrible "sign" or "symbol" of the love of God. *The very fact that God graciously opens the way of reconciliation completely determines the structure of this reconciliation,* also as the satisfaction of God's justice. Men may try to reason away this concept by appealing to the many expressions in the Old Testament which say that God is caused to be favorable, interpreting these as ideas taken over from paganism, but then they have found the idea of an *Umstimmung* in the Old Testament apart from the way God opened himself, and thus they rob this "causing to be favorable" of its true characteristic. But this *Umstimmung* may not be read into the Confessions of the Church either. The Church was concerned with pointing out the way which God opened, and she saw in the reality of the cross the basis for her confession that Christ had become a curse for us.

We have come to the conclusion that the central problem of the doctrine of reconciliation is not solved subjectively (sign, symbol, evoking our love), nor is it solved theopaschitically as God's taking upon himself the sin and guilt and the suffering. Both options are markedly antithetical to the orthodox doctrine of reconciliation.

In response to these critiques it is not possible to give a *rational explanation* of the mystery, concerning which Calvin gave a paradoxical formulation in referring to God's eternal love and the historical act of reconciliation.[53] Nevertheless the Church, although she does not intend to rationalize the reconciliation, has emphasized the one central idea in Scripture which is essential to the biblical teaching concerning reconciliation, namely the revelation concerning Jesus Christ the Mediator.

When we call the confession concerning the Mediator essential, this does not mean that we find this terminology everywhere in Scripture. Here, too, we realize that Scripture does not offer

53. Cf. L. van der Zanden, *De Spits der Verzoening,* 1950, especially the passages which briefly seek to interpret that which Calvin called the mystery, pp. 32-33, concerning that which is eternal in God and historically motivated in connection with God's love and wrath. Cf. also p. 35.

us a system of orderly dogmatic ideas but rather, because of the multiplicity of authors and varying situations, presents the person and work of Christ now in one way and now in another way. But when, in various instances, the idea of the Mediator is explicitly mentioned, we observe how essential this idea is to the message concerning Jesus Christ. Oepke points out how seldom the word "mediator" is used in the New Testament,[54] but he nevertheless comes to the conclusion that the New Testament faith is strictly and exclusively oriented to the idea that Christ is the Mediator. The thing that matters is not the frequency of the word, but the place which Scripture ascribes to Christ. And when we realize this, then those passages that speak of Christ as the Mediator fit into the whole of the biblical witness. We recall Paul's statement in I Timothy 2:5: "For there is one God, one mediator also between God and men, himself man, Christ Jesus," or the expression of the Epistle to the Hebrews: "By so much as he is also the mediator of a better covenant" or "of the new testament" (Heb. 8:6, 9:15; cf. 12:24). It is very evident that Christ's being the Mediator is at once related to our salvation and reconciliation. When Paul speaks of the Mediator he at once adds that the man Jesus Christ "gave himself a ransom for all," and in Hebrews Christ's position as Mediator is connected with the New Testament, by means of which the full richness of salvation comes to expression.

The word "mediator" already implies this, because it indicates a person who stands between two parties in order to reconcile them. Christ's mediatorship implies a complete reconciliation. The idea of a mediator presupposes the annihilation of the distance caused by sin and enmity. Christ's mediatorship is not primarily a cosmic bridge over the tremendous distance between God transcendent and our universe, but rather a soteriological solution to the condition of enmity. For that reason Scripture emphasizes the absoluteness and uniqueness of Christ's mediatorship. When Christ ascribes a "mediating" function to another figure, for example to the prophets and especially Moses, this does not eliminate Christ's unique mediatorship. To the others God does indeed give the task of mediation, of standing between God and man, as is especially evident in Moses, who as a man stood before God. Moses considered himself unfit for the task and hence wanted to be excused from his commission (Exod. 4:13) so that God's anger turned against him (4:14), but nevertheless he became God's "representative" to his people and stood before Pharaoh in a unique situation: "I have made thee a god to Pharaoh" (Exod. 7:1). By the commission which was laid upon his shoulders he was placed between God and men. It was he alone who climbed up to God (Exod. 19:3, 9ff.) and stood both at the side of God and at the side of the people in his mediatorship.

But at the same time the relativity and insufficiency of his mediatorship is evident. Not only did God become angry with this mediator, which brings out his incapability to perform God's commission, but Moses in the exercise of his mediatorship had to experience the limitations of it. After the people had sinned Moses climbed up unto God with the purpose of establishing a possible reconciliation: "Peradventure I shall make atonement for your sin" (Exod. 32:30). And he offers this prayer up unto the Lord: "Yet now, if thou wilt forgive their sin –; and if not, blot me, I pray thee, out of thy book which thou hast written (vs. 32).

What we see here is the contemplation of a possible substitution in order to effect a reconciliation. Yet we see clearly the powerlessness of this mediatorship in spite of Moses' great love for his people, for God did not accept this offer: "And Jehovah said unto Moses, Whosoever hath sinned against me, him will I blot out of my book" (vs. 33).[55] This shows the limitation of Moses' mediatorship, and this limitation is everywhere evident in any human mediatorship. This limitation, however, points toward the only Mediator in whom substitution becomes a unique reality. Gispen says that Moses' plea here surpasses that of Exodus 32:11-13, and "whoever loves sinful Israel to such an extent is truly a type of the Mediator Jesus Christ."[56] Without minimizing Moses' concern in any way, we can nevertheless deduce from God's negative answer that Moses lost sight of the

54. Kittel, TWNT, IV, 622, 628.

55. This prayer of Moses is of an entirely different nature than that of Exod. 32:11ff., where Moses appeals to the impression which the annihilation of Israel would make upon the Egyptians and to God's oath which he swore to Abraham, Isaac, and Jacob. In answer to the latter prayer we read: "And the Lord repented of the evil which he thought to do unto his people." Of this prayer Gispen correctly says: "Moses is the true mediator between the Lord and his people" (*Exodus*, II, 189).

56. Gispen, *op. cit.*, pp. 194, 195. Gispen nevertheless says: "An entirely different question is whether that which Moses proposes is possible."

limits of his mediatorship. At any rate, we see the great difference between him and Christ. The reason for God's refusal, namely, that another cannot bear the sin of the people, not even this mediator Moses, does not imply that God will allow no substitution; instead, it points to the uniqueness of the Mediator Jesus Christ, in whom the relativity of human mediators is eliminated: ". . . himself man, Christ Jesus, who gave himself a ransom for all, the testimony to be borne in its own times" (I Tim. 2:5, 6).

Christ is the Mediator in an absolute sense because he is not simply commissioned as a man, but because in his person he combines true divinity and true humanity. He appears as such in the entire New Testament, even though the word "mediator" appears only sporadically. Here, too, there is an inseparable connection between his person and his work. His reconciling work is based on his being Immanuel – he is our peace.[57]

On the basis of Christ's mediatorship it is evident that the question whether God or man is the object of reconciliation is a false dilemma. Christ is not like a human mediator who tries to influence another person to change his mind, for he is a unique Person. The emphasis is not on abstract mediating, but on *this* Mediator. That is why it is so significant that Calvin and the Confessions constantly emphasize that God himself gave this Mediator. To be sure, this idea must be treated carefully; it should not lead us to careless speculations which tend toward theopaschitism, but on the other hand we must take with entire seriousness the fact that reconciliation is effected in Christ as true man but also as true God.

He is the reality of the New Covenant of which he is the Mediator. He is not just the Mediator according to his human nature, but *he* is the Mediator – *vere Deus, vere homo.* The two natures of Christ cannot be separated in his mediatoral work, for he is not simply *a* mediator but *the* Mediator between God and men with his whole person and in his specific office.[58]

57. Cf. C. Bouma in his commentary on I Tim. 2:5, "The idea expressed by the word *μεσίτης* is, however, often used in the Word of God concerning Christ wherever the idea of substitution (Isa. 53) and of reconciliation is presented."

"For he is our peace" (Eph. 2:14). Says Bouma, "The word (*μεσίτης*) is used in classical Greek of a peacemaker."

58. Cf. K. Schilder in his commentary on the Heidelberg Catechism, pp. 2C lff. Here Schilder discusses the ideas of Stancarus (that Christ is Media r only according to his human nature).

This Mediator is of God made unto us wisdom, and righteousness, and sanctification, and redemption (I Cor. 1:30). Hence the scriptural message concerning the Mediator Jesus Christ contains a warning not to operate carelessly with an incorrect dilemma which opposes God's love to his justice, reconciliation to satisfaction, and God's grace to his wrath. Through the work of this Mediator reconciliation becomes real in the midst of the revelation of God's justice and holiness. The same epistle which so emphasizes the sacrifice and which contains the statement that offends so many, that "apart from shedding of blood there is no remission" (Heb. 9:22), speaks with joy concerning the surety of a better testament (Heb. 7:22). In him is contained our reconciliation; he is the full guarantee of salvation both for the present and the future. We can depend upon this covenant, for it is based not on an abstract idea or a timeless truth but is effected through the historical death of Christ. In him reconciliation and peace are secure. Christ did not wrestle our salvation and peace from an avenging God, but he fulfilled and realized God's oath unto Abraham (Heb. 6:13ff.). Both offer and *expiatio* remind us of the unchangeableness of God's counsel. This is the basis for "the hope set before us: which we have as an anchor of the soul, a hope both sure and stedfast and entering into that which is within the veil" (Heb. 6:18, 19); whither as a forerunner Jesus entered for us. With this kind of a Mediator it becomes clear that we can and must reject the "God himself" of theopaschitism as a trespassing of the limits set by the testimony of Scripture, and that at the same time we can and must maintain that "all things are of God, who reconciled us to himself through Christ" (II Cor. 5:18).

When Paul speaks of God's activity in Christ Jesus he adds, "We are ambassadors therefore on behalf of Christ, as though God were entreating by us: we beseech you on behalf of Christ, be ye reconciled to God" (II Cor. 5:20). These words have time and again evoked the question how this admonition could follow after the statement concerning *God's* activity. Should the preacher not simply broadcast the *fact* of this reconciliation whether men believe or not, whether they have accepted it or still reject it? Why after the *katallagē* still another act, namely an act by man? Is there still room for a human decision after the divine? Does not man's decision undo God's, or at least mitigate its absolute and definitive character? These and similar questions have been asked again and again, especially by those who have concluded to the universality of reconciliation from the fact of the *katallagē* and who therefore maintain that this universality is not endangered by faith or unbelief. Here we touch the core of the doctrine of reconciliation by way of the eschatological *apokatastasis* (restitution), which in our day especially has become the focal point of discussion.

The question concerning *apokatastasis* may originate in several ways, but now we are speaking of that *apokatastasis* which is supposedly connected with Christ's reconciling work. It plays an important role in dialectical theology, especially Barth's, in connection with the election and rejection of Jesus Christ. On the basis of God's activity in Christ Jesus in his absolute substitution, Barth concludes that man must be considered in Christ because Christ alone is the One rejected by God. This rejection of Jesus Christ, on whom descended the sword of God's wrath, concerns a divine decision which we cannot undo by a human decision.[59] How, then, is the *apokatastasis* connected with the fact of the substitution and the reconciliation it implies? This problem has not yet been solved by Barth. On the one hand, he keeps emphasizing the universality of grace in Christ, and on the other hand, because of the actuality of faith, he relates reconciliation to faith and continues to stress the urgent question: "Do you believe this?"

It is not surprising that the battle concerning *apokatastasis* now rages anew in connection with reconciliation. Originally the restitution had been taught on the basis of a general love of God for mankind, without accepting the necessity of substitution, but now according to Barth it became actual on the basis of substitution. Brunner said of Barth's idea that it was "the most radical doctrine of general salvation which thus far has been advocated."[60] Barth's doctrine may not be identified with Origen's, according to Brunner, for Barth goes still further. Brunner considers universal salvation a heresy which denies the reality of God's justice and judgment. At any rate it is noteworthy that

59. See my extensive discussion concerning this in *Faith and Justification*.
60. E. Brunner, *Dogmatik*, I, 338, 345, 346, 376 - 381. Brunner knows, however, that Barth rejects it. Cf. what Brunner says of Barth: "He knows too much of the non-too-illustrious succession of proponents of the doctrine of *apokatastasis* in the history of the Christian Church than to be willingly classified with them" (p. 376, in a discussion of Barth's doctrine of election). Brunner says also that Barth has not said the last word yet. No doubt the appearance of Barth's fourth volume of *Kirchliche Dogmatik* will clarify many questions.

Brunner speaks in far sharper language than Barth, although Barth, too, rejects the *apokatastasis*.[61]

We are, of course, not concerned with an interpretation of Barth's position nor with the controversy between Barth and Brunner. But the cause of the controversy is closely connected with the basic question of the doctrine of reconciliation. That is evident when Brunner writes that we cannot believe in a salvation "which lies outside and beyond faith either for us or for anybody else." The free and sovereign grace of God in Christ is meant "for the world in general, is meant for all, but only in so far they believe." The crux of the matter is the *conditionalis divinus*. Faith as the determining factor regarding salvation cannot be eliminated, although Brunner adds: "It remains an open question whether the possibility of the decision of faith is limited to this life when we look at I Peter 3:19." But reconciliation outside of faith makes salvation an "objective" thing which contradicts the teaching of the New Testament. In the same vein Barth, too, speaks of the "fatal danger" of unbelief, but he emphasizes far more the election of all men in Christ and his substitution for everybody. From this point of view the message of reconciliation inevitably assumes the character of an announcement of a certain state of affairs to which we may or may not assent, but which thereby becomes neither weaker nor stronger because it concerns an ontic situation which cannot be changed by human decisions.[62] The message of reconciliation points to the fact of reconciliation in the rejection of Jesus Christ, and reveals this fact as God's decision concerning salvation. Unbelief is the foolishness not to believe that divine decision which is election; but who can resist God's election? Thus, proceeding from God's election and reconciliation, faith and unbelief are rendered irrelevant.

Such a theory also places us at that peculiar fork in the road of theological thinking, whereby one road leads to the doctrine of a universal reconciliation and the other leads to making reconciliation dependent upon the reality of faith, which thus becomes a constituent of reconciliation. The first road now seems to be especially in vogue: its emphasis on the superior power of the actual reconciliation places faith in the background. We must

61. W. Michaelis in *Versöhnung des Alls. Die frohe Botschaft der Gnade Gottes,* 1950, p. 12, says that Barth "show a far greater reserve regarding this teaching than Brunner."

62. K. Barth, *Die Botschaft von der freien Gnade Gottes,* 1947, p. 6.

not confuse Barth's position, however, with the one which the Canons of Dort reject, namely that God "as far as He is concerned, has been minded to apply to all equally the benefits gained by the death of Christ; but that, while some obtain the pardon of sin and eternal life, and others do not, this difference depends on their own free will, which joins itself to the grace that is offered without exception" (Rej. of Errors, II, 6), because in Barth we find that the free will cannot undo the superior power of the fact of reconciliation. We really cannot see why Barth still objects to the *apokatastasis.* We can see why he hesitates, because thus the existential power of the decision of faith is eliminated, but this argument cannot stem the force of the *apokatastasis*-idea, since reconciliation is concerned with God's activity in Jesus Christ. When the point at issue is the absolute substitution and when the latter makes actual the election of all in Christ, how, then, can objection be made to the *apokatastasis* on the basis of faith or unbelief?

On the basis of Barth's concept of reconciliation it is difficult to see how Paul can urge: "be ye reconciled to God." These words are evidently an essential element of the passage, for they are wrought with the earnestness of the ambassador: "we beseech you on behalf of Christ," and "as though God were entreating by us." Again and again theologians have ripped apart reconciliation and being reconciled, and so have overemphasized either the objectivity of God's activity or man's freedom to decide. But if we take seriously the Word of God in II Corinthians 5:20-21, we must first of all acknowledge that the divine reconciliation does not exclude but includes faith, that an official commission can be given to go out into the world with the message, the *diakonia* of reconciliation. Grosheide paraphrases this passage thus: "let it come to the one, final and complete act of reconciliation with God."[63] But the object of this admonition is still not to advocate that reconciliation is the result of divine and human co-operation, for this would weaken the preceding words: "God was in Christ." And after the admonition, which is squeezed between the mention of God's acts, Paul again points at what God has done in Christ, "that we might become the righteousness of God in him" (II Cor. 5:21).

The admonition "be ye reconciled to God" is therefore not an admonition to co-operation in the work of reconciliation, but the

63. Grosheide, *Commentary,* II, 214, 215.

call to live in faith out of this reconciliation. That it is God who reconciles, Paul cannot wish to cancel by his word *katallagēte.* Grosheide speaks of a mystery and therewith refers to God's act and ours. The relationship between these two is not a matter of co-operation but of God's act, which is acknowledged in the answer of faith as the sovereign act of reconciliation. Exactly in the words "be ye reconciled to God" we see the exclusive grace which comes to us in Christ as reconciliation. According to the structure of this faith it is perfectly clear that it is not a human participation in reconciliation. Elsewhere we have dealt with the correlation between faith and justification, which does not refer to a reciprocal dependence but to a believing acceptance of justification. The same is true of reconciliation. Faith which directs itself toward reconciliation knows that it does not perform a meritorious act, but that the reconciliation embraces and covers all our unprofitableness.

For that reason there is a mission, a word of reconciliation; for that reason there are ambassadors who urge people to acknowledge this act of God. Those who deny this correlation, making reconciliation an objective fact which is merely announced – Christ died for all and all are elect in Christ – change the *kergyma* into a mere declaration and rob preaching of its urgency. Such a concept of reconciliation, in principle, opens the way to the *apokatastasis* until the strange discovery is made that Paul sends out ambassadors with the *word* of reconciliation. Michaelis, who accepts the doctrine of the *apokatastasis,* understands verse 20 in this way: the reconciliation of the world has become a fact and "what is further necessary is that according to 5:20 the knowledge of this reconciliation must be brought to the world."[64] But surely this is a perversion of the text. The message comes to mankind not to "announce" a certain "truth" (namely that Christ died for all) but as a ministry of reconciliation, a proclamation which urges men to the reality of peace through faith in the blood of the cross. The doctrine of *apokatastasis,* as even Barth's doctrine of reconciliation, threatens the *kerygma.*

The word of reconciliation is not comparable to a secular proclamation but to a message which comes in order that man, in faith, might live out of the riches of reconciliation. This restores the unity of II Corinthians 5:18-21, for now faith is seen

64. Michaelis, *Versöhnung des Alls,* pp. 130, 131.

as the echo to the message of reconciliation. Michaelis therefore is correct when he contradicts Brunner: it is not the case, as Brunner says, that a *conditionalis divinus* can be deduced from the concept of reconciliation. Brunner had too lightly combined reconciliation with the condition, "in so far as they believe." But Michaelis himself has no room for ambassadors from God who go forth with the word of reconciliation. Once again we find the thesis that God is exclusively subject of reconciliation. Says Michaelis: "We were enemies of God, but God was not our enemy," whereupon he quotes Barth who says that God is indeed angry, but that that fire "is the fire of his burning love and by no means that of his burning hate." If Michaelis does not accept the *apokatastasis*, at least he is susceptible to it, and this in turn has a profound effect upon preaching (*kerygma*, or announcement of a situation?) as well as upon missionary activity. Among both Jews and Gentiles there are some inside the congregation who know, and others in the world who do not know; the bridging of this contrast "is the problem and task of the original mission," says Barth in a very illustrative passage.[65] This contrast between knowing and not knowing corresponds to election and reconciliation in Jesus Christ (the Rejected One!). But this view robs both *kerygma* and mission of the dynamic, compassionate, and admonishing character which it has in Scripture, and which includes man's responsibility not as human cooperation in salvation but as the way to complete peace with God.

The concept of what Scripture reveals concerning reconciliation will inevitably determine the nature of the proclamation. We are touching here upon the reasons for Berkhof's complaint concerning various alarming elements in present-day preaching, which he ascribes to Barth's theology in its further development.[66] especially "Barth's emphasis on the superior power of God's saving activity" and his idea that unbelief — over against God's unambiguous "yes" — is an "impossible possibility" which cannot defeat God's "yes." In answer to this Berkhof emphasizes the seriousness of man's decision, because God's decision does not cancel ours. In bringing Christ, God does not so much call our attention to the abyss from which we have been saved and the judgment that lies behind us, as to the judgment that lies ahead,

65. Barth, *K.D.*, III, 2, 738, 741.
66. H. Berkhof, *Crisis der Middenorthodoxie*, pp. 37-40.

"namely, if we do not believe that in Christ [the former judgment] lies behind us."

This shows again how central the message of reconciliation really is. Reconciliation can be misconceived by ascribing the final decision to man, but also by objectifying it in preaching and by disqualifying unbelief not as sin and guilt but as a relatively unimportant foolishness (compared with God's decision). Those, however, who understand somewhat the correlations of reconciliation in Scripture, will also understand more and more both the joy and the seriousness of preaching.

We shall never be able to analyze exactly the interrelation between faith and reconciliation. Outside of faith nothing can be understood here. But it is the marvel of the work of the Holy Spirit that those who really respond to the proclamation of reconciliation claim no merit whatsoever for that response, but rather find the essence of their joy and gratitude in God, who reconciled us unto himself. For that reason missions cannot be explained in terms of "knowing" and "not knowing." Of course, this "not knowing" is of concern to the ministry: "How then shall they call on him in whom they have not believed: and how shall they believe in him of whom they have not heard? and how shall they hear without a preacher?" (Rom. 10:14). But *what* they need to hear is not an "announcement." The message they need is the one call of the gospel of reconciliation, the call to the faith that pleases God, because that message alone speaks of his act, the act of his reconciliation.

B. SACRIFICE

When we now speak of Christ's sacrifice, we do not thereby begin a new subject which can be detached from the rest of Christ's work. It is simply another biblical aspect of the one, many-faceted work of Christ. We noticed before that when Paul speaks of Jesus Christ the Mediator between God and man, he immediately adds, "who gave himself a ransom for all" (I Tim. 2:5). Scripture speaks in various ways of the self-surrender, the self-sacrifice of Christ. In the Epistle to the Hebrews it is the extensively-discussed central theme[67] — Christ

67. See, besides the commentaries, A. Seeberg, *Der Tod Christi in seiner Bedeutung für die Erlösung,* 1895, pp. 1-116; H. H. Meeter, *The Heavenly High Priesthood of Christ,* 1916; M. Dibelius, "Der himmlische Kultus nach dem Hebräer Brief" in *Theologische Blätter,* 1942; F. Büchsel, *Die Christologie des Hebräerbriefs,* 1922.

the High Priest – but the subject is by no means limited to this letter. It has been said by some that Christ himself did not announce his death as a sacrifice, but such people have already ruled out *a priori* those many statements of Christ which could refer to the same fact of sacrifice, as, for instance, when at the institution of the Lord's Supper he said, "This cup is the new covenant in my blood, even that which is poured out for you" (Luke 22:20), or when he spoke of giving his life a ransom for many (Mark 10:45) or of giving his life for the sheep (John 10:11, 15; cf. 15:13) as the Good Shepherd. For that reason the opinion that Jesus himself did not connect his death with the giving of a sacrifice can be the result only of a certain concept of sacrifice which is incompatible with the nature of Christ's self-sacrifice.[68]

Behm, for instance, says that according to the institution of the Lord's Supper "Christ's blood offers the guarantee for the realization of the new order of God," but according to him that has nothing to do with a sacrifice. The idea of a sacrifice is also missing in Paul, Peter, I John, and Revelation. To be sure, he must admit that besides illustrations from the realm of justice we also meet with ideas derived from the sacrificial cult, but that does not mean "that cultic sacrifice-ideas are connected with the blood of Christ." He asserts that the Jewish idea of sacrifice faded and weakened among the Jews of a later period and became simply a symbol of personal dedication, and thus the primitive Christian idea of the sacrificial blood of Christ is "only a pictorial representation of the idea of self-surrender, of completed obedience to God which Christ showed in his death on the cross." This is even the case in Hebrews, where, according to Behm, we are dealing with metaphorical language, the main point of which is to emphasize the religious-moral evaluation of the blood of Christ.[69]

68. "Jesus did not consider the realization of the *kainē diathēkē* by his death a sacrifice" (Behm-Kittel, TWNT, III, 184). Cf. also *ibid.*, I, 173, 174.

69. *Ibid.*, II, 174. Behm deduces this from Heb. 9:14, where we read that the blood of Christ cleanses our *conscience* from dead works. But this is connected with the reconciliation of sin in the reality of Christ's sacrifice. Finally Behm discusses Paul's statement in I Cor. 10:16 (the communion of the blood of Christ) and says, "Hence here, too, blood is only a visual sign for death." It is true indeed, that Paul and John are far from advocating a "blood mysticism," but such mysticism is by no means implied in the reality of Christ's sacrifice. Cf., however, Behm in TWNT, I, in connection with Heb. 9:22.

According to this viewpoint we are not dealing with a personal and unique aspect of the work of Christ but with a symbolic indication of obedience. That which is here expressed in no uncertain terms we find also in many other theologians. If they only meant to say that Christ's sacrifice was different from the Old Testament sacrifices, they would reiterate the teaching of Scripture itself, but they may not on the basis of a metaphor change the idea of sacrifice into that of self-surrender. Christ's sacrifice is indeed self-surrender, as Scripture definitely emphasizes, but this self-surrender is not a general human concept which can also be applied to Christ. On the contrary, Christ's self-surrender is the fulfillment of all sacrifices. His sacrifice is not merely an illustration of obedience, as is the sacrifice of the believers of which Scripture also speaks even in Hebrews, saying that doing good and communicating are sacrifices wherewith God is well pleased (Heb. 13:16; cf. the figurative language in Ps. 51:18, in connection with vs. 17). These sacrifices in Hebrews do indeed have something in common with Christ's sacrifice, but they are not of the same kind. To define the idea of Christ's sacrifice on the basis of these sacrifices is to substitute the idea of obedience and thereby to ignore the teaching of Scripture. It is an illicit "spiritualizing" of the sacrifice-idea.

To be sure, theologians of this persuasion will admit that Paul, too, uses terminology derived from the sacrificial rites, for instance in I Corinthians 5:7, "For our passover also hath been sacrificed, even Christ," and Ephesians 5:2, "[Christ] gave himself up for us, an offering and a sacrifice," but "metaphorical sacrifice-idea in Paul's Christology is no more than a way of indicating the basic saving fact of the death of Christ."[70] Moreover, it is pointed out that Paul also uses this figurative language to typify the Christian life. The advocates of this sacrifice-concept obviously have the most trouble with the Epistle to the Hebrews, however, because there the death of Christ is not just mentioned briefly under the metaphor of a sacrifice but is treated in the wide context of the history of salvation and in positive connection with the Old Testament cult of sacrifices. Behm, too, although he speaks of "figurative language," must admit that this epistle "refers back to the cultic sacrifice-idea"; nevertheless, he says, Hebrews does not teach simply that Christ's sacrifice is superior to those of the Old Testament, but rather that Christ's

70. Kittel, TWNT, III, 185.

"free, personal act of self-giving" effected an eternal salvation. He says that the author of Hebrews goes back "to the primitive presentation and the primitive meaning of the sacrifice in the Old Testament, where it was the means of personal communion between God and man," and now the original meaning of the sacrifice is fulfilled in the personal act of Christ.[71] The latter is decisive and as such has nothing to do with the Old Testament cult; hence Behm concludes that the sacrifice-idea in Hebrews as well is "only an expedient to give a figurative representation of the saving work of Christ."

Thus the sacrifice-idea has no objective revelatory significance. It is in a purely formal sense a personal self-surrender. It is no revelation of the reality of the sacrifice of Christ's suffering and death.

Our main objection to this misrepresentation arises from the fact that Scripture does not treat the sacrifice-idea briefly and in analogy to the idea of self-surrender, but speaks of it, rather, in the context of reconciliation. It speaks of the precious blood of Christ, as of a lamb without blemish and without spot (I Pet. 1:19, 20), of Christ who his own self bare our sins in his own body on the tree (II Pet. 2:24), of our passover who is sacrificed for us (I Cor. 5:7), and of Christ the Lamb of God that taketh away the sins of the world (John 1:28, 36).

It is especially Hebrews, however, which makes the idea of analogy or simile inapplicable to Christ's sacrifice. Although the author surely does not identify Christ's sacrifice with the cultic sacrifices of the Old Testament, and definitely emphasizes the uniqueness of Christ's sacrifice which renders all other sacrifices superfluous (Heb. 10:18, "Now where remission of these [sins] is, there is no more offering for sin"), nevertheless he points out the historic significance of Christ's sacrifice in the total scheme of salvation. The idea of the "shadow" of good things to come is something truly different from the spiritualization of Christ's sacrifice in an analogy or simile.[72] This epistle can be understood only in the light of the fulfillment of the shadow. And it

71. *Ibid.*, pp. 185, 186.
72. Cf. the criticism of H. van Oyen in *Christus de Hogepriester*, p. 164, of Behm's theory, for instance of "the sacrificial blood being considered as the symbol for moral obedience and legal faithfulness" by the Hellenized Jews. He also refers to Hebrews 9:22 which "puts every theory concerning symbolism to shame."

is evident that this implies far-reaching consequences for the correct understanding of the work of Christ as a sacrifice.

Those who view Christ's sacrifice as an analogy have the greatest difficulty with the statement in Hebrews 9:22, "and apart from shedding of blood is no remission." This statement makes sense in connection with the real sacrifice of the High Priest, but not when it is considered figurative language. For this letter is not concerned with a useful symbol, but with the progress from old to new, from shadow to fulfillment. The fact that the author thereby goes above and beyond the Old Testament sacrificial cult provides no basis for saying that he is using figurative language, because the redemptive-historical progress from sacrifices to the Sacrifice implies that the Old Testament sacrifices were already instituted in connection with the Sacrifice and now, in the reality of Christ's sacrifice, receive their ultimate fulfillment. It is this fact which is emphasized in the epistle. It is not concerned with subjective impressions or aspects but with a religious orientation to the Priest, the High Priest of our profession (Heb. 3:1). That, indeed, is the theme, the main topic of the letter ("Now in the things which we are saying the chief point is this: We have such a high priest," Heb. 8:1), namely, the glory of this true High Priest whose sacrifice comprises complete salvation. The role of the Old Testament sacrifices was not that of figurative language but of historical reality. They were already of significance because they annually reminded the people of their sin (Heb. 10:3), and in a certain sense they are called sanctifying.

The contrast between the Old Testament sacrifices and Christ's sacrifice is not between meaninglessness and meaningfulness, but is indicated by the words "much more." "For if the blood of goats and bulls, and the ashes of a heifer sprinkling them that have been defiled, sanctify unto the cleanness of the flesh: how much more shall the blood of Christ, who through the eternal Spirit offered himself without blemish unto God, cleanse your conscience from dead works to serve the living God?"[73] At first glance this text might lead us to the conclusion that the sacrifices were meaningless. Such a sacrifice does not cause reconciliation and the taking away of sins, nor can it, for the priest who brings the sacrifices is so imperfect that he must first sacrifice for him-

73. Heb. 9:13-14. Cf. Van Oyen, *Christus de Hogepriester,* and Grosheide, *Commentaar op Hebreeën;* O. Michel, *Der Brief an die Hebräer,* 1949, p. 205.

self and after that for the people (Heb. 9:7). But the author points out that this already showed that under the Old Covenant the way to the sanctuary was not yet opened (vs. 8). To be sure, there is a sanctification (vs. 13), but this was cultic in nature, and with the forceful words "how much more" the author goes on to the powerful effect of the sacrifice of the High Priest who is Christ. It is precisely the Old Testament – "a figure for the time then present, in which were offered both gifts and sacrifices" – which brings out the absolute meaning of Christ's sacrifice. In him the formerly necessary repetition finds its absolute and eschatological termination, for this High Priest does not have to offer for himself first; the power of his sacrifice is manifest in the fact that he truly bears and consequently puts away sin. His sacrifice is the act, the personal act of his life, because he offered himself (Heb. 7:27, 9:14), and did so with his own blood (Heb. 9:12) in order thus to enter into the holy place and to obtain eternal redemption for us (*ibid.*). The repetition is replaced by the decisive, absolute, and joyous "once" (Heb. 9:26; cf. vs. 28). This immaculate sacrifice is the eschatological act of the Messiah – the High Priest – "who at the end of the ages hath . . . been manifested to put away sin by the sacrifice of himself" (vs. 26). "In whole burnt offerings and sacrifices for sin thou hadst no pleasure: Then said I, Lo, I come (In the roll of the book it is written of me) to do thy will, O God" (Heb. 10:6-7).

This is not an absolute disqualification of the cult of sacrifices, as has so often been stated, but the biblical antithesis to the misinterpretation of these sacrifices. Such misinterpretations existed already under the Old Covenant, as is shown by the criticism of the prophets when they spoke for God to the backsliding people of Israel: "What unto me is the multitude of your sacrifices? saith Jehovah: I have had enough of the burnt-offerings of rams, and the fat of fed beasts; and I delight not in the blood of bullocks, or of lambs, or of he-goats" (Isa. 1:11, 12). This refers to the vain oblations, the abominable incense (vs. 13). "I cannot away with it." These sacrifices had been conjoined with worthless prayers and the spreading forth of hands (vs. 15).

The entire service of God is at stake here. The sacrifice is of no avail; it resembles an arrow which falls far from its mark, because it lacks true religion and the perspective of reconciliation. God does not reject the sacrificial service as such, but the legalistic interpretation of it which sees the offer as a performance to make God favorably inclined toward the people. God's judgment and wrath descend upon that attitude, upon the feasts and solemn meetings, the burnt offerings and sacrifices and even upon the songs.[74] For the sacrifices now no longer presuppose God's covenant and grace but have a function *ex opere operato,* in contradiction to the scriptural reconciliation which originates solely in God.[75] It is by his redemptive grace that scarlet sin becomes as white as snow and that crimson becomes white as wool. (vs. 18), and it is the Lord who says: "I have blotted out, as a thick cloud, thy transgressions, and, as a cloud, thy sins; return unto me; for I have redeemed thee" (Isa. 44:22). The human sacrificial act is oriented to the divine reconciling act, the putting away of unrighteousness, the blotting out of sin (Lev. 16:11, 16, 17, 19, 21, 24, 27; 17:11), and not to self-deliverance, not even a self-deliverance in connection with God for which he cannot be thanked because there is nothing to thank him for.

There is indeed a correlation between sacrifice and reconciliation, but everything depends upon how this correlation is understood. Each sacrificial act is of decisive and far-reaching significance, namely, in connection with the question "whether man here by himself performs a meritorious act whereby he is able to blot out his debt and buy off God's wrath, or whether such a reconciling act enters in and accompanies God's free forgiveness whereby he restores communion with the sinner."[76] The issue at stake is the nature of the "causality" of the sacrifices. Exactly because there was a connection between sacrifice and reconciliation, Israel could pervert the sacrifice and misconstrue the con-

74. Cf. I Sam. 15:22, Ps. 50:13 ("Will I eat the flesh of bulls, or drink the blood of goats? Offer (!) unto God the sacrifice of thanksgiving; and pay the vows unto the most High"). Cf. vs. 15, "And call upon me in the day of trouble: I will deliver thee, and thou shalt glorify me"; and especially also Jer. 7:22 (sacrifices and obedience), Amos 5:24 (sacrifices and righteousness). Cf. Grosheide, *Commentaar op Hebreeën,* p. 275.

75. When Van Gelderen discusses the optimistic expectation of the day of the Lord in Amos' time he says, "This basis is the appreciation of the cult as *opus operatum*" (*Amos,* p. 137). Cf. A. A. van Ruler, *De Vervulling der Wet,* 1947, pp. 342f.; Kittel, TWNT, III, 183: "In the legal religion of the post-exilic Jews the cultic sacrifice petrifies to an *opus operatum.*" This term is also found in J. Th. Ubbink, "*De Hogepriester* en Zijn Offer in de Brief aan de Hebreeën" (in *Oud-Testamentische Studiën,* p. 182).

76. W. Eichrodt, *Theologie des Alten Testaments,* III, 19.

nection by ignoring and eliminating the background of all sacrifices. The divine revelation, however, catches up with this strange causality which always betrays itself by the conditions under which it manifests itself, namely, the absence of obedience, joy, faith, and repentance. In this atmosphere the *opus operatum* functions as the misjudgment of God's love and covenant.[77] The scriptural idea of reconciliation makes this antithesis perfectly clear. There we see God's love and holiness when God appears in a cloud upon the mercy seat (Lev. 16:2), but amidst his holiness shines the light of his reconciliation. There is a connection, but it is based on God's commandment as the expression of his love (cf. Deut. 7), the love of him who leads his people, so that the causality can never be abstracted from the covenant of God.[78]

Since, therefore, the Old Testament already condemns the legalistic interpretation and practice of sacrificing, such an interpretation is all the more ruled out after the one sacrifice in Christ has become a historical reality. Here it becomes perfectly evident that the sacrifice offers no merit of ours, any more than the Old Testament sacrifice was a magic means unto reconciliation. The meaning of all sacrifices is revealed in the reality of the precious blood: "we have been sanctified through the offering of the body of Jesus Christ once for all" (Heb. 10:10, 14). After that every repetition is a denial of this definitive sacrifice, this self-abandonment in the shedding of blood, and if there is still such a thing as a sacrifice, then only by way of analogy and figurative language: "I beseech you therefore, brethren, by the mercies of God, to present your bodies a living sacrifice, holy, acceptable to God" (Rom. 12:1; cf. Heb. 13:16). The fact that we now have only an analogy is possible only because Christ's sacrifice is *not* a mere analogy or figure of speech. It cannot be explained as a symbolic self-surrender, which would detach the biblical idea (he offered up himself) from the whole context of Hebrews and from the entire Scripture as well. While the Epistle to the Hebrews and the other New

77. Cf. Kittel, TWNT, III, 183.

78. W. H. Gispen, *Leviticus,* 1950, p. 13: "He institutes a sacrificial service as a service of reconciliation." Gispen points out that we do not read that God instituted the sacrifice. The sacrificial cult is the Divine qualification of what the sacrifices represented, namely gift, reconciliation. Cf., "In Lev. 1-7 we find the further Divine regulation of the already existing custom of sacrificing" (p. 13).

Testament statements concerning Christ's sacrifice do not furnish us with a systematic exposition, as is the case for all other aspects of Christ's work, there is nevertheless harmony in the one, central message concerning the sacrifice "for us" wherein he bears our sins as the Substitute.[79] Thereby Christ has revealed historically the meaning and joy of the entire Old Testament sacrificial cult, so that his sacrifice provides salvation for all time.

This sacrifice need not be repeated, as in the Roman Catholic Church, because this violates the "once for all." Nor may the saving power of this sacrifice be limited to the time when it took place and thereafter. There have been those who asserted, no doubt out of respect for the history of redemption, that the reconciling sacrifice became fully effective only after it took place on Golgotha, and from this they concluded that the believers in the Old Testament could not share fully in the forgiveness of sins because the sacrifice had not yet been made. This idea, which originated out of a protest against the supposed timelessness of Christ's reconciliation, nevertheless obscures the valuable idea of the history of salvation by misinterpreting the significance of this historical sacrifice for all times. Coccejus, for example, was led to accept the idea of a real difference between the forgiveness of sins in the Old and the New Testament. And even though Coccejus and the Roman Catholic Church have little in common, they similarly misinterpret the historical and therefore also the super-temporal significance of this reconciling act. According to Coccejus the Old Testament believers cannot yet share in the forgiveness of sins by the blood of Christ, while according to Rome the reality of the sacrifice must be carried into the history of all times by means of the mass in order to become truly effective.[80]

79. Cf. what Paul says concerning the passover in I Cor. 5:7. "Apparently the apostle could suppose that the congregation would understand the idea without his further explanation. The main thing is that Paul considers it quite natural that Christ's death can be considered as a sacrifice for others" (G. Sevenster, *De Christologie van het Nieuwe Testament*, p. 172). Cf. the fact that the Epistle to the Hebrews deals especially with the sacrifice on the great Day of Atonement.

80. On Coccejus see my *The Person of Christ*, p. 150. Coccejus makes a distinction between two kinds of *remissio peccatorum*, namely, before and after the reconciling work of Christ. He repeatedly emphasizes that he does not deny the forgiveness of sins under the Old Covenant (e.g. in his *Praefatio in epistulam ad Ephesios* [*Opera Omnia*], Amsterdam,

Still other attempts have been made, however, to explain why Christ's death is called a sacrifice. Windisch, for instance, sees behind the Old Testament sacrifice the idea that "blood is able to remove pollution," which is "a fundamental idea of the ancient, especially Jewish and primitive Christian religion." Since the early Christians supposedly believed that sacrificial blood was charged with cleansing power, we find the New Testament speaking of the cleansing power of the blood of Christ.[81]

According to Windisch the author of Hebrews derived his blood-theory entirely from the Old Testament, and thus he believed in a real cleansing by means of blood. Windisch finds, remarkably, only one exception, namely Hebrews 10:4, which says that it is impossible that the blood of bulls and of goats should take away sins. In this passage, according to Windisch, the author "rejects the old sacrifice blood only in order to make the Christian blood-theology more effective."

But this text is essential to the whole argument of this epistle: the clear objective of Hebrews is to emphasize the difference between the Old Testament sacrifices and Christ's sacrifice as the personal act of the High Priest, who effects reconciliation by the surrender of his own holy life. Christ is the High Priest after the order of Melchizedek, not of Aaron, and hence his sacrifice cannot be identified carelessly with others which allegedly depend upon a magical power in the blood. The relation between Melchizedek and Aaron indicates different purposes for their respective sacrifices. If the Levitical priesthood had brought perfection, then there would have been no need for a Priest after the order of Melchizedek (Heb. 7:11). The fact that he did appear, not out of the tribe of Levi but of Judah," from which no man hath given attendance at the altar" (7:13), shows that the nature of this sacrifice cannot be generalized. It cannot be deduced from a "blood-theory."

We do read that without shedding of blood there can be no forgiveness, but this is not a general law which applies to Christ among others. It rather illuminates the nature of Christ's sacrifice within the framework of God's entire reconciling activity.

1673, Vol. IV, p. 38), but only wishes to make a differentiation in this forgiveness. Cf. G. Schrenk, *Gottesreich und Bund im älteren Protestantismus, vornehmlich bei Coccejus,* 1923, pp. 100ff. See also A. Kuyper, *Locus de Christo,* III, vii, 111ff.

81. H. Windisch, *Der Hebräerbrief,* 1931, pp. 82-85.

Christ's sacrifice does indeed involve the blood that cleanses, but the cleansing of this blood is not effected according to the nature of the Levitical sacrifices but "after the power of an endless life" (Heb. 7:16). The sacrificial cult which was imperfect and utterly unable to effect real reconciliation — because it was only the shadow of that which followed — is fulfilled in Christ's sacrifice and confirmed with a divine oath from Psalm 110:4, "Thou art a priest for ever after the order of Melchizedek" (Heb. 7:21). No general law of purifying sacrifices applies to this Priest. The meaning of the sacrifices can be understood only in the fulfillment of these foreshadowings by Christ's sacrifice.[82] The fact that the Old Testament sacrifices did not take away sins but brought them in remembrance proves that they foreshadowed good things to come when the real and decisive sacrifice would be made.[84]

That which seemed to be permanent and "eternal" according to the institution of the Levitical priesthood, and which was nevertheless very relative, revoked by the eternal and decisive and different priesthood of Christ according to the will of God. It did not become meaningless, for it had played an important role in the divine revelation, but its relative character is evident from the description in Hebrews 7:18.[85] Hence, those who ignore Melchizedek and absolutize Aaron will never be able to understand Christ's sacrifice. For then they will not understand the eternal priesthood of Christ whereby the objective is realized, namely, the putting away of sins (Heb. 9:26), the free access to God (Heb. 7:25). This goal is reached by Christ's sacrifice, so that he "shall appear a second time to them that wait

82. Cf. Heb. 8:2. In Heb. 10:1 σκιὰ is contrasted with εἰκών (the image of the things). See on this K. Schilder, *Heidelbergse Catechismus,* II, 321ff.

83. Heb. 10:3. Cf. on humiliation, Lev. 16:19, 30-34.

84. Cf. Heid. Cat., Q. 19, that God gave the holy gospel "which (He) Himself first revealed in Paradise; afterwards published . . . and foreshadowed by the sacrifices and other ceremonies of the law; and lastly fulfilled His only begotten Son" (cf. Belgic Conf., 25).

85. "For there is a disannulling of a foregoing commandment because of its weakness and unprofitableness." This annullment (ἀθέτησις) does not imply a failure with regard to God's activity in the giving of the law and in the sacrificial cult, but the redemptive-historical fulfillment which is indicated and preached by the cult — the ἀθέτησις, the putting away of the sins by the sacrifice of Christ (Heb. 9:26).

for him" (Heb. 9:28). That is possible only because he was once offered to bear the sins of many.[86]

The controversy regarding the meaning of Christ's sacrifice has centered especially upon his bearing the sins of many. On the one hand, we find in our day those who take a radical, almost theopaschitistic view of Christ's substitutionary work, while on the other hand we find those who argue from a certain sacrifice-concept to an elimination of the idea of substitution from the work of Christ.

Brouwer, especially, rejects emphatically the connection between sacrifice and substitution when he answers the question, What is the truth of the Old Testament which comes to its fulfillment in Christ?[87] The earlier idea, that the sacrifice is substitutionary, he considers untenable on the basis of ethnology. Proceeding from the notion of sacrifices in general – because they were not confined to the Hebrews – he views the sacrifice as "an act which is directed against invisible powers in order to protect man's life or to strengthen it, or to avert evil influences." The Hebrew sacrifice must be considered against the background of this pagan concept, whose Canaanitish form received a specific content from the ethical monotheism of the Jahweh cult. Brouwer does not succeed in developing this idea of a "specific content," because when he attempts to explain the significance of the blood in the sacrifice he points to the prehistoric era and says that the shedding of blood is "the giving of a counter-influence whereby evil influences are expelled." According to him there is no such a thing as a substitution-idea, either within or outside of Israel, which is evident from the Passover, in which the blood of the paschal lamb was a protecting symbol. Sacrifice is no substitution but a warding off of evil. It is a gift to the deity of something valuable belonging to man himself. This view of the sacrifice, which eliminates every substitutionary aspect, makes Brouwer write that Christ fulfilled this kind of a sacrifice when he gave his life.

In the light of Scripture, however, several problems arise in connection with this concept, difficulties which Brouwer solves only superficially. For instance, he explains Isaiah 53, which speaks of the "bearing of iniquities," as though this "carrying"

86. Cf. his appearance "without sin" as distinguished from "without sin" in Heb. 4:15 (Grosheide, *Commentary*, p. 267).

87. A. M. Brouwer, *Verzoening*, 1947.

meant "accepting the results of the iniquities, to accept the responsibility for them." He – the Servant of the Lord – accepted his suffering as the result of these iniquities. Thus substitution is replaced throughout by solidarity. It is the solidarity of the highest love, which removes the results of sin. This idea, of Christ's solidarity with our plight, Brouwer discovers everywhere in the New Testament, for instance in the words of Paul where he says that God made Christ to be sin for us (II Cor. 5:21), which he explains as Christ voluntary acceptance of the results of sin. Everything Scripture says concerning what Christ did "for us" means, according to him, "in our behalf," and not "in our stead."

It is obvious, however, that Brouwer has approached Scripture with strong dogmatic prejudices when he reasons away every element of substitution. He says, for instance, that substitution is "impossible" – "Could it be supposed that God's love would punish the innocent for the guilty? And is that not at variance with reality?" Hence in Christ's sacrifice we find no element of substitution but of solidarity; he suffers with us and thus in solidarity conquers the suffering. In substitution the "others" are excluded, but in solidarity everything is more "organic" – the "others" are in that case not exempt; they are sustained and helped in their plight, but fight they must. Christ's solidarity with us was necessary to reveal God's love, not only to announce it, but to show it by his entering into our suffering for sin.

One of the most striking aspects of this viewpoint is undoubtedly that solidarity is linked with the removal of the *results,* the "natural" results of sin. The taking away of the guilt of sin fades completely into the background. This is inevitable on the basis of the "impossibility" of Christ's being a substitute or a Mediator. Thus only the removal of the results of sin enters into focus.

Brouwer further asserts that the idea of "substitution" is both religiously and morally dangerous because it fits only into a system which accepts the transferral of meritorious good works. This criticism of the idea of substitution is in essence identical to that of Socinianism, which is the background dogmatically of Brouwer's viewpoint regarding sacrifice. This explains why he proceeds from the pagan idea of sacrifice to explain that of the Old Testament, even though he says that the latter gave it a new content, (which latter he does not pursue, out of fear that he might thus introduce the idea of substitution after all, as the attempt to incline God to be gracious *by means of someone else*). In his aversion to the idea of substitution he explains every relevant statement of Scripture in that particular light, and is forced to introduce arbitrarily the idea of "results of sin" even where the text provides not the least basis for it. Hence we are no longer surprised to hear him say that in the letter to the Hebrews "the process of Hellenization" has already set in and the departure from the symbol of piety of the prophets has commenced.

It is no wonder that Brouwer no longer has an eye for the ideas of sacrifice and substitution. Those who follow the Socinians in considering substitution impossible are forced to eliminate the sacrifice from the contexts in which Scripture places it, and to change completely, for instance, the image of the Man of Sorrows in Isaiah. Thus Brouwer relegates the mystery of Isaiah 53 to a realm that is diametrically opposed to the magic offering ritual, since the Man of Sorrows is made to bear the results of the sins of others in order "thereby to bring peace and healing to those others." Through solidarity Christ becomes part of a totality, and this idea, quite naturally, also governs Brouwers' idea concerning forgiveness. He says that when the New Testament speaks concerning God's forgiveness, "the condition is only that man comes to the Father in deep, real, self-abandoning penitence." And even though, on the basis thereof, some came to the conclusion that forgiveness requires no "mediator," Brouwer admits that the person and work of Christ involves more than simply the announcement of the forgiving mercy of God. His work is necessary on the basis of the "solidarity of the highest love," which bears the results of sin with and in behalf of the "others" in order to conquer them. It is indeed illustrative that Brouwer's rejection of the sacrifice as substitution goes hand in hand with the view that Christ did not deliver us from the guilt of sin but from its results. Whereas Scripture everywhere speaks of delivery from sin, even in connection with the naming of Christ, Brouwer consistently changes "sin" into "results of sin" and thus mutilates the essence of Scripture's message. That is the companion view of his other one, which holds that our deliverance cannot be from the wrath of God, an idea which, according to him, is nowhere to be found in Jesus' teachings. To be sure, there is mention of the wrath of God in John 3:36, but "this is not a saying of Jesus himself, but is ascribed to John the Baptist by the author."

After this there follows a general leveling down on the basis of these assumptions. For instance, the word "ransom" in Matthew 20:28 is seen in analogy with the Shepherd who gives his life for the sheep, which is merely a "sign of love to his friends." But if we reject the unfounded assumption that solidarity takes the place of substitution, we may approach Scripture far more objectively, for instance where it speaks concerning Christ's sacrifice by which he takes our sins upon himself (Heb. 9:26) and "bare our sins in his own body upon the tree, that we, having died unto sins, might live unto righteousness" (I Pet. 2:24). If we refuse to substitute everywhere the results of sin for sin itself, then the message of Scripture comes to us clearly, as the witness concerning the Lamb of God that taketh away the sins of the world. What is said here concerning Christ concerns the most essential aspect of his coming.[88] All the passages concerning the death of Christ, whatever their context, point to the fact that it was "for us" in the sense of "in our stead."

The distinction has frequently been made between "in our behalf" and "in our stead." Many admit, however, that Scripture does not warrant such a distinction. We read, for instance, that "the Son of man came . . . to give his life a ransom for (*anti*) many" (Matt. 20:28, Mark 10:45), whereas we also read that Christ "died for (*hyper*) all" (II Cor. 5:15; cf. Rom. 5:6; 5:8, and I Cor. 15:3). When Christ gives his life a ransom (*lytron*), then life becomes free because He gives his life. "In their favor it is precisely the case that he takes their place."[89] This correctly says that "in the stead of" and "in behalf of" neither contradict each other nor exclude each other. When we translate both expressions by "for," then this one word signifies a twofold aspect. It is exactly the uniqueness of Christ's act that makes it not an impersonal substitution but one that benefits others.

We are not dealing with Brouwer's idea of replacement, in which one person takes the place of another for a certain reward, but with a substitution which is full of blessing and benefit for those whose place is taken. The substitution has often been caricatured

88. Cf. Sevenster, *Christologie*, p. 236.

89. Kittel, TWNT, p. 373, s.v. ἀντί. Büchsel, too, speaks expressly of "idea of substitution."

and the Church held responsible for this caricature,[90] but the doctrine of substitution is based squarely on the teaching of Scripture. Who could separate "in our stead" from "in our behalf," or even differentiate between the two in the message that Christ became a curse "for us" in that one act which is ever purposeful until the end? In him every mechanical aspect is excluded by his personal act of self-surrender.[91]

This unity between "in the stead of" and "in our behalf" is the fulfillment of all prophecy. Already in the sacrificial ritual we notice a clear sign of substitution when we read, "For the life of the flesh is in the blood: and I have given it to you upon the altar to make atonement for your souls: for it is the blood that maketh atonement by reason of the life" (Lev. 17: 11).[92] An event is depicted that takes the place of another event which could have been expected on the basis of God's holiness. Something takes the place of sinful man, of the sinful people, and thereby the situation before God is entirely changed. Here sin is carried away and forgiveness is tendered. "And the priest shall make atonement for them, and they shall be forgiven" (Lev. 4:20; cf. vss. 26, 31, 35; Lev. 5:10, 13).

The sacrifice was fully "in behalf of" because it took place "in the stead of." Powerless in itself, because it was a shadow of that which followed, it brought the forgiveness which this exchange, this substitution represented concretely. It rested on the taking away of sins, not by human effort but by an act of God: "But there is forgiveness with thee, that thou mayest be feared" (Ps. 130:4). Without faith and gratitude substitution

90. The problem is evident in the books by Vincent Taylor, *Forgiveness and Reconciliation,* 1946; *The Atonement in the New Testament Teaching,* 1946; *Jesus and His Sacrifice,* 1948. In the latter book, pp. 103ff., Taylor acknowledges that "for" in Mark 10:45 means "in the stead of" and adds: "It is wrong to conclude from this linguistic study that the saying must be interpreted in a crudely substitutionary sense," although he admits, "undoubtedly, it contains a substitutionary idea, since something is done for the many which they cannot do for themselves." See also p. 282 (a substitutionary aspect in the suffering of Jesus), but it is "neither crudely substitutionary nor automatic in its action, but something which is to be owned and appropriated" (p. 283).

91. Dr. K. Schilder has objected to the term "substitution" in *Heidelberg Catechism,* II, 47. He prefers the word "substitute." It seems to me that this switching of terminology is fruitless, since also with regard to the word "substitution" we can avoid the idea of replacement.

92. Cf. Th. C. Vriezen, *Hoofdlijnen der Theologie van het Oude Testament,* 1949, p. 243.

cannot be understood; but in faith and thankfulness it is experienced as the miracle, the mystery of Christ's work. Then it is understood that the pivotal thing is the "precious blood [of Christ], as of a lamb without blemish and without spot," who "gave himself for many" (I Pet. 1:19, I Tim. 2:6). Here we are far removed from cold matter-of-factness because of the very personal, moving, and loving act of Christ. Of this Scripture speaks constantly, whether in connection with the sacrifice on the great Day of Atonement, or in connection with the paschal lamb (I Cor. 5:7), or in the picture of the slain Lamb, the Man of Sorrows, who is not now called the sacrificial lamb but rather the Servant of the Lord who was wounded for our transgressions and bruised for our iniquities (Isa. 53:5). The image of the lamb and the sheep in Isaiah 53 points to the patience of the suffering Servant. It is he upon whom the Lord has laid the iniquity of us all (vs. 6).

This substitution, by which the sin of mankind is laid upon the Man of Sorrows, is at the same time the chastisement of our peace (vs. 5), and the light of substitution beams forth in the healing by means of his stripes.

The unique substitutionary act of Christ can be denied only by those who follow the Socinian argument that this is not possible because it is unjust — the one "for" — "in the stead of" — the other! It is considered an error to believe that Christ by his death obtained salvation for us and paid for our sins by his sacrifice.[93] The Socinians maintain that *God* truly *forgives* sin, whereas in the doctrine of substitution we owe our salvation to Christ rather than to God because Christ showed us mercy and God therefore did not have to give us grace, nor could he, after the satisfaction had been effected by Christ.[94]

This seemingly logical argumentation completely denies the trinitarian aspect of reconciliation; it isolates the work of Christ, making it an independent act of legal satisfaction and ignoring the doctrine of the *sent* Messiah. This is evident from the caricatured representation of a God who does not and cannot for-

93. This idea is, according to the Socinians, *fallax, erronea et admodum perniciosa.* Cf. *Catechesis Racoviana Maior*, Chap. VIII, 9, 12.

94. *Ibid.*, VIII, 9, 16. Here too the reference to *pro nobis* is considered unfounded, because it does not mean *vice* or *in loco,* but that Christ died for us so that we could be saved. See further Questions 23-28 of this Catechism, where it says, *Vox redemptionis simpliciter liberationem notat,* and the attack on the idea that God is the "object" of reconciliation. Cf. Polman, *op. cit.*, II, 322ff.

give but only demands satisfaction, making forgiveness superfluous.[95]

The criticism that substitution is morally impossible must also be viewed in this light. Bavinck points out that Socinius' criticism of the doctrine of satisfaction was so sharp and so complete that succeeding critics could do nothing but repeat his arguments.[96] We may indeed call this criticism "complete" because it declared God's actual activity in Jesus Christ impossible – the mystery and miracle of substitution by which chastisement brings peace and stripes healing. The irritable human heart always tends to rebel against this act of offense, and is quite capable of cloaking this rebellion with a theology that claims to defend the grace of God by eliminating substitution. The Socinian opposition must not be isolated as a foreign opinion in the history of theology. It is, essentially, just one form of *the* rebellion of man, which rejects this substitution. In this case it argues by appealing to our sense of justice. And it need not surprise us that those who wish to substitute "solidarity" for this kind of substitution, advance the further consideration that in substitution man is set aside, whereas in solidarity man is aided.

The controversy with the Socinians has been one of the most serious in the history of the Church, for it concerns the heart of the Church's teaching regarding the sacrifice of Christ. Those who protest against substitution in the sacrifice of Christ express the natural, inevitable rejection by the human heart; refusing the gift of God, they are left in the poverty of their debt. God's graciousness and justice are revealed only in the real substitution, in the radical sacrifice, in the reversing of roles. Here we may well quote the words of Paul, "Things which eye saw not, and ear heard not, And which entered not into the heart of man, Whatsoever things God prepared for them that love him" (I Cor. 2:9). Only by the power of the Holy Spirit can these protests against substitution be conquered in the joyful accepting of this gift, namely, the forgiveness of sins. When faith understands the *sola fide*, the *sola gratia* also becomes reality and the words of Christ are comprehended: "If I wash thee not, thou hast no part with me" (John 13:8).

95. Cf. Bavinck, *Gereformeerde Dogmatiek,* III, 330, 389.
96. *Ibid.,* p. 332.

If we view the sacrifice of Christ according to the teaching of Scripture, we cannot for one moment separate this sacrifice from what Scripture says concerning God's activity in Christ. All that is said concerning his sacrifice is presented in the light of God's commandment (John 10:18), and of the justice and love of God which are revealed in Christ. But at the same time we will also see the reality of what Scripture says concerning the love of *Christ*. He himself specifically mentioned this love in his sacrifice: the commandment to his disciples that they must love one another is conjoined with the statement, "as I have loved you" (John 15:12, 13:34, 15:10). And he will manifest this love by laying down his life for his friends – "Greater love hath no man than this, that a man lay down his life for his friends" (15:13) – as the shepherd gives his life for the sheep. His sacrifice will be an act of love which cannot be stopped by the greatest terrors of suffering – the love to the end (13:1). It is the act which matches the act of God's love in sending his Son (3:16); it manifests itself during his entire life, and on the road to the deepest depth of his suffering in the washing of the disciples' feet, and throughout the whole *passio magna* in which even God's forsaking him and the disciples' denying him could not diminish or disturb his love. He did not take with him the loyalty of his friends, but rather their sins, which he carried in his body upon the tree because he had not come to be served but to serve and to seek that which was lost and to call sinners. That is why his love remained unchanged even when he was forsaken by all. His was not a love that depended upon reciprocal love and fluctuated along with it, but a love that bore its own unique characteristic all the way to the end of the sacrifice.

Scripture calls our attention to this one-sided, mysterious love in manifold manners. He loved us – in the words of Paul – "and gave himself for us, an offering and a sacrifice" (Eph.. 5:2). Compare also Galatians 2:20, ". . . the Son of God, who loved me, and gave himself up for me." This love passes knowledge (Eph. 3:19) and protects against all powers both present and future (Rom. 8:35, 39).

To be sure, Scripture also speaks of human love which does not seek itself (I Cor. 13:5), but this higher kind of love is still not of a kind with the love of Christ; at most it is the echo, the answer to his love and is recommended as such (John 15:12; 13:34; Eph. 5:2). It is the imitation of Christ's love, and is based upon his loving sacrifice of reconciliation.[97] This human love never competes with Christ's love, because it is fully patterned after it as Christ's love is correlated with God's: "As the Father hath loved me, I also loved you: abide ye in my love" (John 15:9; cf. Col. 1:13, Eph. 1:6). "Therefore doth the Father love me, because I lay down my life" (John 10:17).

We may never, out of reaction to the humanization and isolation of Christ's love, tamper with the message of Scripture concerning the love of Christ. It is utterly different from human one-sidedness and indulgence and weakness; it is strong in the weakness of his life. It is as a burning fire and a full armor against all demons. It is in this love that Christ has glorified God's name on earth (John 17:4) by finishing his work, and in his action he always knows himself to be the Sent One and ever sees the high purpose of the *passio magna*: ". . . that the world may know that thou didst send me, and lovedst them, even as thou lovedst me" (John 17:23).[98]

It is necessary to stress these aspects of Christ's love as pictured in Scripture in order to avoid the abyss of Gnostic dualism or Marcionism, which separates God from Jesus Christ and thereby distorts both the justice of God and the love of Christ. The love of God and the love of Christ may not be separated from the holiness of God, for the message of this love is identical with the word of the *cross*. It is the Messiah of God who hears the word from heaven: "Thou art my beloved Son, in thee I am well pleased" (Mark 1:11). In the course of this Messiahship the love of God manifests itself in the love of Christ, who in his sacrifice reveals how holy this love is and how mighty is the protection anchored in this love. We are unable to fathom the cross. And we ever feel compelled to speak of the unsearchableness of the ways of God.

But this unsearchableness is not a *dark* mystery. Rather, it is a message to be preached, a message which reveals the depth of the Father heart in a manner that brings our lives to renewal and restoration: "Herein is love, not that we loved God, but that he loved us, and sent his Son to be the propitiation for our sins. Beloved, if God so loved us, we ought to love one another" (I

97. Cf. the chapter on "The Imitation of Christ" in my *Faith and Sanctification*. Cf. Viktor Warnack, *Agape. Die Liebe als Grundmotiv der N.T. Theologie*, 1951.

98. Cf. Kittel, TWNT, s.v. ἀγαπάω I, 49. Cf. also Christ's power to forgive sins, Mark 2:11.

John 4:10, 11). Here we hear the message of God's love and at the same time we hear of the reconciliation through Christ's blood. But this mystery does not break the unity of love's voice. And whoever asks: "Show us the Father, and it sufficeth us," hears the answer from Christ on his way to cross and forsakenness: "he that hath seen me hath seen the Father; how sayest thou, Show us the Father?" (John 14:8, 9).

C. OBEDIENCE

Having discussed the reconciliation and sacrifice of Christ, we now wish to consider his obedience. Again we are not dealing with an entirely new aspect of the work of Christ that can be considered apart from the others, but with a further insight into the one perfect work of Christ which Scripture also presents as his obedience. This obedience of Christ has often been regarded as the essence of his life, to the neglect of other important aspects of his work. Inevitably, this influences greatly the concept of his obedience. In this view Christ's obedience becomes an impoverished moralism, a kind of office-faithfulness devoid of all scriptural depth. But we may not react to this misrepresentation by ignoring the teaching of Scripture regarding Christ's obedience. Indeed, we may say that both Church and theology have continuously emphasized Christ's obedience. Disregarding the question whether the distinction between active and passive obedience is the most effective way to explain Christ's obedience, we nevertheless can see that by the expression "passive obedience" the Church meant to indicate that she would not reduce Christ's obedience to the level of moralism, nor would she allow it to be contrasted with his reconciliation or substitution.

It must be clear to anyone who reads Scripture that we may designate the work of Christ as obedience. In fact, the word "obedience" is actually used. In the noteworthy passage where Paul speaks of Christ's emptying and humbling himself, we read that he "became obedient even unto death, yea, the death of the cross" (Phil. 2:8); and concerning his suffering we read that "though he was a Son, yet learned obedience by the things which he suffered" (Heb. 5:8).[99] He was "born under the law" (Gal. 4:4) and his entire life was a continuously obedient living under the law. From day to day he had to "listen," in the sense of

99. Cf. my *The Person of Christ.*

the words "hear" (*audire*) and "obey" (*obedire*).[100] In Christ there was a profound relationship between "hear" and "obey." He "seeth" what the Father does and "heareth" his Word (John 19:30). Christ was constantly conscious of this dependence and subjection, and spoke frequently of it. In Gethsemane he *subjected* himself to the will of God and ever *sought* it (5:30). Nowhere is this more evident than when he said that it was his meat to do the will of him who sent him (4:34). This sharply brings out the continuity of his accomplishing the will of God; Christ did not obey spasmodically or incidentally. In his high-priestly prayer he spoke of the work which the Father gave him to perform, the work which he finished in order to glorify the name of God on earth (John 17:4; cf. 19:30 – "It is finished").

We are dealing with a *total* life's direction which manifests itself in every day and hour, in ever-changing circumstances and encounters, as the action of the Sinless One, the Holy One of God. His whole life is the ultimate opposite of autonomy. In whatever he said he was dependent upon the Father; he did and said that which the Father had said (John 12:49; cf. 8:28 – ". . . as the Father taught me, I speak these things"). When Christ spoke of the commandment or the commandments of the Father (John 15:10), however, he did mean a legalistic relationship. Indeed, he is the Servant of the Lord, but his obedience was peculiarly filled to the brim with joyful abandonment to his Messianic life's task. Christ said that the world should know that he loved the Father, and that as the Father gave him commandment even so he did (John 14:31).

The commandment to which Christ was subjected was oriented to the unique task which he had to accomplish as God's Messiah. For that reason he could describe the commandment which he had received thus: "I have power to lay it [his life] down, and

100. ἀκουειν and ὑπακοη; cf. Kittel, TWNT, s.v. ἀκουειν. In Ps. 40:6, quoted in Heb. 10:5ff., we read: "Sacrifice and offering thou hast no delight in; mine ears hast thou opened," whereas Heb. 10:5 reads: ". . . but a body didst thou prepare for me," a version which is based on the Septuagint. Kuyper explains the opening of the ears in Ps. 40 (prepared for the service of obedience) to be incorporated in the translation of σωμα in Hebrews (*totum pro parte*). The preparation of the ear in Ps. 40 corresponds to the preparation of the body in Heb. 10 (*Encyclopedie*, 1909, pp. 405-05). Cf. Grosheide, *Comm. on Heb.*, p. 274, note, and Van Oyen, *Christus de Hogepriester*, p. 182, who further refers to Rom. 12:1 (the readiness of the whole human being to do the will of God).

I have power to take it again. This commandment received I from my Father" (John 10:18). And thus, oriented to this pinnacle of his total obedience – obedience unto death – he was oriented to the will of his Father. "He is the One who wholly receives and carries out, who does nothing but obey."[101] He always did those things that pleased the Father (John 8:29), and in so doing he is the Son, the Servant of the Lord. Moreover, this doing the will of the Father bore rich results: "And this is the will of him that sent me, that of all that which he hath given me I should lose nothing, but should raise it up at the last day" (John 6:39).

For that reason Christ's obedience comprises not simply a part of his life, but the totality of his Messianic work. And this obedience can also be said to express the purpose of his coming, being summarized thus: "Lo, I am come (in the roll of the book it is written of me) to do thy will, O God" (Heb. 10:7; cf. vs. 9). *Christ came to do the will of God.* That was the sole purpose, we may say here, because it concerned the will of God which was oriented to the sacrifice. That is why Hebrews 10 speaks of Christ's perfect obedience in inseparable connection with his perfect sacrifice. Again it is his beneficial obedience, because by virtue of this will – accomplished by Christ – "By which will we have been sanctified through the offering of the body of Jesus Christ once for all" (Heb. 10:10).[102] We clearly see, as everywhere in Scripture, how inseparably Christ's obedience is correlated with his suffering and death – his obedience, during his whole Messianic life, unto death, even the death of the cross.

When we mentioned the Scripture references to Christ's obedience we did not yet discuss the one passage which speaks with special emphasis of the significance of this obedience. We are referring to Paul's words in Romans 5:12ff.

This is the passage in which Paul contrasts Adam and Christ, summarizing thus: "For as through the one man's disobedience the many were made sinners, even so through the obedience of the one shall the many be made righteous" (vs. 19). We cannot discuss this entire section exegetically, yet it is necessary that we clearly see what a tremendous importance Paul ascribes here

101. Kittel, TWNT, s.v. θελημα (III, 55).

102. We wish to point out that here, too, we are dealing with God's activity through and in Jesus Christ. Cf. what we said concerning the *Umstimmung.*

to the obedience of Christ. This importance is the greater since this is not an isolated section in Paul's letter, as many claim, but is directly and closely connected with what precedes it, namely, verses 1-11, in which Paul discusses the significance of the death of Christ and our reconciliation and peace with God.

No matter how we interpret the word "therefore" in verse 12, to Paul there is in any case a real connection between his earlier discussion of reconciliation and his subsequent discourse on Christ's obedience.[103] The thing to note is that in the comparison between Adam and Christ he calls attention to both similarity and difference. The similarity is expressed in the words, "by one man." Adam's act of disobedience was not an isolated act of one man, for it brought with it tremendous and far-reaching consequences for all of humanity. Through one man sin entered into the world, and death through sin (Rom. 5:12); and so death passed unto all men. An irresistible power – the power of death – holds mankind in its grip. The grave significance of the act of Adam's disobedience is not weakened by the fact that Paul adds: "for that all sinned." For he does not reason that all men incurred death in the same manner as did Adam, because they, too, sinned; rather, he wishes to stress the correlation between Adam's disobedience and the power of death over all. And even if we may not translate this phrase – as did Augustine – "for that all men have sinned *in Adam*," nevertheless Paul's words emphasize the correlation between all men's sin and Adam's disobedience.[104] That, to Paul, was the decisive

103. This connection is strongly maintained in the commentary by Anders Nygren in *Der Römerbrief*, 1951, who already even in his introduction to Rom. 5:12-21 proceeds from and speaks of the "culmination point of the letter, from which the whole can be best observed" (p. 22). Cf. also p. 153, where Nygren discusses the attempts to deduce Rom. 5 from Jewish and Hellenstic sources, and remarks that Paul "already on the first page of the Bible came across the story of Adam, so that it was not necessary to search for further material relevant to his ideas" (p. 154).

104. The words concerned are ἐφ' ᾧ παντες ἥμαρτον. Cf. Nygren, *op. cit.*, pp. 158-59; Bavinck, *Gereformeerde Dogmatiek*, III, 59ff. (on ἐφ' ᾧ p. 60, as *eo quod, quandoquidem, quia*); S. Greijdanus, *De Toerekeningsgrond van het Peccatum Originans*, 1906, *Comm.* on Rom. 5:12. That the ἥμαρτον cannot be the basis of the death of all follows immediately from the train of thought: death reigned as king from Adam until Moses, "even over them that had not sinned after the likeness of Adam's transgression," (Rom. 5:14). Cf. also Paul Althaus, *Der Brief an die Römer*, 1949, p. 44, and Dodd's attempt to escape Paul's convincing

significance of Adam's disobedience, which, as the act of "one man," is compared with the other act, also by one man — Jesus Christ. Hence we have a remarkable comparison: Christ's act like Adam's, was not merely of individual significance for himself in his relation to God; but unlike Adam's, it was an act of obedience not unto death, but unto life (Rom. 5:18).

A tremendous history is connected with both Adam's act and Christ's. Adam is "a figure of him that was to come," namely Christ (vs. 14). But in the indication of similarity we also see the difference, for the consequences are not the same: "But not as the trespass, so also is the free gift. For if by the trespass of the one the many died, much more did the grace of God, and the gift by the grace of the one man, Jesus Christ, abound unto the many" (vs. 15; cf. vs. 17).[105] Paul's one great concern, here and in his entire letter, is this *abundance*. And this abundance, expressed by the words "much more," suddenly ends the comparison. It is wise to listen attentively to this "much more," which shows that Paul in his analysis of the power of death is not overwhelmed by "the problem" of theodicy. On the contrary, he has a full view of the riches of grace, of which he also speaks elsewhere. Paul does not merely make a comparison between two men who had an equally powerful influence on the human race, for the gift of grace is not comparable to the violation.

---

argument, in *The Epistle of Paul to the Romans,* 1949, p. 79, for instance: "Adam is a myth, though for Paul he *may* have been real," and concerning the "mystical unity" in Adam as "corporate personality" (p. 80).

105. We can only briefly mention the conclusions which Barth draws from what Paul says regarding the relation between Adam and Christ in "Christus und Adam nach Römer 5. Ein Beitrag zur Frage nach dem Menschen und der Menschheit" (*Theol. Stud.,* Heft 35, 1952). The characteristic feature of Barth's exegesis is that he finds herein justification for his completely Christological approach, as well as his basing anthropology on Christology (see his final conclusions on p. 55). Barth's exegesis, it seems to me, is untenable because he introduces ideas which cannot be found in Paul. Barth, namely, draws from the parallel Adam — Christ the conclusion: "Between our former being *outside of* Adam and our present being *in* Christ there is a natural connection. It was, correctly understood, already our former being outside of Christ, our still hidden but nevertheless real being in him" (p. 10). With Barth, therefore, Adam was "only apparenly" a head of mankind (p. 15). In order to understand Adam we must proceed from Christ, and not vice versa (p. 15). The title of Barth's essay has been purposely chosen — *Christus und Adam.*

The power which resulted in life is more abundant than the power which resulted in death.

The reign of grace is greater and more abundant than the reign of sin unto death (vs. 21); justification is more than condemnation (vs. 16); life is more than death (vs. 17). In spite of the similarity, the contrast is decisive. These two turning points in history can be compared with no others.[106] The effects of what Christ did in history reach into the farthest future,[107] not merely to quiet trembling individual consciences through a quiet peace, but to bring the reign of God, and life, and the resurrection from the dead.[108] Adam's act leads into the quicksand of dark death; but the fruitfulness of the work of Christ can neither be measured nor estimated.

It must not be overlooked that Paul in this section (which as a matter of fact may be numbered among his doxologies) correlates the great abundance of Christ with His *obedience*. He recognizes no tension between the abundance of reconcilation and this obedience. They are one in the reality of Christ's life. And it is understandable that the Church also, in preaching and contemplating this work of Christ, has always been concerned with this pure, saving, abundant act of his life, concerning which he himself spoke so earnestly while in the midst of his suffering: his obedience.

In our attempt to do full justice to the unity of Christ's obedience, we may ask whether the usual dogmatic distinction between Christ's active and passive obedience is not subtle, scholastic, unfounded, and irreverent. Is it not sufficient simply to speak of "the obedience of Christ crucified," as it is expressed in Article 23 of the Belgic Confession? It is obvious that this question can be answered correctly only when we know what is meant by this differentiation.

It strikes us at once that there was no intention to eliminate the unity of Christ's obedience by dividing his life into active and passive moments. The word "passive" may give us this

106. Cf. Althaus, *op. cit.*, p. 46, and Nygren on Rom. 5:12.

107. Cf. H. D. Wendland, *Geschichtsanschauung und Geschichtsbewusstein im Neuen Testament*, 1938, pp. 28ff.

108. Cf. Paul on Adam being the first *man* and Christ the last *Adam* (ἐσχατός) (I Cor. 15:54ff.), which ends in the admonition, "be ye stedfast, unmovable, always abounding in the work of the Lord (vs. 58).

impression momentarily, but at closer examination it becomes evident that in spite of this differentiation it was emphasized that Chrst always remained the active, fully-conscious Mediator. It is clearly evident from the entire record of his suffering that a state of mere passivity could not be the basis of this differentiation. And when we understand "passive" in the correct sense as delineated above, we can without any objection call Christ's total obedience an active obedience unto death. His entire suffering is full of this activity, as all his words on the cross show, and already before that Christ had spoken of his holy activity toward the end of his life when he said: "Therefore doth the Father love me, because I lay down my life, that I might take it again. No one taketh it away from me, but I lay it down of myself" (John 10:17, 18).[110] It is by no means the case that after an actively helping, healing, curing, preaching, and praying life, a period of "passivity" finally overwhelmed Christ's afflicted life. True, at a certain moment he was robbed of his freedom and bound, but even then the wondrous mediatorial activity was not terminated but rather was uninterruptedly preserved.[111]

We realize that this unified, uninterrupted obedience involves a mystery, but this mystery nevertheless designates a moment-to-moment reality, for his activity remained manifest in everything that he underwent. "As a lamb that is led to the slaughter, and as a sheep that before her shearers is dumb, so he opened not his mouth" (Isa. 53:7), but who will conclude from the materialization of this prophecy that this "lamb" was passive? It is exactly this being brought and being dumb that constitute manifestations of his complete, uninterrupted activity, just as he remained the Active One when he was made sin.

All this, however, was by no means denied when a distinction was made between the active and passive obedience or even the active and passive aspects of Christ's obedience.[112] Schilder even speaks of "the greatest activity in the utmost passivity at the same time."[113] Moreover, the facts relevant to this distinction were appreciated long before it was made explicitly. Polman

109. The same holds true of the expression "passive obedience," if "passive," is understood as a sort of "passivity."

110. Cf. his refusal to accept the pain-stilling myrrh (Mark 15:23).

111. Cf. K. Schilder, *Christus in Zijn Lijden,* 1951, II, 150-51, e.g. on "the active obedience in the passive." Cf. also II, 219.

112. Bavinck, *Gereformeerde Dogmatiek,* III, 383.

113. *Heidelbergse Catechismus,* II, 217.

correctly points out that Calvin did not make the distinction between active and passive obedience, but spoke only of "the one obedience which embraced His entire life."[114] This does not mean, however, that Calvin rejected what was later meant by this distinction. Calvin indeed strongly emphasized – as did subsequent Reformed theology – the unity of Christ's obedience as wholly oriented to the reconciliation, but even with him the twofold aspect is clearly evident when he views Christ's whole life as obedience. Calvin points out that Scripture constantly correlates grace with Christ's death, but that does not mean that the entire course of his life was not one of obedience. The accepted distinction did not separate an active part from an inactive part; Christ's "passive" obedience was precisely his fulfillment of the law, his accepting and bearing the punishment for sin, and his undergoing God's wrath. Hence we are not dealing with two separable parts of Christ's obedience.

"The active obedience is not an outward addition to the passive, nor vice versa. Not one single act and not one single incident in the life or suffering of Christ can be said to belong exclusively to the one or the other."[115]

From this we may not conclude, however, that the distinction between active and passive obedience is either meaningless or inaccurate. Rather, it is closely linked with the unique position of Christ as Mediator and his Messianic commission. This was quite evident when in various discussions either the active or passive obedience was in danger of being neglected. For instance, there has often been a tendency to accept only an active obedience, in a sense which denies what the passive obedience implies, namely, the bearing of the punishment for sin in the wrath of God. Christ's obedience, in this view, obtained a humanistic or at least moralistic quality. This view emphasized the faithfulness which he had manifested in his "calling," but rejected his substitution. In protest the Church emphasized his passive obedience, and in this struggle it became sufficiently clear what she meant thereby.

On the other hand, the active obedience of Christ has also been denied. According to this camp there was only a passive obedience, which was understood to be Christ's suffering as the

114. Polman, *Onze Nederlandse Geloofsbelijdenis,* II, 52 (Calvin, *Institutes,* II, XVI, 5; cf. III, 14, 12).

115. Bavinck, *op. cit.,* p. 384; cf. "his doing was suffering and his suffering was deed."

undergoing of our punishment. Its adherents rejected the concept of an active obedience, at least in Christ's work for us, since as man he was obliged to obey the law even for himself. They did not deny Christ's actively fulfilling the law, but Piscator (e.g.) denied that this activity was one of the meritorious causes of reconciliation.[116] He remarked that there was agreement that man is justified by the merits of Christ, but that according to some the actual meritorious obedience is the *obedientia passionis et mortis Christi,* while others say that it is the *tota obedientia Christi.*[117] Piscator agrees with the former position, particularly on the basis of I John 1:7, "the blood of Jesus his Son cleanseth us from all sin," and Hebrews 9:22 "apart from shedding of blood there is no remission."

Some theologians did not consider the difference to be serious, but others felt that the unity of Christ's work was at stake.[118] Piscator saw a direct and immediate connection between the death of Christ and our justification, while the Reformed theologians who contested his position emphasized with Calvin one obedience during Christ's entire life.

The remarkable thing was that Piscator, in opposition to Beza, said that justification is an *actio simplex,* and that Olevianus, who agreed with Piscator, also said that what is imputed to us is not *multiplex* but *simplex.* Obviously they felt that the twofold obedience — with regard to justification — was *multiplex* and they

116. Cf. F. L. Bos, *Johann Piscator,* 1932, p. 243, Thesis 7, in which Piscator answers the question whether the holiness of Christ has no bearing on our justification. He denies that: "*ut causas, sine quibus passio et mors Christi non potuisset nobis ad justitiam imputari,*" but this holiness itself cannot be a meritorious cause. Cf. Piscator's subsequent explanation in this letter to the French synod: "*Obedientia vitae*: *quam prestitit legi communi; obedientia mortis*: *quam praestitit speciali mandato Patris de patiendo ac moriendo pro electis*" (Bos, *op. cit.,* p. 118). Only the latter is imputed to us.

117. Thesis 2, *ibid.,* p. 242.

118. In 1587 Beza wrote to Piscator — after previous serious admonitions — that in essence they were in agreement and concerned themselves with the same objective, namely, our salvation (Bos, p. 83). Later it proved that the controversy was taken far more seriously, when Pareus urged Piscator in a letter "not to be misled by Satan. He is definitely going to inflict a mortal wound to your churches if you do not take heed." And he asked the question: If only Christ's death is the cause of our justification, "to what purpose then are his previous humiliation, the form of a servant which he has accepted, his servitude over against the law . . . ?" (Bos, p. 10; cf. p. 11).

contrasted this with the *simplex* of the *obedientia mortis.* The others emphasized the fact, which they considered undeniable, that it was Piscator who destroyed the unity (*simplex*) by positing a twofold obedience, namely, an *obedientia vitae* (for himself) and an *obedientia mortis* (for us). Both groups were therefore concerned with the unity of Christ's work and obedience. But it is clear that Piscator could arrive at the *simplex* only by limiting Christ's meritorious obedience to his *obedientia mortis.* Thus he concluded to the twofold nature of Christ's obedience, and because of this duality he could no longer find the true unity according to the gospel. His appeal to the cleansing blood of Christ could not justify the basis on which his viewpoint rested, especially since Scripture emphatically speaks of Christ "under the law," and that not in an isolated "legal" context as a minor part of Christ's life alongside his reconciling work, but in this context: "But when the fulness of the time came, God sent forth his Son, born of a woman, born under the law, that he might redeem them that were under the law, that we might receive the adoption of sons" (Gal. 4:4, 5).

Here Christ's being under the law is not presented as the legal aspect of his life alongside the reconciling aspect, but in connection with his incarnation and humiliation. That is why not a single part of Christ's life can be separated or even isolated from his reconciling work. Instead, there is a close connection between Christ's holiness and the salvation of man by his blood in the reconciliation by the innocent lamb. Piscator's criticism of the *duplex* would have been correct only if the Reformed theologians had placed the legal and reconciling aspects independently alongside each other, or if they, to say it differently, had separated Christ's fulfilling the will of his Father from what Scripture everywhere says *is* the will of the Father, namely, the fulfillment of the task given by him. It is exactly in this regard that he has fulfilled the deepest meaning of the law. And it is for this reason that the Reformed theologians maintained, and that correctly, the unity of the active and passive obedience of Christ over against Piscator. So, for instance, Bavinck observed that Scripture nowhere makes a distinction between *obedientia vitae* and *obedientia mortis* when it deals with the work Christ was commissioned to do.[119]

Bavinck hits the core of the problem when he points out the

119. Bavinck, *Gereformeerde Dogmatiek,* III, 364.

special relationship between Christ and the law, for his obedience is obedience to the will of God, according to Psalm 40 and Hebrews 10, namely that will of God that came to expression in the command he received from the Father to lay down his life.[120] His fulfilling the law is never isolated from this reconciling task. Rather, his entire life manifests this kind of obedience, and is a life according to and a fulfillment of this meaning of the law, namely, "loving God and his neighbor." His life is one doxology to the glory of the Lord and the holiness of his command. Thus he obeys his parents and lets himself be baptized; thus he honors the Sabbath as the Lord of the Sabbath and manifests his healing work on the Sabbath in the signs of the Kingdom; in short, thus he fulfills the law in his entire Messianic work. Thus fulfilling God's law, Christ went his way in our stead and went God's way in the most absolute and unique obedience of the Servant of the Lord.

It is particularly in the scriptural messages concerning the Servant of the Lord that tremendous problems emerge in the background of the controversy regarding the obedience of Christ. The mistake of those who exclude the active obedience from the work of reconcilation, in the final analysis, is that they separate two aspects that never can or may be separated,[121] namely, that

120. Cf. H. Vogel, "He who wants to separate the one from the other robs both of their saving power. The passive obedience is saving on the strength of the active obedience and the active obedience is prefigured in the passive and is therefore saving" (*Gott in Christo,* 1951, p. 726).

121. In the revelation concerning "the Servant of the Lord" we see most clearly the utmost unity between obedience and humiliation. There is no disconnection whatsoever between Christ's suffering and his knowing that he is the obedient Servant of the Lord. He is the *suffering Servant* of the Lord. All aspects of Christ's work converge in the form of the *ebed Jahve.* Cf., besides the references to Christ in Acts 3:13, 26; 4:27, 30, especially Matt. 12:17ff., with extensive quotation from Isa. 42:1-4 and Matt. 8:17 (Isa. 53:4). The revelation concerning the *Servant* of the Lord is constantly connected with the "for us" of his reconciling work done in this kind of obedience. He is God's "elect" (Isa. 42:1; cf. the derisive term slung at him as being the Christ, the chosen of God, in Luke 23:35) and God's Servant, the Righteous One, who bears our iniquities (Isa. 53:11). Cf. the extensive discussion of this term, and the many references to the N.T., in Kittel, TWNT, V, s.v. *pais theon,* pp. 709ff. On the fulfillment of his task as the Servant of the Lord, see further Isa. 42:1-4; on his trust, Isa. 50:4-11; on his suffering, Isa. 52:13-53:12. Cf. the question discussed by C. R. North, "whether the portrait of the Servant is consistent through the Songs," in *The Suffering Servant in Deutero-Isaiah* (1948), p. 154. This question

part of his obedience which is for himself and that part which is for us. At the same time they separate his being subject to the law as man from his suffering as Mediator, whereas it is precisely the man Jesus Christ who is our Mediator. Hence the result of such a differentiation is that Christ's relationship to the law takes on a legalistic aspect, no matter how emphatically his obedience during his entire life is magnified. This legalistic aspect is the result of accepting a relative, isolated law-relationship as such, outside of and independent of Christ's mediatorial obedience. When such an isolation is accepted, then no full justice can be done to the undeniable fact that Christ's holiness (negatively, his sinlessness) is constantly presented in Scripture in his irrevocable refusal of every attempt to keep him from going the way of his suffering – among other things, the temptation in the wilderness.[122]

Hence we should be grateful that by maintaining both the passive and active obedience of Christ, at the same time the correct view is retained of the unity of Christ's work in obedience. This line of thought is also expressed in the Belgic Confession (Art. 22), which says, "Jesus Christ, imputing to us all His merits, and so many holy works which He has done for us and in our stead" – a statement of which the words "and so many holy works which He has done for us" were omitted apparently, not wholly unintentionally from the *Harmonia Confessionum.* The Synod of Dort, however, maintained and retained this statement, and by adding "and in our stead" once again emphasized the unity of the active and passive obedience, because the objective was not to divide the one obedience into two mutually rather

---

relates also to the various aspects of the Servant of the Lord. When Volz speaks of "contrasts" and on the basis thereof arrives at the idea of a twofold Servant, North correctly observes that "exactly the same might be argued from the contrast between the Galilean ministry of Jesus and his death upon the Cross" (*op. cit.*, p. 154). Cf. W. Manson, *Bist du, der da kommen soll?* (1952), pp. 133-136.

122. See the chapter on "The Sinlessness of Christ" in my *The Person of Christ.*

123. Cf. J. J. van Toorenenbergen, *De Symbolische Schriften der Ned. Herv. Kerk* 1869), p. 36: "The Synod of Dort has emphatically condemned this deletion" (cf. Polman, *op. cit.*, III, 52). Bogerman's proposal simply to speak of "obedience" in order to overarch the different viewpoints (Bogerman was sympathetic towards Piscator's ideas) was rejected, so that the expressive words were again incorporated in Article 22.

independent and separated parts, but to bring out that the obedience of his entire life was in our behalf and for our benefit.

As we thus describe Christ's entire work also as obedience, the image of Christ presents itself precisely as the apostolic witness presents him. In him there was no tension between the fulfillment of the law and the accomplishment of his mediatorial work. His holiness was not simply a presupposition of his mediatorial work, but it manifested itself in that work, which throughout his historical life is the fulfillment of the law. Thus we see Christ in the fulness of his love, and in him we see the meaning of love toward God and towards our neighbor become historical reality. His was a life lived in solitude and in activity; it was a dependent life, of which both solitude and prayer were the prelude to the activity of his mediatorial work.[124] His entire life reflected the holiness of God, and in this clear consciousness of his perfect heart he resisted the hypocrisy of men, of which he spoke with holy indignation. He does not resemble the one son in the parable, who said Yes but did not go and work in the vineyard because he did not want to, but neither does Christ resemble the other son, who did not want to go at first but afterwards went after all (Matt. 21:28-32). The tensions in Christ's life are not those of his sins but of ours. It can be said that with his coming "philanthropy" appeared (Tit. 3:4). God's grace is manifested in his entire life, during which he explained the law to us: the second commandment is like unto the first (Matt. 22:39), and he himself gave a commandment: "This is my commandment, That ye love one another, as I have loved you" (John 15:12). His is a love – the fulfillment of the law – that passes knowledge (Eph. 3:19), and no man has greater love than this, that a man lay down his life for his friends (John 15:13). The contrast between "inward" and "outward" that so often characterizes a person's life is entirely absent in him. *All* the issues of his life were from his *heart,* and when he saw the multitudes, he was moved with compassion on them, because they fainted and were scattered abroad as sheep having no shepherd (Matt. 9:36; cf. 15:32, "I have compassion on the multitude . . ." ; 20:34, compassion materialized in a deed for the blind). Indeed, even those who consider the veneration of "the

124. After a certain activity "he withdrew himself in the deserts, and prayed" (Luke 5:16).

heart of Jesus" liturgy to be indefensible in the light of Scripture, must agree with the expression of a Roman Catholic author who speaks of "the treasures of affection contained in the heart of Jesus."[125]

Those who listen attentively to the scriptural message concerning Christ will continue to maintain the relatedness of his *entire* obedience to the work of reconciliation, precisely in order to preserve this message. To exclude his active obedience from this relatedness, however well intended in order to maintain the *simplex* nature of Christ's obedience, inevitably has led to a violation of this mystery. That is why the distinction between active and passive obedience is a preservation of this mystery. Even so, it still remains possible that with this distinction we nevertheless divide Christ's life's work of obedience into "parts." But in the light of the scriptural testimony it is possible to maintain the unity of his reconciling obedience unto the death of the cross with the richness of his fulfillment of the law throughout his entire life.

We have thus far considered Christ's reconciliation, his sacrifice, and his obedience. It becomes increasingly clear that with all these terms we touch upon the one work of Christ. What is important is not *our* interpretation, the correctness of *our* terminology, or the subjective aspects *we* ascribe to Christ's work, but the one reality which is understood in faith. When we understand something of the riches and abundance of this work of Christ in his threefold office, in his being the Shepherd — the great Shepherd — then the way is cleared to speak, finally, about Christ's work as *victory*.

D. VICTORY

It may seem rather strange that we conclude our discussion of the work of Christ with the word *victory*. It gives the impression that we are suddenly moving to a different level, namely, that of struggle and power. Does not the word "victory" suggest the idea of a hero, and does it not introduce the element of struggle into the categories of the Christian faith, so that Christ's life and death are seen in quite a different light from that of the three preceeding terms? Even though we grant that the existence of

125. *Dictionaire de Théologie Catholique,* VIII[1] 1164.

struggle, concern, and tension in the life of the Son of man, does that mean that we therefore touch upon an *essential* aspect of his life (Heb. 13:20)?[126]

These questions can be answered only in the light of Scripture. We first wish to point out, however, the accusation that the Church and theology have paid far too little attention to Christ's struggle and victory. According to this viewpoint the Church's contemplation of the work of Christ was characterized by one-sidedness, so that it lost sight of certain elemental Christian motifs. Especially Gustav Aulén has constantly pointed this out. He has expressed his objections in the form of an analysis of various types of reconciliation, distinguishing three of them. First there is the Latin type, that understands reconciliation in a legalistic sense in the framework of a court of law.[127] The second is the "ethical" type, which makes reconciliation dependent upon what takes place inside of man. But Aulén points out a third type, namely, what he considers to be the classic motif of reconciliation, which has been grossly neglected in the history of theology and which can be described as the *dramatic* motif of reconciliation. The basic idea is that Christ is Conqueror, the attacker of the powers of evil, i.e., of sin, death, and Satan.[128] The classic motif is the dramatic one, the motif of victory which already in the ancient Church was a vital, dominant idea in Christian thought, but which afterwards became supplanted by the Latin, Anselmian motif of reconciliation. This destroyed the religious depth of the dramatic motif, because the Latin theory was concerned only with a legalistic interpretation of Christ's work. It is especially this type to which Aulén is opposed, because, although it does recognize an act of God, it is "an act of God which is interrupted vertically."[129] For in Anselm's viewpoint it is man (the God-Man Jesus Christ) who does the meritorious, satisfactory work. Christ in his human nature is "the

126. Cf. H. Berkhof, *Christus en de Machten,* 1953.
127. The Anselmian doctrine of satisfaction.
128. Cf. G. Aulén, *De Christelijke Verzoeningsgedachte* (tr. J. Hensel, 1931); "Die drei Haupttypen des Christlichen Versöhnungsgedankens" (*Zeitschrift für systematische Theologie,* 1931); *Het Christelijke Godsbeeld* (tr. J. Hensel, 1929); *Die Dogmengeschichte im Lichte der Lutherforschung,* 1932; and on Aulén, G. Brillenburg Wurth, *De Theologie van Gustav Aulen,* 1931.
129. *Zeitschrift für systematische Theologie,* p. 514.

center of the entire argument" in the Latin theory of reconciliation. The emphasis is no longer exclusively on the activity of God, but the one-sided, purposeful act of God "has found a counterpart down below." Since the emphasis is now on the work of Christ as a *man*, his work is considered on the basis of a legal order.

In the classic motif of reconciliation everything is entirely different. It is not concerned with a legal relationship in Christ's work but with the uninterrupted act of God in Christ for the victory over the powers of evil.[130] In Christ the divine enters the world of sin and death and carries out its victorious work of reconciliation. Only divine power can accomplish this. In this viewpoint the emphasis is not on an accomplishment that is offered to God from below, but on the reconciling activity of God himself.

The classic motif of reconciliation is concerned with drama, warfare, and victory. It is the original motif which the primitive Church, among others Irenaeus, clearly understood, but which later on was lost only to be revived again by Luther's mighty vision of Christ the Warrior against the powers of evil.[131] The work of Christ is a condition of warfare and victory, a tremendous aspect which later on was no longer understood because the dualistic background was lost sight of, and at last, in the eighteenth and nineteenth centuries, the drama of reconciliation was no longer recognized.[132] The dramatic motif of reconciliation is not simply concerned with a dogmatic-historic problem but with *the* New Testament motif of reconciliation. In fact, it is to be expected that a thought that so much prevailed in the ancient Church "had its root in primitive Christianity, and there stood clearly in the foreground." Those who base the Latin motif of reconciliation on the New Testament read the New Testament with preconceived ideas, and thus ignore its teaching.[133] For the dramatic motif is very clearly seen in Paul, John, in Hebrews, the Apocalypse, and no less in the Gospels. We find everywhere

130. "The criterion of the classic type is first of all the uninterrupted activity of God and the interrupted legal order," *ibid.*, p. 532.

131. *Ibid.*, pp. 502, 511; cf. *De Christelijke Verezoeningsgedachte*, esp. ch. 6.

132. Aulén sees in Barth tendencies to return to the old scholastic theology, *De Chr. Verzoeningsgedachte*, p. 147.

133. "The research of recent years has more and more come to see this," *Zeitschrift*, p. 511.

the dualism between the will of God and the hostile powers of evil. In Christ's warfare with Satan, he casts out demons. In this warfare we see not simply an ecclesiastical motif, but "Christianity's classic motif of reconciliation." And when Luther rediscovers the old motif after the historical development of dogmatics in the ancient Church and the Middle Ages, we once again behold the power of the "dramatic theme."

It is the dramatic essence of "A Mighty Fortress Is Our God" that determines Luther's view of salvation by Christ. Central in this viewpoint are the curse, the law, sin, the devil, and the wrath of God. The only power able to meet these is not, legalistically, the human performance, not even that of Christ in his human nature, but the divine power which Scripture ascribes to Christ.[134] The wrath of God is conquered by a divine act. Reconciliation is at the same time deliverance. Christ is the victor over tyranny, the powers of evil, which hold both man and the world in bondage. There is a tension between the divine curse and the divine blessing. The curse must depart when love breaks through the wrath in the victory of *Christus Victor*.[135]

It is not accidental that in our day the restoration of the so-called classic motif of reconciliation is advocated. Ever since Aulén started this movement about 1930, attention has been called more and more to the "powers" that threaten human life. The time of the optimistic theologians seemed past. Otto had talked about the irrational mystery of religion in which God was experienced both as *fascinans* and as *tremendum*, and the justice and wrath of God were re-emphasized. An eschatological way of thinking began to prevail, which discovered destructive forces upon which God's judgment majestically manifested itself. And the work of Christ was presented as the victory over the powers of evil and destruction. Today we hear everywhere about demythologizing, the new aeon which has already supplanted the old, the invasion of the Kingdom, and V-Day, whereby in princi-

134. Luther's deepening of the dramatic motif, according to Aulén, lies in the fact the ancient Church discerned three powers of evil, namely, sin, death, and Satan, but Luther, following Paul, adds the law and the wrath of God (*Chr. Verzoeningsgedachte*, p. 113). Aulén feels that Luther's insight was much deeper than that of the ancient Church.

135. Cf. A. Nygren, "Christ and the Forces of Destruction," *Scottish Journal of Theology*, IV, 4 (1951), and J. S. Stewart, "On a Neglected Emphasis in N.T. Theology," *ibid.*, IV, 3 (1951); also Aulén, *Christelijk Godsbeeld*, pp. 192ff.

ple the decisive battle concerning the "powers" has been fought.[136] Liberation and deliverance are strongly emphasized, while the cosmic significance of Christ's work is again accentuated, in contrast with the individualistic limitations of former times. Are there not powers dethroned? And is it not a danger that faith, in the face of a seeming superabundance of facts, is tempted to believe sooner in the "occupation" than in the liberation? Has faith the power to live in the new aeon, which is not merely in the future but a present eschatological reality which entered and still enters the world with the superior power of Christ's Kingdom?

It is taught that Scripture itself affords the basis for the classic, dramatic motif of reconciliation, since it speaks in many contexts of Christ's warfare and victory. And these references do indeed exist: when we listen attentively to the testimony of Scripture regarding the Messiah, we soon discover that it speaks unmistakably, both in prophecy and in the fulfillment, of the power and the victory of Christ. Already in the promise to Eve we meet a reference to victory, while in the Old Testament the coming Messiah is referred to as the "one that is mighty" (Ps. 89:19). He is the Lion out of the tribe of Judah (Gen. 49:9, Rev. 5:5). When Isaiah pictures the Man of Sorrows as a lamb that is brought to the slaughter, and as a sheep that is dumb before her shearers, this does not mean that he will not divide the spoil with the great (Isa. 53:12). Prophecy testifies that "unto us a Child is born." But among his names is also Mighty God (Isa. 9:6). "Of the increase of his government and of peace there shall be no end, upon the throne of David, and upon his kingdom" (Isa. 9:7).

Edelkoort says of the Messiah figure in the Old Testament that the Messiah is never active but always passive, "not only in Daniel, but also in Jeremiah and Isaiah."[137] Elsewhere he expresses himself more carefully by saying that the Messiah in the Old Testament is "very seldom active," and continues, "sal-

136. Cf., among others, Cullmann, *Christus und die Zeit,* and A. Nygren, *op. cit.,* who uses the illustration for the liberation of a country after the occupation by the enemy: "*the* illustration, the important general illustration which has been given to the people of our time" (p. 365). Cf. J. S. Stewart: "The thrust of the demonic has to be met with the fire of the divine. As indeed it can: since Christ has overcome the world" (*op. cit.,* p. 301).

137. A. H. Edelkoort, *De Christusverwachting in het Oude Testament* (1941), p. 501.

vation is never his doing, his creation, and when mention is made of his kingdom, then he receives it, but he never conquers it."[138] Edelkoort intends to stress with these words the Messiah's dependence, which indeed is already contained in the Messianic commission, but we may not equate this dependence with passivity and receptivity, as Edelkoort seems to do, although he himself speaks of the Messiah as being "equipped with God's power" in the exercise of his royal office. In the Messiah there is no contradiction between receptivity and activity, because in the messianic fulfillment of his commission we see his full activity. And therein we see the harmony of his messianic life, in which there is a unique correlation between weakness and strength.

When the promised Messiah comes, we see him engaged in battle in various ways. At the beginning of his public ministry he is already tempted, a temptation which has direct bearing upon his messianic office; and here we see that his warfare is of a very special sort. In no uncertain terms he rejects the glory of the power over the kingdoms of the world without undergoing suffering (Matt. 4:8-11), and he also thwarts the attempts to honor him as a political messiah and to make him king (John 6:15). Obviously in his entire life he wants nothing to do with mundane heroism and with striving for power. When the disciples entertain thoughts about the glory of the Messiah, then he reminds them of the laws of *his* kingdom: "they who are accounted to rule . . . lord it over them . . . . But it is not so among you. . . . For the Son of man also came not to be ministered unto, but to minister" (Mark 10:42-45).

But this "ministry" by no means excludes his struggle. Christ himself spoke of this more than once when his life was surrounded by opposition as the Kingdom of God came near. Just as the power of darkness was aware of Christ's power in his appearance among his people, so Christ himself entered the battle with full consciousness and cast out the demons.[139] He related

138. *Ibid.*, p. 219; cf. p. 339: "the Messiah is wholly receptive and God, in a tremendous sense, is active."

139. Cf. Mark 1:24 – "What have we to do with thee, Jesus thou Nazarene? art thou come to destroy us? I know thee who thou art, the Holy One of God." Cf. Mark 5:7 – "What have I to do with thee, Jesus, thou Son of the Most High God?"; cf. also the plea of the unclean spirits (5:10, 12). Concerning the demoniac opposition, see 4:15 (in connection with the seed sown), Luke 22:31 (the seating of the disciples), John 13:27 (the betrayal of Judas), Luke 22:53 ("this is your hour, and the power of darkness").

this battle to the coming of the Kingdom: "But if I by the finger of God cast out demons, then is the kingdom of God come upon you" (Luke 11:20; cf. Matt. 12:28 – "by the Spirit of God"). When the Pharisees said that his power over the devil was of demonic origin, he threw this clarifying light upon his power: "When the strong man fully armed guardeth his own court, his goods are in peace: but when a stronger than he shall come upon him and overcome him, he taketh from him his whole armor wherein he trusted, and divideth his spoils" (Luke 11:21-22).[140] Christ speaks of his power here as an irresistible power which is connected with his messianic coming.[141]

We notice something of the triumph during Christ's whole life; yet this triumph does not lessen the depth of his suffering in any way. On the contrary, this triumphant element is inextricably connected with his entire life. When he speaks about his humiliation and glorification as he is about to enter his great suffering, we hear something about this connection: "Now is the judgment of this world: now shall the prince of this world be cast out" (John 12:31; cf. John 16:11 concerning the testimony regarding the Comforter – "of judgment, because the prince of this world is judged"), and to his disciples he can therefore speak the encouraging words: "be of good cheer; I have overcome the world" (John 16:33; cf. John 14:30, "the prince of the world cometh; and he hath nothing in me"), words which he spoke after his prophecy that the disciples would be scattered and would leave him (John 16:32). Christ's references to his power and triumph are never at variance with those to his love, sacrifice, service, meekness, and suffering, for it is exactly in connection with the latter that he speaks of victory. It is a victory that is unique. Only those who misinterpret or lose sight of that uniqueness can ask of this Messiah: "Art thou he that cometh, or look we for another?" (Matt. 11:3). John, who himself had preached the Messiah who was stronger than he (Matt. 2:11), receives an answer that points to the very works that occasioned the question of doubt: "the blind receive their sight, and the lame walk . . . and the poor have good tidings preached

140. Cf. also Luke 10:18-19 concerning Satan's falling from heaven and what Christ said to the seventy: "Behold, I have given you authority to tread upon serpents and scorpions, and over all the power of the enemy." Cf. Acts 10:38 – "who went about doing good, and healing all that were oppressed of the devil."

141. Cf. R. Otto, *Reich Gottes und Menschensohn* (1942[2]), pp. 74ff.

to them. And blessed is he, whosoever shall find no occasion of stumbling in me" (Matt. 11:5-6).

Only in the light of his entire work, his messianic work, can the manifestations of his power over the sick and the demon-possessed be understood. The uniqueness of his struggle corresponds to the uniqueness of this victory, which means that an enemy of immense proportions has been rendered powerless. Yet Christ never displayed his power arbitrarily, for this would contradict the very nature of his power. An evil and adulterous generation that desired a sign received no other sign than that of Jonah the prophet (Matt. 12:38ff.), for Christ was interested only in the beneficent signs of the Kingdom he had come to bring. They are indeed mighty signs, the conquering of sickness, demons, and death, but the true nature of these signs can be understood only in faith.[142] Those who view these signs in unbelief cannot, indeed, deny Christ's superior power, but they can be ready with a negative interpretation of them, as did the Pharisees. In that case one does not *really* see the miracles; even the disciples, at times, saw everything and nevertheless perceived nothing, as at Christ's appearance on the water when they were afraid and did not recognize him, "for they understood not . . . but their heart was hardened" (Mark 6:52). The new miracle was not understood because the previous one had been observed only casually. Then the Master's word, "Be of good cheer: it is I; be not afraid" (vs. 50) was needed to remove their consternation.

To believe in Christ or not to believe in him is therefore not determined by one's concept of his power as such. If we do not know *him,* then we know neither the uniqueness of his struggle and victory nor his power, which is evident in the fact that the powerful raising of Lazarus became the occasion for deliberation to kill this man because he was a reminder of Christ's power (John 12:10; cf. vs. 19). The clearest interpretation of Christ's power in connection with his entire work is, however, found where the healing of many demon-possessed people was taken as the fulfillment of the prophecy concerning the Man of Sorrows, "Himself took our infirmities, and bare our diseases" (Isa. 53:4; Matt. 8:16-17).[143] It is, indeed, real power, but

142. Cf. H. N. Ridderbos, *De Komst van het Koninkrijk,* p. 73 and all of par. 10 on "Jesus' miraculous power."

143. Cf. H. N. Ridderbos, *Matthew,* I, 169: apparently there is a difference between Isaiah 53 and the fulfillment. "In essence, however,

power that is subservient to Christ's messianic task and connected with his sacrifice; therefore it is senseless to meet this Messiah with clubs and swords (Mark 14:48). His power and victory are unique because they are the victorious power of reconciliation and mercy in the way of his suffering and death.

We can summarize this whole matter in the words of John, who describes the object of Christ's coming thus: "To this end was the Son of God manifested, that he might destroy the works of the devil" (I John 3:8). Against the dark background of sin and Satan John points to this goal of Christ's coming. But under no circumstances may we isolate this warfare-motif from what we read elsewhere concerning the object of his coming, for instance, that he came to serve. For, fundamentally, his battle and his service are identical. It is in the way of his service, his sacrifice, that he has destroyed the works of the devil. This Warrior is the Messiah, who can nevertheless hang upon a cross amidst the scorn of bystanders who interpret his cross as the symbol of his powerlessness: "He saved others; himself he cannot save. He is the King of Israel; let him now come down from the cross, and we will believe on him" (Matt. 27:42). Only in faith can the mystery of the power of the Crucified One be understood. The scorn of the bystanders, that aggravated Christ's suffering, reflects at the same time the mystery of his power, namely that he saved *others*.

It is no wonder, then, that Christ's victorious power is described with glowing terms in the apostolic epistles, and that not simply as a single display of might after weakness but as the manifestation of the power of his holy suffering and death, which in the resurrection is confirmed as a true and victorious power. We read of the mystery of victory where it is said that it was not possible for him to be held by death (Acts 2:24). We hear, as it were, the sound of trumpets announcing a real victory, a victory not merely peripheral but central to the message of the gospel and revealing the mystery of his work. He has disarmed the principalities and powers and made a public example of

---

there is no difference." The quotation from Isaiah 53 is applicable here "because the evangelist . . . knows that Jesus could exercise this omnipotence and miraculous power only because of his willingness and readiness also to descend into the depth of suffering" (p. 168).

them, thus triumphing over them.[144] The word which Paul uses for "to triumph" is *thriambeuō,* which points to the glorious and superior nature of his victory, namely, to be bound to the chariot of victory of the Conqueror, a word that Paul also applies to himself: "But thanks be unto God, who always leadeth us in triumph" (II Cor. 2:14).[145] The same triumphal procession displays not only Christ's victory over the powers and principalities, but also the power of God which is continuously seen in the apostles in spite of their own apparent powerlessness.[146]

Hence this triumph is not the outcome of an uncertain battle between two "powers" but the unexpected victory of "the weakness of God," which is stronger than men (I Cor. 1:25). Jesus Christ partook of our flesh and blood "that through death he might bring to naught him that had the power of death, that is, the devil" (Heb. 2:14).[147] The remark has been made that this text concerning Jesus Christ and the devil "is strange, especially in a context that presents Jesus' death as the act of a cult, a sacrifice,"[148] but this proves how manifold the aspects of Christ's entire work are, so that in one epistle they can be described as a holy sacrifice, as the shedding of blood, as suffering without the gate (Heb. 13:12), and at the same time as victory. For this reason he came – *cur deus homo*[149] – to gain the victory and to deliver "all them who through fear of death were all their lifetime subject to bondage" (Heb. 2:15). We see not two diverging lines, but one line –the line of sacrifice and victory: "what is meant is that the complete sacrifice, namely, that God delivers himself up, robs Satan of his power."[150]

144. Col. 2:15. Cf. E. Andrews, *The Meaning of Christ for Paul* (1949), pp. 69ff.
145. θριαμβευω. Cf. J. A. C. van Leeuwen, *Commentarie,* p. 205.
146. Delling speaks of "Jesus' way of the cross" as "the triumphal procession of God" (TWNT, III, 160).
147. Heb. 2:14 – καταργειν; cf. I Cor. 15:26 (abolished death) and II Tim. 1:10 (Christ Jesus, who abolished death). Cf. Delling in TWNT, *s.v.* καταργέω (I, 453). Van Oyen points out that it does not say of the devil that he has ἐξουσια but κράτος (power) of death (*Christus de Hogepriester,* p. 43). But in Col. 1:13 we read "ἐξουσια τοῦ σκότους," which proves that we must be careful in drawing such conclusions. Cf. also Luke 22:53.
148. Bent Noack, *Satanas und Soteria. Untersuchungen zur N.T. Dämonologie,* Copenhagen, 1948, p. 80; cf. the expression "remarkable" in O. Michel, *Hebräenbrief,* p. 86.
149. Windisch, *Hebräenbrief,* p. 23.
150. Michel, *op. cit.,* p. 86.

The light that emanates from Christ's victory is consequently a bright light. It is the light that we also see in the last book of the Bible when we read of the Lion of Judah's tribe (Rev. 5:5), but also of the warfare against the Lamb: "and the Lamb shall overcome them, for he is Lord of lords, and King of kings" (17:14).[151] The terms "Lamb" and "Lion" present no paradox because they form the background of the one work of Jesus Christ. It is the victory of the Lamb that is the light of the coming of God.

There are also passages without specific reference to battle and victory where we notice the marvel of the superior power of Christ as God's Messiah. The glad tidings are that God has delivered us through Christ from the power of darkness, and translated us into the kingdom of the Son of his love (Col. 1:13). This is particularly evident in the passages where Christ's work is described as "buying." Sevenster points out that this phrase is not expressly connected with the death of Christ but that the latter is undoubtedly presupposed.[152] The new Dutch translation renders this phrase thus: "You are bought and paid for" (I Cor. 6:20; 7:23; Grosheide in *Korte Verklaring* has "bought with a price"). This clearly indicates that the transaction is definitive and complete (Grosheide, "The sale is in all seriousness and reality"). In our transition from slavery to liberty his victory is fully revealed. "To buy one free" is the expression that we still hear in the new song: "Thou . . . didst purchase unto God with thy blood men of every tribe . . ." (Rev. 5:9). This purchasing to liberty is the *summa doctrina* of the Christian faith, namely, that this liberty is the same as being Christ's possession and no longer one's own.[153]

Here we see the light of Christ's work shining in the midst of ordinary life. Christ himself spoke of this liberty when he warned against the bondage of sin: "I say unto you, Every one that committeth sin is the bondservant of sin" (John 8:34).

151. Cf. Kittel, TWNT, I, 314, *s.v.* *ἀρνιον*.

152. G. Sevenster, *Christologie van het Nieuwe Testament,* p. 167, on *ἀγοράζω*. Cf. on the meaning of *ἀπολυτρωσις*, in *ibid*, p. 170.

153. Cf. I Cor. 6:19 ("and ye are not your own") with Lord's Day I of the Heidelberg Catechism, in which we find a beautiful combination of the *ἀγοραζω* in Scripture (1. "not my own, but . . ."; 2. "fully satisfied"; 3. "delivered from all the power of the devil"; 4. "heartily willing and ready, henceforth, to live unto Him").

But he added a word that pointed to his conquering power: "If therefore the Son shall make you free, ye shall be free indeed" (vs. 36).

We return for a moment to the so-called classical motif of reconciliation – *Christus Victor.* The objection to this classical motif is not that it sees and preaches Christ as Warrior and Conqueror. We must continue to listen to the biblical message of Christ's victory, and Luther's hymn is not only applicable in the Lutheran Reformation as a specific experience of Christ over against the "powers." The battle-and-victory motif is both Pauline and Johannine, and calls our attention to the profoundest depth of Christ's work which is apparent already in his humiliation, which depth cannot be understood without seeing it as part of Christ's struggle and victory. Hence it is quite logical that the emphasis on Christ as Victor emerged as a reaction against the watered-down and secularized theology of the nineteenth century, which had little or no concept of the eschatological motifs of the gospel and consequently saw little of the struggle and victory of this real Lord over the powers of evil. And when tremendous tensions once more occupied peoples' minds and hearts, it seemed that the classical motif meant no less than the rediscovery of the gospel.

But it is very necessary to observe that the concept of the nature of the "conquered powers" has frequently changed in the course of history. It has become increasingly more evident that we may not think that we have presented the *kerygma* faithfully when we call Christ Victor and speak of his tremendously powerful battle. For the question is *which* powers Christ Jesus has conquered, and how this victory is seen in the total context of the scriptural testimony. Even after having rediscovered the cosmic perspectives of the gospel, we must always formulate our views on the basis of the entire gospel.[154] Precisely while rejecting one-sided views, we must be on our guard against other one-sided views. And in a day of new interest in the epistle to the Colossians, which speaks of "disarmed powers,"[155] and of a new consciousness that according to Scripture there is no theology

154. Cf. M. H. Bolkestein, "Het Woord Gods en de Kosmos," *Nieuw Theologisch Tijdschrift,* 4th ed., pp. 1ff.

155. E. Stauffer, *Theologie des Neuen Testaments,* 1948[5]: "Until now no one has put into effect the historic-theological testament of Colossians" (p. 24), e.g., in connection with "the world-encompassing range of the *sola cruce.*"

without demonology,[156] nor a true insight into Christ's work without considering it in connection with his triumph, his power, and his Kingdom, we must all the more take into account the harmonious balance of God's gospel.

This is especially necessary because the *Christus Victor* theme carries with it the temptation to secularize Christ's triumph by lifting it out of its rich scriptural contexts. The consequences are evident, for example, when the so-called classical or dramatic motif of reconciliation is *contrasted* with the doctrines of substitution and satisfaction. So, in Aulén's view, reconciliation is the "unbroken" line of action on the part of God (the *divine* deliverance) which to be sure does not deny what Scripture definitely presents, namely a *human* Christ, but which nevertheless relegates that aspect to the background. Aulén's (and many others') criticism of Anselm's concept may indeed touch upon many weak spots in it, but this does not change the fact that Anselm's question, *cur deus homo?*, often remains unanswered in this criticism. Those who emphasize – contrary to the confession of the Church – the divine character of reconciliation and deliverance because only God can conquer the "powers," and then reject the *qua homo* because they have misunderstood it on the basis of a wrong view of Christ's work, have lost the necessary resistance against the powerful flood of monophysitism that ultimately could no longer stem the dangers of docetism. It was inevitable that on the basis of this classical motif of reconciliation the image of the true man Jesus Christ became blurred, whereas the Epistle to the Hebrews presents his dethroning of death precisely in connection with his sharing *our* flesh and blood (Heb. 2:14).

Hence Herbert's remark, in an introduction to the English translation of Aulén's book, that the classical motif of reconciliation opens a way to unity between Protestantism and Roman Catholicism,[157] is based on an illusion. For not only does the dramatic motif involve a tension between *love* and *justice* (which in legalism becomes a caricature), but also and especially it overstresses the powers of evil at the expense of the concept of guilt. Reconciliation in Christ does indeed involve "victory," but this victory cannot be viewed simply as a triumph of superior

156. *Ibid.*, p. 50.
157. Cf. F. W. Camfield, "The Idea of Substitution in the Doctrine of the Atonement," *Scottish Journal of Theology*, 1948, p. 283.

divine power which makes unnecessary the idea of substitution. No amount of scriptural references to "triumph" can void the fact that the nature of Christ's victory is thereby distorted. This kind of refutation of Anselm's position is altogether too simplistic, because it overlooks the fact that Anselm, in spite of the fact that in many respects his explanation was open to attack, nevertheless concerned himself with the reality of *guilt,*[158] and in so doing he had not only the Epistle to the Romans but also the Epistle to the Colossians on his side.

The question, therefore, which Camfield asked Aulén, "What does such a victory do to repair the past?"[159] finds no answer in the classical motif of reconciliation, because it ignores the past and takes guilt less seriously than did both the Church and Anselm in their confession of Christ's substitionary suffering. When juridical and forensic terms for Christ's work are replaced by military and strategic ones,[160] we should remember that Scripture also speaks of "disarming" and "dethroning" and in connection therewith of the "armor" of *believers.* But our main objection is to the replacement of the Church's terms by the exclusively dramatic ones, for that changes Christ's "battle" in his work to a "motif" which destroys Paul's message of the "bond written in ordinances" (Col. 2:14-15) and of the chariot of victory, and which no less obviates the *sacrifice* of the High Priest and his dethronement of the devil in Hebrews.

Only when we escape the temptation of the dramatic motif in its abstract, isolated nature can we view Christ's victory in its unique nature according to the Scriptures. For this kind of victory enables us to keep courage because Christ has conquered the world (John 16:33), and at the same time enables us to listen to John's message on the cleansing blood (I John 1:7) in order to confess without worldly airs and without overestimating ourselves: "this is the victory that hath overcome the world, even our faith" (I John 5:4).

Finally, how important this aspect — the victory — is to a correct insight into the meaning of Christ's work becomes evi-

158. See Anselm, *Cur deus homo* (*Floril. Patristicum,* 1929), I, XXI, together with Anselm's remark to Boso: "*nondum considerasti, quanti ponderis sit peccatum.*" Cf. on Anselm, C. R. Walker, "St. Anselm — a Revaluation," *Scottish Journal of Theology,* 1952, pp. 362ff.
159. Camfield, *op. cit.,* p. 284.
160. *Ibid.,* p. 291.

dent in the passage that combines as into one theme the fruit of the entire work of Christ: the victory *in him.* This victory through trust in the victorious Lord is decisively determined by, and included in, his victory. We are, according to Paul, *more than conquerors,* but it is a triumph "through him that loved us" (Rom. 8:37). Because Christ's triumph is wholly unique, so, too, is the believers' victory. They know that the meek will inherit the earth (Matt. 5:6), and that he receives authority who overcomes and keeps Christ's works (Rev. 2:26). Then he will "sit down" with me in my throne, as I also overcame, and sat down with my Father in his throne" (Rev. 3:21; cf. 2:17; 3:5, 12). In this victory of the believers their entire life is described in the power of the work of Christ. In this victory the light of reconciliation beams forth to the outer edges. The passage on victory in Romans 8 follows a passage on suffering: "For thy sake we are killed all the day long; we were accounted as sheep for the slaughter" (Rom. 8:36). In all this lies the victory, which must seem very strange to those accustomed to measure according to worldly standards, since this victory seems to be composed of defeats — "all the day long." But the word for victory[161] does not stretch too far or too high, for it is pronounced against the background of the inviolable truth: "If God is for us, who is against us?" (Rom. 8:31). All pronouncements converge as it were into one focus: He has not spared his own Son, but has delivered him up for us all (Rom. 8:32).

We hear of justification over against condemnation and accusation, of the Crucified and Risen One, of the *sessio Christi* and his powerful intercession, and finally of the love of Christ. Thus *our* victory is protected against all misunderstanding.

Apart from this context our victory becomes an illusion, and the dark shadows of tribulation and anguish, persecution and famine, nakedness or peril or sword descend as the final shadows upon our powerlessness. But *through* this context we are kept from this illusion and our certainty increases, so that we quietly look about us and recognize the "powers" of both the present and the future. We recognize them in the knowledge of the secret, "If *God* is for us . . . ."

This victory does not require us to discard the distinction between the Church "militant" and the Church "triumphant." The Church that knows about the victory is still engaged in war-

161. ὑπερνικωμεν. Rom. 8:37.

fare, and the expression "Church triumphant" reminds us of the eschatological perspective, of the time when not only the charges will be removed, but also the shadows — the many shadows — will flee. *Ecclesia militans* — in this battle the victory is her great comfort. Indeed, the entire work of Christ can be comprehended in this victory. It is the kind of victory which, in the future, will unmask many strange victories as defeats. Will there not be a war against the Lamb of God? But this unmasking is one of the things a child of God need not fear, not even when he meets the Judge of the living and the dead, who is the same as the Crucified One. He is the Giver of the white stone (Rev. 2:17), of the white garments (Rev. 3:5), of the new name (Rev. 2:17), of the hidden manna, of the morning star (Rev. 2:28), and of the crown of life (Rev. 2:10). In the battle we may not lose sight of the victory nor, in being "more than conquerors," of the *battle,* or having to persevere: "To him that overcometh, to him will I give to eat of the tree of life, which is in the Paradise of God" (Rev. 2:7).

INDEXES

INDEX OF PRINCIPAL SUBJECTS

INDEX OF PERSONS

INDEX OF SCRIPTURES